U.S. Government Directories, 1970-1981

U.S. Government Directories, 1970-1981

A Selected, Annotated Bibliography

Compiled
by

CONSTANCE STATEN GRAY
Head, Government Publications Department
University of Louisville Ekstrom Library

Libraries Unlimited, Inc.
Littleton, Colorado
1984

Copyright © 1984 Libraries Unlimited, Inc.
All Rights Reserved
Printed in the United States of America

No part of this publication may be reproduced, stored in a retrieval system, or transmitted, in any form or by any means, electronic, mechanical, photocopying, recording, or otherwise, without the prior written permission of the publisher.

LIBRARIES UNLIMITED, INC.
P. O. Box 263
Littleton, Colorado 80160-0263

Library of Congress Cataloging in Publication Data

Gray, Constance Staten, 1931-
  U.S. government directories, 1970-1981.

  Includes indexes.
  1. Administrative agencies--United States--Directories
--Bibliography. 2. United States--Executive departments
--Directories--Bibliography. I. Title. II. Title:
US government directories, 1970-1981.
Z7164.A2G685   1984   016.35304'025   83-26801
[JK7]
ISBN 0-87287-414-1

Libraries Unlimited books are bound with Type II nonwoven material that meets and exceeds National Association of State Textbook Administrators' Type II nonwoven material specifications Class A through E.

Contents

Introduction vii

Chapter 1
Areas and Places 1

Chapter 2
Associations and Organizations 11

Chapter 3
Businesses and Industries 28

Chapter 4
Data Sources 43

Chapter 5
Establishments and Institutions 57

Chapter 6
Government Agencies, General 73

Chapter 7
Government Agencies, Subject 88

Chapter 8
Individuals 108

Chapter 9
Information Sources and Systems.................................129

Chapter 10
Laws and Regulations...143

Chapter 11
Programs, Activities, Facilities, and Services........................152

Chapter 12
Miscellaneous Subjects..183

Appendix 1 – Regional Federal Depository Libraries................195

Appendix 2 – GPO Sales Publications Reference File (PRF).........199

Appendix 3 – U.S. Government Bookstores......................209

Appendix 4 – U.S. Government Departments and Agencies.........213

Title Index...229

Subject Index..241

Introduction

SCOPE

This bibliography is an annotated list of directories published by departments and agencies of the United States federal government between January 1970 and December 1981. Included are 575 titles received from the Government Printing Office (GPO) as depository items. For the purposes of this volume, directories are defined broadly as alphabetical or classified lists of organizations, individuals, businesses, places, laws, programs, and so forth, which usually state purpose and give addresses, contact persons, and telephone numbers. The items selected either have been designated as directories by their issuing agencies or contain the sort of information that serves users seeking directory-type data.

ARRANGEMENT

An impressive number of directories is published each year by the federal government. Although the subject coverage of these reference tools is broad and the information they contain is of interest to a large audience, they are often underutilized due to difficulty of access. A few guides to government directories have appeared over the years, including *Directories of Government Agencies* (Libraries Unlimited, 1969) and *Guide to U.S. Government Directories, 1970-1980* (Oryx Press, 1981), but they have tended to emphasize issuing agency rather than subject in their arrangements. In reality, library patrons are inclined to search for directory-type data by subject, not knowing or particularly caring who has issued the information. The directories in this volume, therefore, are arranged by category: areas and places; associations and organizations; businesses, corporations, and industries; data sources; establishments and institutions; government agencies (general); government agencies (subject); individuals; information sources and systems; laws and regulations; and programs, activities, facilities, and services. These categories serve as chapter divisions; within each chapter, the directories are arranged alphanumerically by SuDocs classification code.

Because a good number of titles fit into more than one category, a cross-reference system is employed to increase subject access. A full entry is usually given in the category where the title places most emphasis. If a publication places equal emphasis in several categories, then the full entry is given at the item's first appearance, with subsequent listings of the item indicating the class number, title, and a *see* reference leading to the annotation.

viii / Introduction

CITATION FORMAT AND CONTENT

The entries, including *see* reference entries, are numbered consecutively from 1 to 645. The fictitious sample entry below shows the positioning of all possible types of bibliographic information, although each individual entry contains only the bibliographic information that was applicable and available.

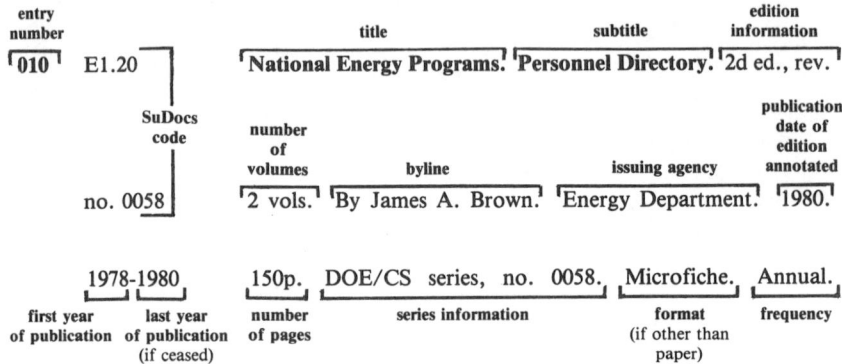

Price Information

Prices are not listed with the entries due to several factors, not the least of which is the GPO *Monthly Catalog*'s statement that "the prices of all U.S. Government Publications sold by the Superintendent of Documents are established by the Public Printer in accordance with Title 44 of the United States Code. Prices are subject to change without notice." Prices will be discussed further in appendix 2, which describes the *Publications Reference File* (GP3.22-3).

SuDocs Code

Due to reorganization of government departments, there may be several different SuDocs numbers for one title. If necessary, these numbers are indicated, including the years they were used.

Edition

The information cited for each publication is for the most recent edition (through December 1981) that the GPO has issued as a depository item. When seeking information about any title, however, one should ask for the very latest edition available.

Personal Author

The names of individual authors, editors, and compilers are given here only when they were listed clearly on the title page. The majority of government directories are compiled through the efforts of large groups, so personal authors are not indicated often in the bibliographic citations of this volume.

Issuing Agency

"United States" or "U.S." is not used as a prefix in the names of the issuing bodies because of the definitive nature of this work. The agency listed in each entry is the most specific issuing body. For example, the publisher of a document with the prefix of A13.2 would usually be identified as the U.S. Department of Agriculture, Forest Service, but entries in this volume list only the Forest Service as the issuing agency. This follows the practice employed in *List of Classes of United States Publications Available for Selection by Depository Libraries* (GP3.24). Appendix 4 lists the issuing agencies with parent bodies for those who require that information.

Date

Beginning dates of some publications were not available for a number of reasons. Executive agencies do not always have this information for their publications, and occasionally when the agencies send a title to GPO for distribution it will be the third or fourth edition of a title published previously by a private organization. Some beginning dates cited are for the series rather than for the title. Official historical information on government publications is very difficult to verify, if it can be found at all.

It should be noted that many titles and subtitles contain dates; for example:

Regional Parks, 1979.

Solar Heating Directory. 1981.

Dates that appear in boldface as part of the title or as a subtitle would merely indicate the time period covered by the directory and are not to be confused with its year of publication, which is positioned after the issuing agency in the citation format (see diagram) and may or may not be the same date as that in the title, depending on when the publication was actually released.

Frequency

The frequency of some titles listed as annuals, semiannuals, or quarterlies may, at first, seem incorrect because the date of the edition annotated is not recent. For example, the date of a title cited as an annual may be 1978. One of several factors might explain this: Federal agencies often fail to send their publications to the GPO, thereby causing a break in continuity; they fail to *x / Introduction*

notify or are very late in notifying GPO when a title's frequency has been changed or its publication has ceased; or they may have every intention of issuing a publication annually, but are remiss or very slow in doing so.

Annotation

Descriptive annotations state the purpose, scope, and arrangement of each directory. The length and type of annotation depend upon the scope and significance of the publication.

APPENDIXES

Appendixes 1 through 4 will assist users in locating most of the items listed in this bibliography. Since items included here are only those sent by the GPO to depository libraries, it should be a fairly easy process; however, items that are listed as out-of-print at GPO will require more searching. These depository items have been distributed according to the rules of the Federal Depository Library Program, which was established by Congress under Chapter 19 of Title 44 of the United States Code. Under this program, government publications are made available to designated depository libraries located in each state and congressional district. There are currently more than 1,350 depository libraries. Of this number, 49 have been designated as regional libraries, which assume responsibility of retaining depository materials permanently and of providing interlibrary loan and reference service in their regions. Copies of documents no longer available through the GPO sales program can usually be found in regional federal depository library collections. Copies of certain technical publications no longer sold by the GPO sales program may also be obtained by writing to the National Technical Information Service, 5285 Port Royal Road, Springfield, VA 22161. Appendix 1 is a list of the regional federal depository libraries. A complete list of all depository libraries can be obtained by writing to the Superintendent of Documents, U.S. Government Printing Office, Washington, DC 20402.

Appendix 2 is an explanation of the *GPO Sales Publications Reference File* (*PRF*), reprinted from the GPO publication *PRF User's Manual. A Guide to Using the GPO Sales Publications Reference File* (GP3.29:P96). This file, a "books-in-print" of federal documents, is a 48x microfiche catalog of publications sold by the Superintendent of Documents. The *PRF* is issued on a bimonthly subscription basis and lists all publications and subscription services currently for sale by the Superintendent of Documents. Forthcoming sales items and items that have been declared out-of-print for up to two years are also included in the *PRF*.

Government bookstores located in Washington, D.C., and other cities throughout the United States are also sources of federal publications. Appendix 3 is a list of these bookstores with addresses.

Appendix 4 is a list of the government departments and agencies that are the issuing bodies of the items listed in this bibliography. Those no longer in existence are indicated by a dagger (†), and those that have changed names or whose functions have been transferred to other agencies are cross-referenced

Introduction / xi

to the current agency. Issuing agencies are also possible sources of publications that may not be available from the GPO. As documents librarians will tell you, it never hurts to try the issuing agency. Current addresses for all government agencies can be found in the Federal Register Office's publication *Government Manual* (GS4.109), which can usually be found in any public or university library regardless of whether it is a depository library.

INDEXES

Two indexes have been included to further facilitate the usefulness of this volume: an alphabetical title index and a subject index, both of which use entry numbers, not page numbers. The subject index provides comprehensive subject coverage of each title. A majority of the subject headings have been taken from the subject key words indicated for each title. Other subject headings are more or less modified versions of the Library of Congress subject headings. *See* and *see also* references are used throughout the subject index to increase access.

ABBREVIATIONS

Identified below are the abbreviations used in the text:

ed. - edition

et al. - and others

FTS - Federal Telecommunications System, a government network of leased long-distance circuits allowing government employees to make official calls to all telephones in the continental United States

n.d. - no date

n.p. - no pagination

rev. - revised

v.p. - various pagination

vols. - volumes

1
Areas and Places

This section concerns itself with world areas, cities and towns, recreation areas, historic sites, national parks and forests, Indian reservations, and the like.

001 A13.2   **Camp and Picnic in the National Forests of the Intermountain**
        In8-5   **Region.** Forest Service. 1981. 82p.

This directory lists the features of developed campgrounds and picnic sites in the national forests of the Intermountain Region. The Intermountain Region of the Forest Service, U.S. Department of Agriculture, includes eighteen national forests in southern Idaho, Utah, western Wyoming, and Nevada, and two national recreation areas: the Sawtooth, located in Central Idaho, and the Flaming Gorge, located in Wyoming. The sites are arranged by state and include the following information: name, map location, elevation, season of use, day limit, camping and picnicking availability, water facilities, waste disposal, number of units, and special features. Also included is a list of forest supervisors' offices with addresses and telephone numbers.

002 A13.2   **Recreation Sites in Southwestern National Forests, 1980.**
        R24-28   Forest Service. 1981. 47p. Annual.
        1979-

The Southwestern Region of the Forest Service includes the twelve national forests in Arizona and New Mexico. Nearly twenty-one million acres in these two states—in general, the coolest and best-watered areas in an arid land—make up the Southwestern national forests. This publication is divided into three parts. Part 1 contains general information about the areas, fees, maps, rules, and the like. Parts 2 and 3 cover the recreation sites in Arizona and New Mexico, respectively. These two sections describe the national forests, which are arranged alphabetically by name. Each entry includes the following information: office address and telephone number, description and map of the area, climate, nearby towns, and a table of recreation sites within the forest stating ranger district, location (miles and direction from reference town), elevation, season of use, period of stay, and special items. Also included is a list of the ranger district offices with addresses and telephone numbers.

003 A13.2   **Tahoe National Forest Camping and Picnicking.** Forest
        T13   Service. 1979. 23p.

2 / 1—Areas and Places

The Tahoe National Forest is located northeast of Sacramento in the central Sierra Nevada range and extends from Lake Tahoe to north of the prominent Sierra Buttes. Within the boundaries of the Tahoe National Forest, roughly 800,000 acres are public lands and 400,000 acres are privately owned. Use of these private lands is subject to permission from the landowner. The Forest Service maintains many public campgrounds, nearly all of which have fireplaces, tables, water, and toilets. Their locations and descriptions are listed in this guide. The volume includes regulations for the use of national forest recreation sites and areas, and describes each campground and picnic ground by giving its elevation and location, and listing whether it has fishing, swimming, boat rental, trailer units, camp units, and water and toilet facilities. One map of the area is included.

004 A13.13 **Campground Directory. Idaho Panhandle National Forests.**
Idl-6 Forest Service. 1981. 12p.

This directory will help the reader choose a campground or picnic area in the Idaho Panhandle national forests. At many of these sites, other recreation opportunities will also be found. For detailed information about hiking, boating, berry picking, and other recreational activities, stop in at the nearest ranger district office. This volume contains a list of the ranger district offices with addresses, telephone numbers, and directions for getting to them. The information provided for each site includes its name, elevation, location, whether there is a fee, attractions, facilities, and other features. A map of the area is included.

005 C1.8-3 **Federal and State Indian Reservations and Indian Trust Areas.**
In2 Commerce Department. 1974. 604p.

Contained in this directory is useful and conveniently arranged information about Indian tribes and Alaskan natives. The volume is arranged alphabetically by states where the tribes and natives are located. The Alaska section is arranged alphabetically by the name of the village corporation and the native villages within each corporation. The information given for each village includes the name of the native group, 1970 population (native, nonnative), areas, and land status. The listings of Indian tribes in other states include such items as name and address of reservation; whether it is a federal or state reservation; population; land status (who owns the land), and total area; history of the area; vital statistics (population, labor force, education); and descriptions of each areas' culture, government, tribal economy, climate, transportation, community facilities, and recreation.

006 C13.52 **Guideline Codes for Named Populated Places and Related**
no. 55 **Entities of the States of the United States.** 2 vols. National
v. 1 & 2 Bureau of Standards. 1978. Federal Information Processing
Standards (FIPS) publication no. 55. Irregular.

Provided in this guideline are codes for named populated cities, towns, villages, and similar communities, whether incorporated or unincorporated, and several categories of named entities that are similar to the above types of communities in one or more important respects. It includes important military and naval installations, townships, Indian reservations, named places that form parts of other places, and places important for transportation, industrial, or commercial purposes (i.e., airports, shopping centers, and unpopulated railroad points). Arranged alphabetically by state and place within state, each entry provides the place's name and standard code, the standard code for the state and the county (or counties) in which the place is located, the postal zip code of the servicing post office(s), and a cross-reference to *Worldwide Geographic Location Codes* issued by the Office of Finance of the General Services Administration.

007 C46.2 **Directory of Economic Development Districts and Area Grantees.** Economic Development Administration. 1977. 49p. Irregular
Ec7-4
1969-

This directory lists alphabetically by state the districts, area grantees, regional commissions, Economic Development Administration (EDA) regional offices and officials, and the Appalachian Regional Commission, with names, addresses, and telephone numbers. Each state entry contains the governor's name, the state EDR official's name, address and telephone number, and the Economic Development District officials and addresses. Also included is an alphabetical name index for district and area grantee officials.

008 C46.25 **Directory of EDA Qualified Areas under the Public Works and Economic Development Act of 1965, as Amended May 1978.** Economic Development Administration. 1978. 170p. Annual.
1965-

This is a listing of the areas officially designated as Title IV redevelopment areas at the time of publication, as well as those areas qualified for Title IV designation under the Public Works and Economic Development Act of 1965, as amended, but not yet officially designated as such. Only those areas with designation dates in the listings' third column were officially designated. The directory is arranged alphabetically by state and then by county. Each entry includes county name, basis of qualification, date of designation, and maximum grant rate (percent). Also indicated for the state is the regional office.

009 C56.202 **Centers of Population for States and Counties, 1950, 1960, and 1970.** Census Bureau. 1974. 96p.
P81-3

This report was published to provide information for many data users who have sought this information in unpublished form in the past. It is not meant to espouse the gravity center of population concept as a preeminent measure for analyzing population distribution and change. The concept of the center of population as used by the Bureau of the Census is that of a balance point; that is, the center of population is the point at which an imaginary flat, weightless, and rigid map of the United States would balance if weights of identical size were placed on it so that each weight represented the location of one person. The report presents both a graphic and tabular description of the population centers of each state in 1950, 1960, and 1970. Also included is a table giving the 1970 population centers for each county, by latitude and longitude.

010 D101.22 **United States Army Installations and Major Activities.** Army Department. 1980. 32p. Pamphlet no. 210-1. Irregular.
no. 210-1
1977-

Contained in this pamphlet is an alphabetical listing of U.S. Army installations and major activities, giving their mailing addresses. It is not intended to be a complete list of all real property holdings of activities under the control of the Department of the

4 / 1 – Areas and Places

Army. Each entry provides the name of the installation or major activity, abbreviation for jurisdiction, and post office address. Jurisdiction abbreviations are defined in table 1; table 2 lists installations and activities in the continental United States, and table 3 lists installations outside the continental United States.

011   D114.2   **Guide to U.S. Army Museums and Historic Sites.** 2d ed.
          M97   Compiled by Norman Miller Cary, Jr. Center of Military
          1968-   History. 1975. 116p. Irregular.

Registered museums that make up the U.S. Army Museum System, as well as the historic sites located on Army property that are currently in *The National Register of Historic Places* or have been nominated for inclusion in that register are listed here. Part 1 lists all registered Army museums alphabetically by the state in which they are located and then by Army post within each state. All Army National Guard museums are also listed by state. Part 2 lists Department of Defense museums by service and then by state. Information on other federal museums with extensive military collections is in part 3, while part 4 contains data on military-oriented private, state, and municipal museums, again alphabetically by state. Part 5 deals with historic sites on Army property alphabetically by state and then by post. Part 6 lists a number of information sources on military history, historic sites, and museums. Part 7 is a bibliography containing a brief listing of books, pamphlets, periodicals, as well as U.S. Army and Department of Defense regulations concerning museums and historic sites. The maps in appendixes 1 and 2 are included to help the traveler who wishes to visit museums or historic sites located on Army installations. (The first edition was entitled *Directory of U.S. Army Museums.*)

012   I20.47   **Indian Land Areas, General: Indian Lands and Related Facil-**
          In2-4   **ities as of 1971.** Indian Affairs Bureau. 1975. n.p.

This is a map, 26 by 43 inches, which, in addition to showing Indian land areas and related facilities, contains a list of the Bureau of Indian Affairs field offices with addresses (area offices and agency offices), arranged alphabetically by state. Indicated on the map are reservations, national forests, monuments, parks, wildlife refuges, and the interstate highway system.

013   I29.2   **Visitor Accommodations, Facilities, and Services, 1980/81.**
          Ac2-2   National Park Service. 1980. 114p. Irregular.
          1976-

The Department of the Interior grants to private companies or individuals the privilege of providing facilities and services that are considered necessary for the accommodation and convenience of park visitors. The areas of the National Park System are open to visitors all year, climatic conditions permitting. Visitor facilities are also open all year unless otherwise noted. Listed in this booklet alphabetically by areas are the overnight accommodations and other facilities and services concessioners provide for travelers in the National Park System. The parks are arranged alphabetically by name; each entry provides the park's office address, and an alphabetically arranged list of concessioners with contact person and address, and services provided. Rates are also given.

014 I29.2 **The Presidents, from the Inauguration of George Washington to the Inauguration of Jimmy Carter. Historic Places Commemorating the Chief Executives of the United States.** Rev. ed. Robert G. Ferris, series editor. National Park Service. 1977. 606p. The National Survey of Historic Sites and Buildings, v. 20. Irregular.
H62-9
v. 20
1976-

This book, which focuses on the sites and buildings associated with United States presidents, provides a new and unique dimension in understanding the presidents and should further stimulate public interest in their careers. It will also guide citizens who wish to visit the various National Park System areas and national historic landmarks that honor them. The volume is divided into three parts. Part 1 presents a historical background of the presidents; part 2 presents in chronological order biographical sketches of the presidents; and part 3 lists alphabetically by state the historic sites and buildings relating to the presidents. Also included are a suggested reading list, criteria for selection of historic sites of national significance, and a map of the United States showing the historic sites of national significance.

015 I29.2 **National Historic Landmarks. A Preservation Program of the National Park Service.** National Park Service. 1976. 150p.
L23-4

National historic landmarks are visible reminders of the events, persons, places, and objects that have affected broad patterns of American history, illustrated man's craftsmanship and artistry, and reflected America's evolving culture. They include historic and prehistoric villages of the American Indian, sites of battlefield conflict, and homes of political leaders, soldiers, scientists, artists, and humanitarians. Leaders of business, labor, and education are also represented. The works of master architects and buildings that reflect outstanding examples of a particular period or style of architecture may be found. This booklet lists the national historic landmarks alphabetically by state. The historical name of the landmark is given with its location and the historic date or historical period involved. This is followed by a short statement on the significance of the property. The final date given is that on which the property was designated as a national historic landmark by the Secretary of the Interior.

016 I29.2 **Index: National Park System and Related Areas, as of June 30, 1979.** National Park Service. 1979. 94p. Biennial.
N21-26
1975-

The National Park System of the United States comprises nearly 320 areas covering some seventy-six million acres in forty-nine states, the District of Columbia, Guam, Puerto Rico, Spain, and the Virgin Islands. These areas are of such national significance as to justify special recognition and protection in accordance with acts of Congress. These areas may be designated as national parks, monuments, lakeshores, seashores, rivers, wild and scenic riverways, historic sites, military parks, battlefield parks, battlefield sites, battlefields, historical parks, memorials, parkways, recreation areas, and wilderness areas. These areas are arranged alphabetically by state. The entry for each area includes its name, address, acreage, authorization date, and a brief descriptive statement. Also included is an alphabetical listing of names of the areas.

017 I29.8 **Guide and Map: National Parks of the United States.** National Park Service. 1980. n.p. Irregular.
P23-4
1974-

6 / 1—Areas and Places

This guide presents the most current information on facilities within the various park areas. Generally the services listed are only those within the park itself, so you can expect that parks close to urban areas will have a greater variety of accommodations and tourist services outside the park than is represented here. The guide is arranged alphabetically by state and gives each park's address and identifies services. The map indicates interstate highways and locations of parks.

018   I29.9-2   **Access National Parks: A Guide for Handicapped Visitors.**
       H19-2   National Park Service. 1978. 197p.

Access National Parks is a handbook of accessibility for handicapped visitors to the National Park System, intended to serve as a tool to improve their visits to the national parks. The volume details information about the accessibility of facilities, services, and interpretative programs in almost three hundred areas of the National Park System. It includes, alphabetically by state, each area's office address and telephone number, location, average elevation (where altitude is a consideration), availability of first aid and medical services, and a description of special programs (wheelchair accessibility data, etc.). Regional maps are provided as well as an alphabetical name key to the sites.

019   I29.71   **Camping in the National Park System.** National Park Service.
       1970-   1981. n.p. Annual.

Contained in this booklet is basic information about the facilities and recreational opportunities available to users of National Park System camping areas. Arranged alphabetically by the name of area, the entries provide the following information: address, location, camping season, campground type, limit of stay (number of days), map references, number of sites or spaces, group camps, campsite fee; trailer village vehicle site and fee, the availability of water and toilets, sanitary station, showers, laundry facilities, stores, food services, swimming, boating, and fishing; and general notes. A map is provided for location references, plus definitions and other general information.

020   I49.2   **Directory. Pacific States Region—National Wildlife Refuges**
       P11   **and Fish Hatcheries.** Fish and Wildlife Service. 1980. 32p.

Arranged alphabetically by state in the Pacific region (California, Hawaii, Idaho, Nevada, Oregon, Washington), this directory lists the field stations for national wildlife refuges and fish hatcheries. The public is encouraged to visit these areas as they are excellent places to view and photograph birds and other wildlife, and often recreational opportunities, such as fishing, hunting, camping, and picnicking, are available there. The refuges and/or hatcheries are presented in alphabetical order by name within each state. Information given includes address, telephone number, directions for getting there, primary wildlife or fish, habitat (acres, etc.), recreation and education available, and special notes. Also included are maps of the states indicating areas and routes.

021   I53.7-2   **Idaho Recreation Guide.** Land Management Bureau. 1979.
       Idl-2   47p. Microfiche.

Information on outdoor recreation sites in the state of Idaho is contained in this booklet. It lists the features of developed campgrounds in the national forests, national resource lands, and state lands of Idaho. Campgrounds with developed wells or piped water systems are noted in this directory. An index map is placed at the beginning of the volume, indicating by number the map areas along a particular route in Idaho. Campgrounds are listed in the directory by their numerical order on the map. Access to campgrounds and picnic grounds are listed by major U.S. and state highways. Information for each recreation site includes name (indicating type of site), access, elevation, season of use, limit of stay, number of units (tent, trailer, picnic area), facilities available, and activities and attractions. Directions and mileage are given for all off-highway campgrounds and other recreation sites. Winter sports information is contained in a separate section of the directory.

022　　I53.11　　　　**Camping on the Public Lands.** Land Management Bureau.
　　　　　C15　　　　　1980. n.p.

Camping on the Public Lands presents a map and a listing by state of the public lands in the eleven westernmost states (Washington, Oregon, California, Nevada, Arizona, New Mexico, Colorado, Utah, Wyoming, Idaho, and Montana) plus Alaska. The areas are arranged alphabetically, giving location and special facilities. General information is provided for all public lands administered by the United States Bureau of Land Management.

023　　I70.17　　　　**The National Register of Historic Places.** 2 vols. Heritage
　　　　　1959-　　　　 Conservation and Recreation Service. 1976, 1979. Irregular.

Volume 1 of this title was issued in 1976 by the National Park Service and was classed I29.76. It contains descriptions of all properties added to the register through December 31, 1974. Volume 2 was issued in 1979 by the Heritage Conservation and Recreation Service (class I70.17), and contains descriptions of properties added from January 1, 1975 through December 31, 1976. The National Register Program of the Department of the Interior's National Park Service serves as an important tool to protect our cultural resources. Listings in *The National Register* are added when areas of historical significance become part of the National Park System by acts of Congress and executive orders, when they are designated as national historic landmarks by the Secretary of the Interior, or when they are nominated to *The National Register* by state and federal agencies. The register is arranged alphabetically by state and territory. Following the listings for states and territories is a listing for the outer continental shelf. Preceding each state or territory is a profile of the historic properties listed in the register for that jurisdiction. The essays summarize cultural and historical events exemplified by properties in *The National Register*. Most states are divided into counties, which are listed in alphabetical order. Properties not located within a municipality are listed under the nearest city or town, while properties within municipalities are listed by street address. The date of construction of a building, structure, or object is listed when known. A description of each property is given, followed by a summary of the significance of the property or those associated with it. Following each entry is information about ownership and accessibility to the public. An alphabetical index is provided.

024　　L37.2　　　　**Directory of Important Labor Areas.** 7th ed. Employment
　　　　　D62　　　　　and Training Administration. 1978. 138p. Irregular.
　　　　　1954-

This directory provides a consolidated listing of the geographical boundaries of all labor areas covered by the Employment and Training Administration's (ETA) area

8 / 1 — Areas and Places

classification program at any time from July 1951 through December 1977. It includes definitions of all Standard Metropolitan Statistical Areas (SMSAs). The listing of an area in this publication indicates that the area is a designated SMSA or has been officially defined and classified as an area of substantial or persistent unemployment, eligible for assistance under various federal programs since July 1951. Part 1, which concerns boundaries of labor areas, lists and defines alphabetically by state and then by area all counties and minor civil subdivisions covered by the ETA's official labor area classification and definition program. Part 2, an index to counties, lists alphabetically by state all counties or parts of counties included in any SMSA or any other area officially classified as an area of substantial or persistent unemployment through December 1977.

025   P1.10-8   **National Five Digit ZIP Code and Post Office Directory.**
      1979-   Postal Service. 1981. 2014p. Annual.

The *National ZIP Code Directory* was issued from 1965 through 1978 to consolidate and update the information previously published in the state zip code directories issued in 1963. Beginning with the 1979 issue, this directory was combined with the *Directory of Post Offices* (P1.10-4, 1955-1978). The result is an official list of post offices and place names (former post offices frequently used and recognized as delivery addresses) with items of information relating to each. Arranged alphabetically by state and then by city, it gives zip codes for streets (named streets first, followed by numbered streets). Added features include a separate section on apartments, motels, hotels, buildings, government offices, hospitals, and colleges and universities. The U.S. Postal Service publishes the *National Five Digit ZIP Code and Post Office Directory* annually to furnish correct and current five-digit zip code and mailing information to the mail user and the public in general. The directory contains complete information relating to the five-digit zip code system and information required by the mailer concerning U.S. Postal Service facilities and organization. The directory is divided into eleven sections. Section 1 provides information about the directory; section 2 has information on proper addressing; section 3 contains information on the mail services; section 4 lists the service improvement programs; section 5 gives Postal Service organization information; section 6 lists special zip codes; section 7 contains the state lists of post offices and post offices with street listings (the major section). Sections 8 through 11 include post office delivery statistics, an alphabetical list of post offices, a numerical list of post offices, and names of discontinued postal units.

026   PrEx1.10-8   **Highway Rest Areas for Handicapped Travelers.** President's
      H53   Committee on Employment of the Handicapped. 1977. n.p.
      1975-   Irregular.

In order to help handicapped travelers better plan their trips and to avoid the inconvenience of inaccessible rest facilities, this guide was published. The number of accessible rest stops has doubled since this booklet was initially published. The present edition contains more than eight hundred accessible rest areas in forty-eight of the fifty states. It is arranged alphabetically by state in chart form, giving the route or highway number, the direction or directions served, the location (e.g., three miles south of Tennessee state line), and the number of the milepost. The U.S. Federal Highway Administration gathered this list of accessible areas for the President's Committee from state highway departments.

1 — Areas and Places / 9

027   PrEx2.2   **Standard Metropolitan Statistical Areas.** Rev. ed., 1975.
        M56   Management and Budget Office. 1976. 108p. Irregular.

The concept of a metropolitan area is one of an integrated economic and social unit with a recognized urban population nucleus of substantial size. The concept of Standard Metropolitan Statistical Areas (SMSAs) has been developed to meet the need for the presentation of general-purpose statistics about metropolitan areas by agencies of the federal government. The statistical concept of a metropolitan area is based upon a body of published objective criteria. The criteria are subject to continuing review, and changes are made as appropriate. Part 1 of this publication reproduces the criteria. Part 2 lists the titles and definitions of the 276 SMSAs presented in this volume. For each SMSA, the table lists the Federal Information Processing Standards (FIPS) code, the component counties or county equivalents (or, in New England, cities and towns), central cities and other places of twenty thousand or more within the SMSAs, and the 1970 population for each geographic area. Parts 3 through 9 respectively present criteria followed in establishing Standard Consolidated Statistical Areas; titles and definitions of Standard Consolidated Statistical Areas; counties of each state within SMSAs (excluding New England); cities and towns of each New England state within SMSAs; a list of New England county metropolitan areas; definitions affected by criterion 5 or 8; and changes in SMSAs, 1950 through 1975. An appendix explains the FIPS codes, Bureau of the Census's minor civil divisions (MCD) codes for New England counties, and the central county codes. A map of the United States is also provided indicating SMSAs.

028   PrEx3.10   **National Basic Intelligence Factbook.** Central Intelligence
        N21   Agency. January 1980. 222p. Semiannual.
        1976-

This book is a compilation of political entities worldwide. It is prepared for the use of U.S. government officials and others seeking information about the world's nations. Arranged alphabetically by entity name, each entry provides information about land, water, people, government, economy, communications, and defense forces. A small map of the area is also provided. Larger reference maps of Canada, Middle America (which includes the lower half of the United States and Central America), South America, Europe, the Middle East, Africa, the USSR and Asia, and Oceania are also included. Abbreviations for international organizations and commodity organizations are included in a separate section, as well as United Nations organizations, and a table of approximate metric conversions.

029   S1.119-2   **Status of the World's Nations.** State Department. 1980. 19p.
        W89   Irregular.
        1973-

An alphabetical listing of nations, dependencies, and areas of special sovereignty, this publication states the capital, population, and land area of each. Also included is an alphabetical and chronological checklist of newly independent nations since 1943. The information in this booklet is provided as reference material only. The number of nations has more than doubled since the end of World War II: on the eve of the war, seventy nations were generally accepted as independent in the world community; by August 1, 1980, there were 165. Each state that is a member of the United Nations is designated with an asterisk.

10 / 1—Areas and Places

030 Y3.F31-22:9 **A Directory of Research Natural Areas on Federal Lands of the United States of America.** Federal Committee on Ecological Reserves. 1977. 280p. Irregular.

Described here are the research natural areas on federal lands, which represent important resources for investigations requiring natural areas unaltered by human intervention. They are also vital repositories of genetic information and invaluable components of our national natural heritage. Arranged alphabetically by state and name of site, it gives acreage, county, latitude, longitude, elevation, contact (owner/administering agency), primary features, and other items.

2
Associations and Organizations

Addresses and directors of associations and organizations, as well as information about organizations concerned with particular subjects, are constantly sought by library patrons, and, consequently, by librarians. This chapter lists directories of many groups that are not easily found elsewhere.

031 A1.38 **Horse Publications and Visual Materials: 1980 Listing.**
no. 1393 Agriculture Department. 1980. 113p. Miscellaneous publica-
1980- tion no. 1393. Biennial.

Listed in this publication are private organizations, state governments, and state extension services at land-grant universities in the United States that have publications, visual materials, or resource persons that may be consulted for information on horses. Information regarding availability of publications and visual materials was provided by the source organization, or a notation is made that no information was provided. Organizations are arranged alphabetically by type (such as breed registry organizations), and addresses and telephone numbers are provided.

032 A1.38 **Swine Publications and Visual Materials: 1980 Listing.** Agri-
no. 1397 culture Department. 1980. 47p. Miscellaneous publication
1980- no. 1397. Biennial.

The purpose, scope, and arrangement of this publication relating to swine parallels that of entry 031 above.

033 A1.38 **Beef Cattle Publications and Visual Materials: 1980 Listing.**
no. 1398 Agriculture Department. 1980. 88p. Miscellaneous publication
1980- no. 1398. Biennial.

See entry 031 above for the purpose, scope, and arrangement of this publication, which concerns beef cattle.

034 A1.38 **Sheep Publications and Visual Materials: 1980 Listing.** Agri-
no. 1399 culture Department. 1980. 36p. Miscellaneous publication
1980- no. 1399. Biennial.

This booklet about sheep has the same purpose, scope, and arrangement as entry 031 above.

12 / 2—*Associations and Organizations*

035   A43.4   **Directory of Selected Private Civic-Service Organizations for**
        no. 581   **Cooperative 4-H Programing.** Extension Service. 1977. 76p.
        1977-   Circular no. 581. Irregular.

Designed to inform 4-H agents about volunteer organizations that have local units in communities throughout the nation, this directory describes those organizations in terms of their membership, structure, programs, and publications. The information came from a study conducted by Cheryl Sue Fox, a federal summer intern, 4-H, 1975. Addresses are given in an alphabetical arrangement by name of the organization.

036   A67.26   **Food and Agricultural Export Directory, 1978/79.** Foreign
        no. 201   Agricultural Service. 1978. 102p. Miscellaneous publication
        1969-   no. 201. Annual.

The purpose of this directory is to provide updated information for firms engaged in exporting, and to encourage those who are not exporting to use the directory to help them get into the growing foreign market for U.S. agricultural products. The directory lists federal and state agencies, trade associations, and other entities offering advice and services in exporting all types of agricultural products, from soybeans to frozen pies. It is arranged first by the federal agencies concerned, and followed by state organizations and export groups, state departments of agriculture and associated organizations, U.S. market development cooperators, contractors under Market Development Export Incentive programs, international brokers and sellers, and U.S. Department of Commerce district and regional offices, a partial listing of foreign embassies in the United States, newly opened foreign embassies in the United States, transportation services, and export publications. Addresses, telephone numbers, and contact persons are given.

037   C1.2   **OMBE Funded Organizations Directory.** Minority Business
        M66-10   Enterprise Office. 1979. 40p. Irregular.
        1973-

This publication lists by administrative region and alphabetical index various business assistance organizations funded by the Office of Minority Business Enterprise (OMBE). The organizations are arranged according to the category of program services they provide primarily (i.e., business development centers, business resource centers, minority business and trade associations, and private resource programs), with an alphabetical index. Information given includes name of organization, address, telephone number, and chief executive officer. Addresses, telephone numbers, and contact persons are also given for regional and field offices of OMBE in each region.

038   C3.238-4   **National Clearinghouse for Census Data Services.** *See*
                                 entry 151.

039   C13.10   **Directory of United States Standardization Activities.**
        no. 417   National Bureau of Standards. 1975. 223p. Special publication
        1967-   no. 417. Irregular.

Standardization activities of trade associations, technical and other professional societies representing industry and commerce, and state and federal governments are summarized in this directory. It also covers nonengineering and nonindustry organizations. The directory contains current descriptive summaries of more than 580 organizations arranged in alphabetical order in three sections covering associations, state agencies, and federal agencies. Also included is an association index by subject areas, and a subject index.

040   C13.10   **Directory of Law Enforcement and Criminal Justice Associa-**
         no. 480-20   **tions and Research Centers.** National Bureau of Standards.
         1978-   1978. 46p. Special publication no. 480-20. Irregular.

Listed in this directory are national nonprofit professional and volunteer social action associations and research centers active in the fields of law enforcement and criminal justice. The international and foreign organizations listed either have a large number of American members, have a U.S. chapter, or are doing work that is applicable to the United States. The local organizations listed either cover several states or are of national interest. The organizations are arranged alphabetically, giving address, telephone, year founded, officer, purpose, activities, and so forth. A subject index is included.

041   C51.2   **International Directory of Appropriate Technology**
         D63   **Resources.** Compiled by Brij Mathur. A VITA publication.
                        National Technical Information Service. 1980. n.p.

A Volunteers in Technical Assistance (VITA) publication, this volume provides information on those organizations known to be involved in some aspect of "appropriate technology," and should facilitate the sharing of information and technical resources. The directory is divided into three parts. Part 1 lists the organizations alphabetically by countries. Part 2 provides lists of publications, reports, papers, and so forth, published by these organizations. Part 3 is a subject index to facilitate use of the material. The volume contains more than 250 entries and each entry provides the following information, if available: name of the organization, address, contact person, type of organization (whether government, quasi-government, private, or university), number of employees, areas of interest, services provided, library and inquiry service, and publications (i.e., newsletter/periodical), with title, frequency, and cost.

042   C55.292   **Annotated Acronyms and Abbreviations of Marine Science**
         Ac7   **Related International Organizations.** 2d ed. Rev. by Charlotte
         1969-   M. Ashby. Environmental Data Service. 1976. 113p. Irregular.

Descriptive entries are grouped into three sections: (1) organizations, (2) programs, projects, and expeditions, and (3) miscellaneous terms. Two indexes are provided: one lists acronyms and abbreviations in alphabetical order, the other lists full titles in alphabetical order, giving acronyms and/or abbreviations. Part 1 offers a full description of the organizations and their marine science activities. Part 2 is an alphabetical arrangement by name of international programs, projects, and expeditions, giving date (if available), nature of the project, and cooperating nations. Part 3 lists in alphabetical order those terms used in international marine science activities, particularly those concerned with the international exchange of oceanographic data.

043   C61.8   **Official U.S. and International Financing Institutions. A**
         F49   **Guide for Exporters and Investors.** 3d ed., rev. International
         1976-   Trade Administration. 1980. 12p. Irregular.

This guide was published in response to the many requests from exporters and investors for information on sources of financing, insurance, and procurement for U.S. exports and investments. The publication was designed to assist U.S. exporters and investors in entering international markets and to compete successfully for worldwide business. The organizations listed include: Export-Import Bank (EXIMBANK); Foreign Credit Insurance Association; International Development Cooperation Agency; Agency for International Development; Trade and Development Program; Overseas Private Investment Corporation; U.S. Agriculture Department's PL-480, Food for Peace and Commodity Credit Corporation; the World Bank Group (International Bank for Reconstruction and Development, International Development Association, International Finance Corporation); Inter-American Development Bank; Asian Development Bank; and African Development Fund. Each entry contains purpose, resources, program volume, current interest rates and fees, maturities, supported export value, guides for exporters, addresses of information and contact points, and eligibility requirements.

044 CR1.10 **Civil Rights Directory.** Rev. ed. Civil Rights Commission.
no. 15 1981. 549p. Clearinghouse publication no. 15. Annual.
1970-

The United States Civil Rights Commission has jurisdiction to study discrimination and denials of equal protection of the law on the basis of race, color, religion, national origin, sex, age, and handicap. The organizations (both governmental and private) listed in this directory are engaged in program activities in these areas. The directory includes only those agencies and organizations whose responsibilities and services are related directly to civil rights. The book has five sections, the first of which deals with federal government agencies that are responsible for enforcing, administering, monitoring, and coordinating equal opportunity laws, executive orders, and policies. Preceding the list of agencies, which are arranged alphabetically by name, is a list of civil rights authorities under which the federal agencies operate. Section 2 lists the state and local government agencies alphabetically by state. Section 3 is an alphabetical arrangement by name of private organizations and women's organizations. Section 4 lists research organizations alphabetically by name, and section 5 is an alphabetical arrangement of other organizations. Each entry lists the address, telephone number, chief executive officer with title, a brief description of the organization, purpose, activities, geographic areas served, and publications.

045 CS1.2 **Directory of Unions and Associations with Exclusive Recogni-**
Un3-16 **tion in the Federal Service.** Civil Service Commission. 1978.
22p.

This directory lists national and international unions and associations that have, either directly or through local units, exclusive recognition with departments and agencies of the executive branch of the federal government and the U.S. Postal Service. The listing is in alphabetical order by abbreviation of the organization name.

046 E1.28 **Directory of Key Foreign Personnel—Solar Commercializa-**
DOE/TIC **tion.** *See* entry 113.
11302

047 E1.28 **Market Development Directory for Solar Industrial Process**
SERI/SP **Heat Systems.** *See* entry 115.
434-454

2—Associations and Organizations / 15

048 E1.28 **Solar Energy Information Locator.** *See* entry 307.
SERI/SP
751-210

049 E1.33-2 **Consumer Energy Atlas.** *See* entry 308.
no. 10879-01

050 ED1.8 **Resource Guide: Recreation and Leisure for Handicapped**
R26-2 **Individuals.** Education Department. 1980. 102p. Irregular.
1979-

Resource Guide was created to meet the need for sources of information on programs, funding resources, and governmental publications for those interested in recreation programs for the handicapped. The publication is divided into three sections: information resources, a funding guide, and a list of publications available from federal sources. The first section describes the information resources that are primarily national in scope and cover the subject of recreation for all handicapping conditions. Each organization listing contains name, address, telephone number, statement about history and functions, what it provides, and how to use it. The second section contains program descriptions excerpted from the 1980 edition of the *Catalog of Federal Domestic Assistance* (entry 601). Each description provides an information contact with address and telephone number. The third section is an alphabetical list of publications available from federal sources. The publications section includes name, agency author, number of pages, date of publication, price, annotation, and order information.

051 ED1.30 **Directory of Education Associations, 1980-81.** Compiled by
1965-66- Lois V. Lopez. Education Department. 1981. 129p. Annual.

Updated annually, this directory lists the names, addresses, and telephone numbers of education associations and their chief officers. Also included are titles of their publications and frequency of issue. Entries are arranged in alphabetical order within six sections: national and regional; national honor and professional; state; foundations; religious; and international. The index is alphabetical by association name and by key word in the name. Before the 1979-80 edition, the volume was entitled *Education Directory: Education Associations* and was issued by the U.S. Office of Education.

052 ED1.102 **Directory of Library Networks and Cooperative Library**
L61 **Organizations, 1980.** National Center for Education Statistics.
1980. 181p.

The organizations that appear in this directory are primarily or exclusively libraries. They also have the following in common: (1) they engage in cooperative activities that are beyond the scope of traditional interlibrary loan services as stated in the American Library Association code; (2) their activities extend beyond reciprocal borrowing; (3) the organization operates for the mutual benefit of participating libraries; and (4) the scope of the organization is interinstitutional. The publication consists of the main body (a listing showing the general profile of each responding library organization in the world), and the following three alphabetical indexes: (1) all organizations by state with entry numbers indicating their location within the directory; (2) organizations' acronyms followed by their full names and entry numbers; and (3) services and activities indicating entry number. The main body entries include state, entry number, acronym, address, city, zip code, director's name and title, telephone number, participants, present and planned activities, year operations began, whether computerized, frequency of operation, paid staff, annual operating cost, and teletype number.

| 053 | EP1.2
Or3
1975- | **Environmental Organizations Directory. A Directory of Environmental Organizations for Alaska, Idaho, Oregon, and Washington.** Environmental Protection Agency. 1979. 37p. Irregular. |

Organizations are arranged alphabetically by state. Included are separate listings for the environmental defense centers, environmental management planning agencies, regional air pollution control agencies, state agencies, student groups, and U.S. Environmental Protection Agency regional offices. Information given for each entry includes contact person, address, telephone number, number of members, and a description of programs and activities.

| 054 | EP1.2
P76-14 | **A Survey of International Intergovernmental Organizations: The Strategies That They Use to Abate Pollution.** By Melvin L. Myers. Environmental Protection Agency. 1978. 133p. |

International intergovernmental organizations are surveyed as policy instruments for abating pollution in this volume. It lists sixteen international organizations and the Law of the Sea Conference, and provides a ranking of organizations based on their potential effectiveness in abating pollution. The report surveys the background and structure of, and the strategies used by, each organization. A bibliography for each organization and a general bibliography are also provided. The volume includes such organizations as the Food and Agricultural Organization (FAO), the World Health Organization (WHO), the North Atlantic Treaty Organization (NATO), and other specialized United Nations groups.

| 055 | EP1.17
no. SW157.8 | **Resource Recovery Plant Implementation Guides for Municipal Officials: Further Assistance.** Compiled by Denise Hawkins. Environmental Protection Agency. 1975. 29p. SW (Solid Waste Management) series no. 157.8. Irregular. |

The Environmental Protection Agency (EPA) has compiled this source as a three-part guide. The first section is a listing of contacts in localities actively planning resource recovery systems. These entries include the consultants they have employed, the systems they have selected, and the companies chosen to construct their systems. Part 2 lists those companies that are marketing resource recovery systems; part 3, organizations and associations that can provide information about resource recovery. Part 4 is a bibliography of articles and publications, both technical and nontechnical, with pertinent information on resource recovery. Arranged alphabetically by state and community, part 1 indicates the type of system selected, address, telephone number, consultants, and systems vendors. It also includes the consultant's primary contribution to the project. The list of part 2 is an alphabetical arrangement of companies by name, giving contact person, address, telephone number, processes used, and products. Part 3 is an alphabetical arrangement by name of the organization, listing executive officer, address, and telephone number. The bibliography in part 4 is arranged by general topics and then by specific subject areas of concern.

056 FEM1.102   **Arson Resource Directory.** Fire Administration. 1980. 161p.
      Ar7   Microfiche. Irregular.
      1980-

An explanation and full identification of key resources—organizations and individuals—that are active and successful in arson prevention and control are found in this directory. It is a "switchboard" to help readers get in touch with experts and resources and to assist them in coordinating their efforts with others to become more effective in stopping arson. It includes programs and agencies on the local, state, national, and international level. Part 1 contains the major programmatic areas across the nation concerned with arson prevention and control; part 2 identifies miscellaneous groupings of federal, public, and private resources other than those falling into the programmatic areas; and part 3 is an alphabetical index of organizations, programs, and resources listed in the directory.

057 HE1.54   **Catalog of Human Services Information Resource Organiza-**
      no. 15   **tions. An Exploratory Study of Human Services Information Clearinghouses.** Health and Human Services Department. 1980. 343p. Human Services Monograph series, no. 15. Irregular.

This catalog contains descriptive profiles of 157 organizations that disseminate human services-related information on a national, regional, or statewide basis to researchers, practitioners, administrators, and the general public. It represents an attempt to identify the myriad of federally supported human services information clearinghouses as well as many privately supported clearinghouses and similar organizations that provide information resources in the human services area. In addition to clearinghouses, the types of information resource organizations included in the catalog represent information analysis centers, special libraries, "document depots," resource centers, abstracting and indexing services, and diffusion networks. Chapter 1 is an introductory chapter; chapter 2 presents a conceptual framework within which to view various types of information resource organizations; and chapter 3, the main body of the catalog, includes profiles of all human services information organizations identified in this study. The profiles are arranged alphabetically by the name of the organization.

058 HE20.3002   **Directory of Community High Blood Pressure Control**
      B62-13   **Activities.** 2d ed. National Institutes of Health. 1977. 367p.
      1976-   Irregular.

The organizations listed in this resource are concerned primarily with the prevention and control of high blood pressure. Organizations are listed in alphabetical order by state and by city within each state. Information includes organization name, address, description, activities, contact person, telephone number, and area served.

059 HE20.5102   **Directory of Family Planning Grantees and Clinics.** 3d ed.
      D62-3   Community Health Services Bureau. 1979. 105p. Irregular.

The purpose of this directory is to facilitate communication among the various family planning clinics supported by the Bureau of Community Health Services. It includes listings for more than two hundred grantees and more than thirty-six hundred clinics. The directory is divided into two parts. The first consists of a list of the family planning grantees arranged by region and alphabetically within region by state, city, and organization name. The second part lists the family planning clinics supported by the grantees. The clinics are also arranged by region and alphabetically within region by state, city, and organization. The grantees in part 1 have been indicated by a *G* (for grantee), followed by a number located above the upper left corner of the address and name of the grantee. Corresponding numbers in part 2, located above the upper left corner of the clinic address, are used to indicate clinics supported by that grantee. Each entry contains organization name, address, and zip code.

060   HE20.5102   **A Directory of National Health, Education, and Social Service Organizations Concerned with Youth.** Community Health Services Bureau. 1979. 56p.
         N21h-5

This directory was developed as a resource for national and local organizations, interested groups, and individuals concerned about the needs of teenagers, the problem of unwanted pregnancies, and other issues affecting youth today. Direct service organizations and indirect service organizations (those that provide auxiliary services) make up the two sections of the directory. Organizations are arranged alphabetically by name within each category. Information given includes address, telephone number, director, membership, purpose, activities, and publications. An appendix gives a partial list of U.S. Department of Health, Education, and Welfare programs that provide health services for youth, and which develop policies related to youth.

061   HE20.6502   **Consumer Health Education. A Directory.** National Center for Health Services Research. 1975. 45p.
         C76

In this directory we find summaries of some of the things that have been, and are being, done by nonprofit organizations (such as voluntary health agencies, professional groups, foundations, and citizens associations) to bring health education materials to the widest range of interested people. It is arranged alphabetically by name of the organization and gives addresses, telephone number, objectives, and description of its activities, including publications and contacts.

062   HE20.8102   **Public and Private Sources of Funding for Sexual Assault Treatment Programs.** National Center for the Prevention and Control of Rape. 1981. 35p.
         Se9-3

The purpose of this publication is to assist rape crisis centers and other sexual assault treatment and service programs in obtaining financial support. While it is not a comprehensive listing of funding resources, it is a guide to possible resources in the federal government and in the private sector. The first of three sections provides brief descriptions of selected federal agencies or programs administered directly from the federal level, as well as those dispersed in block grants through individual state mechanisms. Section 2 covers private funding sources, giving names and addresses. Section 3 contains several appendixes: a bibliography of funding resources, an annotated grant proposal outline, and fundraising approaches to secure continued rape crisis center success.

063   HE20.8215   **Drug Abuse Prevention: A Guide to Speakers.** National Clearinghouse for Drug Abuse Information. Report series 19, no. 1. 1972. n.p. Irregular.
         Ser. 19
         no. 1

Arranged alphabetically by state and subsequently by the name of the organization, this directory reflects only those drug abuse programs that have reported an active speakers' bureau. It provides identifying data on programs, including program director, program name, address, and telephone number.

064 HE23.2   **Directory of National Information Sources on Handicapping**
   H19-3   **Conditions and Related Services.** Handicapped Individuals
   1976-   Office. 1980. 236p. Irregular.

This directory is a major effort to document at the national level information resources existing for handicapped persons and those working on their behalf, as well as direct service providers. The organizations and agencies listed have been arranged into various categories: information/data banks (including federal projects), database vendors, facilities, schools, clinics, federal government (other than information units), advocacy, consumer, professional and trade, voluntary health, and service organizations, and, in the appendixes, religious organizations and sports organizations. There is an alphabetical list of groups as well as a subject index indicating organizations concerned in those areas. The directory contains abstracts on 285 organizations, providing name, address, telephone number, handicapping conditions served, brief history, purpose, and objectives of the organization, and the information services provided.

065 HH1.2   **Registry of Private Fair Housing Organizations/Groups.**
   F15-7   Prepared by the National Newspaper Publishers Association. Housing and Urban Development Department. 1977. 134p.

Private fair housing organizations/groups were voluntarily established to promote the materialization of fair housing locally and throughout the nation. Their activities may include, but need not be limited to, one or more of the following: education, monitoring, information service, and referral service. All of those activities are strongly supportive of the Department of Housing and Urban Development's affirmative and enforcement efforts under Title VIII of the Civil Rights Act of 1968, the federal fair housing law. The registry was developed for governmental entities, the building and real estate industries, minority/majority home and apartment seekers, and others who promote the idea of fair housing for all people. The registry is arranged alphabetically by city within states. Each entry includes the organization's name, address, telephone number, office hours, contact person, organizational structure, affiliations, when founded, area served, personnel percentage of activity devoted to fair housing, types of fair housing programs, target discrimination areas, specific fair housing activities, and fair housing services provided. An appendix lists those organizations that did not respond to the questionnaire and their status as providers of fair housing services remains unverified. These organizations are also arranged alphabetically by state, then by city and name, giving contact person and address.

066 HH1.2   **Directory of International Organizations Concerned with**
   M56-2   **Metric Building.** Housing and Urban Development Department. 1979. 14p. Microfiche.

The focus of this publication is information on twenty-four worldwide and regional groups concerned with metric building. Section 1 lists the worldwide groups alphabetically by name, giving address, a brief description of the organization, when founded, purposes, activities, where located, and its acronym. Section 2 deals with regional groups and provides the same type of information as the first section. The directory was originally prepared as an appendix to *International Trends and Developments of Importance to the Metrification Plans of the U.S. Construction Community*, by Charles T. Mahaffey (National Bureau of Standards, 1977).

067 I49.2 **Liaison Conservation Directory for Endangered and Threat-**
    En2-8 **ened Species.** *See* entry 337.

068 I66.2 **Private Assistance in Outdoor Recreation. A Directory of**
    P93 **Organizations Providing Aid to Individuals and Public**
    1970- **Groups.** Outdoor Recreation Bureau. 1975. 63p. Irregular.

Listed here are a number of professional societies and national organizations providing low-cost publications and other aids to the planning, development, and operation of outdoor recreation areas. Arranged alphabetically by type of sport, the directory gives addresses, purposes, assistance available, and publications.

069 J1.2 **Directory of Organizations Serving Minority Communities.**
    Or3 Justice Department. 1971. 88p.

To be found in this source are the names and addresses of many federal agencies, private organizations, colleges and universities, newspapers, and radio and television broadcasters serving women and blacks, Spanish surnamed people, American Indians, and Oriental communities. The first section contains the names and addresses of the headquarters offices of federal agencies with special interest in minority communities as well as private organizations with nationwide affiliations or special channels of communication with minority groups. Local organizations and local chapters of national organizations are listed by state and city in the second section.

070 J21.2 **Directory of Nonprofit Immigration Counseling Agencies.**
    Im6-5 Immigration and Naturalization Service. 1981. 71p.

Voluntary agencies, legal services corporations, and ethnic, religious, and community organizations concerned with immigration are listed in this publication. These groups either counsel persons on immigration matters or refer them to more experienced agencies. Most of the organizations included here participate in the INS Outreach Program, which provides them with specialized training, technical assistance, mailings, access to forms, and other related services. The organizations are arranged alphabetically by regions (Eastern, Northern, Southern, and Western), by state within region, and by city within state. An additional section names other counseling agencies that were placed on the INS Outreach Program list too late for this printing. Appendixes list INS district offices, overseas offices, and other offices from which immigration counseling can be obtained, as well as INS publications used by voluntary counseling agencies. All entries contain address and telephone number.

071 J26.2 **Directory of Community Crime Prevention Programs:**
    C73-5 **National and State Levels.** By James L. Lockard, et al. National Institute of Law Enforcement and Criminal Justice. 1978. 129p.

Compiled to provide individuals and community groups with information about ongoing crime prevention programs, this directory lists the organizations concerned.

2—*Associations and Organizations* / 21

They are arranged alphabetically by name within national and state categories, giving program title, address, telephone number, services, goals and objectives, and so forth. Several appendixes augment the actual program descriptions. Appendix 1 provides an overview of the LEAA's role in community crime prevention by describing the Community Crime Prevention Division of the National Institute of Law Enforcement and Criminal Justice, and the Office of Community Anti-Crime Programs. Appendix 2 is a list of organizations which, while not within the parameters of the main directory, provide technical assistance, funding, educational literature, documents, publications, training, and training materials for those seeking further information about community crime prevention.

072   L1.2   **Register of Reporting Labor Organizations.** Labor Department. 1980. 320p. Irregular.
       R26
       1964-

Identified in this volume are labor organizations (unions) that filed reports under the reporting requirements of the Labor-Management Reporting and Disclosure Act (LMRDA), as amended, or the Civil Service Reform Act of 1978, with the U.S. Department of Labor's Office of Labor-Management Standards Enforcement. The register is arranged alphabetically by location, including the fifty states, several U.S. territories and possessions, and a number of foreign countries. The location shown for each union indicates the state and the city where that union is chartered to operate. Within each state or other jurisdiction, the listing of reporting unions is arranged under the headings of AFL-CIO trade councils and directly affiliated locals, affiliated labor organizations, and unaffiliated labor organizations. Subordinate units are listed in numerical or alphabetical sequence depending on the designation system employed by the parent union. Where a union's reports show no affiliation, the union is included under Unaffiliated Labor Organizations, arranged alphabetically by key words in its name.

073   L1.2   **Register of Federal Employee Unions.** Labor Department. 1975. 36p.
       R26-2

Listed here are federal employee unions that filed reports with the U.S. Department of Labor under the reporting provisions of Executive Order 11491, as amended, and the applicable regulations (29CFR 204.3 through 204.25). The unions listed were active as of January 1, 1975. The register is arranged alphabetically by location—state and city.

074   L1.66   **A Directory of Public Employee Organizations. A Guide to the Major Organizations Representing State and Local Public Employees.** Labor-Management Services Administration. 1974. 61p.
       Em7-2

Information on the organizational structure, location, and policies of public employees organizations is provided in this directory. The listing is limited to organizations that, either in whole or part, organize or represent public employees at state and/or local levels. It does not include those organizations that primarily represent federal employees. Only the very largest organizations are listed. The information includes headquarters address, publications, origin, conventions, membership, and jurisdiction.

22 / 2 — Associations and Organizations

075 L1.66 **A Directory of Public Management Organizations.** Labor-
M31 Management Services Administration. 1973. 47p.

Listed in this guide are the principal national public management organizations that have a substantial and continuing interest in public employee-management relations. The following information is provided for each organization: address and telephone number of the headquarters and any branch offices; brief description of the organization and its purpose; type of individual or agencies that are eligible for membership; membership requirements; organization structure; offices, titles and names of incumbents; programs and services of the organization; publications issued; information on annual conference, if any; and place and date of origin of the organization are also listed.

076 L2.3 **Directory of National Unions and Employee Associations.**
no. 2079 1979 ed. Labor Statistics Bureau. 1980. 139p. Bulletin no.
1971- 2079. Irregular.

The first of five parts in this volume reviews the structure of the labor movement in the United States, concentrating particularly on the AFL-CIO. Part 2 lists national unions and professional and state employee associations as defined by the Bureau of Labor Statistics (BLS), giving the names of the major officers and officials as well as the number of members and locals or affiliates of each organization. (Other pertinent details are presented in several appendixes.) Part 3 provides a brief summary of significant developments in organized labor; part 4 presents information on union and association membership; and part 5 discusses the various functions and activities that unions perform. Indexes of organizations and officers and officials listed in the directory are provided at the end of the volume. Appendixes include information about membership outside the United States, organizations reporting 100,000 members or more, female members, female officers and officials, white-collar members by occupation, membership by industry group, membership by state, and other topics. Before the 1975 edition, this directory was classed L2.2:Un33-9. Other editions published as BLS bulletins are nos. 1750, 1937, and 2044.

077 L36.102 **Recruitment Sources for Women.** Women's Bureau. 1978.
R24 12p.

Contained in this list are names and addresses of organizations that can provide assistance to employers seeking women candidates, particularly for professional, technical, and managerial positions. The list may also be used as a source by individual women who wish to have their names or resumés referred to employers. It is arranged alphabetically by name of the organization under the headings General, State, and Local, with a list of regional offices.

078 L36.102 **Commissions, Committees, and Councils on the Status of**
St2-2 **Women.** Women's Bureau. 1978. 8p.

This is an alphabetical list by state of the organizations on the status of women. The leaflet gives chairpersons, executive directors, and/or other staff. Provided are addresses and telephone numbers. It is attachment B to L36.102:R24 (see entry 077).

2—Associations and Organizations / 23

079 L37.102 **Directory for Reaching Minority and Women's Groups.**
M66 3d ed. Employment and Training Administration. 1979. 284p.
1970- Irregular.

Found in this directory is a compilation of organizations, institutions and individuals vital to those who are involved in equal employment or civil rights work or may seek assistance in resolving problems in such areas. The volume gives names, addresses, and telephone numbers alphabetically by state and city. It also includes federal, state, county, regional and municipal agencies; community action, ethnic service, civil rights, human resources, educational, business, industry, and media names and addresses. The title was formerly *Directory for Reaching Minority Groups*.

080 LC19.4-2 **National Organizations Concerned with Visually and Physi-**
no. 78-2 **cally Handicapped Persons.** Compiled by Carol Keys. Rev. ed.
1978- National Library Service for the Blind and Physically Handicapped. 1979. 17p. Reference circular 78-2. Irregular.

Many of the organizations listed in this circular offer various services to handicapped persons. Others are associations of professional and volunteer workers who serve the varied needs of handicapped persons or their representative organizations. Non-governmental organizations are the subject of part 1; part 2 concentrates on federal agencies concerned with handicapped persons—both those groups that serve in an advisory capacity as well as those offering direct services. The organizations in part 1 are arranged alphabetically by the name of the organization; the information given there includes address, principal publication, and a brief statement of services provided.

081 LC19.4-2 **Sports and Games for Handicapped Persons.** Compiled by
no. 79-1 Merrillyn Gibson. National Library Service for the Blind and
Feb. 1979- Physically Handicapped. December 1979. 20p. Reference circular 79-1. Irregular.

Section 1 of this circular lists those organizations that offer sports activities, equipment, or information about specific sports. Information is also given about national and international multisport competitions, arranged alphabetically by the type of sport. Section 2 lists the sources for purchasing table games that have been adapted to facilitate their play by handicapped persons. Information centers and clearinghouses are covered in section 3, and section 4 is a list of periodicals concerned with sports and recreation for the handicapped. Addresses are given for all of the organizations.

082 PM1.8 **Hispanic Employment: A Recruitment Sources Booklet**
H62 **Including Recruitment Sources in Puerto Rico.** Personnel Management Office. 1980. 136p.

A variety of information is contained in this booklet, including population figures as of 1976 for states with large concentrations of Hispanics; Hispanic national, state, and local organizations; and radio and television stations serving the Hispanic community. It also provides information on Hispanic enrollment at junior colleges, four-year colleges and universities, and a percentage breakdown of major fields of study at these institutions. The major portion of the work lists Hispanic organizations. The national list includes the major Hispanic organizations having branches in several states or having a program of national scope. The state and local section includes those organizations that operate at the state and local level in the United States. This listing is

24 / 2—*Associations and Organizations*

arranged by states and cities within each state. Addresses have been provided for all organizations with telephone numbers, if available. Only those states with significant numbers of Hispanic organizations have been included.

083   Pr39.2   **Women. A Documentary of Progress during the Administration of Jimmy Carter, 1977-1981.** Barbara Haugen, editor. President of the United States. 1981. n.p.
        W84

This volume is a composite of women's activities during the years 1977-1981. It not only lists the women in government, but accomplishments of women in other areas. The several directories that are listed in this work include organizations that seemed of such significance to warrant inclusion in this list. The major list is a guide to women's resources, which was compiled in the fall of 1980. These organizations are indexed alphabetically by principal interest and are listed in alphabetical order in the guide. Information given includes address, telephone, and contact person(s).

084   Pr39.8   **Who's Involved with Hunger: An Organization Guide.** Rev. ed. Edited by Patricia L. Kutzner, assisted by Christina Miller and Mark Lewy. The Presidential Commission on World Hunger. 1979. 35p.
        W89-3/H89-4

Organizations that are concerned about world hunger are listed in this guide. The organizations are arranged under five headings: Government Organizations; Private Agencies—Global Focus; Appropriate Technology Organizations; Private Agencies—National Focus; and Private Agencies—U.S. Regional. It contains a section on local, state, and regional organizations in the food/nutrition/and poverty field within the United States. The information given includes date of establishment, address, telephone number, director, and contact person(s). Activities and publications are also included. An alphabetical index by name of the organization is provided.

085   PrEx1.10   **Membership Directory.** *See* entry 410.
        M51-2

086   S1.67-4   **Directory of Contacts for International Educational, Cultural and Scientific Exchange Programs.** 6th ed. State Department. 1975. 71p. Irregular.

This is a listing of the private and governmental agencies active in the conduct of international exchange-of-persons programs. Divided into four sections, the first lists the government agencies with addresses, contact persons, and telephone numbers. Section 2 lists the commissions, committees, and advisory groups of U.S. government agencies. Section 3 lists intergovernmental agencies with contact persons and telephone numbers. Section 4, the largest, lists in alphabetical order the private agencies and organizations. Information given includes addresses of the main office and regional branches, if applicable, officers of the organization, and telephone. Also given are the scope, purpose, and activities of each organization.

087   S1.70   **United States Contributions to International Organizations. 29th Annual Report for Fiscal 1980.** State Department. 1981. 117p. International Organization and Conference series, no. 154. Annual.
        no. 154
        1952-

2—Associations and Organizations / 25

This publication more closely resembles a handbook than a directory; however, it contains directory-type information for many international organizations that probably will not be found elsewhere. The organization section is divided into five parts, including United Nations and special programs; specialized agencies and the International Atomic Energy Agency; Inter-American organizations; other regional organizations; and other international organizations. Information given for each organization includes the following: abbreviation or acronym, address of main headquarters, executive head, origin and development, purpose, structure, and initial date of U.S. participation. The table of contents is the guide to the arrangement.

088   T22.2   **Cumulative List of Organizations Described in Section 170(c)**
          Or3   **of the Internal Revenue Code of 1954. Revised to October 31,**
          1971- **1981.** Internal Revenue Service. 1982. 1114p. Publication no. 78. Annual.

Publication no. 78 is updated and issued annually. Three cumulative quarterly supplements are published each year, containing additions and name changes. Other changes (i.e., address) are reflected in the complete annual issuance in January. The directory contains a list of organizations eligible for receiving tax-deductible contributions, including both those groups that hold IRS determination letters and those whose ruling remains outstanding. The preface to the annual issue explains the rules covering deductions. The organizations are arranged alphabetically under their legal names, giving location (city and state).

089   VA1.22   **Service Organizations' Representatives Currently Recognized**
          no. 2-151 **in the Presentation of Claims before the VA. List of Claims**
          1978-   **Agents Recognized by the VA.** Veterans Administration. 1981. 37p. Information bulletin 2-151. Annual.

This is a complete list of the accredited representatives of each of the organizations recognized by the Administrator of Veterans Affairs under the provisions of Title 38, United States Code, Section 3402. Monthly supplements are issued between annual lists. The organizations are arranged alphabetically by name, followed by an alphabetical list of representatives. Claims agents, including addresses, are listed at the end of the publication.

090   Y3.Eq2:2   **A Directory of Resources for Affirmative Recruitment.** Equal
          R24   Employment Opportunity Commission. 1975. 91p.

Although not a complete or comprehensive listing, this publication is a starting point for employers seeking to expand their affirmative recruitment sources. Directories and professional rosters that can be helpful in identifying recruitment sources are listed in section 1. Section 2 covers some of the organizations that make specified types of referrals on a national, regional, or local basis. Each entry contains the address, contact person, telephone number, a statement of purpose and services provided, and whether a fee is charged. See also entry 079.

091   Y3.P94:2   **Directory of Labor-Management Committees.** 2d ed. National
          L11-2   Center for Productivity and Quality of Working Life. 1978.
          1976-   211p. Irregular.

26 / 2—*Associations and Organizations*

Included in this list are those organizations formed to "encourage, support, and initiate efforts in the public and private sector specifically designed to improve cooperation between labor and management in the achievement of continued productivity growth." These joint labor-management committees are also concerned with the quality of working life, including morale and working conditions. They provide a vehicle for two-way communication, and become forums for employees and management to share ideas for improving the success of enterprises and the security and satisfaction of jobs. This is only a partial listing of the currently active committees. The committees are listed alphabetically by state, and within states, alphabetically by city. In almost all cases, entries include employers and unions, date of committee origin, number of employees affected, type of committee, and whether the committee was covered by a provision in the union contract. Whenever possible, information is also given on the committee's structure and history, issues handled, and results. Names, addresses, and telephone numbers of labor and management contacts are given as well as third parties when they are involved. The directory is indexed by type of labor-management committee, by unions, and by company.

092 Y3.P94:2 **Directory of Productivity and Quality of Working Life**
P94-6 **Centers.** National Center for Productivity and Quality of Working Life. 1978. 68p.

The directory has been prepared to foster the mutually supportive relationships among the productivity and quality of working life centers of the nation. It was also designed to be of value to innovative managers in the public and private sectors by making readily available sources of information on the various aspects of productivity and quality of working life issues. The centers are arranged in alphabetical order, followed by appendixes listing foreign productivity and quality of working life centers, and a geographical index by state of the centers. The information given for each organization includes address, telephone number, background, structure, funding/support, objectives, program activities, and publications/AV materials.

093 Y3.Sp2-7:2 **Directory of Spanish Speaking Organizations in the United**
D62 **States.** Cabinet Committee on Opportunity for the Spanish Speaking. 1970. 224p.

Demands for information from organizations, agencies, and individuals who desire to work for the progress of the Spanish-speaking people in America prompted the compilation of this directory. There is an alphabetical index of organizations, an alphabetical listing of national organizations, and an alphabetical listing of organizations arranged descendingly by state, city, and organization. Only 207 organizations are listed. Information given for each organization includes name, address, telephone number, principal officer, scope, date established, primary ethnic membership, meeting schedule, whether descriptive literature is available, objectives, and branch offices, if any. See also entry 082.

094 Y3.W58-22:2 **National Organizations Issues Resource Book.** White House
Or3 Conference on Families. 1980. v.p.

Compiled as resource material to provide the White House Conference on Families National Advisory Committee with some basic information on issues, this volume contains the issues priorities for American families of over one hundred national organizations. This volume includes a wide range of organizations, representing the arts, communications, business, labor, religion, family advocacy, and many others. The organizations are arranged in alphabetical order as indicated by the table of contents. Information provided for each organization includes address, telephone number, membership, contact person(s), and issues. In some instances, policy, program, and strategy recommendations are also given. Some statements of purpose are given.

3
Businesses and Industries

Although some of the publications listed in this chapter do not give addresses of the business and industry organizations they cover, most present some means by which the companies can be identified and/or located (i.e., SIC code, occupational code). Many of the titles found here present information about businesses owned by members of minority groups and women.

| 095 | A13.2
Se3-7 | **Seed and Planting Stock Dealers: A Directory of Dealers That Sell the More Common Forest and Shelterbelt Seeds and Plants.** Forest Service. 1979. 22p. |

The purpose of this directory is to provide a list of vendors that sell the more common forest tree and shelterbelt seeds and plants. Arranged alphabetically by state, it gives the name, address, telephone number, and code number of each dealer. There is also a table of information supplied by dealers regarding the material they have available, and a species listing, which indicates the code numbers of dealers who sell the seed or planting stock.

| 096 | A103.9
1954- | **Meat and Poultry Inspection Directory.** Food Safety and Quality Service. June 1978. 493p. Occasionally on microfiche. Semiannual. |

This publication includes a list of establishments operating under federal meat inspection, public stockyards operating under animal disease eradication inspection, licensed manufacturers of biological products, pathological laboratories, trained diagnosticians, and state officials in charge of animal disease control. The establishments are arranged by number and cross-referenced in two other lists (by name and number, and by state and city). Also included is a list of foreign meat and poultry establishments. Veterinary services indicate regional and assistant directors, area officers, veterinarians in charge, lines of work and area of coverage, veterinarians specially trained in the differential diagnosis of foreign animal diseases, regional epidemiologists, veterinarians specially trained in the differential diagnosis of poultry diseases, and addresses and telephone numbers of Food Safety and Quality Service regional offices. The U.S. Food and Drug Administration field offices are also listed.

3 — *Businesses and Industries* / 29

097   C1.2   **American Association of Spanish-speaking and National**
     Am3   **Association of Minority Certified Public Accounting Firms.**
          Minority Business Enterprise Office. 1978. n.p.

Part 1 of this directory lists the member Spanish-speaking firms in alphabetical order by company name, giving their addresses and telephone numbers. Part 2 lists the members of the National Association of Minority Certified Public Accounting Firms in alphabetical order by state, indicating the name of the firm along with its address and telephone number.

098   C1.2   **Directory of Minority Media.** Minority Business Enterprise
     M66-11   Office. 1973. 89p.

This publication was designed specifically to avail established and potential advertisers an additional tool to broaden their advertising campaigns. As of 1973, there were over two hundred black-oriented newspapers published in the United States, and black-oriented radio stations exist in all areas with a substantial black population. This volume lists in part 1 the newspapers and periodicals by minority focus (American Indian, black, Oriental, and Spanish-language publications). They are arranged alphabetically by state and city, giving title of the publication and address. Part 2 lists the radio and television stations by the same arrangement. Part 3 is a statistical summary of family expenditures between 1960 and 1970, and income and general characteristics of the black and Spanish-heritage population in 1970.

099   C1.2   **National Directory of Minority Manufacturers.** Minority
     M66-14   Business Enterprise Office. 1974. 121p.

The Minority Business Enterprise Office prepared this directory to assist procurement personnel in both the public and private sectors to identify viable minority manufacturing firms that are available for contracting purposes. It does not represent the totality of minority manufacturing companies. In this volume a minority manufacturing firm is defined as one that is owned 50 percent or more by a minority individual (American Indian, black, Oriental, Mexican, Central or South American, Cuban, or Puerto Rican). The directory is arranged by company, followed by five separate indexes to assist in locating the company and product desired: alphabetical company index, alphabetical product description index, geographical index by city within state, numerical standard industrial classification (SIC) code index, and numerical federal supply classification index. Each company entry states address, contact person (with telephone number), date established, number of employees, annual sales figure, floor space (in square feet), whether it has a government contract, code for category of minority owner, SIC code, type of product, principal products and federal supply classifications (FSCs), and materials and/or processes. Each entry also contains a minority code number indicating the category of minority.

100   C1.60-3   **Geographical Areas Serviced by Bell and Independent Tele-**
     no. 73-1   **phone Companies in the United States.** By B. A. Hart. Tele-
     1973-   communications Office. 1973. 117p. OT report 73-1.
              Irregular.

This particular study was undertaken because there was no single source of information on geographic coverage of individual telephone companies in the United States. The geographic coverage of all telephone companies in the United States is presented in a series of maps. These consist of U.S. maps of operating areas served by the major companies, and individual state maps depicting the operating areas served by Bell and each of the numerous independent companies. A state-by-state listing of more than fifteen-hundred telephone companies and their headquarters is also given.

101 C13.10 **Catalog of Security Equipment.** By John V. Fechter and
       no. 480-35 Elizabeth M. Robertson. National Bureau of Standards. 1978. 52p. NBS special publication 480-35. Irregular.

The purpose of this catalog is to familiarize the general public with the kinds of security equipment available for specific needs and to identify manufacturers of the security products. Following a brief discussion of topics related to each category of security equipment, there is a description of specific equipment items in that category. The price range of each item is included in parentheses after each entry. Manufacturers and distributors of the items of security equipment are listed at the end of each section alphabetically by product. Manufacturers' addresses and telephone numbers appear at the end of the catalog in alphabetical order. There is also a subject index of products.

102 C39.202 **Directory of Minority Contractors with a Maritime Capability.**
       M66   Maritime Administration. 1977. 81p. Irregular.
       1973-

In this directory is a list of minority vendors and subcontractors serving the maritime industry of shipbuilding and ship operating companies, primarily in the eastern states. The firms are arranged alphabetically by product and/or service. Information given includes name of firm, address, chief executive officer, SIC code, products, and list of previous customers. New to the 1977 publication are the lists of previous customers and the separate sections on minority business organizations (OMBE-funded organizations and minority banks) by state. The publication also lists Office of Minority Business Enterprise regional offices, SBA regional and district offices, American Savings and Loan League members, and minority insurance companies.

103 C46.8 **Buyers Guide to Products Manufactured on American Indian**
       In2-5 **Reservations.** Economic Development Administration. 1979. 71p.

These listings describe current employment and production activities of firms operating on American Indian reservations. Part 1 lists the companies by product classification (SIC code) and indicates the page number on which the company can be found in part 2, which gives the name of the company, name of the reservation, address, contact person(s) and office held, telephone number, list of products, number of employees, and SIC codes. Part 2 is arranged alphabetically by state.

104 C61.2 **A Directory of U.S. Export Management Companies.** International Trade Administration. 1981. 188p. Microfiche. Irregular.
       Ex7-5
       1975-

The directory is divided into three parts. Part 1 is an alphabetical listing of all the companies and the product index number assigned to the firm. Part 2 lists the firms in numerical order by product index number. Information in this section includes address, contact executive, telephone number, telex and cable numbers, and a brief description of products handled. Part 3 is a product index containing an alphabetical listing of products and index numbers of the firms that handle those products.

105 C61.10-2 **Commercial News USA. New Products Annual Directory for 1980.** International Trade Administration. 1981. 350p. Annual.
       1979-

The purpose of the monthly *Commercial News USA* magazine is to provide U.S. export offers suitable for dissemination throughout the worldwide Commercial Newsletter Service to over 200,000 foreign business officials, government representatives, and other prospective buyers. This new-product and trade information is made available to foster U.S. commercial interest in foreign markets. In addition, it informs the U.S. Foreign Service of new Commerce Department trade promotion programs and policy development. This directory includes all the new products listings published in issues of *Commercial News USA* from January through December 1980. The 1980 directory constitutes a single-source document that can serve as a convenient guide to new American products. The directory is organized into thirty-one types of industries (agricultural machinery and equipment, sports, recreation, hobbies, automotive, etc.). Within each category the product is named and described, price indicated, bank reference given, and contact and address provided. Also included is an alphabetical listing of companies and their addresses, indicating the 1980 issue of *Commercial News USA* in which they appear.

106 C62.14 **Franchise Opportunities Handbook.** Industrial Economics Bureau. 1981. 358p. Annual.
       1978-

The purpose of this volume is to assist in the establishment of minority group businesses. Information is given on how to franchise, other sources of information about franchising, government assistance programs, and nongovernment assistance programs. Franchising participants or companies are indexed alphabetically and by category. The main body of the volume lists franchise company data and is arranged alphabetically by the name of the company. Data includes address, contact person(s), description of operation, number of franchisees, how long in business, equity capital needed, financial assistance available, training provided, managerial assistance available, and when the information was submitted to the publishers of the volume.

107 CAB1.26 **List of Certificated U.S. Air Carriers.** Civil Aeronautics Board. September 1980. 9p. Semiannual.
       1977-

Listed in this publication is the current address of certificated air carriers (route carriers, charter carriers, and cargo carriers). Before 1980, it was entitled *List of U.S. Air Carriers* and also included air freight forwarders and names of presidents of companies with official abbreviations and authorizations. The carriers and addresses are listed alphabetically by name within the three categories.

108 CSA1.2 **Accessibility Assistance. A Directory of Consultants on Environments for Handicapped People.** Compiled by Margaret Milner, National Center for a Barrier Free Environment. Community Services Administration. 1978. 202p.
       Ac2

The principal section of this volume is a geographical arrangement by state (in alphabetical order) that gives address, telephone number, professional category of the

32 / 3 — Businesses and Industries

consultant, type of services available, and a brief summary of experience with accessibility projects. Also names and addresses of one or two references are provided for each firm. Other sections list consultants alphabetically by professional or agency category and an alphabetical name index. Both of these sections have page references to the consultant profile listings in the geographical section.

| 109 | D1.46
no. 5100.6
v. 2
1980- | **Contractors Listing. Volume II of Directory of Federal Contract Audit Offices.** Defense Contract Audit Agency. 1980. 352p. Pamphlet no. 5100.6, v. 2. Irregular. |

Volume 2 of this set is an alphabetical listing of contractors including addresses and telephone numbers of defense and nondefense contractors that have been audited by the Defense Contract Audit Agency (DCAA) based on assigned audit cognizance or arrangements that have been made for audits of contracts awarded by other organizations. In order to find the auditing office of a particular contractor, locate that contractor's entry in volume 2 to determine the organization code assigned to the audit location; then find the organization code in the organization code index in volume 1, which will list the page number of the auditing office. Information given for each contractor includes name, address, telephone number, and audit office code number.

| 110 | D14.10
no. 74 | **DCPA National Directory of Fallout Shelter Analysts and Their Associated Architectural and Engineering Firms.** Defense Civil Preparedness Agency. 1978. 370p. Miscellaneous publication no. 74. Irregular. |

This directory lists firms that have indicated they employ staff architects and/or engineers who have successfully completed a course in fallout shelter analysis (FSA) sponsored by Defense Civil Preparedness Agency (DCPA). The directory is divided into sections corresponding to the eight DCPA regions and arranged alphabetically by states within each region. After the name of each firm, a roster of the individuals who are FSAs and work for that specific firm are provided. The address of the firm is given along with information as to whether the individual is a qualified instructor or attended certain courses. A roster of other FSAs living within the state but not associated with an architectural or engineering firm are listed alphabetically at the end of each state, with only name and place given. Two other sections list foreign analysts with locale, and other firms with FSAs.

| 111 | E1.2
C73-3 | **Commercially Available Small Wind Systems and Equipment. A Checklist Prepared by the Rocky Flats Wind Systems Program.** Energy Department. 1981. 21p. |

Found in this volume are wind machines and equipment being marketed in the United States as of the publication date. The systems included are all rated at less than one hundred kilowatts or nonelectrical equivalent. Information is given on firms dealing in small wind machines, anemometers and recorders, wind machine towers, batteries, inverters, plans, and kits. The small wind machines section is divided into electrical output wind machines (giving model name, usually comparing name and number, size rated by kilowatt, rotor diameter, number of blades, rated speed, and cut-in speed); mechanical output wind machines (giving name and model number, capacity, elevations, pipe diameter, rotor diameter, rated wind speed, and cut-in wind speed);

electrical wind machine manufacturers; mechanical wind machine manufacturers; and wind machine dealers/distributors. Information for all firms includes name, address, products, telephone number, and, when available, contact person.

112 E1.26   **National Solar Heating and Cooling Commercial Demon-**
       no. 0057   **stration Program. Key Personnel Directory.** Energy Depart-
       1978-   ment. 1979. 137p. DOE/CS series, no. 0057. Irregular.

The purpose of this directory is to identify those firms and individuals who are principal participants in the Department of Energy's (DOE) solar heating and cooling demonstration projects for federal and nonfederal commercial buildings. The listing provides identification of several participants in each active DOE commercial demonstration project. When available, identifying information has been provided for owners, architects, solar designers, mechanical engineers, builders, and other key personnel directly involved in each project. Part 1 is an index to projects of nonfederal commercial buildings, federal commercial buildings, and federal residential buildings arranged alphabetically by state giving location, proposer, building type, solar application, and solar manufacturer. Part 2 is also an alphabetical arrangement by state, giving name of project and address, owner, solar designer, architect, mechanical engineer, builder, contract officer representative, and other key people with addresses, contact persons, and telephone numbers. An appendix lists additional sources of information and solar projects other than those sponsored by the DOE. Both parts are arranged in three sections covering nonfederal commercial buildings, federal commercial buildings, and federal residential buildings.

113 E1.28   **Directory of Key Foreign Personnel – Solar Commercializa-**
       DOE/TIC   **tion.** Energy Department. 1980. 227p. Contractor Research
       11302   and Development report DOE/TIC 11302. Irregular.
       1980-

This directory was specifically designed as a reference manual that can be used by U.S. industries and government in the development of an international solar energy commercialization strategy. Section 1 is an alphabetical listing by country that includes in-country manufacturing, financial institutions, nonprofit associations, installations and maintenance, research and development organizations, key government offices, and location of diplomatic representation. Names, addresses, and telephone numbers are given for the firms, as well as contact person(s), when available, and area of activity. Section 2 is an alphabetical arrangement of companies denoting country, an alphabetical arrangement of associations, and a list of agents/industry representatives for U.S. companies in foreign countries, and telex numbers.

114 E1.28   **Large-Scale Alcohol Fuels Plants Directory.** Compiled by
       SERI/SP   Arthur Adams, Solar Energy Research Institute. Energy
       290-1467   Department. 1981. 108p. Contractor Research and Develop-
       1981-   ment report SERI/SP 290-1467. Irregular.

Found in this directory are the results of a survey of ethanol and methanol plants in the United States producing at least 100,000 gallons per year. It includes 299 plants from 44 states. Plants are listed in the directory according to location, by state and then city. If a city for the plant has not been selected yet, the plant is listed at the beginning of its state. If a state has not been selected, the plant appears at the front of the directory. Such plants are labeled "Site Not Selected." Information given for each plant listing includes plant location, information contact with address, operational stage, type of alcohol produced, proof of alcohol, production (stating 1980 and 1981 capacity), primary feedstock, secondary feedstock, byproduct, and capitol cost. Indexes at the rear of the directory list the plants by sequence number according to byproducts, capacity, company, and feedstock. Asterisks are used in the indexes to indicate operational plants.

115 E1.28 **Market Development Directory for Solar Industrial Process**
SERI/SP **Heat Systems.** Prepared by the Solar Energy Research Insti-
434-454 tute. Energy Department. 1980. 377p. Contractor Research
1980- and Development report SERI/SP 434-454. Irregular.

The purpose of this directory is to provide a basis for market development activities through a location listing of key trade associations, trade periodicals, and key firms for three target groups (potential industrial users, potential industrial process heat (IPH) system designers, and solar IPH equipment manufacturers). Chapter 1 lists trade associations and their publications for selected four-digit SIC industries. Eighty SICs are included in this chapter, and some key statistics and a location list of the largest plants (in comparison to the number of employees in each state) are included for fifteen of the eighty SICs. Address, telephone number, and chief executive officers are given. Chapter 2 lists architectural/engineering and consulting firms known to have solar experience. Professional associations and periodicals to which information on solar IPH systems may be directed also are included in this chapter. Chapter 3 contains a listing of solar equipment manufacturers and their associations.

116 E2.2 **Staff Report on Retired Hydropower Plants in the United**
H99 **States.** Federal Energy Regulatory Commission. 1980. 51p.

This listing of retired plants includes more than three thousand sites, giving a brief summary of pertinent data for each. Table 1 indicates, by state, the number of sites and the previously installed capacity at retired hydropower plant sites that may have potential for redevelopment. Every state except Mississippi has one or more retired hydropower plant sites. Table 2 lists the number of retired hydropower plants and the previously installed capacity by major drainages. Table 3 lists information for each retired plant in the Federal Energy Regulatory Commission (FERC) inventory of retired state plants, and is arranged by state and river basin code. Information given here includes plant and site name, latest known owner of powerhouse, name of stream where plant is located or name of stream where water is diverted to site, name of state using FIPS abbreviation code where powerhouse or site is located, nameplate capacity in kilowatts, difference in elevations between the top of the power pool and tailwater with no discharge, date when last unit was retired or placed in permanent standby or when generation was permanently stopped for any reason, FERC map number, and plant status/classification indicating viability for development, remaining structures, and reason for retirement.

117 E3.2 **Small Producer Certificate Dockets Sequenced by Docket**
P94 **Number Authorized for Use in Reporting to the Federal**
Energy Regulatory Commission. Prepared by John Ryan and Marvin Hirsh. Energy Information Administration. 1979. v.p.

3 — *Businesses and Industries* / 35

A companion volume to E3.2:P94-2 (entry 118) and E3.35 (entry 123), this resource is a listing in numerical sequence of all small producer certificate dockets assigned by FERC through the filing date of the last listed docket. It is arranged in numerical order by producer code number.

118	E3.2 P94-2	**Small Producer Certificate Holders and Co-owners, Listed Alphabetically. Authorized for Reporting to the Federal Energy Regulatory Commission.** Prepared by John Ryan and Marvin Hirsh. Energy Information Administration. 1979. 395p.

The publication contains in alphabetical order all applicants and co-owners in small producer certificate applications filed with the FERC through February 5, 1979. Information given includes the six-digit producer code number, the CS docket number, date application was filed, date of the order issuing the small producer certificate, if issued; date certificate was issued; date certificate was denied, terminated, or rejected; date a mailing was returned because respondent address was not correct; and date a respondent changed its name because of a succession or a redesignation.

119	E3.11/7-4 1980-	**Coal Distribution Companies in the United States—1980.** Energy Information Administration. 1981. 107p. Annual.

Identified here are organizations in the United States that submitted distribution data directly to the Energy Information Administration (EIA) on form EIA6, "Coal Distribution Report." The term *coal distribution companies* includes coal mining companies, wholesale coal dealers (including brokers), and retail coal dealers. The companies are arranged in alphabetical order, giving the address and identifying the coal-producing district(s) served. Definitions and geographical locations of the coal-producing districts are given following the company list.

120	E3.11/7-5 1979-	**Directory of Coal Production Ownership, 1979.** Energy Information Administration. 1981. 43p. Microfiche. Irregular.

Production ownership patterns in the coal industry are identified in this report as accurately as possible. This directory would be of interest to anyone who is interested in accurately tracing the ownership of coal companies to parent companies, or who is concerned about the structure of ownership in the U.S. coal industry. This audience includes coal industry specialists, coal industry policy analysts, economists, financial analysts, and members of the investment community. The information and analysis contained in this report are not available from any other EIA office or government agency. The report is organized into three sections. The first describes the report and contains an analysis of the composition of coal production ownership; the second section contains a description of the methodology and data sources utilized in compiling the directory, and also provides examples of how to use the directory; and the third section contains the directory proper in two parts. In the directory section, table 1 presents the 162 parent operating companies, arranged in order of their production rank, showing ownership of the operating company, the source of the data concerning ownership, and its Securities and Exchange Commission (SEC) classification. Table 2 is an alphabetical grouping of each of the 312 individual producing units shown in table 1.

| 121 | E3.21
El2/supp.
1977- | **Plant and Ownership List Supplementary to the Maps #1-11, Entitled Principal Electric Facilities, 1978. Based on Data to June 1977.** Energy Information Administration. 1978. 87p. Irregular. |

The first part of this volume lists alphabetically the company ownership list together with the four-letter codes and the states within which each utility operates. Part 2 lists the generating plants by assigned numbers in ascending order within each state. Information given includes the name of the plant, reliability council symbol, megawatt capacity and type of plant symbol, utility code (ownership) number of the map on which it appears, and location code on the map. Information on maps indicates transmission kilowatt lines and generating plants' capacity. The types of stations shown by symbols are conventional steam electric, nuclear steam electric, reciprocating internal combustion engine, combustion turbine, hydroelectric station, combined cycle, and capacity under construction.

| 122 | E3.29
1977- | **Inventory of Power Plants in the United States. 1980 Annual.** Energy Information Administration. 1981. 333p. Annual. |

This publication is designed to provide a current record of electric power-generating capacity in the United States. It contains a comprehensive list of existing, standby, out-of-service, and retired electric generating plants, as well as projections for new units planned by utilities. The report is divided into five chapters: (1) "Introduction," (2) "Summary," (3) "Electric Generating Units," (4) "Jointly Owned Units," and (5) "Projected Units." Chapters 3, 4, and 5 are organized alphabetically by state; within each state, generating units are listed alphabetically by electric utility system. Information given for each unit includes state, company, plant, county, unit number, nameplate rating in megawatts, unit type, primary fuel, alternative fuel, status, date, whether jointly owned, and last update.

| 123 | E3.35
1979- | **Buyer/Seller Codes Authorized for Reporting to the Federal Energy Regulatory Commission.** Prepared by John Ryan, Sr. and Marvin Hirsh. Energy Information Administration. 1980. 148p. Annual. |

The buyer/seller codes in this publication are six-digit code numbers assigned to buyers and sellers of natural gas. It is a companion volume to E3.2:P94-2 (entry 118), and is arranged alphabetically by name. Names of individual persons are listed in alphabetical order, last name first. Company names are listed in alphabetical order, exactly as the legal company name is written, within the constraints of a thirty-five character line.

| 124 | EP1.2
M66-11 | **Professional Minority Consulting Firms.** Environmental Protection Agency. 1980. 66p. |

The Environmental Protection Agency (EPA) works to facilitate procurement opportunities within the minority business community. This directory is intended to assist program personnel in further identifying and assisting minority businesses to obtain a fair share of the agency's contract work. Part 1 of the directory is an alphabetical listing by name of the minority companies, indicating page number where detailed data can be found. The Small Business Administration's (SBA) 8(a) Program companies are designated by an asterisk. Part 2 is an alphabetical arrangement of the

3—*Businesses and Industries* / 37

companies, indicating key executive officer, address, telephone number, and a list of areas of expertise or activity.

125   EP1.17   **Resource Recovery Plant Implementation Guides for Municipal Officials: Further Assistance.** *See* entry 055.
no. SW157.8

126   FHL1.31   **Members of the Federal Home Loan Bank System. 1978.** Federal Home Loan Bank Board. 1979. 99p. Microfiche. Annual.

Classified by type of institution, this directory lists savings and loan associations. Part 1 is an alphabetical listing by state and then by city of savings and loan associations insured by the Federal Savings and Loan Insurance Corporation (FSLIC). Information given includes docket number, name of the association, and address. Part 2 lists the uninsured savings and loan associations that are members of the Federal Home Loan Bank (FHLB) system. Each entry is arranged alphabetically by state and city, and gives association name and docket number. Part 3 lists alphabetically by state and city the member mutual savings banks and life insurance companies. Bank name and docket number are given. The appendix lists registered savings and holding loan companies. They are arranged alphabetically by state and city, with holding company name and number.

127   GS1.2   **Women and Business. A Directory of Women-owned Businesses in Washington, Oregon, Idaho, and Alaska.** General
W84   Services Administration, Region 10, 1979. 63p.

This list of women-owned businesses is arranged alphabetically by name under five categories: construction, manufacturing, transportation, retail-wholesale, and services. Information given for each firm includes name, address, telephone number, name of owner(s), chief executive officer, and a brief description of the type of business and services offered.

128   GS1.2   **Directory of Women Business Owners.** General Services
W84-2   Administration, Region 2. 1980. 24p.

This is a directory of women-owned businesses primarily of the General Services Administration's (GSA) Region 2 (New York and New Jersey). Divided into two sections by commodities and services, part 1 list the Region 2 companies. Part 2 lists like businesses in the other areas of the country. All companies are arranged alphabetically under their designated headings, such as advertising, janitorial services, typing, and so forth. Information given for each company includes name, address, and contact person.

129   HE19.102   **Alphabetic List of Lenders.** Education Office. 1979. 508p.
Al7

Institutions and organizations that have awarded students loans for the furtherance of their education are listed here and in two companion volumes. (See entry 130). This volume lists the lenders alphabetically by name. Information provided for each lender includes address, lender number, lender type (national bank, state bank, savings and loan, credit union, insurance company, etc.), parent type, whether federal or guaranteed loan, interest billing, federal claims, and ineligibility reason.

38 / 3—Businesses and Industries

130 HE19.102   **State/City List of Lenders.** Education Office. 1979. 536p.
St2

This volume and HE19.102:N91-2 (*Numeric List of Lenders, 1979*), are companion volumes to *Alphabetic List of Lenders* (entry 129), and they provide the same information (see annotation for entry 129). The difference is that the numeric list is arranged numerically by lender number, and the state/city list is arranged alphabetically by state and then by city and name of organization.

131 HH1.2   **Registry of Minority Contractors and Housing Professionals.**
M66-4   10 vols. Housing and Urban Development Department. 1973.

These directories are divided in ten separate volumes by region with each volume having two major parts or sections. Part 1 lists by metropolitan areas names of contractors in alphabetical order. Many of the larger metropolitan area listings are broken into subareas (e.g., South Side Chicago, East Chicago). This section also lists the business specialty of each company. Part 2 provides additional background information on each of the businesses listed in part 1. Businesses, with ID codes for cross references, are arranged here in alphabetical order, giving name, address, telephone number, type of ownership, minority group, number of employees, years in operation, if licensed or registered, and if carries liability insurance. It also indicates profession or business, category of clients (individual, private, or public), financial support organization, contact person, and other information.

132 I1.84-3   **Source Directory. Native American Owned and Operated**
1967-   **Arts and Crafts Businesses.** 1980-81 ed. Interior Department. 1980. 23p. Irregular.

The entries in this directory are native American-owned and -operated arts and crafts businesses that offer a wide variety of creative products for sale. Included are (1) artist and craftsmen cooperatives; (2) tribal arts and crafts enterprises; (3) businesses privately owned and operated by native American craftsmen and artists; and (4) businesses privately owned and operated by native American merchants who retail and/or wholesale authentic native American arts and crafts products. Also included are several nonprofit organizations that work directly with native American groups to develop products and markets. The majority of the sources listed maintain retail shops, and visitors to the areas where they are located are especially welcomed. The entries are arranged alphabetically by state as follows: name of source, mailing address, city, zip code, (highway location, Indian reservation), hours/season, telephone, type of organization or owner/manager (tribe), product's main category, mail order catalog, and price list information. The directory is also illustrated with pictures of some products. The title was formerly *Source Directory. Indian and Eskimo Organizations Marketing Native American Arts and Crafts.*

133 J1.41   **Directory of Security Consultants.** Prepared by Elizabeth
no. 0309.00   Robertson and John V. Fechter. National Institute of Law Enforcement and Criminal Justice. 1975. 59p. Law Enforcement Standards Program report no. 0309.00. Irregular.

The resources listed in this directory should be of help to the general public, community authorities, police, businesses, and others wishing to identify effective strategies to eliminate or protect targets of opportunity, in addition to identifying measures and mechanisms to stimulate community support of such strategies. Arranged into three categories (consultants in the industrial commercial/environment, in the college/university environment, and consultants with specialized functions), with listings ordered alphabetically by the name of the firm, the directory provides title, acronym, address, telephone number, description of services, publications, year operations began, persons on staff, geographical area of operations, and dates and locations of annual meetings. Also included are alphabetical, geographical, and subject indexes.

134 L1.2   **Try Us. 1975 National Minority Business Directory.** 6th ed.
     D62   Labor Department. 1975. n.p. Irregular.

Contained in this directory are three thousand listings of minority-owned firms classified by products or services and a "try-us" number. Included are an alphabetical listing of products/services with "try-us" numbers, an alphabetical listing of firms with "try-us" numbers, and the main body of the volume, arranged in alphabetical order by product/service. The main section lists product/service and SIC code, and the firms are arranged by "try-us" numbers within each state. Information given includes name, address, telephone number, contact person, and a brief description of services. Also included is date of establishment, number of employees, and sales figures. An alphabetical subject index of products cross references the "try-us" numbers. In back of the volume are pictures and/or illustrations of products and facilities.

135 SBA1.2   **Directory of Operating Small Business Investment Companies.**
     D62-2   Small Business Administration. 1979. 72p. Microfiche.
     1978-   Irregular.

Small business investment companies (SBICs) whose licenses issued by SBA remain outstanding are listed here. Exceptions are those companies that are in process of surrendering their licenses or are subject to legal proceedings that may result in the termination of their activity as small business investment companies. Part 1 is a list of the small business investment companies arranged alphabetically by state; part 2 is a list of the 301(d) licensees arranged alphabetically by state (limited to assisting small business concerns owned by socially or economically disadvantaged persons). In part 1, the companies are listed alphabetically by name with president or chief executive officer, address, telephone number, license number, private capital, SBA leverage, investment policy, and owner code (key to the owner code is given at the end of the directory). Part 2 also indicates the total number of 301(d) SBICs by state, total private capital, and total obligations to the SBA. Also indicated are totals by private capital size group, by type of ownership, and private capital by type of ownership.

136 SBA1.2   **Firms in the 8(a) Business Development Program as of**
     F51   **March 31, 1980.** Small Business Administration. 1980. 262p.
     1979-   Irregular.

All 8(a) firms are arranged alphabetically by state within Small Business Administration (SBA) regions of the United States. Information for each firm includes case number (control number assigned to identify a company), company name, telephone number, minority code, business class (industrial classification code), chief executive officer, street address and zip code, noun description of company, and business plan approval date.

137   SE1.2   **SEC Corporation Index. Active Companies and Companies**
       C81-10   **That Have Become Inactive since March 31, 1975, as of March 30, 1979.** Securities and Exchange Commission. 1979. v.p.

This corporation directory shows the assignment of cases to the branches of Corporate Analysis and Examination of the Division of Corporation Finance and the Division of Investment Management in alphabetical order by name of the issues of securities. It also includes a separate listing of foreign governments and foreign private issuers. The index shows the name of the issuer, or registrant, with address; file number of the docket in which the periodic reports are filed; issuer code number used to arrange the names of the issuer in alphabetical order in the index; code number of the branch to which the case is assigned for examination and other processing; code number of the acts under which the issuer has made, or is required to make, filings for which the Division of Corporation Finance is initially responsible; state in which the executive office of the issuer is located; code number for the fiscal year end of the issuer; and classification code used by the Division of Corporation Finance to locate cases where similar disclosure problems may have been encountered in the examination by an earlier coding system.

138   SE1.2   **List of Companies Registered under the Investment Company**
       In8-11   **Act of 1940, as of March 30, 1979.** Securities and Exchange
       1977-   Commission. 1979. 70p. Occasionally on microfiche. Irregular.

Part 1 is an alphabetical list of companies registered, giving class (whether management closed-end diversified, management closed-end nondiversified, etc.), date of registration, file number, and name of branch chief. Part 2 is an alphabetical list of deregistrations, giving file number, date of registration and deregistration, and release number. Part 3 is an alphabetical list of withdrawals giving file number, date of registration, and date of withdrawal. Parts 4 through 7, respectively, list companies exempt pursuant to Section 6, companies exempt pursuant to Section 3(b)(2), companies granted Section 7(d) orders permitting their registrations as foreign investment companies, and exchange funds. Part 8 is an alphabetical list of companies whose shares are offered at no sales load, and gives addresses.

139   SE1.2   **Classification, Assets and Location of Registered Investment**
       In8-12   **Companies under the Investment Company Act of 1940. As of**
       1970-   **September 30, 1978.** Securities and Exchange Commission. 1979. 76p. Annual.

The main body of this directory lists closed-end companies, open-end companies, unit trusts, and face-amount certificate companies alphabetically by region. Information given includes address of principal office, net assets as of September 30, 1978, and date of registration. There is an alphabetical index of companies, giving page number and denoting small business companies. There is also a summary of investment companies by regional office and a ten-year 1969-1978 table.

140   SE1.2   **Index of Active Registered Investment Companies under the**
       In8-16   **Investment Company Act of 1940 and Related Investment**
       1978-   **Advisers, Principal Underwriters, Sponsors (i.e. Depositors) and Underlying Companies as of March 30, 1979.** Securities and Exchange Commission. 1979. 161p. Irregular.

In five parts, cross-referenced, are the names of active registered investment companies and their respective investment advisers, principal underwriters, sponsors (i.e., depositors), and underlying companies, listed in alphabetical order.

141 SE1.2 **Investment Adviser Directory as of December 31, 1978.**
In8-17 Securities and Exchange Commission. 1979. 200p. Irregular.

Contained in this directory is an alphabetical listing by name of all investment advisers registered with the Securities and Exchange Commission, showing the name, principal address, type or organization (sole proprietorship, partnership, corporation, other trusteeship, associations, etc.), and SEC file number for each registrant. It also shows the date on which the investment adviser became registered with the commission.

142 SE1.27 **Directory of Companies Required to File Annual Reports with**
1971- **the Securities and Exchange Commission under the Securities Exchange Act of 1934. Alphabetically and by Industry Groups.** Securities and Exchange Commission. December 31, 1981. 387p. Annual.

Listed in this volume are 8,916 companies with securities listed on national securities exchanges, companies with securities that are traded over-the-counter and are registered under Section 12(g) of the Securities Exchange Act, and certain companies required to file pursuant to 15(d) of the Securities Exchange Act as a result of having securities registered under the Securities Act of 1933. The alphabetical list of companies lists industry code (manufacturing or nonmanufacturing), docket number, and fiscal year. The industry groups are based on the Enterprise Standard Industrial Classification developed by the Office of Management and Budget, Executive Office of the President. There are eight industry groupings and a section for nonclassifiable companies.

143 T63.102 **Financial Organization Directory.** Government Financial
F49 Operations Bureau. 1976. 363p. Irregular.

This directory shows the central mailing address and employer identification number for every financial organization that has concurred in the composite check procedures. Financial organizations are listed in this directory under the main office location. The directory also provides information on those few financial organizations that have advised the bureau that they cannot receive composite checks at a central point. The organizations are arranged alphabetically by state, city within state, and title of financial organization within the city. Financial organizations are cross-referenced to its central mailing address.

144 TD4.8-5 **Federal Aviation Administration Certificated Maintenance**
no. 140-7A **Agencies Directory.** Federal Aviation Administration. March 1, 1980. 85p. Advisory circular (AC) no. 140-7A. Irregular.

Provided in this circular is a consolidated directory of all Federal Aviation Administration certificated repair stations (appendix 1) and parachute lifts (appendix 2). These maintenance agencies were certificated under the authority of Federal Aviation Regulation (FAR) parts 145 and 149, respectively. Each section is arranged alphabetically by state and firm within each state, giving address and code numbers for ratings and services provided. Foreign repair stations are also listed. Definitions of the codes used are given in the introduction.

42 / 3—Businesses and Industries

145 Y3.F31-8:18 **Operating Banking Offices, December 31, 1980.** Federal
1973- Deposit Insurance Corporation. 1981. 689p. Irregular.

This publication contains a listing of all operating banking offices in the United States and other areas. Information given includes whether bank carries federal deposit insurance; whether it is a state or national or mutual bank; whether a member of Federal Reserve System; number of branches, offices, facilities, and so forth. The directory is arranged alphabetically by state and city and name of the bank.

146 Y3.F31-20:2 **Directory of Minority Vendors. State of Oregon, July 1979.**
M66 Prepared by Minority Business Opportunity Committee, Portland Federal Executive Board. Federal Executive Board. 1979. 85p.

More than three hundred minority firms capable of providing goods and services to other commercial, industrial, and government entities are listed here. Minority businesses in this directory mean those businesses owned at least 50 percent by minority group members, or in the case of publicly owned businesses, at least 51 percent of the voting stock is owned by minority individuals. The firms are arranged alphabetically under six SIC code classifications (construction, manufacturing, transportation and communication, wholesale and retail, general services, and professional services). Each listing gives address, telephone number, contact person, date established, and types of jobs preferred. Also included is an alphabetical listing of companies, and a list of minority business resources.

147 Y3.N88:10 **Owners of Nuclear Power Plants.** By R. S. Wood. Nuclear
no. 0327 Regulatory Commission. December 1979. 47p. NUREG 0327
1977- rev. 2. Irregular.

Included here are all plants operating, under construction, docketed for NRC safety and environmental reviews, or under NRC antitrust review. The directory does not include those plants announced but not yet under review or those plants formally cancelled. Part 1 lists plants alphabetically with their associated plants and percentage ownership. Part 2 lists applicants alphabetically with their associated plants and percentage ownership. Part 1 also indicates which plants have received operating licenses (OLs). No cities or addresses are given.

4
Data Sources

Sources of data on all aspects of life today are most important to all researchers. Being able to put your finger on the exact source that gives the information needed is quite unusual and greatly appreciated. This chapter lists directories that will help you locate facts quickly.

148 A1.76 **Guide to USDA Statistics.** Agriculture Department. 1972. 59p.
no. 429 Agriculture handbook no. 429. Irregular.

This guide is abstracted from *Major Statistical Series of the U.S. Department of Agriculture: How They Are Constructed and Used*, Agriculture handbook no. 365. It is intended as a convenient reference for those who want to locate a particular series. Each series is listed alphabetically and is described briefly, telling what it is, what it measures, what it includes (such as subindexes or companion series), limitations or cautions as to use, and where current data are published. The Major Statistical series handbook consists of eleven volumes, each issued as a separate publication: (1) *Agricultural Prices and Parity*; (2) *Agricultural Production and Efficiency*; (3) *Gross and Net Farm Income*; (4) *Agricultural Marketing Costs and Charges*; (5) *Consumption and Utilization of Agricultural Products*; (6) *Land Values and Farm Finance*; (7) *Farm Population and Employment*; (8) *Crop and Livestock Estimates*; (9) *Farm Cooperatives*; (10) *Market News*; and (11) *Foreign Trade, Production, and Consumption of Agricultural Products*.

149 C3.2 **Housing Data Resources. Indicators and Sources of Data for**
H81-3 **Analyzing Housing and Neighborhood Conditions.** Census Bureau. 1980. 42p.

This report is one of a series of publications describing current urban issues in areas such as education, housing and neighborhood development, and social services. The purpose of this report is to suggest indicators and sources of data useful to policymakers, planners, or researchers for planning programs, evaluating need, or monitoring changes in socioeconomic and physical conditions in the city. Major sources of data available to a city are described in this report. These include federal and local sources, as well as information available from trade associations and private companies.

44 / 4—Data Sources

| 150 | C3.145
no. 78
1971- | **Guide to Recurrent and Special Governmental Statistics.** Census Bureau. 1976. 205p. State and Local Government Special Studies, no. 78. Irregular. |

Summarized in this guide are tabular presentations produced as part of the Census Bureau's program of state and local government statistics. It is divided into two sections: one for recurrent reports, and the other for special studies. Within these sections are chapters referring to the most recent issue of the various reports published in this statistical series. Each chapter is essentially a synthesis of the original report, and contains the title, table of contents, and a sample of every table published in the original report. Section 1 contains the recurrent reports; special studies are explained in section 2. The introduction is a good guide to the data sources listed.

| 151 | C3.238-4
1981- | **National Clearinghouse for Census Data Services. Address List.** Census Bureau. 1981. n.p. Annual. |

Listed in this title are organizations registered with the National Clearinghouse, which provide specialized assistance in obtaining and utilizing statistical data and related products prepared by the Census Bureau. This assistance may range from informational services, such as seminars or workshops, to technical services, such as providing tape copies or performing geocoding. Divided into two parts, the first is a listing by state, and the second is a list of organizations by services provided. (Addresses, telephone numbers and contact persons are given.) The letters A through M are used to indicate the services provided, and these codes are summarized at the bottom of each page in the state listing. Services provided may include one or all of the following: preparation of computer tape copies, printouts, or special files and extracts; preparation of microfiche copies, printouts from microfiche, or other micrographic services; preparation of analytic reports, area comparisons, or area profiles; online access to data; training programs or other information services in accessing and/or using census data; special services (such as geocoding, site selection, market area analysis, redistricting, or other activities using census products). For earlier editions see entry 152.

| 152 | C3.238-4
A79
1977-1980 | **Summary Tape Processing Centers and State Data Centers. Address List.** Census Bureau. 1980. 8p. Annual. |

The organizations listed in this publication provide services designed to assist data users in obtaining and utilizing statistical data and related sources prepared by the Census Bureau. The services range from assistance in selecting the right statistical report to sophisticated computer tape processing. Summary Tape Processing Centers (STPCs) are organizations that have advised the Census Bureau that they have tape files of data prepared by the bureau and, at minimum, perform processing services for data users. State Data Centers (SDCs) are generally consortiums of state organizations (e.g., state planning agency, state library, and major state university) that provide tape processing, training, and other user services. The organizations are arranged in alphabetical order by state, and each organization address is followed by codes that summarize its characteristics. The codes are summarized at the bottom of alternate pages and in the introduction. To keep informed about new summary tape processing centers or SDCs and to receive future revisions of this list, subscribe to *Data User News*, the monthly newsletter of the Census Bureau. For later editions, see entry 151.

153 C3.262   **Directory of Data Files.** Prepared by Molly Abramowitz and
     1979-   Barbara Aldrich. Census Bureau. 1979. v.p. Irregular with
              quarterly updates.

Described in this publication are the Census Bureau's holdings of machine-readable data and how they can be obtained. Both general information about Census Bureau statistical programs and specific information about individual files are provided. The major portion of this publication is an overview of the various census statistical activities and abstracts of the files, which are products of those activities. The overview and abstracts are organized according to the following major subject areas: agriculture data, economic data, general data, geographic data, governments data, population and housing data, and software data. Each subject area is subdivided alphabetically by the titles of individual censuses or surveys. The abstracts for individual files are in alphabetical order within categories. Each abstract consists of the bibliographic citation for the file and the following information: subject-matter description, geographic coverage, reference materials, related printed reports, related machine-readable data files, and file availability. Appendix A provides definitions of Census Bureau geographic concepts. Appendix B is an annotated bibliography of reference materials for Census Bureau data, appendix C contains in chart form the number of reels necessary for each file at various technical specifications, and appendix D contains order forms for the data files and an example of a completed form. The directory is updated quarterly by revised pages.

154 C13.10   **Critical Surveys of Data Sources: No. 1 - Mechanical Proper-**
     no. 396-   **ties of Metals.** By R. B. Gavert, et al. 1974. 81p. **No. 2 -**
     1, 2, 3, 4 **Ceramics.** By Dorothea M. Johnson and James F. Lynch.
     1974-   1975. 47p. **No. 3 - Corrosion of Metals.** By Ronald B. Diegle
                 and Walter K. Boyd. 1976. 29p. **No. 4 - Electrical and Mag-**
                 netic Properties of Metals. By M. J. Carr, et al. 1976. 83p.
                 National Bureau of Standards. Special publication no. 396-1,
                 2, 3, 4. Irregular.

This series is designed to provide guides to data covering selected areas of materials and properties. These surveys assess the scope, assets, and deficiencies of the most prominent sources of such information. Included are handbooks, technical sources, compilations, information centers, foreign information sources, technical societies, and trade associations. Information given for each entry, if applicable, includes name, publisher or custodian, scope, properties covered, sources of data, size of data bank, data storage and search, selectivity of the data, time lines of the data, availability, cost of access to data, and general comments. A separate appendix lists those sources that were found to offer only generalized guides to the literature. There is a materials index and properties index.

155 C13.10   **Computer Science and Technology: Guide to Computer Pro-**
     no. 500-22 **gram Directories.** Compiled by Addie G. Chattie. National
                 Bureau of Standards. 1977. v.p. Special publication no.
                 500-22. Irregular.

Described in this publication is the National Bureau of Standards' (NBS) collection of catalogs or directories listing software, both proprietary and in the public domain. These computer programs are available from private organizations, academic institutions, and government agencies. Section 1 is an annotated listing of the sixty-three software catalogs in the guide. Information includes title, corporate author address, telephone number, and type of publication (report, book, notebook, etc.), with report number (if applicable), author, frequency, date, status, descriptive abstract, and subjects. Section 2 is an annotated listing of supplementary publications that present material on available software. The format is similar to that of section 1 and includes similar data, where appropriate. The publications are listed in alphabetical order by title. Section 3 is an annotated listing of computer users groups. Data on each users group includes name of organization, contact person, corporate affiliation, status, and descriptive abstract. The arrangement is alphabetical by acronym or name. Section A1 is the application program index. Section S2 is the systems program index. The introduction explains how to use the guide.

156   C51.11   **NTIS Sumstat Catalog. Federal Summary Statistical Data**
         Su6   **Project. Summary Statistical Data Files on Magnetic Tape**
                       Publicly Available from the Department of Commerce.
                       National Technical Information Service. 1972. v.p.

This catalog was the first step of a project to improve access to machine-readable, summary statistical data files (excluding personal files) produced by the U.S. government, and made available to the public without restrictions. It does not cover printed publications. The catalog is divided into an abstract section and four indexes. The abstract section is arranged in alphabetical/numerical order within each subject field. Indexes include generating agency, subject, responsible individuals, and number. There is a section on how to use the catalog. See also entry 157.

157   C51.11-2   **A Directory of Computer Software and Related Technical**
         1974-   **Reports.** National Technical Information Service. 1980. v.p.
                       Biennial.

These directories are unique guides to machine-readable data files, databases, and software agencies. All released data meets the requirements of the Privacy and Freedom of Information Acts. Before 1980, the abstracts were arranged in three main sections ("Economics," "Social Sciences," and "Science and Technology"); alphabetically by subject fields, and then alphabetically by the directory or order number. Five indexes are included for easier access (agency, hardware, language, number, and subject). The 1980 edition includes only machine-readable software and related technical reports; and its arrangement is alphabetical and numerical by subject fields. The title of this publication in 1974 was *Directory of Computerized Data Files and Related Software from Federal Agencies,* and from 1976 to 1978 was entitled *Directory of Computerized Data Files, Software and Related Technical Reports.* See entry 156 for earlier information.

158   C51.15   **Directory of Federal Statistical Data Files.** National Technical
         1981-   Information Service. 1981. 510p. Occasionally on microfiche.
                       Irregular.

Designed to assist users in acquiring information on data released by the federal government in machine-readable form, this directory consists of abstracts that describe statistical and related files produced by the federal government. The directory reflects an effort to integrate all individual agency sources of information through a centralized source. The main purpose of this sourcebook is to provide more descriptive information on the availability and content of federal statistical machine-readable data files that may be acquired by the public or from which information may be obtained. Most of the files named in this directory have been prepared by or for federal executive agencies. The directory is organized into three primary sections: a section on its scope and use; a section containing file abstracts; and a section containing several appendixes. As shown in the table of contents, the abstracts are organized by agency. Each abstract for the data files includes the following: bibliographic citation, file reference, general description, geographic coverage, time coverage, technical characteristics; reference materials, related reports, related files, contacts, and availability. The appendixes include file titles by agency, subject matter index, subject matter by agency index, and glossary.

159   C55.202   **The Interim Climate Data Inventory: A Quick Reference to Selected Climate Data.** By C. F. Ropelewski, et al. Environmental Data and Information Service. 1980. 176p.
           C61-6

The primary purpose of this publication is the distribution of information collected at the Climate Data Management Workshop held in Harpers Ferry, West Virginia, in May 1979. During that workshop, representatives from federal and state agencies, private industry, and the academic research community identified and described climate data sets held by their respective organizations. The information in the publication is limited to descriptions of data sets available at the workshop. The volume is made up of definitions of data set attributes; summary tables (including data sets listed by parameter, geographical areas, data holding centers by country, and abbreviations and acronyms); appendix 1, dealing with other information sources; and appendix 2, which is the data set descriptions. Data set descriptions include title, parameters, period of observation, geographical area, data type, data organization, media, volume, remarks, holding center, and data set identifier. They are arranged numerically by working group subject.

160   C55.219-2   **Marine Geology and Geophysics Data Services and Publications.** Environmental Data and Information Service. 1981. 14p. Key to Geophysical Research Documentation no. 14. Irregular.
           no. 14

Described in this catalog are the National Geophysical and Solar Terrestrial Data Center's (NGSDC) products and services in the marine geology and geophysics disciplines. The sections in this catalog outline certain popular data services offered by NGSDC. General facts about information accompanying the data sets, areas of coverage, source of data sets, and available formats are given. Data inventories or searches are, in general, provided free of charge initially, in anticipation of later purchases or exchanges of data. Inquiries about the data sets and their prices may be made by telephone or by mail.

161   C56.210-2   **Guide to Foreign Trade Statistics: 1975.** Census Bureau. 1975. 208p. Irregular.
           1972-

The foreign trade statistics program, conducted by the Census Bureau, involves the compilation and dissemination of a large body of data relating to the imports and exports of the United States. The program includes a variety of data presented in many different arrangements and released in the form of reports and machine tabulations that are distributed to Department of Commerce field offices and Bureau of Customs offices for public reference use. This publication is intended to serve as a guide to the various

48 / 4—Data Sources

sources of foreign trade statistics and to inform users of the content and general arrangement of the data. Divided into seven chapters, each (except chapter 1, which is the introduction), describes and includes visual samples of the documents. Chapter 2 describes the foreign trade statistics program. The other chapters contain information about published foreign trade reports, foreign trade reference material, origin of exports and destination of imports, classification schedules, and availability of special services.

162   C57.2   **A Guide to Federal Data Sources on Manufacturing.** Domestic
      M31   and International Business Administration. 1977. 197p.

The purpose of this guide is to provide to the user of federal statistics a framework in which to evaluate the numerous statistics on the manufacturing sector. It attempts to show the basic types of data available in each publication and the timeliness and detail of the statistics, point out significant differences between statistics from different sources or surveys, and selectively provide definitions when they will contribute to understanding the significance of the data types included in a specific publication. The chapters deal with economic indicators, classifications, manufacturing characteristics, production, employment, foreign trade, prices, and finance. Common to each chapter are a brief introduction; definitions, where they are considered helpful; a list of each data source by title, when the series began, and where it is obtainable; a narrative section on principal data type; and a tabular section that shows detail and reporting unit as well as the specific data type. The introduction is a comprehensive guide that includes a list of Government Printing Office bookstores, Census Bureau regional offices, Commerce Department district offices, and Bureau of Labor Statistics regional offices.

163   C57.8   **Measuring Markets: A Guide to the Use of Federal and State**
      M34   **Statistical Data.** Industry and Trade Administration. 1979.
              101p.

This publication describes data sources containing statistics that will assist management in making sound business decisions in areas such as market shares, the allocation of advertising expenditures, the alignment of sales territories for the purpose of achieving maximum sales at minimum costs, and the selection of sites for plants, stores, or distribution centers. Part 1 describes types of markets, sales goals, market potential, sales territories, and market research data. Part 2 discusses five major types of market research data (population, income, employment, sales, and taxes) and presents a tabular listing of data sources. The listing provides a description of these sources, geographic coverage of the data, frequency of publication, issuing agency, and, where applicable, SIC industry coverage. Part 3 contains twelve case examples with accompanying statistics, illustrating the use of such information for market analysis. The concluding section is a bibliography listing both government and nongovernment publications pertinent to market research.

164   D1.6-2   **How to Get It: A Guide to Defense Related Documents.**
      In3   Defense Department. 1980. 530p. Microfiche. Irregular.
      1980-

Published as an aid for those who have to identify or acquire government-published or -sponsored documents, maps, patents, specifications or standards, and other resources of interest to the defense community. The contents are limited to technical documents and information resources prepared for, needed by, or of particular interest to the Department of Defense and its contractors (or potential contractors), especially in support of research, development, test and evaluation programs. The entries are arranged alphabetically in a single list by document type, source, acronym, series designation, or short title. Each entry consists of the item and detailed acquisition information such as source, order forms to use, cost, where indexed, and telephone numbers for additional information. A glossary and bibliography are included.

165 D301.6-5 **Environmental/Socioeconomic Data Sources.** Air Force
En8 Department. 1976. 170p.

In order to implement and conform to the National Environmental Policy Act (NEPA) and the President's Council on Environmental Quality's policies, the Air Force must have the capability to evaluate the full range of environmental considerations prior to making decisions. To achieve this capability, the Air Force has developed an instructional document called the *TAB A-1, Environmental Narrative*. This guide to sources was developed to supplement the *TAB A-1*. It concentrates on data, particularly census data, that could be useful in completing the human environment section in the *TAB A-1*. The volume is divided into four chapters: (1) "Preliminaries": what the Bureau of the Census has to offer, local planning agencies and chambers of commerce, other local resources, and other federal data; (2) "Getting Started": defining the total region of influence and relevant jurisdictions, getting the basic census publications, and more; (3) "Helpful Hints": where to find specifics you need in census publications; and (4) "Helpful Information": a detailed description of federal data sources, how to obtain census publications, and a guide to Census Bureau data (including demographic, economic, housing, government and public finance data as well as data summaries).

166 E3.39 **Energy Data Contacts Finder.** Energy Information Adminis-
1981- tration. 1981. n.p. Irregular.

The publication is a listing of energy specialists by their technical subject areas, as well as subject specialists at the National Energy Information Center (NEIC). Subjects are data programs, coal, electric power, natural gas, nuclear power, petroleum and petroleum products, alternate fuels, energy statistical support, forecasting and analysis, and conservation, consumption, and utilization. Programs and telephone numbers are given.

167 ED1.102 **Directory of Library Networks and Cooperative Library**
L61 **Organizations.** *See* entry 052.

168 EP1.21-10 **Online Literature Searching and Databases at the U.S.**
1976- **Environmental Protection Agency Environmental Research Center Library. Cincinnati, Ohio.** Compiled by Mary L. Cakins. Environmental Protection Agency. 1978. 35p. Annual.

The library of the Environmental Research Center in Cincinnati, Ohio, is the scientific and technical information focal point for the EPA. As such, it provides technical information backing to all EPA libraries and all EPA scientists, engineers, and researchers. The purpose of this publication is to explain the online searching services available at the Cincinnati library, to outline the procedure for requesting a literature search, and to provide brief descriptions of the available databases. The databases are arranged in tabular form, in alphabetical order, giving name of database, years covered, vendor, meaning of name, number of citations or records, producer, and description.

169 FE1.2 **Directory of Federal Energy Data Sources. Computer Products and Recurring Publications.** Federal Energy Administration. 1976. v.p.
F31-2

The purpose of this directory is to announce two major types of federally sponsored, energy-related information: energy information on magnetic tape, and recurring publications that contain energy-related numerical data. The information on magnetic tape is primarily in the form of data files. However, there are also computer programs, database reference services, and mathematical models. The items are listed under broad subject categories. The citations include title, responsible agency, dates of coverage, accession number, availability information, and abstract. Each entry is indexed by subject, originating agency, and accession number.

170 HE1.2 **Asian American Reference Data Directory.** Health, Education, and Welfare Department. 1976. 482p.
As4

In this title we find a research, planning, and evaluation tool intended for use by the Office of Asian American Affairs (OAAA), other federal offices, and state and local governments, as well as institutions and individual scholars. It also serves as a data bank maximizing the response capability of OAAA's staff to the many inquiries from other federal agencies, researchers, and the Asian American community. The directory contains abstracts of some 480 of the major reference materials related to the health, education, and social welfare characteristics of Asian Americans. The directory also includes reference materials in such areas as demography, socioeconomics, employment and training, culture, immigration, and housing. The key to using the directory is the four indexes: subject, geographic, subgroup, and name (authors, project names, and major funding organizations). Each entry provides the author, title, publisher, funding source, ethnic, racial subgroup identification, major and minor subject descriptors and a geographic reference, a list of pertinent major data variables (tabular material) available, information on the availability of the source document itself, and narrative descriptions of the material contents, methodology, and findings and conclusions. Most of the materials cited are printed documents; online data files are also described. Related materials, such as online data files and published reports or related reports by one or more authors utilizing the same database, have been combined within a single abstract.

171 HE19.302 **Directory of Federal Agency Education Data Tapes.** 2d ed., 1979. Compiled by Edward D. Mooney. National Center for Education Statistics. 1980. 229p. Irregular.
Ed8-3
1976-

Identification and description of education databases is the purpose of this volume. The databases are available on computer tape from federal agencies conducting relevant research and maintaining data systems. NCES organized the Federal Interagency Consortium of Users of Education Statistics, with a membership of more than thirty agencies involved in the collection and use of education data, which submitted these database abstracts. In general, the databases consist predominantly of quantitative data, thus, bibliographic databases such as the Educational Resources Information Center (ERIC) of the National Institute of Education are not included. The directory is organized by level of education and substantive area as follows: elementary and secondary education; postsecondary education (including higher, adult continuing, and vocational/technical education); demographic, vital, health, and welfare; manpower supply and demand; libraries; federal outlays for education. The database abstracts are arranged alphabetically by disseminating agency within each level of education and substantive area. Database abstracts include name of disseminating agency, contact for tape access, contact for general information, objectives, date(s) of data collection, periodicity of data collection, methodology, significant variables, cost of the tape, data characteristics, and auxiliary services including publications available.

172   HE20.6208   **Facts at Your Fingertips. A Guide to Sources of Statistical**
      F11   **Information on Major Health Topics.** 5th ed. National Center
      3d ed. 1978- for Health Statistics. 1981. 180p. Irregular.

This guide lists sources of statistical information on some of the major health topics. It attempts to identify areas or topics of interest and to describe the kinds of data now available or in preparation. Under each topic, the NCHS publications or data are cited first, followed by other Department of Health and Human Services sources, other federal agencies, and private organizations or associations. The arrangement is alphabetical by topic. Included is an alphabetical list of the topics.

173   HE20.6209/   **Current Listing and Topical Index to the Vital and Health**
      List   **Statistics Series, 1962-1977.** National Center for Health Statis-
      1962-71-   tics. 1978. 25p. Irregular.

Data from the surveys and studies conducted by the National Center for Health Statistics (NCHS) are published in its Vital and Health Statistics series. The master series now includes more than four hundred individual publications, grouped into several subseries. This publication is an index to health topics covered in the Vital and Health Statistics series and the Advance Data series according to demographic and socioeconomic variables. The index is in two sections. Although there is some overlapping, section 1, in general, includes topics and variables related to the health conditions of the populace. Section 2 covers the characteristics of health facilities and health care manpower. The index is not exhaustive. It treats in detail those topics and variables most frequently requested by users of the center's data. See also entry 172.

174   HE20.6602   **Sources of Data Related to Dentistry: A Catalog.** Health Man-
      D43-18   power Bureau. 1980. 119p.

This catalog is designed as a data access tool to meet the needs of health planners, researchers, and administrators who are involved in dental care delivery planning. The data sources described here were not compiled on a state or regional basis, but have application nationwide. The catalog is organized according to subject areas that represent aspects of dental health planning. Each source is categorized according to the primary emphasis of its data content. Because many data sources contain data on more than one subject area, the last page of many sections contains cross-references to data sources described under other subject areas, which also contain data relevant to the particular (secondary) subject area. The data source sheets, organized one per data source, contain descriptions of the data attributes that are intended to aid the catalog user in determining the applicability of the sources to their data requirements, as well as the source's availability. The catalog includes title of data source; organization/person responsible for developing the data; year of most recent data collection; update; geographic area covered; geographic level of aggregation; data form; data origin; personal identification; target units of measurement; major variables; publication information or resulting publication; and contact for obtaining data and restrictions.

175   HE20.6613
no. 7
1977-
Nursing-related Data Sources. Rev. ed. Compiled and edited by Helen H. Hudson. Health Manpower Bureau. 1979. 135p. Nursing Planning Information series, no. 7. Irregular.

The purpose of this revised directory is to identify and update sources of data relevant to the study of nursing resources and other areas of concern in the planning process. It is not intended to be an exhaustive listing of all data sources or publications related to nursing manpower, but is intended to emphasize the major studies or surveys conducted or supported by the Interagency Conference on Nursing Statistics (ICONS) members. There is an alphabetical index to data sources that identifies the subject classifications (Nursing Personnel, Nursing Education, the Health Case Delivery System, and/or the Client Population). Part A of the volume alphabetically lists the thirty-five major data sources submitted by ICONS members. It also lists the following kinds of information: type and description of the study on survey, history, frequency, and latest edition; methodology used in collecting the data and from whom; persons or agencies to contact for further information about the study or survey, availability of the actual data files, and related publications; and a summary of the subject areas in which data were collected, or data items that can be released on tapes. Part B lists abstracts of surveys and studies conducted by agencies other than the members of ICONS. The information is essentially the same as that given in part A, but has been briefed and consolidated under three general areas: subject classification, general description, and contacts for additional information. There is also a list of other selected references: sourcebooks, guides, directories, and publications not directly related to the data sources abstracted in this directory.

176   HE23.3102
St2
Inventory of Federal Statistical Programs Relating to Older Persons. Prepared by the Task Force on Statistics of the Interdepartmental Working Group on Aging. National Clearinghouse on Aging. 1979. 113p.

The resources listed in this document will serve as a means for persons and organizations in the field of aging to keep abreast of the changing characteristics of the elderly population. It is an attempt to gather into one place all federal surveys and programs containing data related to the elderly population. The inventory of federal statistical surveys or programs in this book consists of twelve categories of information describing the surveys or programs of each of the participating federal agencies. There is an alphabetical list of member agencies or departments with statistical surveys or programs and page numbers. The presentation is alphabetical by agency and in columnar form. Information includes survey or program title, purpose of data collected, scope and method of data collection, limitations and reliability of the data, lowest geographic level, age detail, frequency of data collection, method of data storage, availability of unpublished data, time lag of data, publication program, and information contact.

180 L2.34-2   **A Directory of BLS Studies in Employee Compensation, 1947-**
     Em7   **1971.** Labor Statistics Bureau. 1972. 20p. Irregular.
     1972-

This directory lists studies that have been published as bulletins, reports and articles from the *Monthly Labor Review* of the Bureau of Labor Statistics. The studies are arranged under five main subjects: employee compensation and payroll hours; annual earnings and employment patterns; earnings and hours frequency distributions non-occupational studies; employee benefit plans; and special studies. Title, year, price, and availability of each study is indicated. The directory is updated periodically.

181 L2.34-2   **Directory of BLS Studies in Industrial Relations, 1960-74.**
     In2-2   Labor Statistics Bureau. 1975. 16p. Irregular.
     1975-

These studies listed here have been published as bureau bulletins, reports, articles and reprints from the *Monthly Labor Review*. The subject areas covered include collective bargaining agreements, union and association activities, and work stoppages. Each entry lists title, bulletin number or magazine issue, and price, if available. Updated periodically.

182 L2.34-2   **Directory of Industry and Municipal Government Wage**
     W12   **Surveys and Union Wages and Hour Studies, 1960-75.** Labor
     1967-   Statistics Bureau. 1976. 19p. Irregular.

Listed are the industry wage surveys, municipal government wage surveys, and union wage and hours studies conducted by the Bureau of Labor Statistics, all of which appear in their reports, bulletins, and *Monthly Labor Review* articles. Part A lists the industry wage surveys that cover approximately fifty manufacturing and twenty nonmanufacturing industries and are usually nationwide in scope. Part B lists the municipal government wage surveys and information on earnings of municipal employees in fifty-one cities, including twenty-six cities with populations of 500,000 or more. Part C lists the union wages and hours studies that provide occupational information on minimum wages and maximum schedules of hours at straight-time rates agreed upon through collective bargaining between trade unions and employers in selected cities of 100,000 inhabitants or more. Each entry lists the product or subject area covered by the wage survey, year, status of publication or bulletin number, data covered, and *Monthly Labor Review* reference. The municipal government wage surveys are arranged alphabetically by city. Updated and revised periodically.

183 L2.34-2   **Directory of Area Wage Surveys July 1970 to December 1972.**
     W12-4   Labor Statistics Bureau. 1973. 41p. Occasionally on micro-
     1968-   fiche. Irregular.

Publications listed here have resulted from the bureau's annual area wage survey program. Since 1960, the regular area wage survey program has been designed to provide estimates relating to all Standard Metropolitan Statistical Areas in the United States. After completion of all of the individual area bulletins for a round of surveys, two summary bulletins are issued. The summary bulletins and special *Monthly Labor Review* articles published since 1960 are listed in a separate section of the directory. The section on individual area surveys is arranged alphabetically by state and area, and gives period covered, type of survey, number of BLS bulletin, and price. The summary

177   I19.2   **Sources of U.S. Geological Survey Publications.** Geological
        So8-2   Survey. 1978. n.p.

This leaflet describes the data centers and lists addresses of other sources of Geological Survey information. It lists offices and addresses for ordering books, maps, and periodicals; and lists the USGS public inquiries offices that provide general information about the Geological Survey's activities and its publications, with addresses and telephone numbers. Also included are the descriptions and addresses of the following data sources: National Cartographic Information Center, Office of Water Data Coordination, National Water Data Exchange, EROS Data Center, Water Information Group, and Geologic Inquiries Group.

178   L2.3   **Directory of Data Sources on Racial and Ethnic Minorities.**
        no. 1879   Labor Statistics Bureau. 1975. 83p. Bulletin no. 1879. Irregular.

In this bulletin, users of statistics on racial and ethnic minority groups are provided with a comprehensive annotated reference to many sources of data on minority groups published by the federal government. The directory identifies and describes a large and diverse number of recent demographic, social, and economic data sources published by a number of federal agencies, and directs users to appropriate sources consistent with their needs. The four major sections cover blacks; persons of Spanish ancestry; other races; and other ethnic groups, respectively. Each of these sections has its own introduction and each section is arranged by reports from the *Census of Population and Housing 1970*, reports from the current population survey, and selected other data sources. Appendixes assist in locating sources including data locator tables, which facilitate the location of minority group data from the 1970 census, and recent current population surveys.

179   L2.3   **A Counselor's Guide to Occupational Information.** Labor
        no. 2042   Statistics Bureau. 1980. 60p. Bulletin no. 2042. Irregular.

A listing and description of occupational guidance and related material available from federal government agencies is contained in this publication. The listings include government career guidance material issued up to the summer of 1979. Each entry gives availability information. The guide is divided into eight chapters. Chapter 1 covers occupational information, including material that describes the nature of work in occupations: the education, training, special skills, and personal qualities usually needed to enter them; and the job outlook, opportunities for advancement, earnings, and so forth. Chapter 2 discusses opportunities for self-employment, summer jobs, overseas jobs, and part-time and temporary jobs. Chapter 3 includes materials covering special categories of workers, including college graduates, minorities, veterans, young workers, and women. General material on apprenticeship, education, and financial aid for students is the subject of chapter 4. Chapter 5 covers materials on job search: finding jobs, applying for them, taking tests, and interviewing. Chapter 6 includes materials on career education, and chapter 7 lists sources of statistics that can be useful for counselors. Chapter 8 provides references to other bibliographies. Four appendixes list state employment security agencies, state occupational information coordinating committees, examples of state occupational information, and federal agencies.

reports and articles section is divided into two parts. Part 1 deals with BLS bulletins that cover the areas studied during the survey year. Each entry gives dates of survey period, title of bulletin and bulletin number, and price and subject areas covered in the bulletin. Part 2 lists the related analytical articles that appeared in the *Monthly Labor Review*. Given here is the survey period covered, title of the article, and the issue of the *Monthly Labor Review* in which it appeared. Updated periodically.

184   L2.64-2   **Directory of Wage Chronologies, 1948 to June 1975.** Labor
       1965-   Statistics Bureau. 1975. 12p. Occasionally on microfiche. Irregular.

Presented in summary form are changes in wage and related compensation practices made by specific employers or groups of employers, usually through agreements reached as a result of collective bargaining. Before July 1965, basic wage chronologies and their supplements were published in the *Monthly Labor Review* and released as bureau reports. Those published later are available only as bulletins (and their supplements). The chronologies are listed alphabetically by employer group under active and discontinued chronologies. Information includes dates of chronologies, report or bulletin number, issue of *Monthly Labor Review*, and price, when available. There is also an index by industry group.

185   L2.71   **Directory of Occupational Wage Surveys.** Labor Statistics
       no. 606   Bureau. 1980. 96p. Report no. 606. Annual.
       1974-

This directory combines the listings of industry wage surveys, arranged by industry (manufacturing and nonmanufacturing); municipal government wage surveys, listed alphabetically by city; union wage and hour studies by industry or trade; area wage surveys by Standard Metropolitan Statistical Area and cross industry; and the national survey of professional administrative, technical, and clerical pay by occupation. Each entry includes date, status of publication or BLS bulletin number, and *Monthly Labor Review* reference. There is also a section on special *Monthly Labor Review* articles.

186   L36.102   **References and Data Sources for Implementing an Affirmative**
       R25   **Action Program.** Women's Bureau. 1978. 5p.

Presented here is a list of sources that may be helpful in formulating and implementing programs of equal employment opportunity and affirmative action. It is divided into sections that reference publications containing data on individuals who may qualify as prospective applicants. Listed also are data sources pertaining to labor force analysis and educational attainment. Each source listed includes the name, a brief description, and information about availability.

187   L37.8   **Guide to Local Occupational Information.** 5th ed. Employ-
       In3   ment and Training Administration. 1976. 163p. Irregular.
       1966-

Found in this publication is a list of selected state employment service studies, bulletins, brochures, and other releases providing concise summaries of job duties, employment prospects, training and experience requirements, training facilities, and so forth in a particular area or state. The guide lists publications by job titles in part 1, by occupational group in part 2, and by states in part 3. Part 4 is a list of occupational guidance publications covering selected industries, occupational fields, or special worker groups. On the inside of the back cover is an alphabetical listing of state employment security agencies with addresses.

188 NS1.2 **Federal Environmental Data: A Directory of Selected Sources.**
En8-2 By Capital Systems Group, Inc. National Science Foundation. 1977. 136p. Microfiche.

This directory describes major environmental databases maintained by U.S. government agencies. It has been compiled to assist various individuals and organizations outside the federal establishment in locating and utilizing the extensive environmental data resources that are available. The project staff has selected the databases for inclusion based on judgments concerning the usefulness of the data, its relevance to the environmental community, and its availability to the public. For the most part, the databases described have been drawn from five federal agencies: the Department of Agriculture, the Department of Commerce, the Department of the Interior, the Energy Research and Development Administration, and the Environmental Protection Agency. A few important databases from other federal agencies have also been included. The directory is divided into six major sections, one for each of the five major agencies, and a sixth containing sources found elsewhere. Each section is prefaced by a brief, general description of its major environmental data holdings, followed by individual profiles of the information sources, arranged alphabetically by their acronyms. Each profile contains certain standard items of information: source name, source agency, objective, general description, size, update frequency, time reference, cost, turnaround time, product, and person to contact. To facilitate referencing the directory's information, each source's acronym and index terms are given in the upper right hand corner of the profile. An alphabetical index appears at the back of the directory.

189 S1.2 **The Information Resources and Services of the United States:**
R31-3 **An Introduction for Developing Countries.** State Department. 1979. 50p.

This publication is intended to introduce the scientific and technical information resources of the United States as well as the services and organizations that will assist information seekers in developing countries to access, interpret, and use the information resources of the United States. The first part of this book discusses the nature of U.S. resources and services, and provides an introduction to the source listings in the appendix. There is also a selected list of directories of U.S. information resources and services. Tables 1 and 2 list, alphabetically by subjects, selected major computer-based information resources (i.e., bibliographic and numeric, or factual, databases). The tables indicate for each database the subject and scope, organization that produces it, and organizations through which the database is available to the public. Table 3 is an alphabetical list of selected information service organizations (including those from tables 1 and 2), indicating the nature of their client services, and addresses.

5
Establishments and Institutions

Laboratories, schools, colleges, libraries, and health facilities are the types of places that appear in the directories listed in this chapter.

190	A13.2 Sch6 1970-	**Forestry Schools in the United States.** Rev. ed. Forest Service. 1980. 34p. Irregular.

This is an alphabetical listing by state, and by colleges and universities within each state, of the forestry curriculums offered by the individual schools. Certain schools are indicated as being accredited by the Society of American Foresters. Each entry includes the department concerned, name of university with mailing address, degrees offered, requirements, and facilities.

191	A101.2 D63-2 1975-	**Directory of Animal Disease Diagnostic Laboratories.** Animal and Plant Health Inspection Service. 1977. 174p. Irregular.

The information contained herein is provided as a guide to where various types of laboratory diagnostic tests are available, and as an overview of what types of procedures are being performed at any given laboratory. Included in this directory is information on laboratories performing diagnostic tests for diseases of domestic and wild animals as well as diseases of animals that affect man. Divided into three sections, section 1 lists the laboratories; section 2 lists National Diagnostic Reference Centers; and section 3 is an index to the laboratories by type arranged alphabetically by state and city referring to section 1. In section 1, the laboratories are arranged alphabetically by state and city in which they are located. Information provided in this section includes name of laboratory, name of director, address, telephone number, affiliation, who may submit specimens, the major species accepted for examination, and the services offered.

192	A103.9	**Meat and Poultry Inspection Directory.** *See* entry 096.

193	C13.2 St2-2 1965-	**A Directory of Standards Laboratories.** 5th ed. Prepared by the National Conference of Standards Laboratories (NCSL). National Bureau of Standards. 1971. 42p. Irregular.

58 / 5 — Establishments and Institutions

Designed to serve as a classified index of standards laboratories in this country, this title provides those seeking information on calibration service with a list of available services in the laboratories contained in the well-known *ASTM Directory of Testing Laboratories*. The first section lists the laboratories alphabetically by name of the parent organization and charts the various calibration capabilities of members and other participating standards laboratories. The second section contains three lists. The first gives standards laboratories in alphabetical order, with the name, address, and telephone number of the person to contact for additional information. The second list is arranged alphabetically by the NCSL delegate name with company name and telephone number. The third list is geographically arranged in zip code order using company name.

194   CS1.7-4   **A Guide to High School Recruitment: School Districts with Significant Hispanic Student Enrollment.** Civil Service Commission. 1976. 53p.
         H53

Considering that many students do not continue on to college, secondary school systems offer a splendid recruitment opportunity for various job categories that the federal government has to offer. This source will enable recruiters to find Hispanic candidates for employment. The listing identifies public school districts and high schools in the United States that have a Hispanic student population in excess of 15 percent of the total student body and/or a significantly large absolute number of Hispanic students. Schools are arranged alphabetically by state, school district, and school. Data for Puerto Rico and U.S. parochial schools are not cited. Information given includes the school district, high school name, county, and recruitment code. The recruitment code refers to the Hispanic student enrollment. This information was taken from the *Directory of Public Elementary and Secondary Schools in Selected School Districts, 1972* (refer to entry 197).

195   E1.28   **National Solar Energy Education Directory.** 3d ed. Prepared in cooperation with the office of U.S. Congressman George E. Brown, Jr., and the Congressional Solar Coalition. A product of the Solar Energy Research Institute. Energy Department. 1981. 279p. Contractor Research and Development report SERI/SP 751-1049. Annual.
         SERI/SP
         751-1049
         1979-

Listed in this directory are all solar energy or solar-related programs and course opportunities offered at the postsecondary level. These fields may encompass any of the following solar energy technologies: active or passive space heating or cooling, domestic hot water, biomass (including alcohol fuel production), ocean energy systems, photoconversion and thermoconversion processes, photo-voltaic systems, process heat, solar thermal power, and wind energy systems. The listings are arranged alphabetically by state; within each state, schools are listed alphabetically according to institution type (colleges and universities, junior/community colleges, vocational/technical schools, and other educational institutions and organizations). Information provided includes: name, address, telephone number, tuition information, program category information, and course category information. Three indexes are included to help find listings for specific schools, program offerings or degrees, and institutions and organizations.

5 — Establishments and Institutions / 59

196 E1.28
SERI/SP
751-1049
1979-
Solar Energy Technical Training Directory. 3d ed. A product of the Solar Energy Research Institute. Energy Department. 1981. 75p. Contractor Research and Development report SERI/SP 751-1049. Irregular.

Programs and courses in this volume were taken from the *National Solar Energy Education Directory* (see entry 195). It includes those schools that offer a technical degree (usually a certificate, associate, or equivalent) in a solar or solar energy-related area. In most cases they are junior or community colleges. All schools are listed alphabetically by state, giving name, address, telephone number, tuition information, program category title and information, and course category. An index lists the schools alphabetically.

197 ED1.2
El2
1968-
Directory of Elementary and Secondary School Districts and Schools in Selected School Districts: School Year 1978-1979. 2 vols. Education Department. 1980. Irregular.

The Office of Civil Rights (OCR) of the Department of Education is responsible for monitoring recipients of federal funds to assure compliance with Title VI of the Civil Rights Act of 1964, prohibiting discrimination on the basis of race or ethnicity; Title IX of the Education Amendments of 1972, prohibiting discrimination on the basis of sex; and Section 504 of the Rehabilitation Act of 1973, prohibiting discrimination on the basis of handicap. These periodic surveys of public elementary and secondary schools are published as a result. This document contains data submitted by the school districts surveyed, as well as national and state level summaries of that data. The 1978 survey collected data from a sample of 6,049 public elementary and secondary school districts that enroll three hundred or more pupils. The directory contains two kinds of tables: directory and summary. The directory tables are arranged in alphabetical order by state. Within states, the order is generally alphabetical by school district name, although in some states the order is not strictly alphabetical. For each district there are three components: district identification, summarized data for the school district as a whole, and enrollments in individual schools. The racial/ethnic categories are American Indian or Alaskan Native, Asian or Pacific Islander, Hispanic, Black, and White. The summary table section explains and presents eight tables that summarize at the national and state levels the data collected for this survey. The tables concern national and state enrollment and program summaries; state enrollments as a percentage of national totals; subject matter participation; participation in interscholastic athletics; participation in courses historically having disproportionate enrollment by sex; pupils requiring and participating in special education; participation in special education by time spent in program; and accessible schools and school facilities. The title of this publication was formerly *Directory of Public Elementary and Public Schools in Selected School Districts.*

198 ED1.2
H19
Directory of Special Purpose Facilities for the Education of the Handicapped. 1978-1979. Education Department. 1981. 473p. Microfiche.

This publication presents summations of data collected through the Special Purpose Facilities Civil Rights Survey, 1978-1979. Institutions receiving federal financial assistance in the fifty states and the District of Columbia were surveyed. Racial, ethnic, handicapped, and sex data are included. Five tables are included. Table 1 presents a

60 / 5—Establishments and Institutions

national summary of the facilities presenting total number, total limited-English-speaking educational enrollment, and total handicapped staff by race and handicapping condition. Table 2 is a regional summary and table 3 a state summary of the same data. Table 4 is an alphabetical arrangement by state of states sending children out-of-state for assistance. It gives the states the children are sent to and the number and percent by race. Table 5 (the main body of the directory) presents the facilities alphabetically by state. Within each state the facilities are arranged alphabetically by name, and the information given includes region; address; type of ownership; alternative place; enrollment (residential or educational) by race, sex, and handicapping condition; staff; residential age span; total limited-English-speaking educational enrollment, educational programs offered, and total handicapped staff.

| 199 | ED1.38 1971- | **Accredited Postsecondary Institutions and Programs—Including Institutions Holding Preaccredited Status as of September 1, 1980.** By Leslie W. Ross and Yvonne W. Green. Education Department. 1981. 210p. Irregular, 1971-1977; Annual, 1979- . |

Listed in this volume are postsecondary educational institutions and programs that are accredited by, or that have preaccredited status awarded by, the regional and national accrediting agencies formally recognized by the Secretary of Education. Divided into two parts, part 1 lists those institutions with programs accredited or preaccredited by regional commissions and associations. Part 2 lists the professional, technical, occupational, and specialized schools or programs accredited and preaccredited by national specialized accrediting agencies arranged alphabetically by state, accrediting agency, and name of institution, giving location, zip code, and year accredited. Part 2 is an alphabetical arrangement of program, accrediting agency, state, and institution. Appendixes list alphabetically the accrediting agencies and associations with addresses, telephone numbers, and contact persons.

| 200 | ED1.111 1965-66- | **Education Directory, Colleges and Universities 1980-81.** By Carolyn R. Smith and Geneva C. Davis. National Center for Education Statistics. 1981. 574p. Annual. |

Listed in this directory are those institutions in the United States and its territories that are legally authorized to offer and are offering at least a one-year program of college-level studies leading to a degree. Institutions are listed alphabetically under the state in which they are located. A branch of an institution is listed as a separate unit following the parent institution. The information presented for each institution includes its area code, telephone number, address, congressional district and county in which it is located, Federal Interagency Committee on Education (FICE) code number, entity number, date established, fall enrollment, undergraduate tuition and fees, sex of student body, calendar system, control or affiliation, highest level of offering, type of program, and recognized accreditation. In the introduction there is a list of nationally recognized accrediting agencies and associations and an explanation of the data. Among the appendixes there are lists of statewide agencies for postsecondary education, higher education associations, and FICE codes. Included is an alphabetical index of institutions. The title of earlier editions was *Education Directory: Higher Education.*

201 EP1.2   **State and Local Environmental Libraries. A Directory.** 2d ed.
     L61-3   A joint publication of the Environmental Protection Agency
     1972-   and the National Oceanic and Atmospheric Administration.
                  1976. 24p. Irregular.

This directory is a listing of those libraries with a common interest in the collection and documentation of environmental literature. General university libraries have not been included, nor have documents divisions of these and public libraries. Specialized departmental libraries of both university and public libraries have been included where they specifically relate to environmental activities. The list is arranged alphabetically by state and library, providing each institution's name and address, with name of the librarian, and telephone number, when available.

202 EP1.8   **Guide to EPA Libraries.** 4th ed. Environmental Protection
     L61-2   Agency. 1977. 44p. Irregular.
     1974-

Libraries within the EPA library system are listed in this publication, grouped by those located at headquarters, the ten regional offices, the four environmental research centers, and satellite laboratories and offices. Provided is the history of each library and a description of its collection and services, whether transferred from a predecessor agency or established since the creation of the Environmental Protection Agency. A list of libraries by code number is provided, as well as a geographical index by state. The librarian and staff are given, and the telephone numbers are FTS (Federal Telecommunication System) and CML (commercial) numbers.

203 HE1.214   **National Directory of Educational Programs in Gerontology.**
     1976-   1st ed. Betsy M. Sprouse, editor. Aging Administration. 1976.
                  1615p. Irregular.

This directory is designed to inform educators, professionals, and students of the nature and location of gerontology-related courses, degree programs, research programs, and educational service and training programs. The directory contains information on the gerontological activities of 1,275 colleges and universities in the United States—approximately one-third of the total number of higher education institutions. It is divided by states, and also includes the District of Columbia, the Canal Zone, Guam, Puerto Rico, and the Virgin Islands. The states and territories are arranged in alphabetical order, with college and university entries listed in alphabetical order within each state or territory. The entries include the institution's name and address, a contact person for the program, courses, research programs, and so forth. The table of contents lists the institutions alphabetically by state. An alphabetical college index and a subject index are also included.

204 HE3.51-5   **Directory of Medicare/Medicaid Providers and Suppliers of**
                  Services, 1975. 10th ed. Social Security Administration. 1976.
                  463p. Irregular.

In this directory is a compilation of names and addresses of all medical facilities that participate as providers and suppliers of services in the Health Insurance for the Aged and Disabled Program and the Medical Assistance Program. The directory is arranged in alphabetical sequence by state, by city within state, and by the name of the facility for each type of provider or supplier. They are identified in the following manner:

hospitals, skilled nursing facilities, intermediate care facilities, institutions for the mentally retarded, home health agencies, outpatient physical therapy, independent laboratories, portable X ray units, and renal disease treatment centers. For later editions, see entry 228.

205   HE19.102   **Educational Institution Numeric List.** Education Office. 1979.
          N91   313p.

Presented in this directory by FICE code is a list of educational institutions from the *Education Directory, Colleges and Universities 1978-79* (see entry 200). It describes their eligibility for student loans. Information for each institution includes address and eligibility code. Companion volumes are listed in chapter 3, entries 129 and 130.

206   HE19.302   **Traditionally Black Institutions of Higher Education: Their**
          B56   **Identification and Selected Characteristics.** By William H. Turner and John A. Michael. National Center for Education Statistics. 1978. 10p.

A first of its kind of publication, this pamphlet identifies 106 traditionally black institutions (TBIs), describes the procedures used to compile the list, and presents selected items of descriptive information about each institution. The schools are arranged alphabetically within each state and included are each institution's name, location, year established, control type (public or private), whether two-year or four-year, 1976 opening fall enrollment (by percentage black, sex, and attendance status), first-time freshmen enrollment, and the name of the chief executive officer (1978).

207   HE19.302   **Colleges and Universities Offering Accredited Programs by**
          C68   **Accreditation Field, Including Selected Characteristics, 1977-78.** By Arthur Podolsky. National Center for Education Statistics. 1978. 116p.

Included in this volume are selected characteristics of higher education institutions and their branches offering accredited programs, as published in the *Education Directory, Colleges and Universities 1977-78* (see entry 200). The institutions are shown in state order and alphabetically within states for each accreditation. For each institution listed, the following characteristics are given: location, enrollment size, control and type of institution, and tuition. Professional and specialized schools and programs are accredited by the associations listed after the accreditation field. The associations are also listed alphabetically in the appendix. The index indicates where to find data for all the professional accreditations the institution has and is arranged alphabetically by institution name.

208   HE19.302   **Free Universities and Learning Referral Centers, 1978.** By
          Un8   Robert Calvert, Jr., and William A. Draves. National Center for Education Statistics. 1979. 36p.

A free university is generally defined as an organization offering ungraded, unaccredited classes to the general public, and in which anyone can teach and anyone can learn. Learning referral centers provide educational referrals to individuals seeking information from other individuals offering teaching skill or tutorial services. They serve as education brokers. These institutions first developed during the period of student protests of the 1960s; they were student-led and served the student community

5—Establishments and Institutions / 63

and/or the general public. This publication is divided into several sections that report on such items as the number of these types of institutions, registration, staff, fees and budgets, programs, problems, and directions for the future. Sections 8 and 9 are the directory and listing of new institutions. The directory sections list the institutions alphabetically by state and city, giving address and telephone number.

209 HE19.322 **Institutions of Higher Education Index by State and Congressional District.** By Carolyn R. Smith. National Center for Education Statistics. 1977. 50p. Biennial.
       1971-

This publication is a companion volume to the *Education Directory, Colleges and Universities* (see entry 200). Arranged by state and congressional districts, the index reports the names of the senators, representatives, and other elected officials of that particular Congress, their states and congressional districts, and each institution of higher education located therein. Information given includes the name of the institution, type of control, student body, and the city of location.

210 HE19.337 **Directory of Postsecondary Schools with Occupational Programs, 1978.** 4th ed. By Evelyn R. Kay. National Center for Education Statistics. 1979. 376p. Biennial.
       1971-

Public and private schools that offer postsecondary occupational education are listed in this directory. It is intended to meet the needs of manpower and educational planners at the federal, state, and local levels as well as others who require precise information on the current and potential supply of skilled workers. The schools are listed alphabetically under the states and cities in which they are located. Each school listing is by a school number, and the information given includes name of school, address, county, zip code, telephone number, ID number, accreditation, programs offered, type of school, control or affiliation, enrollment, and eligibility with loan organizations. Two indexes are provided: a school index, which is an alphabetical list of all schools in the directory, followed by a state abbreviation and school number as a reference to its location in the directory, and a program index, which lists program offerings followed by references to the schools that offer these programs. The supplement to this volume (*Programs and Schools, 1978*), provides one-line listings: name, address, and ID number for all schools that offer each of the occupational programs. The list of programs in the supplement is identical to that which appears in the program index in the directory. The program index is arranged alphabetically by state abbreviation and school number.

211 HE20.2402 **Directory of General Hospitals Providing Walk-in Emergency Mental Health Services.** National Institute of Mental Health. 1973. 49p.
       Em3

This directory is intended to provide information on the availability of emergency mental health services provided by units of nonfederal general hospitals in the fifty states and the District of Columbia. For the purpose of this directory, emergency mental health services are defined as specific programs whose primary purpose is to provide psychiatric care in emergency situations by staff specifically assigned for this purpose. Hospital programs that provide only holding bed facilities and programs primarily for drug and alcohol abuse are excluded. The entries in the directory are arranged alphabetically by city within state. Information given for each entry includes name and address of unit; telephone number(s) of unit; hours and days of operation; geographic and other restrictions; and name and address of parent facility.

64 / 5 — *Establishments and Institutions*

212 HE20.2402   **Directory of Institutions for Mentally Disordered Offenders.**
        Of2-2   National Institute of Mental Health. 1972. 24p.

A listing of mental health and correctional institutions providing psychiatric care for adult mentally disordered offenders is presented in a convenient format in this publication. Included are mental health institutions and the correctional facilities that provide psychiatric care for mentally disordered offenders. These include federal, state, and municipal facilities; VA hospitals and correctional facilities connected with the armed forces are excluded. The information is listed alphabetically, first by state and then by institution, under mental health and correctional facilities. The data includes location, capacity, type of institution, administrative officials, and population classified by sex.

213 HE20.3702   **Soviet Biomedical Institutions: A Directory.** A publication of
        So8-4   the Geographic Health Studies Program. John E. Fogarty International Center for Advanced Study in the Health Sciences. 1974. 553p.

This directory has been prepared in order to provide U.S. biomedical scientists with a guide to the organization, personnel, geographic distribution, subordination, and research activities of selected medical and biological institutions in the Soviet Union. It contains descriptions of approximately twelve hundred Soviet biomedical institutions (including research, educational, and service facilities) and learned societies. The institutions in the main section of the directory are arranged by function, type, and specialization, and are keyed, by number and letter, to the outline immediately preceding the main section of the directory. An explanation of the number and letter system (code) employed in the guide is presented in the introduction. Very comprehensive technical notes are provided. The data elements for each institution in the main section of the directory include name, subordination, location, components and personnel, and statements of research activities in selected institutions. The appendixes include a geographic index that is an alphabetical listing of Soviet republics, cities within republics, and names of institutions (transliterated and translated) located in each city; a subordination index that lists alphabetically, by city and name, all identified institutions subordinate to the USSR Ministry of Health, USSR Academy of Medical Sciences, and USSR and Republic Academies of Sciences; and a listing of all institutions in the directory arranged alphabetically by translated name. Each of the appendixes also lists the number and letter codes for all institutions to facilitate locating them in the main section of the directory.

214 HE20.4002   **Directory of Blood Establishments Registered under Section**
        B62   **510 of the Food, Drug, and Cosmetic Act.** 4th ed. Food and
        1976-   Drug Administration. 1979. 811p. Annual.

Provided in this directory is information on the structure, function, and performance of the blood service complex. This publication is part of a continuing program to collect data relating to blood banking in the United States. Included are summary tables of statistics for establishments, products, and functions. Appendix B provides definitions of establishments, products, and functions. Military establishments are also included and identified, as well as establishments in a few foreign countries. The listing is arranged alphabetically by state and city. Information provided for each entry includes name, address, zip code, registration number, responsible head, type of establishment, products, and functions.

5 — *Establishments and Institutions* / 65

215   HE20.4002   **Establishments and Products Licensed under Section 351 of**
        Es8   **the Public Health Service Act.** Food and Drug Administra-
        1971-   tion. 1977. 182p. Irregular.

In this publication are listings of establishments holding licenses issued under the Public Health Service Act, Section 351, and the biologic products these establishments are licensed to manufacture. This publication consists of the following sections: Part 1 — an alphabetical list of licensed establishments, operating locations, and mailing addresses for directing written inquiries; part 2 — licensed establishments listed numerically by license number and the products each establishment is allowed to manufacture; part 3 — an alphabetical list of biologic products with the license number and name of each establishment licensed to manufacture each product; part 4 — an alphabetical list of biologic products by category; part 5 — an alphabetical list of NDA-approved drug products (New Drug Applications approved under Section 505 of the Federal Food, Drug and Cosmetic Act), and the NDA sponsor; and part 6 — an alphabetical list of NDA sponsors including operating locations, mailing addresses, and drugs manufactured. Before 1975, this publication was issued by the National Institutes of Health.

216   HE20.4003/   **Directory/Poison Control Centers — United States and Terri-**
        2-2   **tories, 1981.** National Clearinghouse for Poison Control
        1978-   Centers. 1981. n.p. Annual.

This directory lists poison control centers compiled from information received from the centers, state coordinators, and state departments of health. It is revised periodically in an attempt to keep it current. The centers are arranged alphabetically by state, by city within state, and by institution. The address and telephone number of each state coordinator is given preceding each state listing. Information given for each entry includes name and address of institution, and telephone number. The publication was formerly issued as a National Clearinghouse for Poison Control Centers bulletin, HE20.4003-2, 1978-8.

217   HE20.5102   **Clinical Genetic Service Centers. A National Listing.** 1st ed.
        G28-3   Community Health Services Bureau. 1980. 117p.

Listed in this guide are institutions in the United States providing services in one or more of the follolwing areas: clinical genetics (including diagnosis and treatment), genetic counseling, prenatal diagnosis, cyto-genetics, and biochemical genetics. It is intended as a reference tool for locating and contacting these institutions. The first section of the directory lists only those institutions offering services for a range of genetic conditions. A supplement identifies the federally funded programs for hemophilia and sickle cell anemia. The entries are arranged alphabetically by state, by city within state, and by institution. Information given for each institution includes name and address, department(s) where services are available, services provided, contact person(s), and telephone number.

218   HE20.6202   **Directory. Family Planning Service Sites — United States.**
        F21   National Center for Health Statistics. 1978. 177p.

Names and addresses of the 4,660 medical service sites that responded to the 1975 survey of the National Inventory of Family Planning are included in this directory. These sites are arranged alphabetically by state or outlying area, city, and name of the site. These sites generally offer any of the following services provided by a physician,

66 / 5 — Establishments and Institutions

nurse-midwife, registered nurse, or other authorized personnel, including medical history; physical examination; laboratory testing; testing, consultation, and treatment including continuing medical supervision; issuance of drugs and contraceptive supplies; and appropriate medical referral when indicated.

219 HE20.6602 **Allied Health Education Programs in Junior and Senior Colleges.** Health Planners ed., 1975. 2 vols. Health Manpower Bureau. 1978.
Ed8

Volume 1 contains an inventory of programs including enrollment and graduate data, and volume 2 contains summary tables on programs by health profession, number of enrollers, and graduates. It also contains data on constraints affecting program growth. The data in volume 1 is provided in two sections. Section 1 lists by state each institution's health occupations program offerings and provides academic, enrollment, and past and projected graduate data for ongoing programs. Section 2 provides descriptive data about those programs surveyed that were planned. Companion volumes are entries 220 and 222. Full explanatory notes are given for each volume and section.

220 HE20.6602 **Allied Health Education Programs in Junior and Senior Colleges.** Guidance ed., 1975. Health Manpower Bureau. 1978. 609p.
Ed8/
Guidance

This companion directory to entries 219 and 222 provides information primarily for counselors. The data is provided in three sections. Section 1 lists by state each institution's health occupations programs, offerings, and the name and title of each institution's contact person. Section 2 provides a list of active programs by occupational category, academics, student aid, and cost data for ongoing programs. Section 3 lists the planned programs by occupational category and provides descriptive data.

221 HE20.6602 **A Directory of Preceptorship Programs in the Health Professions.** 2d ed. Health Manpower Bureau. 1977. 75p. Irregular.
P91

Provided in this directory is useful information for students seeking to identify available off-campus clinical experiences and to faculty seeking resource information on different types of preceptorship programs at other institutions. The directory is divided into three sections. Sections 1 and 2 list alphabetically by state and institution those programs open to students from other institutions, and those programs closed, or limited to students enrolled at the sponsoring college or university. Section 3 lists those institutions that have indicated an interest in beginning a cooperative program with another health professional school. Each entry in sections 1 and 2 provides name of the institution; contact names and addresses; a brief description of the preceptorship offered; the sponsoring school or organization; location of preceptorship sites; length of assignment; availability of stipends, transportation or lodging; the funding source for the program; and whether the program is open to students from other institutions.

222 HE20.6602 **Health Occupations Training Programs Administered by Hospitals, April 1976, a Directory.** Health Manpower Bureau. 1977. 362p.
T68

Information on 4,552 allied health and nursing training programs administered by hospitals in the United States as of April 15, 1976, is listed in this volume. The directory consists of two sections and explanatory notes are provided for each section. Section 1 is designed primarily for guidance counselors, students, and health planners, and contains an alphabetical listing of training programs classified within major occupational categories. Information is provided on academic description and program size. The alphabetical arrangement includes state, city and name only of hospital. Section 2 is designed primarily for hospital administrators and health planners, and presents an alphabetical listing by state and city of those hospitals with training programs. In addition to the address of the hospital, it provides information on control or ownership, the type of service provided, number of beds, and program titles. An appendix contains a glossary of occupational titles and a list of titles of programs reported by respondent hospitals, not contained in the glossary. The index lists all hospital training programs included in the directory alphabetically, indicating page number. A companion directory, *Allied Health Education Programs in Junior and Senior Colleges* (1975), is discussed in entry 219.

223   HE20.7002   **Directory of STD** [Sexually Transmitted Disease] **Clinics.**
       Se9   Centers for Disease Control. 1981. 396p.

This directory has been compiled with information obtained from state and local health departments and includes all counties in the United States. Divided into two sections, section 1 is an alphabetical listing by state, county, and city of each facility, and section 2 is an alphabetical listing by state, county, and city of hot line services. In section 1, at the beginning of each state's listing, the state department of VD control is identified. The definitions of the abbreviations used are shown at the end of each state's listing. Also included is facility name, address, telephone number, days and hours open, appointment, cost, and services provided.

224   HE20.8102   **Directory. Federally Funded Community Mental Health**
       C73   **Centers, 1981.** National Institute of Mental Health. 1981. 98p.
       1973-   Biennial.

Brought together in this directory is a list of the centers that the National Institute of Mental Health has funded since 1963 through construction, staffing, and initial operations grants. At the present time, more than 750 programs are operational, providing services designed to meet the needs of their communities. The list is arranged alphabetically by state and by facility within state. Information for each facility includes its name, address, name of current director, board chairperson, office telephone number, twenty-four-hour emergency telephone number, type and number of grants, and type of support.

225   HE20.8123   **Mental Health Directory 1977.** National Institute of Mental
       1964-   Health. 1977. 620p. Irregular.

In several sections, this directory provides a listing of state mental health authorities, voluntary mental health associations, self-help organizations for mental health, mental health-related information sources in the federal government, national agencies listed by special problem categories, and organizations, professional associations, and state mental health facilities and services. This main section of the directory, listing mental health facilities and services by state is intended to provide a central source of information on mental health facilities throughout the United States. For purposes of this directory, a mental health facility is defined as in administratively distinct governmental, public, or private agency or institution whose primary concern is the provision of direct mental health services to the mentally ill or emotionally disturbed. In this section, states and cities within states are arranged alphabetically. Within cities, the facilities are arranged as psychiatric hospitals; general hospitals; residential treatment centers for emotionally disturbed children; outpatient psychiatric clinics; mental health day/night facilities; federally funded community mental health centers; and multi-service mental health facilities. Information given for each entry includes name, address, telephone number, geographic area served, auspices, services maintained, eligibility restrictions, and type of services provided (i.e., inpatient, day treatment, and emergency service).

226   HE20.8129   **Directory of Halfway Houses and Community Residences for the Mentally Ill, 1977.** National Institute of Mental Health. 1978. 38p. Irregular.
1977-

This directory provides information on the availability of halfway houses and community residences for mentally ill persons throughout the fifty states and the District of Columbia. It is intended for use by persons in the social service, medical, and other professions who have occasion to refer clients to such facilities, by families of potential halfway house clients, by potential clients themselves, and by other interested parties. Within each state the facilities are listed alphabetically according to city and by establishment name within city. Information given for each facility includes its name, address, telephone number, type of facility, organization legally responsible for the facility's operation, number of beds, sexes served, ages served, services provided, and admission requirements.

227   HE22.202   **Directory of Adult Day Care Centers.** Health Care Financing Administration. 1980. 162p. Irregular.
Ad9
1978-

Given in this directory are overviews of the 618 ongoing programs in the nation that provide services to approximately 13,500 persons daily. Senior center programs are not included, nor are day care programs for the mentally retarded and those day centers providing primarily psychiatric or mental health services to adults. The volume indicates state program totals and sources of program funds; states in which programs receive Titles XIX and XX reimbursement for adult day care; primary funding sources for adult day care; and state associations for adult day care. The center listings are alphabetical by state, and the information given includes the establishment's name, address, telephone number, program director, date started, sponsoring organization, funding sources, nature of program, and average daily census.

228   HE22.202   **Medicare/Medicaid Directory of Medical Facilities.** Health Care Financing Administration. 1981. v.p. Annual.
M46
1977-

Information in this publication is arranged by regions of the United States, listing facilities in alphabetical sequence by state, city within state, and facility name within city. Information given is address with a provider numerical index that indicates effective date, termination date, termination code, billing election code, radiological and laboratory codes, type of facility (hospital, long-term care, home health agency, outpatient physical therapy); control (ownership); long-term care facilities; and accreditation. Bed size data and laboratory speciality/subspeciality is also given. See entry 204 for earlier publications.

5—Establishments and Institutions / 69

229   HH1.2   **Housing Management Training Programs. A Directory 1977.**
M31-3   Housing and Urban Development Department. 1978. v.p.

Presented in this directory are the results of a survey of colleges and universities that offer special programs in housing management. Private housing management organizations are also included. Thirty programs are listed alphabetically by state, and then alphabetically by the name of the institution. Each entry provides the name of the school, organization, or association with address; contact person with telephone number; name of program; content of program; format/duration of program; fee; and degree or certificate. An alphabetical subject index is included for easy access.

230   J26.2   **Directory of Criminal Justice Degree Programs Offered by**
C86-5   **Institutions of Post-Secondary Education Participating in the Law Enforcement Education Program (LEEP): Program Year 1978-79.** Law Enforcement Assistance Administration. 1979. 137p.

The information here on criminal justice degree programs and degree levels was obtained from the institutions' applications for funding for program year 1978-79, submitted in the spring of 1978. Due to this, the data provided in the directory reflects the institutions' intent to offer such degree programs; some may not be operational. LEEP provides grants and/or loans to public law enforcement and criminal justice personnel and students who are committed to careers in the criminal justice system. Institutions are listed alphabetically by state and by the name of the institution within each state. Information given includes name of institution, city, zip code, program(s) offered, and degree level.

231   L1.2   **Directory of Job Corps Centers.** Manpower Administration.
J57-12   1975. 27p. Irregular.
1971-

This directory is an alphabetical arrangement by state, and by municipality within states, of the active Job Corps Centers, including Civilian Conservation Corps Centers. Information given for each entry includes type of center, when activated, capacity and sexes, whether residential or nonresidential, operator, courses, address, telephone number, and occasionally travel directions. Also listed in the directory are the addresses of the Job Corps regions within the ten regions of the United States.

232   LC19.2   **Address List: Regional and Subregional Libraries for the Blind**
Ad2   **and Physically Handicapped, March 1981.** National Library
1979-   Service for the Blind and Physically Handicapped. 1981. 27p. Semiannual.

The regional libraries and subregional libraries listed here provide, in cooperation with the Library of Congress, a free library service to persons who are unable to read or use standard printed materials because of visual or physical impairment. In addition, these libraries offer handicapped readers' reference and readers' advisory services. The libraries are arranged alphabetically by state. Within states, the regional library appears first, followed by subregional libraries listed alphabetically by city. (Subregional libraries are usually departments of public libraries.) Information given for each entry includes name, address, telephone number, and contact person.

233 LC19.2 **Library Resources for the Blind and Physically Handicapped.**
L61-5 **A Directory of NLS Network Libraries and Machine-Lending**
1979- **Agencies, 1980.** National Library Service for the Blind and Physically Handicapped. 1980. 111p. Annual.

With the cooperation of authors and publishers who grant permission to use copyrighted works, the National Library Service for the Blind and Physically Handicapped (NLS) provides free library services to blind and physically handicapped persons. NLS selects and produces full length books and magazines in braille and on recorded disk and cassette. The reading materials produced are then distributed to a cooperating network of regional and subregional libraries that circulate them to eligible borrowers by postage-free mail. Network libraries also offer reference, readers' advisory, and other services. The directory is arranged alphabetically by state. Within each state, the regional library appears first, followed by subregional libraries listed alphabetically by city. Separate machine-lending agencies are listed as the final entry for the state. Appendixes 1, 2, and 3 provide statistics on readership, circulation, budget, staff, and collections for each library. Each entry in the directory section includes name, address, telephone numbers (NATS and TTY), area services, name of librarian, hours, type of book collection, special collections, and services.

234 LC39.9 **Maritime Folklife Resources. A Directory and Index.** Prepared by Peter Boutis with the assistance of Mary Hufford.
no. 5 American Folklife Center. 1980. 129p. Publication no. 5.
1978- Irregular.

This directory and index is the product of the National Maritime Folklife survey conducted by the American Folklife Center of the Library of Congress between January and September of 1979. The survey questionnaire focus extended from vessels—their artifacts and the lives of those aboard them—to data on communities, which for economic or recreational reasons engage in water-related activities. In most cases, institutions and programs are listed according to the name reported on the completed questionnaire. Museums and special centers have been alphabetized by their own designated title, even if they are affiliated with a university or other larger institution. Archives that are attached to an academic department or a university's library have been alphabetized under the name of the university. The directory includes a glossary of vessel types; an index to key holdings, which identifies the institutions by holdings; a state index, which identifies the institutions by state and city; and the alphabetical directory of museums and other institutions. The entries in the directory section list name, address, telephone number, and days and hours open. A brief description of the institution and its holdings, special features, and membership, if applicable, are also included.

235 TD1.2 **Directory of Transportation Education, Institutions Offering**
Ed8 **Programs at Degree and Non-Degree Levels, Including Seminars, Institutes and Workshops.** 1st ed. Transportation Department. 1976. 204p. Irregular.

Listed in this directory are those postsecondary institutions in the United States that offer degree-level programs in transportation and related areas, as well as regularly scheduled transportation and related seminars, workshops, or institutes. All modes of transportation are included: air, highway, pipelines, rail, water, urban/mass, and intermodal. In sections A and B, the institutions are listed numerically by the FICE code and are grouped by states, alphabetically. Each entry gives the division or department offering the course(s), address, contact person, telephone number, and program information. In section A, the program information indicates the specific academic offering along with letter codes to indicate its relationship to a particular mode of transportation or area of emphasis, as well as the degree level for each offering. Section B program information includes frequency of offering, period in academic year when normally offered, mode of transportation to which it pertains, and whether a certificate is awarded on completion of the program. A modal index at the end of the book lists institutions offering courses by type of mode alphabetically giving FICE code.

236 TD2.2 **A Directory of Business Education Programs and Courses of Academic and Commercial Interest for Small and/or Minority Entrepreneurs in the State of Maryland.** Prepared by Charles Toogood and Joseph C. Reid, Baltimore Minority Business Opportunity Committee (M.B.O.C.) of the Federal Executive Board. Federal Highway Administration. 1981. 73p. Microfiche.
 D62

A useful guide, this directory assists small and/or minority business entrepreneurs, government agencies, and persons who intend to enter into small businesses in identifying business, education, and training resources that are presently available throughout the state of Maryland. It incorporates business courses and educational programs that are specifically designed to assist, but are not limited to, minority business owners wishing to acquire the additional skills necessary to compete in American business enterprise. The directory is divided into seven sections. Section 1, "Evening Academic School Resources," concerns secondary school resources, evening trade schools, and youth, adult, and evening training centers. Section 2, "Colleges, Universities, and Private Institutions," deals with post-secondary schools, including small colleges, universities, and two-year institutions. Also listed are private institutions that offer training and study programs for the small- and minority-business entrepreneurs. Federal, state, and local government agencies are the topic of section 3. Section 4 is about the Maryland Center for Public Broadcasting (PBS). Section 5, "Professional Trade Resources," contains a list of trade unions, private businesses, and the like. Section 6 is index 1, an alphabetical listing of programs and courses. Section 7 contains index 2, an alphabetical listing of agencies and institutions within each section. Each section contains a list of names, addresses, telephone numbers, and personal contacts at each of the institutions providing specialized business courses or training programs. Each section also contains a brief description of the training courses or programs offered in addition to other information, such as fees and how long the courses will continue.

237 TD4.8-5 **List of Certificated Pilot Schools. 1980.** Federal Aviation Administration. 1980. 52p. Advisory circular (AC) no. 140-2. Annual.
 no. 140-2

This circular provides a listing of pilot schools that are FAA-certificated as of May 1980 under Federal Aviation Regulations, Part 141, and a listing of aircraft dispatcher and flight engineer courses that are FAA-certificated. Each new edition supersedes all other editions. There are three appendixes. Appendix 1 gives an explanation of the codes used in the publication; appendix 2 lists the pilot schools in alphabetical order within the state, U.S. possession, or territory in which they are located, and gives school's name, mailing address, certificate number, and ratings or courses offered. Appendix 3 lists the aircraft dispatcher and flight engineer courses in alphabetical order within the region in which they are located. Each listing includes the name of the business, its mailing address, courses offered, and the FAA office that issued its certificate.

238 TD4.8-5 **Directory of FAA Certificated Aviation Maintenance Tech-**
no. 147-2   **nician Schools, 1980.** Federal Aviation Administration. 1980. 4p. Advisory circular (AC) no. 147-2. Annual.

All FAA-certificated aviation maintenance technician schools certificated as of March 1, 1980 under the authority of FAR, Part 147, are listed in this directory. Each new issue cancels the previous issue. FAA certification does not necessarily mean college credit will be extended by universities, nor does it indicate approval by other state or federal agencies. The schools are arranged in alphabetical order within the state in which they are located, giving name, mailing address, and ratings code letters.

239 TD4.25 **Directory of Aviation Majors and Curricula Offered by**
D62 **Colleges and Universities.** Federal Aviation Administration.
1973-   1979. 69p. Irregular.

Included in this listing are institutions offering both two-year terminal courses of instruction and those leading to baccalaureate and higher degrees. The institutions are listed by the various names of the programs and have been categorized into seven groups. Other nomenclature is also listed to provide the student with some degree of selectivity. Within each subject category, the institutions are arranged alphabetically by state, giving the name of the institution, city, zip code, aviation and related courses, majors, and certificates and/or degrees offered. There is no index or table of contents.

240 Y4.P93-1 **Government Depository Libraries. The Present Law Gov-**
D44 **erning Designated Depository Libraries.** Joint Committee on
1972-   Printing, Congress. 1981. 123p. Annual.

Five sections comprise this volume. Sections 1 and 2 give an overview of the depository library program, including some procedures for handling government publications and the legislation, laws, and statutory authority relating to depository libraries. Section 3 lists the depository libraries by state and city, and section 4 lists the libraries by state and congressional district. In section 2, the libraries are arranged alphabetically within city, and the information given includes name, address and/or zip code, date established as a depository, telephone number, and depository library number. Section 4 contains each library's location, name, whether designated by representative or senator, law school, year of designation, and also indicates whether there is a vacancy for another depository library. Section 5 lists the GPO bookstores and distribution center by state, giving name, address, zip code, and FTS and commercial telephone numbers.

6
Government Agencies, General

This chapter lists officials and describes the organization of government agencies—federal, state, and local.

241 A1.89-3 **Directory of the Agricultural Research Service, 1974.** Agriculture Department. 1975. 165p. Irregular.
Ag8
1968-

Organized into five main sections, this directory is designed to provide information about Agricultural Research Service (ARS) personnel. The first section covers the ARS headquarters staff and includes the Office of the Administrator, national program staff, program analysis and coordination staff, Information Division, International Programs Division, the Office of the Deputy Administrator for Management, and the management divisions, General Services Division, and Personnel Division. The other four sections cover the Northeastern region, North Central region, Western region, and Southern region. Each regional section is grouped according to its areas. Areas are broken down to include the office of the area director, and the various laboratories and locations. A detailed map of each region is included in the directory. Individuals are listed giving title, telephone number, and address code. Addresses may be found by using the code and the address list near the end of the volume. Also included is an alphabetical index of names indicating pages where persons can be found.

242 A1.111 **The Location of New Federal Offices and Other Facilities. Annual Report Pursuant to Title IX Section 901(b) of the Agricultural Act of 1970 as Amended by Section 601 of the Rural Development Act of 1972. Fiscal Year 1979.** Agriculture Department. 1980. v.p. Annual.
1974-

This volume reports the efforts during the fiscal year of all federal departments and agencies to locate their new offices and other facilities in rural areas. Executive Order 11797, dated July 1974, delegated the Secretary of Agriculture the responsibility for preparing and submitting the annual report to Congress. The reports of the departments and agencies have been summarized for quick reference. Part 1 consists of narratives, directives, and policy statements, reflecting efforts of all concerned in implementing the policies and procedures of the act. Part 2 is a statistical outline, alphabetically by agency, of all new facilities established or relocated during the fiscal year. Definitions of rural and urban areas, location selection codes, and usage codes are included. Also indicated is the number of employees.

74 / 6—Government Agencies, General

243   A13.36-2   **Forest Service Organizational Directory. August 1981.**
          Or3-2   Forest Service. 1981. 164p. Irregular.
          1970-

This directory shows the organization of the Forest Service with the addresses and telephone numbers of the main field offices and units. It lists the personnel chiefly responsible for the various units, key functions, lines of work, and research projects. Arranged by the Washington office, state and private forestry areas, regions, and research units. Included is an alphabetical index of personnel, index of national forest administrative units, and field office addresses.

244   A13.65-2   **Intermountain Region Offices.** Forest Service. 1980. n.p.
          In8-2   ˙Irregular.

In this leaflet is an alphabetical arrangement of Intermountain regional offices by name of national forest. Each district office is listed with address and telephone number.

245   A103.2   **Directory and Field Office Listing.** Food Safety and Quality
          D62   Service. 1979. 58p. Irregular.
          1979-

Addresses and telephone numbers of the personnel and laboratories of the various divisions and units of the Food Safety and Quality Service are indicated in this directory. It is divided into sections covering the Office of the Administrator; administrative management; state, city, and territorial locations; commodity services (Food Quality Assurance Division, Fruit and Vegetable Quality Division, Meat Quality Division, and Poultry and Dairy Division); Compliance Program; Meat and Poultry Inspection Program; and Science Program.

246   C1.2   **Directory of Key Contacts and Services. Who's Where in**
          D62   **Commerce.** 3d ed. Commerce Department. 1980. 70p.
          1979-   Irregular.

The title of this publication was formerly *Resources & Services for Economic Development Directory of Key Contacts and Services Available to State and Local Governments.* The directory describes Commerce Department resources and services local government officials can use for their own development strategies. It provides an agency-by-agency breakdown of key resources, services, and contact points for information and assistance. The department's resources and services can be divided into three broad areas: information and data vital for policymakers and planners; financial and technical assistance for business, economic, and export development; and applied technology for industry and local tax base enhancement. Commerce agencies are not limited to offering only one or another of these services, however; some combine three types of assistance, therefore a matrix has been devised to help readers find those areas most related to their needs. The main body of the directory lists the agencies under the aforementioned three broad areas, giving resources, contact person, address, telephone number, and district offices and regions. Other items included are a department organizational chart, agency abbreviations, a matrix of multiunit resources and services, a list of the duties of the Office of the Secretary, secretarial representatives by region, and a map of standard federal regions.

247 C1.8-3 **The Guide to the U.S. Department of Commerce for Women**
W84-2 **Business Owners.** Commerce Department. 1980. 42p.

Prepared primarily for the female business owner, this guide identifies U.S. Department of Commerce programs that can help women business owners. The programs that have been identified are not specifically mandated by legislation to assist women's business enterprise; however, the department does have the commitment and program resources available to assist women's business enterprise. The purpose of each of the department's agencies (or organizations) is stated, followed by a description of applicable programs available to the woman entrepreneur. Programs that can assist women business owners are categorized as either financial assistance or business assistance programs. Each agency section ends with a reference to the *Catalog of Federal Domestic Assistance* (see entry 601). In the appendix, the name, address, and telephone number of each agency's Washington and regional contacts are listed. Also in the appendix are members of the Commerce Task Force on Women's Business Enterprise, members of the Interagency Committee on Women's Business Enterprise, the text of the President's Executive Order 12138, a current organizational chart of the department and a description of the Minority Bank Deposit Program.

248 C55.102 **National Weather Service Offices and Stations.** 20th ed.
Of2 National Weather Service. 1980. 40p. Occasionally on micro-
1971- fiche. Irregular.

The purposes of this publication are to list all first- and second-order offices and stations operated by, or under the supervision of, the National Weather Service; to show the type and location of each station; and to indicate briefly the nature of the observational program provided by each station. (First-order refers to a station manned by full-time Weather Service employees; second-order refers to all other stations that are supervised by the National Weather Service). The stations and offices are arranged alphabetically by state and place within each state. Information includes the station name, airport name, call letters, type of station, international index number, latitude and longitude, elevation and elevation type, and upper air and radar observational data.

249 CAB1.28 **Telephone Directory. July 1980.** Civil Aeronautics Board.
1980. 44p. Quarterly.

Listed in this volume is an alphabetical directory of individuals indicating addresses and telephone numbers along with an organizational directory of offices and services. Room numbers and office/bureau abbreviations are also indicated. The directory also contains an alphabetical list of other government agency telephone numbers and hours of service. General information on dialing, emergency numbers, and so forth is included.

250 CC1.53 **The Telephone Directory. April 1, 1981.** Federal Communications Commission. 1981. 38p. Occasionally on microfiche. Quarterly.

There are three sections in this directory: one with general information, another with telephone information, and the major section, containing listings. The general information section lists such items as building locations, symbols for the organization, and emergency numbers. The telephone section gives general information and use of telephone, long-distance calls, dial-9-calls, and so forth. The listing section includes employee and miscellaneous services listing; functional listing; alphabetical name listing (which also indicates department, room number, and building); organizational chart, organizational listing (which includes individuals, telephone extension numbers, and room numbers); and the field locations and facilities (which lists regional directors, district offices, limited offices, monitoring stations, and special enforcement facilities). Contact people, addresses, and telephone numbers are given.

251   CS1.7-4   **Guide to Characteristics of Civil Service Regions. Statistical Data as of December 1975.** Civil Service Commission. [1976]? n.p.
        R26

This document is a compilation of the major federal employee population centers, comprising ten thousand or more employees, and the federal agencies consisting of at least three thousand employees within each U.S. Civil Service Commission region. This directory gives regional statistics for each region, but basically it identifies the ten regions of the CSC, stating the type of office and locating it on a map, and listing the areas where CSC offices are located in each region. Also listed are the major installations within the region, arranged alphabetically by region. The statistics given include total area (square miles), total population, total number of persons employed at federal installations and/or facilities, states and agencies, and number of Veterans Assistance Centers. Addresses are given.

252   D1.7   **Telephone Directory. December 1981.** Defense Department. 1981. v.p. 3 per year.

Information is given on emergency calls, national communications system voice precedence system, bus maps, bus schedules, Automatic Voice Network (Autovon), and telephone numbers of other government agencies. General information includes building abbreviations and locations, zip codes, and DoD bus route numbers, long distance area codes, and international time map. The alphabetical section lists names and abbreviations for buildings and telephone numbers. The organizational section has an index and includes persons for each office/agency.

253   D1.46-4   **Directory of DCAA Offices. October 1981.** Defense Contract Audit Agency. 1981. v.p. Occasionally on microfiche. 3 per year.
        1980-

DCAA is organizationally divided into headquarters, field detachments, and six regions. Within each region are field audit offices (FAOs) consisting primarily of branch and resident offices under which suboffices may be established. Offices responsible for providing procurement liaison services are designated as suboffices reporting to a branch. Within each regional section of the directory, FAOs are listed by regional/organization code (R/ORG) sequence. In addition, the directory includes an alphabetical index and an R/ORG index, which may be used in locating a specific office. Within the alphabetical index, resident offices and procurement liaison locations are listed collectively under "RES OFC" and "LIAISON OFC," respectively. There is also an index by name of field audit and suboffice managers. Addresses, telephone numbers, and contact persons are given. Also included are organizational charts, a list of headquarters personnel, a map of DCAA regional boundaries, and geographical areas of responsibility. This publication was formerly issued as DCAA pamphlet no. 5100.1.

254   D7.6-12   **DoD Activity Address Directory.** 2 parts. Defense Department. 1976. Microfiche. Quarterly.

This directory is published by direction of the Assistant Secretary of Defense (Installations and Logistics) under authority of DoD directive 4000.25, dated March 23, 1971. The directory contains activity address codes and the associated in-the-clear activity addresses to which materials, documentation, and billings are directed. The activity address code is a distinctive six-position alpha-numeric code assigned to identify specific units, activities, or organizations. The format for the directory is prearranged by the Central Control Point (CCP). Part 1 is a code-to-name directory, and addresses in part 2 are arranged by the military services, other DoD components, and civil agencies, and are listed in sequence by zip code. A very thorough introduction is provided in section 1 of part 1.

255   D301.35   **USAF Installation Directory.** Air Force Department. 1981.
      87-13   113p. Pamphlet no. 87-13. Microfiche. Annual.
      1978-

Contained in this directory are all separately located and defined areas of real property in which the Air Force exercises a real property interest. It has been compiled from the USAF installations characteristics reports submitted by the major commands in accordance with AFM 87-18, and reflects the latest information contained therein. Arranged alphabetically by installation name, the directory lists the installation code, command code, county or district where located, state and nearest city, name of the parent installation, and type, classification, and status of the installation. Also included is a list of installations arranged alphabetically by major installations with off-base installations.

256   E1.12-2   **Brookhaven National Laboratory Telephone Directory. 1980.** Energy Department. 1980. v.p. Annual.

Along with the alphabetical listings (which include staff person, telephone extension, mail drop number, and street address of building) and the organizational listings (which give name of agency or office and telephone extension), this directory includes many other items to assist with using the directory and contacting the personnel. Some of the items provided are area code map, alphabetical list of buildings, emergency numbers, housing, time-zone maps, metric conversion table, residences, and zip codes. A comprehensive index at the beginning will be most helpful to all users.

257   E1.49   **Doing Business with the Department of Energy Directory.**
      no. 0047   Energy Department. 1980. 31p. DOE/PR series, no. 0047. Irregular.

Listed in this directory are DOE offices and contacts that are concerned with procurement, small business, small disadvantaged business, and women-owned businesses. Part 1 lists the DOE headquarters program offices with addresses, room numbers, telephone numbers, and contacts. Part 2 lists the DOE procurement offices (operations, project, area offices, and regional representatives). Part 3 lists the government-owned, contractor-operated (GOCO) and major on-site contractors; and part 4 lists other major DOE contractors. Parts 2 and 3 give the office manager and address, procurement office contact, and SB/DB contact. Part 4 gives the company's name and address, and the contact for business purposes, with telephone.

78 / 6—Government Agencies, General

258 E4.11 **Roster. Emergency Electric Power Administration.** Economic Regulatory Administration. July 1980. v.p. DOE/RG series, no. 0041. Irregular.
     no. 0041

This directory lists the EEPA national headquarters staff; EEPA area map; EEPA directors, deputies, regional power liaison representatives, state power liaison representatives, and major utility representatives; EEPA state power liaison representatives (alphabetically by states); and the Federal Emergency Management Agency (FEMA) regional map and regional offices, in that order. Given is name, address, and telephone number, and whether the position is vacant, along with person acting or alternate.

259 ED1.24 **Telephone Directory.** Education Department. 1980. 69p. Occasionally on microfiche. Annual.

Included in this directory are addresses, telephone numbers, specific organizations, and building and room numbers of Department of Education employees in an alphabetical directory. It is arranged in the following sections: general information and services; emergencies; organizational chart; Office of the Secretary and principal staff; organizational abbreviations; alphabetical listing; regional offices; councils and commissions; buildings occupied by the ED; and other selected Washington area agencies with telephone numbers, office hours, and zip codes.

260 EP1.12 **Telephone Directory, Summer 1980.** Environmental Protection Agency. 1980. 107p. Quarterly.

In this directory are listings of hospitals, airlines, railroads, buses, shuttle bus services, and taxi services, as well as other general information materials. The main sections are the organizational directory and the alphabetical personnel directory. Buildings, room numbers, and telephone numbers are given.

261 FEM1.14 **Telephone Directory, 1980.** Federal Emergency Management Agency. 1980. 31p. Annual.

Divided into four sections, this directory contains an emergency numbers section; a headquarters-organizational section; a regional offices and federal regional centers section; and the alphabetical personnel section. Each section gives key personnel, organization affiliation, building room number, and telephone number.

262 GS4.109 **United States Government Manual, 1981/82.** Federal Register Office. 1981. 948p. Annual.
     1935-

This is the official handbook about the federal government, containing sections describing the creation, authority, organization, and functions of the agencies in the legislative, judicial, and executive branches. A typical agency description includes address, telephone number, a list of principal officials, a summary statement on the agency's purpose and role in the government, a brief history of the agency (including its legislative or executive authority), a description of its programs and activities, and a section on sources of information. This last section provides information on consumer activities, contracts and grants, employment, publications, and many other areas of interest to citizens. Regional offices may also be included. The section on the legislative branch includes the names of all senators and representatives listed alphabetically, along with state, district (where applicable), and room number. Supplemental information

6—*Government Agencies, General* / 79

following the major sections includes addresses, officials, and brief descriptions of quasi-official agencies and selected international organizations; selected boards, committees and commissions; commonly used abbreviations of the names of agencies and departments; organizational charts of the departments, and selected agencies. Also included is a list of executive agencies and functions of the federal government abolished, transferred, or terminated subsequent to March 4, 1933. Included are name, subject, and agency indexes. Copies of the Declaration of Independence and the Constitution of the United States are included.

263   GS4.119   **Directory of Federal Regional Structure, 1981/82.** Federal
         1978-   Register Office. 1981. 202p. Irregular.

The standard federal administrative regions were established to achieve greater uniformity in the location and geographic jurisdiction of federal field offices. This publication provides a directory of federal agency regional structures designed to give practical information about regional offices of federal departments and agencies. Included in the directory is a map showing the ten standard federal regions, followed by tables listing the key personnel, addresses, and telephone numbers for agencies with offices in those regions. In addition, maps and tables are provided for those agencies with regional structures other than that of the standard regional system.

264   GS12.12   **Telephone Directory, Central Office and Region 3.** Automated Data and Telecommunications Service. 1976. 112p. Annual.

An alphabetical directory of names and an organizational directory of the General Services Administration, its divisions, and regions are contained in this volume. It includes such general information as dialing instructions, building locations, and an area code map. Information for each individual includes telephone number, building, and room number.

265   HE1.28   **Telephone Directory.** Health and Human Services Department. 1980. v.p. Occasionally on microfiche. Annual.

Found in this directory are such items of information as building addresses, symbols, telephone dialing instructions, transportation services, and regional offices personnel, with addresses and telephone numbers, as well as an organization chart and other miscellaneous informational items. The main sections are the alphabetical personnel section and the organizational section. Each of these sections gives organization affiliation, room number, building, and telephone number.

266   HE20.3002   **Medical Staff Directory: The Clinical Center.** National Insti-
         M46-4   tutes of Health. 1980. 98p. Annual.
         1980-

Presented here are the active medical staff (clinical directors, senior staff, and junior staff) and the guest medical staff (physicians and dentists of recognized ability who are not employees of NIH, but who participate in the scientific and/or clinical activities of institute clinical center programs as guest workers, as visiting staff [including fellows, associates, and scientists], or as NIH contract employees). Part 1 is an alphabetical listing of practitioners that gives name and home address, telephone number, zip code,

6—Government Agencies, General

office building, room number, and institute branch. Part 2 is a list of practitioners by organizational component, arranged alphabetically by component.

267   HE20.3016   **NIH Almanac. 1981.** National Institutes of Health. 1981.
         1964-   169p. Annual.

The *NIH Almanac* does for the National Institutes of Health (NIH) what the *NCI Fact Book* does for the National Cancer Institute (see entry 270). Originally intended for the use of information staffs, administrators, and other federal employees who often need access to pertinent facts about the NIH, it has now become a most useful source to others outside the departments, including news media and administrators. Although the almanac includes data found in other basic NIH publications, it is intended to complement rather than replace them, and to offer in one volume all important historical data and other reference material. The volume has sections on historical data of the organization, appropriations, support of medical research, the staff, real property and facilities, field units, lectures, nobel laureates, honors, exhibits, and symposiums. The historical data section gives biographical sketches of the directors and deputy directors of NIH, and a list of all directors, associate directors, secretaries of the Health, Education, and Welfare and Health and Human Services departments, and surgeons general of the Public Health Service. The organization section gives the mission, important events, legislative chronology, biographical sketches of directors, appropriations, grants, and programs of each NIH division and institute. The staff section gives historical figures for employees and staff.

268   HE20.3017   **Scientific Directory 1981; Annual Bibliography 1980.** National
         1956-   Institutes of Health. 1981. 484p. Annual.

Primarily intended for reference use by research workers in the biomedical sciences; this volume presents a broad outline of NIH organizational structure, the professional staff, and scientific and technical publications covering work done at NIH. The material is arranged by components, with the directory and bibliography entries presented together at the laboratory or branch level within each component. Also presented is comparable information for NIMH (National Institute of Mental Health), although it is no longer a component of NIH (see the agency listing in appendix 4). The directory has an alphabetical index of names of scientific staff members, other key individuals, visiting scientists, and guest workers with tenure of a year or more. An asterisk before a name identifies the chief of a section.

269   HE20.3037   **Telephone and Service Directory. 1981-2.** National Institutes
         1981-   of Health. 1981. 272p. Occasionally on microfiche.
                      Semiannual.

This directory has an alphabetical personnel directory section that lists addresses, organization affiliations, buildings, room numbers, and telephone numbers, and organizational listings that indicate key personnel, building, room number, and telephone and tube number. Also of interest is the pneumatic tube station directory and the "yellow pages," which are designed to answer questions on how to use central services or where to get information about services or subjects of general interest. In the "yellow pages," items are arranged alphabetically and are cross-referenced under multiple headings to facilitate access to the information. There is a classified alphabetical index that supplements these "yellow pages." Other general information is given,

6—*Government Agencies, General* / 81

as well as telephone numbers of other government agencies within the Bethesda, Maryland, area.

270 HE20.3174   **National Cancer Institute Fact Book. (NCI Fact Book.)**
       1978-   National Cancer Institute. 1978. 45p. Occasionally on microfiche. Irregular.

Although much of this volume is concerned with budget data, grants, contracts, and historical data, it is an excellent source for locating and identifying the personnel and agencies within the institute. The first section is devoted to general information, and not only gives statistical data on cancer deaths, dollar funding, historical events, and program strategies, but contains a directory of personnel, NCI executive committee, National Cancer Advisory Board, organizational charts for NCI and its divisions, research positions, and building locations and square footage. The directory of personnel gives building number and telephone number. The organizational charts explain the functions of each division and office, and lists the directors.

271 HE20.4037   **FDA Location Directory.** Food and Drug Administration.
       1979-   1980. v.p. Occasionally on microfiche. Annual.

Names, addresses, telephone numbers, and other data about persons and organizations within the FDA are contained in this directory. Section 1 contains an FDA organization chart, a map of FDA regions and districts, plus mailing addresses and general telephone instructions for FDA headquarters buildings, Federal Telecommunications System (FTS) area codes and time zones, and FDA telecommunications systems. The second section provides an FDA headquarters classified listing, and the third, an alphabetical listing of FDA headquarters employees. Section 4 deals with FDA field operations (FDA headquarters field activities), FDA regional addresses, mail routing codes, key field personnel and resident inspection posts, and section 5 is an alphabetical listing of FDA headquarters field activities employees. All alphabetical listings give name, mail routing codes, buildings, room numbers, and telephone numbers. There is also a list of FDA buildings with addresses, telephone numbers, and symbols.

272 HE23.11   **HDS Telephone Directory. Spring 1981.** Human Development Services Office. 1981. n.p. Quarterly.

This is primarily an alphabetical directory of personnel giving telephone numbers, organizations for which individuals work, room numbers, and buildings. Also included is an organizational directory listing agencies, positions and personnel with room numbers, buildings, and telephone numbers. There is a list of building addresses and abbreviations.

273 HH1.92   **Telephone Directory. 1981-2.** Housing and Urban Development Department. 1982. 25p. Occasionally on microfiche. Irregular.

Provided here is an alphabetical listing of Housing and Urban Development Department headquarters employees. Also included is a brief directory by service. For each employee the following information is given: complete official name, organization where employed, room number, and telephone extension number.

274   I1.2   Directory of Personnel Offices. Regional and Headquarters.
D62-4   Interior Department. 1978. 20p.

Included in this directory are the location of personnel offices of the various agencies of the Interior Department beginning with the Office of the Secretary through to the Office of Surface Mining Reclamation and Enforcement. The information given for each agency includes the name of the office, division or branch, address, telephone number, title of responsible official, appointing authority (for position), and area of jurisdiction.

275   I1.2   Information Sources and Services Directory. Interior Depart-
In3-2   ment. 1979. 300p.

The purpose of this directory is to give access to the information sources that are products of the Department of Interior's many functions and responsibilities. Its intended audience is individuals and organizations requiring the kind of information and services that the Interior Department, by law and by custom, provides. In conducting the management of the natural resources of the United States, the following specific areas are covered: public lands and their natural wealth, fish and wildlife, the National Park System, heritage conservation, and the federal responsibility to native Americans. The directory is divided into five parts: main text; organizational index (arranged by bureau and office, with individual elements listed alphabetically below the main heading and entry numbers on the right); subject index; geographical index by state; and field office locations. The main text is organized by component, and each has an entry number. Each entry of a particular division's components is arranged alphabetically by name and/or state and gives mailing address, telephone number, information products and services, subject coverage, time span of coverage, and geographic coverage. Using any of the indexes leads one to the entry number of the main text.

276   I49.2   Directory. Region 6. Fish and Wildlife Service. 1980. 76p.
D62-2   Microfiche.

This directory contains the personnel and organizations of Region 6 of the Fish and Wildlife Service of the Department of the Interior. It provides a complete table of contents, an alphabetical listing of names and agencies, a regional office listing, offices in various cities in the region, a listing of state fish and game agencies in Region 6, Washington area offices, and other offices of special interests and scope. The alphabetical listing only refers to a page number in the directory where detailed information may be found under the organizations. Organizational listings provide addresses, telephone numbers, titles and names of personnel, and FTS and commercial telephone numbers.

277   I53.2   Bureau of Land Management Office Directory. Land Manage-
D62   ment Bureau. 1976. 40p.

This directory lists, in the following order, the BLM's Washington office, Denver Service Center, Boise Interagency Fire Center, state and district offices, and Outer Continental Shelf (OCS) offices. Information given for each section, except district offices and OCS offices, is the address, staff members' names and titles, telephone extension number, office hours, and home address and telephone number. For district offices and OCS offices, information includes the name and address of office, telephone number, the name and home telephone number of office head, and office

6—Government Agencies, General / 83

hours. States included are Alaska, Arizona, California, Colorado, Idaho, Montana, Nevada, New Mexico, Oregon, Utah, and Wyoming. OCS offices are located in New York, New Orleans, Anchorage, and Los Angeles.

278   Ju10.20   **Telephone Directory. December 1980.** Administrative Office of the United States Courts. 1981. n.p. Semiannual.

Contained in this volume is a list of services, arranged by component, which gives the names of the units, branches, and sections involved, along with personnel and telephone numbers. It also has an alphabetical directory of the Administrative Office, the Federal Judicial Center, and the Supreme Court, giving locations and telephone numbers. The alphabetical directory for the Administrative Office also includes the divisions and sections. There is an organization chart and list of buildings with addresses.

279   L1.67   **Telephone Directory, Fall 1980.** Labor Department. 1980. 235p. Occasionally on microfiche. Semiannual.

Presented in this directory is general information for locating and contacting personnel and offices of the Labor Department and its many agencies. It includes an organizational directory section and an alphabetical individual directory. The alphabetical directory gives each agency's abbreviation, building, and room number. The organizational section identifies directors and chiefs of each office or division, with room numbers and telephone numbers. There is a list of building abbreviations and locations and principal regional and field offices with addresses, personnel, and telephone numbers.

280   L36.2
         D62
         1979-   **ESA Directory of Offices.** Employment Standards Administration. 1980. 99p. Annual.

The national and regional offices of the Employment Standards Administration of the Department of Labor are listed in this publication. The national office section lists the various offices and divisions, naming personnel with room numbers and telephone extensions. The regional sections are arranged numerically by regions 1 through 10, and lists the names of the states within the regions. This section identifies the regional office address and names the personnel with telephone numbers and field stations. Also listed are addresses for the Wage and Hour Division, Federal Employees' Compensation district offices, and Office of Federal Contract Compliance Programs offices within each region. Directors and assistant directors are indicated for these offices.

281   LC1.40
         1981-   **Library of Congress Directory.** Library of Congress. 1981. 59p. Microfiche. Annual.

The main section of this resource is an alphabetical directory of names and agencies, offices, and sections of the Library of Congress, listing agency affiliation, room numbers, and telephone numbers. Three appendixes include one that identifies the symbols used in the directory, an alphabetical directory by services, and an alphabetical government agency directory, listing telephone numbers, mail stop numbers, and zip codes. There is an organizational directory listing, and other items of interest include eating facilities, location of annexes, nonlibrary organizations in the Library of Congress, and working hours of the principal government agencies.

84 / 6 — Government Agencies, General

282 NAS1.18 **The Writers Guide to NASA.** National Aeronautics and Space
W93 Administration. 1978. 28p.

This booklet is another of NASA's efforts to serve the interests of the public by offering free and open access to its development and operations facilities and communications with its people. The guide outlines what NASA does, where it conducts its operations, and whom one should contact for information on any specific program or project. Included is a map of the United States with a key to the location of major NASA installations and a list of information sources. The major section is arranged first with NASA headquarters information, and then alphabetically by name of the installation. Information for each place named includes location, description, mission, and a list of public affairs contacts with telephone numbers, both office and home.

283 NAS1.24 **Telephone Directory. Headquarters. August 1981.** National Aeronautics and Space Administration. 1981. 56p. Quarterly.

Items contained in this directory include frequently called numbers, telephone information, a NASA organizational chart, a metro map of regional rapid rail, an alphabetical list of official mail codes, a classified listing of the organization, an alphabetical listing of headquarters employees, an alphabetical listing of HQ contractor employees, equal opportunity personnel information, time zone and telephone area codes, and official installation addresses and telephone numbers. Other sections deal with support services, U.S. Postal Service mail pickup schedule for HQ, teleconference information, Washington agency directory (other agencies), NASA and DoD bus schedule, and emergency number information.

284 NCU1.14 **Telephone Directory, 1981-2.** National Credit Union Administration. 1981. 26p. Occasionally on microfiche. Quarterly.

Included here is an organizational, alphabetical, and regional directory of the NCU Administration, as well as a telephone listing of federal credit unions in various departments of the government (intra-agency telephone listing and post office stops). The regional directory section indicates the supervisory examiners, examiners, and consumer examiners.

285 PM1.2 **Classified Information Directory for the Central Office.** Personnel Management Office. 1980. 16p.
In3

Provided in this directory are the addresses of headquarters and officials of the OPM, and an organization chart. Also included are alphabetical subject chapters on what the Office of Personnel Management does, explaining each subject category thoroughly. An alphabetical index of topics that may be of interest to anyone seeking help at OPM is provided. Each topic indicates a room number for the headquarters building, and a telephone number. A list of OPM regional offices in the United States is given, indicating region, address, telephone number, states covered, and names of officials.

286 S1.21 **Telephone Directory. Spring 1981.** State Department. 1981. 144p. Occasionally on microfiche. Quarterly.

Several other agencies are included as part of this State Department directory. They are: Overseas Investment Corporation, U.S. Arms Control and Disarmament Agency, U.S. International Communication Agency, Board of International Broadcasting, and

6—Government Agencies, General / 85

ACTION. Addresses, room numbers, telephone numbers, and agency affiliations are given in the following sections: an alphabetical directory of services; an alphabetical directory of personnel; an organizational directory; a list of officers, alphabetical by country; a list of commissions, committees, and advisory groups; and listings of Department of State field offices, liaison offices in the Department, and chanceries. There are also lists of government information numbers, office hours and mail stops, and office symbols.

287 T1.28 **Telephone Directory. Fall 1980.** Treasury Department. 1980. 172p. Occasionally on microfiche. 3 per year.

In addition to the alphabetical listing of names and the organizational sections, this directory contains a government agency listing of telephone numbers, zip codes, and office hours. A directory of principal field offices, an international time table, calendars for the years 1800 through 2000, a U.S. area code map, and building abbreviations and locations are also included.

288 T17.15 **Telephone Directory.** Customs Service. 1981. 173p. Annual.

This directory provides a listing of principal officials at the service's headquarters and in customs field offices. The first section lists principal service headquarters officials in an organizational format. Following this section are customs field offices, organized by region and city. The first section is preceded by a list of the FTS operator numbers that correspond to those cities having either a district or regional customs office. Next are listings of facsimile telephone numbers, followed by radio sectors, air units, Customs Service Academy, dog training center, twenty-four-hour telephone numbers, teletype system stations, international mail branches, preclearance stations, and a city cross-reference guide. Addresses are given for each entry.

289 TD1.9 **'81 Directory. July 1981.** Transportation Department. 1981.
 1968- 204p. Quarterly.

Contained in this publication is a list of services, a classified directory, and an alphabetical directory, as well as other useful miscellaneous information for employees of this department. One such item is a list of individuals who are trained in cardiopulmonary resuscitation (CPR), which tells how they can be reached. Also included is a selected Washington agency directory, giving switchboard number, office hours, post office stop number, and zip code.

290 TD4.52 **FAA Directory. May 1981.** Federal Aviation Administration.
 1978- 1981. 195p. Quarterly.

There are six major sections in this directory. They pertain to: (1) Washington/region/ center headquarters; (2) field facilities; (3) regional area maps and organization charts; (4) personnel; (5) special interest groups; and (6) glossary. The directory shows the Washington headquarters section first. Headquarters data are arranged as follows: administrator, deputy administrator, assistant administrators, and associate administrators, with offices/services arranged alphabetically under their associate administrator. Region and center sections follow. Each regional section begins with the region's organization chart and area map. Two regional subsections follow. The first subsection shows regional headquarters data. The second subsection shows the region's field facilities. The regional field facility subsection contains field offices and facilities at the sector

86 / 6 — Government Agencies, General

level and above. It is arranged in alphabetical order by state, city within state, and type of facility within city. The city with which the field facility is associated is listed in one column. The associated city name relates to the regional area map; the field facility's physical location is provided under the location column. The alphabetical section is a listing of all people identified in the sections described above. A section on special interest groups contains pertinent information about various facilities. The glossary gives a brief functional description of various facilities. The back cover of the directory has been indexed so that any directory segment can be located easily.

291   Y1.2   **Telephone Directory. Spring 1981.** House of Representatives.
         T23   1981. 297p. Quarterly.

This directory contains the officers of the House, the representatives, the House committees, with subcommittees and an alphabetical listing of their staffs; House leadership staffs; representatives' staffs; standing committees, members and staff; select committees, members and staff; joint committees, members and staffs; staffs of House officers; general support officers; House commissions, caucus section; officers of the Senate; senators; Senate committees and subcommittees with chairmen; executive branch, including cabinet members; and other government agencies. Also included is selected information of a general nature, such as capital buildings and grounds, emergency numbers, miscellaneous city numbers, abbreviations, metro subway map, and long-distance area code and time zone map.

292   Y1.3   **Telephone Directory. November 1981.** Senate. 1981. 160p.
         T23   Occasionally on microfiche. Semiannual.

The directory contains, in the following order, a list of senators with room and telephone numbers; officers of the Senate and House; an alphabetical listing of Senate staff; senators' staffs arranged by senators' names; Senate committee members and committee staff (members); Senate leadership, officers, and offices; general support; members of the House of Representatives; committees of the House of Representatives; government agencies; selected city numbers; abbreviations; Centrex dialing instructions; FTS dialing instructions; location of buildings; and civil defense instructions.

293   Y3.N88:10   **U.S. Nuclear Regulatory Commission Functional Organiza-**
         no. 0325   **tion Charts.** 3d ed., rev. Nuclear Regulatory Commission.
         1978-   1981. 56p. NUREG series no. 0325. Irregular.

In this publication we find charts of the various agencies and regional offices of the U.S. Nuclear Regulatory Commission. It ranges from the office of the chairman to all other subject areas of concern. Each chart for an office indicates a chief official and describes the main purpose and function of the office.

294   Y3.N88:14   **Telephone Directory. Communications Information.** Nuclear
                      Regulatory Commission. 1981. v.p. Annual.

The directory is organized into five sections, the first of which gives general information and contains NRC building locations, regional map, security guard location, shuttle bus service, selected Washington agency directory, and other useful and helpful miscellaneous information. The second section gives NRC organizational symbols and listings, and contains an organizational chart. An NRC alphabetical listing, giving

6—*Government Agencies, General* / 87

telephone extension, locations, room, mail code, and organization, comprises section 3. Section 4 lists NRC resident personnel by region and by site name in alphabetical order, then alphabetically by site name alone. Section 5 is the functional directory, which is arranged alphabetically by function.

295   Y3.P38-2:9   **Telephone Directory. March 1981.** Pension Benefit Guaranty Corporation. 1981. 49p. Quarterly.

Included here are telephone, office, and room number information for the Pension Benefit Guaranty Corporation's employees in the following sections: organizational; alphabetical by office; and alphabetical by individual. Also included is information on office codes, mail/messenger schedules, telephone procedures, support services, emergency information, and an organizational chart.

296   Y4.G74-9   **Organization of Federal Executive Departments and Agencies.**
         Ex3/supp.   **Data as of January 1, 1979.** Senate Committee on Govern-
         1977-   mental Affairs. 1979. n.p. Annual.

Presented is a chart of the organization of the federal executive departments and the independent agencies and commissions. It lists each agency or office, and gives the number of employees working there. Also indicated are the number of field or regional offices. It states a cumulative figure for employees in the United States and personnel outside the United States, as well as the number of employees for the Executive Office of the President. The members of the Senate Committee on Governmental Affairs, with their states, are named. The supplement to this organizational chart is a Committee Print entitled *Agencies and Functions of the Federal Government Established, Continued, Abolished, Transferred, or Changed in Name by Legislative or Executive Action during Calendar Year _____*. This list is prepared by the Office of the Federal Register, National Archives and Records Service, GSA, for the committee. Public Law numbers, executive order numbers, and statute citations are indicated. References to the *Weekly Compilation of Presidential Documents* are also indicated.

7
Government Agencies, Subject

This chapter lists and describes the organization and officials of government agencies—federal, state, and local—of a specific subject nature.

297 A98.9 **WIC Program Directory of Local Agencies.** Food and Nutrition Service. 1978. 100p. FNS no. 177. Irregular.

This WIC (Special Supplemental Food Program for Women, Infants and Children) Program directory of local agencies is to be used as a tool for referring migrant WIC participants to WIC Programs as they move during the migratory work season. The directory is divided into four sections, which contain the following information: Section 1 provides a list of the WIC Program directors in the thirteen states serving migrants. It is arranged by region and gives addresses and telephone numbers. Section 2 is a list of state agency codes throughout the United States, organized alphabetically by state. Section 3 comprises the main body of the directory and is a listing of the local agencies by state and county, arranged alphabetically by state and county. It includes a listing of counties in each state, the county code, the address and telephone number of the local agency, the local agency code, and other counties served by the local agency. In addition, the counties served by the local agency are cross-referenced individually. Section 4 is a list of the Commodity Supplemental Food programs in the thirteen states serving migrants (Colorado, Illinois, Indiana, Iowa, Kansas, Michigan, Minnesota, Missouri, Nebraska, North Dakota, Ohio, Texas, and Wisconsin).

298 A98.15 **Directory of Cooperating Agencies.** Food and Nutrition Service. 1981. 134p. Annual.

This publication is an alphabetical arrangement by state of those state agencies that cooperate with the Federal Food and Nutrition Service of the United States Department of Agriculture in administering nutrition activities of the federal government. Agencies within each state are listed by State Department function, and the information given for each agency includes principal contact person, address, telephone number, and federal program responsibility abbreviation.

299 C3.186 **State and Local Agencies Preparing Population Estimates and Projections: Survey of 1975-76.** Census Bureau. 1978. 80p. Current Population Report series P-25 (Population Estimates and Projections), no. 723. Irregular.

In this survey an attempt has been made to inventory the availability of population estimates from state and local government sources. It goes into great detail in presenting the results of a mail survey of state and local governmental agencies, giving such information as methodology, accuracy of methods, and demographic detail. However, for the purposes of this bibliography, the publication presents important directories of agencies that work in this field. These lists are presented in tabular format, except for the Federal-State Cooperative Program's agencies, contacts, and telephone listings. The directories list: (1) state and local agencies making population estimates; (2) agencies making population estimates for Standard Metropolitan Statistical Areas (SMSAs); (3) state and local agencies making population projections; and (4) the above-mentioned list of Federal-State Cooperative Program agencies. The first list is an alphabetical arrangement by state, containing agency name and address, areas covered by estimates, level of estimates, and detail and methods used by level. The second directory section is an alphabetical arrangement by name of the SMSA, listing the name of the agency making the estimate, and area covered. The third lists alphabetically by state, and agency name within state, the agency name and address and the area covered by the projection. The Federal-State Cooperative Program list is an alphabetical arrangement by state of the contact agencies, giving address, contact person, and telephone number.

300 C47.12 **Consumer's Guide to Travel Information. Helpful Informa-**
　　In3 　　**tion Sources.** Travel Service. 1978. n.p.

The purpose of this directory is to provide sources of up-to-date information about the destinations and attractions for travel. This is a helpful guide to federal and state government agencies that can provide information and assistance in planning your trip. Divided into three sections, the first contains information on the National Park Service, the U.S. Forest Service, other federally maintained lands and waterways, and American Indian Lands. It gives addresses of the national park regions, selected areas in the National Park System, Forest Service regions, and other contacts. The second section is an alphabetical list, by state, of state government tourism offices and, if applicable, their toll-free numbers. Section 3 discusses other information sources for travel information.

301 C47.12 **Consumer's Guide to Travel Information. State and Terri-**
　　T64-2 　　**torial Tourism Offices.** Travel Service. 1978. n.p.

This list of state tourism offices has been compiled to provide the consumer with a guide to public travel information sources. Most of these offices will provide maps, brochures, and additional tourism information concerning their state or territory. They may be contacted by telephone or by mail. This leaflet is arranged alphabetically by state, giving the name of the state office, address, telephone number, and toll-free number, if available.

302 C61.8 **A Guide for Business. U.S. Commercial Service Offices and**
　　C73 　　**the Foreign Commercial Service Posts.** International Trade Administration. 1980. 24p.

The U.S. Commercial Service (USCS), through its forty-seven district offices, facilitates the entry of nonexporters into international markets and helps develop additional exports for more experienced companies. The Foreign Commercial Service (FCS) is dedicated to serving the overseas needs of U.S. business and is a key element in the President's Trade Reorganization Plan of 1979. The USCS and FCS, supported by the Trade Development staff in Washington, provide U.S. business with direct access to a worldwide network of commercial services and to a fully integrated export marketing and delivery system. This directory contains a list of these offices. Part 1 lists the U.S. Commercial Service Offices alphabetically by state and city within state, giving directors' addresses and telephone numbers, including FTS numbers. Part 2 lists the U.S. Foreign Commercial Service posts alphabetically by country and then by city, giving address, telephone and telex numbers, commercial officer(s), occasionally the workweek, and, when applicable, the director of the export development office.

303   CC1.2 R11-14 1978-   **Directory of Field Contacts for the Coordination of the Use of Radio Frequencies.** Federal Communications Commission. April 1, 1981. v.p. Microfiche. Irregular.

This directory was compiled to assist, as appropriate, in the local preliminary coordination of contemplated frequency usage, the local selection and scheduling of the use of assigned frequencies, and the local resolution of cases of harmful interference. The directory is divided into four sections. The first contains the headquarters address and telephone number for frequency management personnel of the major federal government agencies, arranged alphabetically by the agency. Section 2 contains a half page for each state, the District of Columbia, and outlying areas, arranged alphabetically. Listed under each of these are the names of departments or agencies of the federal government that have field contacts who are concerned with some use of radio frequencies in that jurisdiction. Listed to the right of each department or agency are numbers that refer to the field contacts of that department or agency for the jurisdiction. Section 3 lists the field contacts of the departments and agencies of the federal government, arranged alphabetically by the department or agency. Under each is the title, address, and telephone number of the field contacts for that department or agency. Also shown are the geographical areas under the cognizance of each contact, and in some cases, the frequency bands or types of operation involved. Section 4 lists the field contacts of nonfederal frequency advisory committees. The information is arranged by service, and within each service, alphabetically by state. The names and addresses of coordinators whose geographical area of jurisdiction includes more than one state is repeated for each such state. Following the list of area coordinators is a list of services and contacts for those services where nationwide coordination is accomplished through a centralized coordination office; it is arranged by region.

304   CS1.2 M54-2   **Directory of State Merit Systems.** Civil Service Commission. 1975. 26p.

State merit systems that serve state and local government agencies subject to the standards of the Merit System of Personnel Administration (45 CFR 70) are listed here. The directory also names the agencies served by each state merit system. State agencies providing personnel services for such locally administered programs as welfare, health, and civil defense are listed in the directory; however, individual municipal and county civil service systems that serve local grant-aided agencies have been omitted. The agencies are arranged alphabetically by state. Information consists of the agency name, agencies served, the executive officer, title, address, and telephone number. Also included in this volume are the United States Civil Service regions, giving headquarters, addresses, telephone numbers, chief executive officers, and areas served.

305 D1.2   **Small and Disadvantaged Business Utilization Specialists:**
     B96   **Designated to Assist Small, Minority and Labor Surplus Area**
               Businessmen. Department of Defense. 1979. 69p.

The purpose of this directory is to offer full and free competition, with equal opportunity, to all interested qualified suppliers to compete for DoD contracts. It contains a list of Department of Defense procurement offices throughout the United States. The small and disadvantaged business specialists at each of these offices are available to assist businessmen in obtaining information and guidance on DoD procurement procedures (how to be placed on the bidder's mailing list) and identification of both prime and subcontract opportunities. The location of Army, Navy, Air Force, and Defense Logistics Agency procurement and contract administration offices and the names of the small and disadvantaged business specialists are listed in this pamphlet by state and city, alphabetically. Some of the procurement offices listed purchase only those supplies and services that are required to meet local needs. Others have the broader assignment of central procurement responsibility for particular commodity requirements of one or more of the military departments on a national or global basis. Also included in this volume is a regional listing of Small Business Administration field office addresses with telephone numbers, and a list of the General Services Administration regional offices and Business Service Center, giving addresses, telephone numbers, chief officer, and states covered by the region.

306 E1.26   **State Energy Officials Directory.** Energy Department. May
     no. 0167 1980. 62p. DOE/CS series, no. 0167. Irregular.

Provided in this publication is an alphabetical arrangement by state and territory of the officials in each state involved in energy or energy-related matters. Indicated on a table for each state are the following: the state's federal region; Governor's Conference Association; governor's name, party, and term; state energy director with address and telephone number; the governor's representative to the Regional Energy Advisory Board; and other state energy officials, with names, titles, addresses and telephone numbers. Also included in the directory is a list of the federal Department of Energy officials with telephone numbers and room numbers, as well as an alphabetical list of associations with chief executive offices, addresses, and telephone numbers.

307 E1.28   **Solar Energy Information Locator.** 2d ed. A product of the
     SERI/SP   Solar Energy Information Data Bank, Solar Energy Research
     751-210   Institute. Energy Department. 1980. 58p. Irregular.

Listed in this volume are organizations that offer solar energy, or solar-related publications, or solar information services to the public. The locator tells where to start and where to obtain further information, and includes indexes. Section 1 includes organizations that provide free information on solar, or all, energy sources. These agencies will answer general questions, refer the user to additional sources, and provide overviews of government solar policies and activities. The organizations covered in this section are from the Solar Energy Data Bank and state government organizations in this area. Section 2 lists organizations more specialized in activity that restrict services to a specific region, or charge for information products and services. The organizations covered here are from national government; regional government; other government-related organizations, and universities; regional depositories of U.S. documents; and private organizations. Also included in this section are lists of solar energy periodicals

92 / 7—*Government Agencies, Subject*

and directories of citizens' solar energy organizations. Section 3 lists solar information sources by organization, solar technology, and subject. Information given for each organization listed includes address, areas of interest, information services, and publications.

308   E1.33-2   **Consumer Energy Atlas.** Energy Department. 1980. 251p.
no. 10879-01   DOE/CA series, no. 10879-01. Irregular.

The *Consumer Energy Atlas* was designed to help consumers find answers to energy-related questions. More than ten thousand energy-related experts are included. These experts include members of over fifty federal agencies and departments, over one hundred congressional committees and subcommittees, and covers all fifty states and hundreds of nongovernmental groups and publications. The atlas is actually four directories in one: the consumer information section, which provides contents for the answers to the most often asked energy-related questions from energy conservation funding to nuclear power; the alphabetical section, which lists all personnel with telephone numbers and is cross-indexed to the organization section; the organization section, which has complete office listings, titles, addresses, and telephone numbers; and the subject index section, which lists more than two hundred fifty energy-related categories, and is cross-indexed to the organization section. The organization section is divided into federal government departments and administrative agencies, congressional offices, state government organizations, alphabetically by state; and national energy organizations, alphabetically. Each organization entry includes address, telephone(s), purpose, and contact persons. Also included is an alphabetical list of energy publications, giving name, address, and subscription information.

309   E3.2   **Directory of Energy Data Collection Forms.** 2d ed. Energy
D26-3   Information Administration. 1981. 58p. Occasionally on
1980-   microfiche. Annual.

Forms meeting the following criteria are included in the directory: (1) they are either managed by the EIA, or used as input to EIA publications, and (2) they are now used as active, or were listed as active, in *EIA Data Collection Forms* (the title of this publication's first edition). Four major sections make up this directory. Section 1 gives descriptions of data collection forms and is the primary section. This section is arranged sequentially by form number, and each entry contains a description, or abstract, of the form; the energy source(s) and function(s) covered by the form; the identification of group(s) responding to the form; reporting requirements; the legislative mandate under which the data in these forms were collected, and the frequency at which they were collected; the names and numbers of previous publications resulting from the forms; and of parent reporting systems. Section 2 groups the data collection forms by energy source and function; section 3 lists the data collection forms linked to systems and publications; and section 4 contains the data collection form changes.

310   E3.33   **Energy Information Directory.** 3d and 4th quarters. Energy
1980-   Information Administration. National Energy Information
Center. 1981. 61p. Quarterly.

The National Energy Information Center (NEIC), as part of its mission, provides energy information and referral assistance to federal, state, and local governments, the academic community, business and industrial organizations, and the general public.

This directory lists many of the government offices involved in energy matters. The offices are classified according to their specialties. For the purposes of this publication, each office has been given an alphanumeric identification symbol (A-01, A-02, etc.). The subject index uses these symbols instead of page numbers in referring the reader to relevant entries. Most entries provide an abbreviated office address. For the complete address, consult the building location index. Following the name and title is the DOE routing symbol, which refers to the organization and is a part of the mailing address. Each entry also includes an executive officer, telephone number(s), and a statement of purpose and services. Organization charts for the Department of Energy and the Energy Information Administration are included, as well as appendixes that list state energy offices, DOE research and development field facilities, and Energy Extension Service (EES) state contacts. The directory is published quarterly, and was formerly entitled *Energy Information Referral Directory*.

311 EP1.2   **Directory of Air Quality Monitoring Sites Active in 1977.**
     Ai7-5   Environmental Protection Agency. 1978. 770p. Annual.
     1972-

Included in this volume is a listing of all monitoring sites active in 1977 that have submitted a SAROAD (Storage and Retrieval of Aerometric Data) site information form. In addition to the site listings, this document reflects useful information on pollutant(s) sampled. Data are submitted to the EPA from local, state, and federal air pollution-control agencies, as well as a limited number of private institutions. Arranged alphabetically by state, the organization of this directory is based on the SAROAD site code; therefore to find a specific sampling location, it is necessary to thoroughly understand the site code. The site codes are described in the introduction to the volume. Some of the information given includes address, city or area covered, county, station type, agency type, latitude, longitude, city population, and area population. For historical information relating to sites active before 1977, but not during 1977, consult prior publications, 1972-76.

312 EP1.2   **Directory of Environmental Groups. Region 7.** Environmental
     D62   Protection Agency. 1980. 65p. Microfiche.

Contained in this directory is a list of the organizations, both public and private, that are involved in environmental concerns of EPA Region 7. The states involved are Iowa, Kansas, Missouri, and Nebraska. Listed are the federal agencies concerned with environmental matters; regional offices of EPA for regions 1-10; Region 7 Environmental Protection Agency offices, divisions, and contact persons; and state environmental offices and citizens' groups. Each entry contains the name of the organization, mailing address, and telephone number.

313 EP1.2   **Directory of State Agencies Engaged in Environmental**
     En8-8   **Monitoring.** Environmental Protection Agency. 1973. 82p.

This directory is a catalog of the professional personnel at the state level who are responsible for environmental control and monitoring programs in the areas of air pollution, water quality, water supply, solid waste management, pesticides, radiation, and noise. The listings, which are arranged by state, include the name of the state health officer and other program heads with addresses, telephone numbers, and office hours. Where telephone numbers are not given, initial contact should be made through the state health officer. Complete addresses are given only for state health officers; the remaining individuals are identified by title, with addresses given only when different than the officer's address. Also included is a list of EPA Surveillance and Analysis Division directors by EPA regions, giving names, addresses, and telephone numbers.

314   EP1.2
L11-5   **Federal Laboratories and Research Facilities with Noise Capabilities. A Directory.** Environmental Protection Agency. 1979. 90p.

This document inventories various federal laboratories and research facilities with noise research or noise testing capabilities. It is intended to furnish government officials and others with basic information, providing a starting point for making further inquiries. It is not a comprehensive compendium affording in-depth perspectives of activity. The directory contains a basic inventory, organized alphabetically by federal department, which identifies the laboratories considered in the directory. It gives the address and the chief noise concern of each laboratory, as well as the name and telephone number of whom to contact at the laboratory; an organizational index that identifies the area and level of noise efforts at each of the laboratories inventoried; an index of noise activities, which identifies noise activity areas, categories of activities, and the facilities performing them; a noise instrumentation and special facility index, which identifies equipment and research facilities associated with each laboratory; and a geographical index, which contains maps of the standard federal regions and locates on each map the federal laboratory with reported noise capabilities.

315   EP1.2
W29-35
1974-   **Water Quality Management Directory.** 4th ed. Environmental Protection Agency. 1980. 163p. Irregular.

State and local designated water quality management agencies are listed in this directory. Its purpose is to facilitate the exchange of information about water quality management. As in past editions, the directory includes information necessary to contact those agencies and people directly involved in water quality management programs, as well as an appendix of all 208 grant awards. Agency addresses are listed under the state in which they are located, and states are listed alphabetically within the ten federal regions. A map is displayed with each state, indicating areas undergoing areawide water quality management planning. The agency listing presents the state water quality management agency first, followed by the state's agencies. Local agencies are indented five spaces and are generally listed in order of designation. To the right of the agency address are counties included in the planning area. Information on grant awards is presented separately in the appendixes. Also included are tables of contents alphabetized by state and by agency.

316   EP1.77
1974-   **Environmental Program Administrators.** Environmental Protection Agency. 1979. 63p. Annual.

In this publication we find a listing of state officials and their respective areas of responsibility that has been assembled to facilitate and improve interstate cooperation and intergovernmental communications. The compilation is subdivided into five sections. The first three sections are arranged according to the uniform federal region configuration (i.e., regions 1 through 10 with the states located within each region listed alphabetically). Section 4 is a compilation of interstate agencies having environmental

7—*Government Agencies, Subject* / 95

program responsibilities, while section 5 lists EPA regional offices. Section 1 covers environmental water quality, water supply, and industrial waste; section 2 covers air quality, solid waste, noise, and pesticides; and section 3 covers radiation and state analytical laboratories. Information given includes addresses and telephone numbers. Also included is an alphabetical index, grouped by state.

317 EP1.79-2 **Directory of Federal Coordinating Groups for Toxic Substances.** 2d ed. Environmental Protection Agency. 1980. 105p. Toxic Integration Information series EPA-560/13-80-008. Irregular.
no. 80-008
1979-

Compiled to provide a ready reference about federal toxic chemical coordinating groups, this directory should also facilitate further communication between agencies and the groups themselves. Included are committees, task forces, and other groups that perform coordinating functions in conjunction with federal toxics control and testing agencies. There are federal, state, nonprofit, and private sector members in these groups. The committees and groups are arranged in alphabetical order by name. Information given includes acronym or initials, if applicable; authorization; mission and purpose; and officers and members, with address and telephone number(s). Also included is an alphabetical index of personnel. The first edition was entitled *Directory of Federal Coordinative Groups for Toxic Substances*.

318 EP1.95 **Environmental Hotline '81.** Environmental Protection Agency, Region 5. 1981. 97p. Annual.
1980-

This publication is a directory of more than six hundred private groups and public agencies that are dedicated to protecting the nation's environment through ongoing, active programs. The listings cover the six states of Region 5: Illinois, Indiana, Michigan, Minnesota, Ohio, and Wisconsin. The directory is divided into two basic categories: (1) federal and regional government agencies, and (2) citizens' groups that are concerned about the environment. The directory contains state-by-state listings of those categories plus colleges and universities, and environmental libraries. Each listing includes address, telephone number, and a contact person for the libraries and citizens' groups. Also included are twenty-four-hour emergency numbers—federal and state.

319 FE1.2 **Directory of Federal Agencies Engaged in Energy Related Activities.** Federal Energy Administration. 1975. 80p.
F31

Identified in this publication are key personnel of federal and state governments who are engaged in energy-related matters. Arranged first by the Federal Energy Administration (FEA), and the Executive Office of the President, the sections then are alphabetical by executive departments, followed by independent agencies, boards, commmissions, committees, and state energy offices. FEA regional offices are also listed. The appropriate agency or office within each department is identified along with the concerned contact person, mailing address, and telephone number.

320 FE1.2 **Directory of State Government Energy-related Agencies.** Federal Energy Administration. 1975. 237p.
St2

This publication represents the comprehensive effort of the National Energy Information Center (NEIC) to serve as a national central clearinghouse for energy information. It provides information on state government energy-related organizations, their responsibilities, key personnel, and programs. The main section is an alphabetical arrangement by state of the state government energy agencies. The information provided in this section includes name, address, and telephone number; responsibilities; membership, if applicable; budget and staff size, if available; key personnel, with titles; major programs; and publications and other products. The other eight sections contain an alphabetical state-by-state listing of state agency contacts for energy conservation, energy facilities siting, comprehensive land-use planning, coastal zone management, review of environmental impact assessments, and public utility regulation. Also listed are energy-related committees of the state legislatures and state legislative service agencies, including sources for obtaining copies of bills. Each entry in these sections includes name of agency, address, telephone number, and contact person.

321   FEM1.2   **Directory of Governors and State Officials Responsible for**
      D62   **Disaster Operations and Emergency Planning.** Federal Emer-
      1979-   gency Management Agency. 1981. 29p. Microfiche. Irregular.

This directory, which will be issued periodically, is a state-by-state listing of the governors and officials for disaster operations. Part 1 lists the governors alphabetically by state, and part 2 lists the disaster officials alphabetically by state. Part 1 contains the governors' names, official addresses, their regions within the United States, year term began, how many years, and telephone number. Part 2 indicates the state and region, the responsible official's name and title, name of the agency, address, and telephone number. The 1979 edition was issued by the Housing and Urban Development Department's Federal Disaster Assistance Administration as HH12.2:G74.

322   GS1.2   **Federal Information Centers.** General Services Administra-
      F31   tion. 1980. n.p. Annual.
      1976-

The Federal Information Centers supply answers to questions about the federal government, no matter how simple or complex. Every center offers government publications on consumer information, energy conservation, and a variety of other useful topics. Some have specialists who speak languages other than English. The centers are located in metropolitan areas across the country, and additional cities have toll-free telephone access to them. They are arranged alphabetically by state and place within states. Each entry includes place, telephone number, address, and toll-free information, if applicable.

323   HE1.2   **Directory of State and Local Resources for the Mentally**
      M52-16   **Retarded.** Health, Education, and Welfare Department. 1970.
                124p.

Contained in this directory is a checklist of state and local agencies, facilities, and other resources that render specific services to the mentally retarded. Since this directory is concerned with resources that are primarily in existence for mentally retarded persons, many resources that serve them as a part of their total program do not appear here. The directory is arranged alphabetically by state, containing information on the following topics: mental retardation state coordinating agencies; state agency-administered programs related to the mentally retarded in the fields of education, vocational rehabilitation, health, mental health, public welfare, and special programs (maternal and child health services, disabled children's services, and child welfare services); nongovernment state resources; clinical programs for the mentally retarded; residential facilities for the mentally retarded; and special facilities (university-affiliated, community, and other specialized rehabilitation facilities). Each entry lists the name of the agency, its address, and, if applicable, area served, ages accepted, admission policies, fees, and service restrictions.

324   HE1.502   **Directory: Federal, State and Local Government Consumer Offices.** Consumer Affairs Office. 1977. 53p. Annual.
St2
1973-

The purpose of this directory is to provide a basic source of information on government involvement in consumer protection for consumers, businessmen, and consumer organizations. The directory is divided into two sections, the first of which contains, in alphabetical order, those federal agencies of special interest to consumers. The second section is an alphabetical listing by state of all state, county, and municipal government consumer offices that have been reported to the Office of Consumer Affairs as operational. Branch offices follow the listing for the lead office. Each entry includes the address, telephone number (and toll-free number, if there is one), and name of the responsible official. Also found in section 1 is an alphabetical arrangement by state of Federal Information Centers. The title was formerly *Directory of State, County and City Government Offices.*

325   HE20.2015-2   **Directory of State, Territorial, and Regional Health Authorities. 1971-72.** Health Services and Mental Health Administration. 1972. 122p. Annual.
1971-72
1961-1971-72

Divided into eight sections, this directory contains a listing of (1) state health officers, showing the headquarters address and telephone number; (2) current organizational structure of each individual state health department and health authority responsible for each departmental unit; (3) designated state and territorial agencies for comprehensive health planning; (4) areawide comprehensive health planning agencies; (5) state agencies, other than health departments, administering disabled children's services programs; (6) state agencies, other than health planning departments, administering hospital and medical facilities construction programs; (7) state agencies, other than health departments, administering mental health programs; and (8) regional medical programs. Also included is an organizational chart and a list of regional offices of the Health Services and Mental Health Administration, with their addresses, telephone numbers, and directors. All sections are arranged alphabetically by state. Addresses, telephone numbers, and responsible individuals are given in all sections except section 2, where only responsible individuals are given with their degrees.

326   HE20.6102   **Health Systems Agencies, State Health Planning and Development Agencies, and Statewide Coordinating Councils. November 1, 1980.** Health Planning Bureau. 1980. 44p. Annual.
D62
1977-

Information on 203 Health Systems Agencies (HSAs), 57 State Health Planning and Development Agencies (SHPDAs), and 56 Statewide Health Coordinating Councils (SHCCs) is contained in this directory. Of the 203 HSAs, 180 are private, nonprofit agencies, 5 are units of local government, and 18 are public regional planning bodies. The HSAs are arranged alphabetically by state and numerically according to the health service area within each state. The SHPDAs and the SHCC chairpersons are listed in separate sections alphabetically by state. The HSA entries include name, address, telephone number, chief executive officer, funds authorized, type of agency (nonprofit, etc.), congressional districts covered, population, initial designation date, initial full designation date, and annual designation date. The SHPDA entries include name, address, telephone number, director, fund authorization, initial designation date, and full designation date. The SHCC entries include name, chairperson, and mailing address. Because the federal program is administered through the ten DHHS regional offices, the addresses of those offices and a list of states within each region are included.

327   HE20.6202   **Where to Write for Birth and Death Records: United States and Outlying Areas.** Rev. ed. National Center for Health Statistics. 1979. 8p. Irregular.
B53
1955-

Official certificates of every birth and death are permanently filed in the central vital statistics offices of the states, independent cities, or outlying areas. This pamphlet is an alphabetical arrangement by state of those vital statistics offices in each state or area. Each entry provides the following information: cost of full copy of birth or death certificate, cost of short form, name and address of the vital statistics office, and remarks as to how long records have been kept, cost of additional copies, and other resources.

328   HE20.6202   **Where to Write for Divorce Records: United States and Outlying Areas.** Rev. ed. National Center for Health Statistics. 1979. 5p. Irregular.
D64
1958-

This is an alphabetical arrangement by state of the state or local offices capable of supplying copies of divorce certificates. For more detailed information, see entry 327.

329   HE20.6202   **Where to Write for Marriage Records: United States and Outlying Areas.** Rev. ed. National Center for Health Statistics. 1979. 6p. Irregular.
M34
1958-

This directory is arranged alphabetically by state, listing fees for copies of marriage certificates, addresses of vital statistics offices, and remarks. For more detailed information, see entry 327.

330   HE20.7102   **Occupational Safety and Health Directory 38th Issue, 1980.** National Institute for Occupational Safety and Health. 1980. 105p. Annual.
Oc1-4

This directory lists the names, titles, addresses, and telephone numbers of key personnel of the National Institute for Occupational Safety and Health (NIOSH); the Labor Department's Mine Safety and Health Administration (MSHA), and Occupational Safety and Health Administration; the Occupational Safety and Health Review Commission; and governor-designated and other state agencies, as well as local agencies, responsible for worker safety and health. The directory is divided into five parts. Part 1 is an alphabetical arrangement by state of state-designated agencies, state units, and local units. Part 2 lists NIOSH headquarters, main laboratories, Appalachian Center, and regional offices. Part 3 lists OSHA headquarters staff and regional and area offices. Part 4 presents the Occupational Safety and Health Review Commission with regional offices; and part 5 lists the personnel of MSHA, and the districts and subdistricts of Coal Mine Health and Safety, and Metal and Nonmetal Mine Safety and Health.

7—Government Agencies, Subject / 99

331　HE20.8215　**Directory of Women's Drug Abuse Treatment Programs.**
　　　Ser. 44　　　National Clearinghouse for Drug Abuse Information. 1980.
　　　no. 2　　　　95p. Report series 44, no. 2. Irregular.
　　　1979-

The programs listed in this directory represent a wide variety of treatment designs. While some can be considered exclusively women's programs, others are co-sex programs with a special therapy group designed for women in the program. The directory is arranged alphabetically by state, including Puerto Rico and the Virgin Islands. The state agency responsible for drug abuse activities is given first and then the other programs of each state are listed in alphabetical order, giving address, telephone number, and services of the organization, plus a description of the programs.

332　HE23.102　**International Directory of Mental Retardation Resources.**
　　　D62　　　　2d ed., 1977-78. Edited by Rosemary F. Dybwad. President's
　　　1971-　　　Committee on Mental Retardation. 1978. 360p. Irregular.

Leaders in the field of mental retardation had increasingly expressed the need for information on what was being accomplished, and by whom, in various parts of the world. Remarkable progress, based on increased knowledge of the potential development of mentally retarded persons, has been witnessed in the growth of service programs in many countries. This directory is the result of an effort to have a systematically organized method of identifying and locating persons and agencies in the various countries throughout the world. The volume is divided into two parts, with an appendix. Part 1 lists the international organizations (the United Nations and UN specialized agencies, intergovernmental agencies, international nongovernmental organizations, and others), with address, date of origin, chief executive officer, purpose, and activities related to the mentally retarded. Part 2 contains the individual country reports, alphabetically by name. If available, each entry contains a brief description of the country (area, population, and so forth); government agencies with mental retardation responsibilities; voluntary organizations (citizen, professional, and private foundation) with primary concern in mental retardation; other national voluntary organizations (citizen and professional) that include mental retardation programs; research; publications; brief descriptive notes on program areas (case findings, diagnosis and assessment, consultation to parents, education, work training and employment, developmental disabilities, medical care, residential care, financial assistance, recreation, research, personnel training, planning, standards, monitoring, and accreditation); and information for visitors. The appendix contains suggestions on planning trips to other countries.

333　HE23.3002　**Directory. State Agencies on Aging and Regional Offices.**
　　　D62　　　　Aging Administration. 1978. n.p.

This leaflet is an alphabetical arrangement by state of agencies concerned with aging, listing their names, addresses, and telephone numbers. The regional offices of the Administration on Aging are listed by the ten regions, giving areas covered, addresses, and telephone numbers.

334　HH1.2　　　**Directory of Public Housing Agencies.** Housing and Urban
　　　P96-7　　　Development Department. 1980. 120p. Occasionally on micro-
　　　1977-　　　fiche; also on paper. Irregular.

Public housing agencies are listed in this directory by state and alphabetically by locality within state. Provided are names and addresses of each public housing agency engaged in low-income housing programs.

335   I19.4-2   **Worldwide Directory of National Earth-Science Agencies.** Compiled by Wenonah E. Bergquist, et al. Geological Survey. 1978. 77p. Geological Survey circular no. 771. Irregular.
no. 771
1975-
(no. 716)

This directory is an alphabetical arrangement by country of the governmental earth-science agencies around the world that have functions similar to those of one or more of the operating divisions of the U.S. Geological Survey. The name of each country is followed by the list of appropriate agencies, giving addresses and chief officer. The location of each country is shown on an index map, which is keyed to one of eight reference maps showing major regions of the world. Wherever feasible, names of agencies in countries whose languages are based primarily on the Latin alphabet are given in the language of the country. English translations have been added in brackets where they seem necessary for easy understanding. Names of agencies in countries whose language uses an alphabet other than Latin are given in English. Also given with each entry is a code letter that indicates the principal function(s) of each agency (geology, cartography, hydrology, minerals, and petroleum regulation). The directory also contains an alphabetical index by name of major international organizations whose work is similar to that of those in this directory; it includes addresses and principal officer.

336   I19.4-2   **Catalog of Selected Offices of the Office of Surface Mining, Bureau of Land Management, and Geological Survey Relating to Coal, 1981.** 1980. 41p. Geological Survey circular no. 840. Irregular.
no. 840

Contained in this publication is an alphabetical arrangement by state of the field offices of the federal Department of the Interior's Office of Surface Mining, Land Management Bureau, and Geological Survey that are concerned with coal. Regional, district and field offices, and state directors, where appropriate, are listed, indicating addresses and telephone numbers. Also found in the volume are statements of each of the federal agencies' functions and a listing of headquarters offices with principal officer, title, and telephone number. Also included are maps showing Office of Surface Mining and Geological Survey regions, and a map showing Land Management Bureau field offices.

337   I49.2   **Liaison Conservation Directory for Endangered and Threatened Species.** 4th ed. Fish and Wildlife Service. October 1980. 129p. Occasionally on microfiche.
En2-8

The purpose of this directory is to assist the implementation of the U.S. Fish and Wildlife Service's Endangered Species Program. It is provided as a personal handbook for biologists, administrators, and other conservation-minded persons to facilitate joint efforts to cooperate in achieving the program goal. More than two hundred fifty federal, state-territorial, and private conservation organizations are listed in this directory. With minor exceptions, each organization has designated a staff member to serve as its liaison with the Fish and Wildlife Service's Office of Endangered Species. The volume is arranged into six main sections. Section 1 contains, after a brief statement of purpose, the units of the Office of Endangered Species, Federal Wildlife Permit Office, and Division of Law Enforcement, along with the regional and area offices of the U.S. Fish and Wildlife Service. Entries include responsible persons, addresses, and telephone numbers. Section 2 lists the liaison representatives from the executive departments of the United States government, indicating titles of individuals, with addresses and telephone numbers. Section 3 names liaison representatives of United States government-independent agencies, listing quasi-government groups in alphabetical order. Included are names, titles, addresses, and telephone numbers. Section 4 is an alphabetical arrangement, by states and territories, of the official (governmental) and consultative liaisons within each state. Information given includes the organization's name, address, telephone number, specialty, and whether flora- or fauna-related. Section 5 is an alphabetical listing of private organizations' liaison representatives, indicating name, title, address, and telephone number. Section 6 is an alphabetical listing of endangered species and their recovery plan contacts, listing name, region, address, and telephone number. Also included is an alphabetical personal name index.

338 J1.39 **Criminal Justice Agencies: In Regions 1-10.** 10 vols. National
nos. 1-10 Criminal Justice Information and Statistics Service. 1975.
1971- Irregular.

These reports present an updated listing of the individual names and addresses of criminal justice agencies in the states comprising Law Enforcement Assistance Administration (LEAA) regions 1 through 10. They list 57,575 criminal justice agencies administered by state and local governments. Included are enforcement agencies, courts, prosecution and legal service agencies, defender agencies, correctional agencies and institutions, probations and parole agencies, and a miscellaneous category. Tables showing the number of these agencies at each level of government are included for individual states and for the United States as a whole. The agencies for each state are listed together in the same sequence as stated above, except that the correctional institutions are divided into categories of adult, juvenile, and other. Under each category, the agencies are listed by state level, county level (alphabetical by name of county), municipal level (alphabetical by name of city), town or township level (alphabetical by name of town or township), special district level, and independent school district level. Each entry includes name of agency, address, zip code, and county and chief administrative officer. Also given is the National Crime Information Center (NCIC) identification code, which explains state, county number, unit number of agency by type within each level of government and county, level of government, and type of agency.

339 L1.66 **A Directory of Public Employment Relations Boards and**
Em7 **Agencies. A Guide to the Administrative Machinery for the Conduct of Public Employee-Management Relations within the States.** Labor-Management Services Administration. 1971. 31p.

The purpose of this directory is to provide a guide to the administrative structure and functional responsibilities of agencies for the conduct of public sector labor relations within each state. It is not meant to be a statutory analysis, nor does it deal with the extent of activity or the impact of these agencies upon the climate of public employee/management relations within their respective jurisdictions. For each state included in this directory, legal and Government Employee Relations Report (GERR) citations for the various state laws are provided in footnotes. The publications cited generally include the rules and procedures, decision reporting systems, and annual reports for each administrative agency. A guide called Key to Administrative Agency Coverage deals with the coding system developed to indicate agency jurisdiction. The agencies are arranged alphabetically by the states that have statutes dealing with public employee management relations. For each state, a brief statement on the labor relations statutes is given, listing name, chief officer, address and telephone number, and function, followed by the agency.

340   L36.3   **Labor Offices in the United States and Canada.** Rev. ed., 1978. Employment Standards Administration. 1979. 146p. Bulletin no. 177. Irregular.
no. 177
1972-

Listed in this directory are federal, state, and provincial offices and agencies in the United States and Canada that are responsible for the performance of labor or labor-related functions. It does not include agencies below the state level. The term *labor office* has been used in its broadest sense. Included are primary labor agencies, such as departments or bureaus of labor, as well as other separate commissions, boards, or agencies with functional responsibility for such programs as employment services (including employment offices and unemployment compensation); regulation of private employment agencies; equal employment opportunity and civil rights; labor-management relations; mediation and arbitration; occupational safety and health; mine safety; workers' compensation; and vocational rehabilitation. The directory is divided into four main sections concerning federal labor offices in the United States, arranged alphabetically by state and territory; federal and provincial labor offices in Canada; associations of state governmental labor officials; and other associations. Each entry includes name of agency, address, telephone number, and names and titles of responsible officials. Parenthetical explanations have been added wherever the name of an agency does not describe its labor function.

341   L37.18   **Directory of Local Employment Security Offices. October 1979.** Employment and Training Administration. 1980. 118p. Irregular.
1977-

In this directory users will be helped to locate or contact any of the 3,469 offices in the Employment Security System. The publication can be used when a worker plans to move from one state to another, when a worker wants to file an interstate unemployment insurance claim, when an employer wants to locate a new branch in a different state and get help in staffing it, or when a JS, UI, or WIN staff member needs to know the location of local offices in a different state in order to help a worker or an employer. The employment security agency of each state implements a federal/state program that provides the following applicant and employer services to clients: unemployment insurance (UI) services, employer services (ES), and Job Service's (JS) employment service WIN program. The directory is arranged alphabetically by states and territories, and then alphabetically by local areas. Each entry lists the address, zip code, telephone number, and functions.

342   Pr39.8   **Who's Involved with Hunger: An Organization Guide.** *See* entry 084.
W89-3/H89-4

7—Government Agencies, Subject / 103

343 Pr39.15 **Consumer's Resource Handbook, 1979.** Special Assistant for
C76 Consumer Affairs Office. 1980. 76p.

Consumers will find this handbook helpful when trying to locate the right source of assistance, from both governmental and nongovernmental sources, for satisfactorily resolving problems with products and services. The handbook is also a directory of federal agencies, giving brief descriptions of the services and information they offer. Additionally, the handbook lists state and local government offices. Divided into three sections, the first outlines steps one can take to resolve consumer problems, and highlights the many offices and organizations (both governmental and private) that consumers can contact for assistance. Section 2 lists and describes federal offices. These descriptions are arranged alphabetically by subject areas ranging from advertising to weights and measures. Addresses and telephone numbers of all listed offices are given and toll-free numbers are printed in boldface type for each identification. Addresses and telephone numbers of federal regional offices are listed alphabetically by the agency concerned. Section 3 lists some eight hundred state and local offices where consumers can get help in resolving problems. An introduction to this section explains what these offices generally do and how consumers can contact them. This section also includes listings of state offices dealing with specific subject areas, including state offices on aging, state-chartered banks, energy, insurance, transportation, and utilities. Arranged alphabetically by state and then by subject area, each entry in this section includes name and title of contact person, name of agency, address, telephone number, and toll-free telephone number (if available). Also included is a list of Federal Information Centers with telephone numbers.

344 PrEx2.2 **National Directory of Clearinghouses.** Management and
C58 Budget Office. July 1980. v.p. OMB circular no. A-95.

Clearinghouses are listed in this circular arranged alphabetically by state according to the ten standard federal regions. The clearinghouses are established pursuant to part 1 of the procedures promulgated by the Office of Management and Budget circular no. A-95 (revised). Areawide clearinghouses in metropolitan areas are established pursuant to the requirements of Section 204 of the Demonstration Cities and Metropolitan Development Act of 1966. State and other areawide clearinghouses are designated by governors of the states pursuant to the rules and regulations developed by the Office of Management and Budget under authority of Title IV of the Intergovernmental Cooperation Act of 1968. Within each region, the states are listed alphabetically, indicating the state clearinghouse name, address, and telephone number; then the areawide clearinghouses are listed with addresses, telephone numbers, and names of places of jurisdiction. Metropolitan areawide clearinghouses are listed first, then, others. Also listed in the directory as appendix A, are members of the Federal Regional Council A-95 Coordinators. Indicated are names, regions, addresses, and telephone numbers.

345 PrEx2.10 **Federal Statistical Directory.** 25th ed. Management and
1935- Budget Office. 1976. 248p. Irregular.

Designed primarily to facilitate communication among the various federal offices working on statistical programs, this directory lists, by organizational units within each agency, the names, office addresses, and telephone numbers of key persons engaged in statistical programs and related activities of agencies of the executive branch of the federal government. This includes such activities as planning and operation of general-purpose data collection programs; planning and evaluation of statistical systems, including data processing and progress reporting; publication and dissemination of general-purpose statistical information; development and application of statistical methods; analysis and research that make extensive use of statistical data and methodology; and responsibility for clearance of report forms under the Federal Reports Act of 1942, as amended. Other information included for each individual are the functional title, room number, and building. The directory also includes a list of buildings with locations in the Washington, D.C., area and a list of zip codes for government offices. There is an alphabetical name index that gives telephone number, and agency abbreviation. Editions of this directory after 1976 are published by the Commerce Department.

346 TD1.2 **Transportation Energy Activities of the United States Depart-**
     En2-6   **ment of Transportation. A Technical Assistance Directory of Programs, Projects and Contacts.** Transportation Department. 1981. 93p. Microfiche.

Provided in this report is a summary of current DOT-sponsored energy-related research technical assistance, planning activities, and information sources. Most of the programs described here are efforts of the DOT. A selected number of innovative state, regional, and local programs have also been included. The directory is arranged into four chapters. Chapter 1 is concerned with sources of direct assistance from DOT. It lists contacts, addresses, and telephone numbers for regional representatives, ride-sharing agencies by state, and other agencies of DOT. Chapter 2 lists national and state hot lines and information centers; and chapter 3 is a subject arrangement of DOT reports and documents in the area of energy and transportation. Chapter 4 lists the research and demonstration projects that are current and significant and/or recently completed activities. It is not a comprehensive account of all research. The activities are listed by sponsoring agency and include title or subject area, time frame, funding amount, contractor/ grantee, and DOT project.

347 TD1.2 **Metropolitan Planning Organizations and State Transporta-**
     M56-3   **tion Agencies – Directory.** Transportation Department. 1980. 143p.

This directory is intended to provide information on state and local agencies involved in the intermodal transportation planning process. Information was submitted by state and local sources and Department of Transportation organizations, especially the Intermodal Planning Groups (IPGs) in the ten federal regions. All of the listings of metropolitan and state organizations and officials are arranged alphabetically by state within each of the ten standard federal regions. The directory includes a map of standard regional boundaries and a state index to sections 1 and 2. Section 1 lists the metropolitan planning organizations (MPOs), which are the forums in each urbanized area for cooperative transportation decision making by principal elected officials of general-purpose local government. The officials listed include the administrator of the designated agency, the policy committee chairperson, and the name of the designated metropolitan area A-95 agency for each urbanized area. Addresses and telephone numbers are included. Section 2 lists the state transportation officials: the chief executive of each state transportation agency and key planning officer. Addresses and telephone numbers are included.

348 TD4.8-5
no. 150/
5000-3
Address List for Regional Airports Divisions and Airports District/Field Offices. December 22, 1981. Federal Aviation Administration. 1982. 18p. Advisory circular (AC) no. 150/5000-3. Irregular.

Provided here is a document that can be used by the public, contractors, and sponsors to locate addresses and telephone numbers of the regional airports divisions and airports district/field offices that have jurisdiction over specific geographical areas. Included in this volume are both commercial and Federal Telecommunications System (FTS) telephone numbers. Arranged by region, the information includes regional maps, states and areas covered, addresses of regional offices, and telephone numbers. Also included is an FAA regional boundary map.

349 TD4.8-5
no. 150/
5200-24
Address List of State Offices of Emergency Medical Services. October 11, 1977. Federal Aviation Administration. 1977. 6p. Advisory circular (AC) no. 150/5200-24. Irregular.

This advisory circular transmits the address list of all state agency-delegated coordinators of emergency medical services, including the District of Columbia, Virgin Islands, Puerto Rico, and Guam. It is arranged alphabetically by state and territory. Each entry includes the title of the chief officer, name of agency, address, and telephone number.

350 TD5.44
National Contingency Plan (National Oil and Hazardous Substances Pollution Contingency Plan) Emergency Response Contacts Listing Directory. Coast Guard. May 1981. 379p. Microfiche.

Telephone numbers and important national emergency response centers for reporting oil and hazardous substances spills, and the like, are listed in this directory. The directory is arranged alphabetically by name of the federal and/or state agencies. Each entry includes name of agency, agency type (state, federal, etc.), states covered, name of primary contact (with work hours and work telephone number(s), home telephone number(s), and answering service hours and telephone number, if applicable). A first alternate contact is listed with telephone number(s) and answering service, and a mailing address of the organization. Occasionally second alternate contacts are listed. Also indicated is the date the information provided was updated.

351 TD5.44:4
National Contingency Plan (National Oil and Hazardous Substances Pollution Contingency Plan) Emergency Response Contacts, Federal Region IV. Coast Guard. 1981. 67p. Microfiche.

This is an alphabetical arrangement by states of Region 4, and responsible federal agencies that have emergency response numbers covering this area of concern. The same type of information is given here as is given in the national listing (see entry 350).

352 VA1.19
no. 20-70-2
1972-
Public Records Directory. Rev. ed. Veterans Administration. December 20, 1979. 16p. VA pamphlet 20-70-2. 1980. Irregular.

This directory is published for the information of all elements of the Veterans Administration. It is designed to provide a listing of the offices charged with the custody of

106 / 7—Government Agencies, Subject

public records of births, deaths, marriages, and divorces. Also included after the state listings are American Samoa, Canada, Canal Zone, Guam, Puerto Rico, Republic of Philippines, and Virgin Islands. Unless otherwise noted, certified copies of such public records will be furnished without charge if the document is to be used in determining eligibility for a VA benefit. The directory is arranged alphabetically by state, and the agency listings include name and address, with pertinent comments where necessary.

353   Y3.El2-3:14   **Election Directory '80.** Federal Election Commission. 1980.
         1978-   153p. Occasionally on microfiche. Annual.

The purpose of this directory is to identify the appropriate state agency or official who is responsible for performing a specific election function. The duties listed for each agency include those mandated by statute, required by regulation, or initiated by officers in charge. While the directory includes some elaboration of state activity, a complete description of any particular function should be obtained from the appropriate state official. The directory is composed of two parts. Part 1 gives a narrative description of the composition, functions, and duties of each state agency responsible for voter registration, the administration of elections, campaign finance, and/or campaign disclosure regulation. Part 2 provides the name, address, telephone number, and title of each official at the federal and state levels of government with election-related duties or responsibilities. It also includes chairmen of election committees in the state legislatures, state legislative reference services, and officers of associations of election officials. Part 1 is arranged alphabetically by state and part 2 lists the federal agencies first and then the states alphabetically, including the District of Columbia, Guam, Puerto Rico, and the Virgin Islands. This publication has been published annually, but due to budgetary cutbacks, no 1981 edition was published. However, editions from 1982 on will be published in a simplified version containing only the information found in part 2.

354   Y3.Se4:24   **List of Local Boards of the Selective Service Systems. January**
         1971-   **1975.** Selective Service System. 1975. 65p. Irregular.

Contained in this volume is an alphabetical arrangement by state of local selective service boards. Included are the administrative site number, local board number, county or area under which it has jurisdiction, mailing address, telephone number, and state code number. Also included is the address and telephone number of the state's headquarters.

355   Y3.W29:2   **Water Resources Coordination Directory. October 1980.**
         C78   Water Resources Council. 1981. v.p. Irregular.
         1971-

This coordination directory is issued by the Water Resources Council for the use of agencies represented on the council and all other federal, state, local, and private interests concerned with the investigation and management of water and related land resources. It provides a description of agency areas of interest and responsibility, and should facilitate communication with various governmental entities and representatives having interest in water and related land resources. Sections 1 through 4 list the names, agencies, addresses, and telephone numbers of the Water Resources Council, River Basin commissions, Federal Interstate River Basin Compact commissions, and inter-agency committees. Section 5 lists the state agencies alphabetically by state and subject area, giving agency name, title of contact person, address, and telephone number(s).

Sections 6 through 10 list the other federal agencies that are involved in this area, plus their state components. Each federal agency listing contains at the beginning a description of its involvement in water related activities.

| 356 | Y4.Ag4-2
Ag4-9
1978- | **A Directory of State and Area Agencies on Aging.** Rev. ed. House Select Committee on Aging, July 1981. 134p. 97th Congress, 1st Session. Committee Print. Irregular. |

This document provides a source of contacts in each state or community for assistance in problems of the aged as well as linkage with programs designed to serve them. An earlier edition (1978) was called *The Emerging Aging Network*. The network now includes 56 state units on aging and 665 area agencies on aging. The directory presents an alphabetical arrangement by state, listing the name, address, and telephone number for the state office on aging and the name of its director. Also contained is a map of the state from which one can determine the planning and service area (PSA) covering the community or county. An area agency on aging has been designated for all PSAs, and the directory lists the name, address, and telephone number of each area agency, along with the name of its director. Included is a description of the area agency's structure (government agency, council of governments, private nonprofit group, etc.). Each state's listing also tells which of the ten federal regions the state belongs to. In a separate listing after the states, addresses for each of the federal regions is provided.

8
Individuals

This section is primarily concerned with lists of persons whose careers make them important sources of information to the public. Basically the scope is national, but it may be state or local. Some of these items may overlap with items in other categories.

357   A1.76 no. 305 1965-66- **1980-81 Directory of Professional Workers in State Agricultural Experiment Stations and Other Cooperating State Institutions.** Rev. ed. Agriculture Department. February 1981. 236p. Agricultural handbook no. 305. Annual.

This directory, prepared by the Cooperative State Research Service, lists those professionals at state agricultural experiment stations alphabetically by state and college, with subdivisions under each college or station by agriculture subject matter. The U.S. Department of Agriculture and its involved agencies are listed prior to the state listings, giving the professionals, subject area, agency, and telephone number. The college listings contain addresses; names of schools or divisions; general administration at the university, with telephone numbers; and the professionals in each subject area with position and/or assignment. Included is an alphabetical name index and a key to abbreviations.

358   A1.89-3 Ag8 **Directory of the Agricultural Research Service.** *See* entry 241.

359   A13.69-2 L47 **Regional Directory—Leafy Spurge Control . . . Rocky Mountain Forest and Range Experiment Station.** Forest Service. 1980. 52p. Occasionally on microfiche.

Contained in this directory is a list of the individuals in the seven Rocky Mountain states, and some in other states and foreign countries, who are involved in the areas of pest research and management, specifically with leafy spurge, a tenacious and poisonous weed infesting nearly 2½ million acres of rangeland in North America. Although about 90 percent of the leafy spurge problem is concentrated in seven states and four provinces in Canada (North Dakota, Montana, Nebraska, South Dakota, Minnesota, Idaho, Wyoming, Manitoba, Saskatshewan, Alberta, and British Columbia); it is found in the United States in 456 counties in 20 states, and in all the provinces of Canada. The directory has two parts: part 1 is an alphabetical listing by name, and part 2 is a listing by state and foreign country. Names, addresses, affiliations, if applicable, and telephone numbers are given.

360   A106.2   **Home Economics Communicators.** Science and Education
       H75   Administration. 1981. 25p. Microfiche.

Located here is an alphabetical arrangement by state of those individuals involved in the field of home economics (HE) who are communication specialists of some sort. They are listed by HE editor and other state, area, and county extension staff members who have major HE information assignments. Information given includes name, percent of time devoted to HE information, information specialty (i.e., radio, television, news, publications, all media), and address and telephone number.

361   A106.2   **Directory of State Extension Horticultural Specialists.** Science
       H78   and Education Administration. 1980. 50p. Microfiche.

Presented in this publication is an alphabetical arrangement by state of the horticultural specialists in that state. Within each state, the individuals are arranged alphabetically by name with the project or group leader and/or department chairman or head at the top of the list. Information provided for each person includes name, title, and mailing address, telephone number, percent of time devoted to extension work, and horticultural specialty (whether fruits, nursery, potatoes, general, soils, etc.).

362   A106.14-2   **Soil, Water, Air Sciences Directory.** 1st ed. Science and Edu-
       1979-   cation Administration. 1979. 54p. Annual.

This publication provides a listing of professional research personnel of the Soil, Water, Air Sciences Program by state office, giving telephone numbers. It includes administrators of the Science and Education Administration, its program, and regional offices with an alphabetical index by name. Information given includes addresses, telephone numbers, and areas of specialty.

363   C1.2   **Directory of Key Contacts and Services. Who's Where in Com-**
       D62   **merce.** *See* entry 246.

364   C1.2   **Membership Directory. President's Export Council, Regional**
       D62-2   **Export Councils, District Export Councils.** Commerce
                   Department. 1975. 66p.

The Department of Commerce has the primary responsibility for carrying out our national export expansion programs. To achieve success in these programs, they enlist the aid and support of the business community. To this end, the department has, since the early 1960s, supported an export council organization that has served as a vital link in the joint government/industry export expansion endeavor. This list then contains the names, titles, companies, and addresses of the individuals who are members of these export councils. The directory is arranged alphabetically by name under the President's Council, region, and districts within each region. The regions are: Eastern, Mid-Atlantic, Southeastern, North Central, Central, and Western. The officers of the councils are listed first. (See also entry 369.)

365   C13.46   **A Survey of the National Metric Speakers Bureau.** National
       no. 960   Bureau of Standards. 1977. 50p. Technical note no. 960.
                   Irregular.

110 / 8 — Individuals

The National Metric Speakers Bureau was established by the Metric Information Office of the National Bureau of Standards (NBS) in January 1976 in response to the rapidly growing interest in the metric system and metrication. The number of speakers at the end of 1976 was 273, with at least one in every state. A survey of all of the speakers was conducted during November and December 1976. The purpose of the survey was to determine how the Speakers Bureau is working, and how it can be made to work better. This report summarizes the findings of the survey, gives a survey of the sources of information on the metric system and metrication, and presents a roster of speakers of the National Metric Speakers Bureau. It is this roster of speakers that helps to make this publication a directory. As previously stated, the first part of the survey analyzes the information received about metric speakers, followed by appendixes A through D. Appendix B lists alphabetically by state the names of the speakers who responded to the survey and gives the number of speakers located in each state. Appendix D lists alphabetically by state the roster of speakers of the National Metric Speakers Bureau and gives name, address, and telephone number(s).

366   C13.58   **Fire Research Specialists: A Directory.** By Nora H. Jason.
　　　　no. 77-1264   National Bureau of Standards. 1977. 133p. Interagency report no. 77-1264. Irregular.

This directory lists specialists from the United States and Canada who have made recent contributions to fire-related literature, to the teaching of fire science or related subjects, or who have participated in or supported fire research programs. This work is an update of the *Directory of Workers in the Fire Field*, by Boris W. Kavsdinoff, Stephen B. McLeod, and Richard G. Katz (NASA CR-121129; 1973). The directory is divided into three parts. The first part, the specialists index, is arranged alphabetically. The first line notes the name, followed by the area(s) of specialization represented by arabic numerals. These arabic numerals are used throughout the directory and are defined in a separate listing. The second and subsequent lines give each specialist's affiliation, mailing address, and telephone number. The second part, the subject specialty index, alphabetically lists the subject areas and the corresponding specialist names. Entries are limited to two areas of specialization per individual. The third part, the affiliations index, alphabetically lists the corporate sources, noting the specialists therein. If a specialist was not affiliated with an organization, the term "consultant" was used to group these individuals in the affiliations index.

367   C21.9-2   **Attorneys and Agents Registered to Practice before the U.S.**
　　　　1973/75-   **Patent and Trademark Office.** Patent and Trademark Office. 1980. 338p. Irregular.

An extract of the official Patent and Trademark Office registers as of March 31, 1980, this publication contains the names and addresses of a majority of the registered patent attorneys authorized to represent inventors. The publication is composed of two parts: Part 1 is an alphabetical list by surname of individual attorneys and agents in the United States or its territories and foreign countries, giving city and zip code. Part 2 is a geographical listing, arranged alphabetically by state and numerically by zip code, of patent attorneys and agents in the United States. Attorneys and agents with offices elsewhere than in the United States are listed alphabetically by country, following the U.S. listing. Entries in this part contain name, complete address, registration number, and telephone number. In the listings, a number sign (#) appears beside the name of each registrant who is registered as a patent agent, and an asterisk (*) appears in the listings beside the name of each registrant who is an officer or employee of the U.S. government.

368   C55.2   **Marine Advisory Service Directory.** National Oceanic and
       M34   Atmospheric Administration. 1980. 58p.

This directory lists those specialists in the marine sciences fields who are a part of the National Oceanic and Atmospheric Administration's (NOAA) National Sea Grant College Program. Marine personnel are listed in part 1 alphabetically by state, giving name, affiliation, address, telephone number, title, percent of time spent in advisory capacity, and specialty(ies). A key to the specialties is provided. Part 2 is an alphabetical listing by name, giving title, telephone number, and state. Three other sections list the specialists in NOAAs Sea Grant Office, with telephone numbers and specialties; Marine Advisory Service Program leaders ordered alphabetically by state, with addresses and telephone numbers; and Sea Grant directors arranged alphabetically by state, with addresses and telephone numbers.

369   C61.2   **District Export Councils Membership Directory.** International
       Ex7-3   Trade Administration. 1980. 154p.

Listed in this directory are the local action business groups known as District Export Councils (DECs), which serve as vital links in the joint government/industry export expansion endeavor. There are forty-seven DECs that work to stimulate greater awareness of the importance of exporting to our economic system. Working in cooperation with the Commerce Department's International Trade Administration District Offices, the councils encourage and support export expansion activities. The total membership of the DEC is approximately thirteen hundred business and trade experts. Membership includes representatives of firms involved in product exports, service organizations, and state and local governments. The list is arranged alphabetically by state and some local areas. Information given includes names, titles, affiliation, addresses, and telephone numbers.

370   CS1.2   **A List of Speakers on Issues Concerning Hispanic Women.**
       H62-2   Civil Service Commission. 1977. 38p.

Statistics show that Hispanic women are on the bottom rung of the employment and economic ladder. They are also very sparsely represented in the federal government. The Civil Service Commission in 1974 established a task force to assist agency EEO and personnel staffs to help this group of women achieve equality of opportunity, and to gain for the federal government a valuable human resource. This list of speakers, a recommendation of the task force, is but one of these efforts. The list is arranged alphabetically by the ten federal regions (Atlanta, Boston, Chicago, Dallas, Denver, New York, Philadelphia, St. Louis, San Francisco, and Seattle) and the Washington, D.C., area. Each entry contains name, title, telephone number, address, specialty, and other information such as fee, whether will travel, and whether bilingual. An appendix provides practical suggestions developed by the task force for use by federal agencies in dealing with the employment concerns of Hispanics.

371   D14.10   **DCPA National Directory of Fallout Shelter Analysts and**
       no. 74   **Their Associated Architectural and Engineering Firms.** *See* entry 110.

112 / 8—Individuals

372   D103.43   **Directory of Environmental Life Scientists.** 9 vols. Army
no. 1105-2-3   Corps of Engineers. 1974. Pamphlet EP (series), no. 1105-2-3.
v. 1-9   Irregular.

This publication provides a directory of environmental life scientists for engineers, biologists, and resource managers. Its purpose is to help link environmental scientists to Corps of Engineers personnel. The ten thousand scientists who responded to the survey have provided information about themselves and their work to assist user groups in contacting them. The directory is divided into nine volumes containing states of the nine Corps of Engineers regions. Each volume is divided into three sections. Section 1 contains five parts: an alphabetized listing of scientists and four cross-reference tables. Section 1 describes only the scientists within one region. The largest amount of data in each directory volume consists of the five tables in section 1. Table 1 in section 1 is the largest of the five and the most detailed. It contains the following sixteen data elements that describe the respondent: name, birthdate, graduate degree, subject specialty, telephone number, address, principal field, competence, experience as an employee and as a consultant; research activities; interest in working with whom; impact assessment experience; and geographic familiarity. Section 2 of the directory contains data about 150 scientists who are citizens of other nations and also contains five tables. Section 3 contains data about 175 organizations that wished to be included in this directory. This section lists alphabetically by name organizations, private firms, and scientific teams, giving address, date formed, and a brief statement of major concerns. Tables 2 through 5 in section 1 are index tables by competence in ecosystem management, keywords, impact assessment experience, and scientific field and geographic familiarity.

373   D114.2   **Secretaries of War and Secretaries of the Army. Portraits and**
Se2   **Biographical Sketches.** By William Gardner Bell. Center of
                     Military History. 1981. 176p.

This book should be useful in connection with presidential nomination of Army secretaries, as a handbook for the congressional armed services committees, and as a reference work throughout the Army. Students and scholars in such diverse fields as history, political science, American studies, and art and portraiture will find the book of interest. It should also be a unique research and reference tool for governmental, academic, and public libraries, and a work of interest to the general public. This volume provides brief biographical statements on the secretaries of war and the secretaries of the Army in chronological order and presents a portrait and brief statement about the artist. Other sections in the volume contain secretaries of war ad interim and acting secretaries of the Army; a chronological list of presidents of the United States, secretaries of war, and secretaries of the Army; and a general bibliography as well as a bibliography of secretaries and artists.

374   E1.19   **High Energy Physicists and Graduate Students. 1978 Census.**
DOE/ER   Energy Department. November 1978. 381p. DOE/ER series,
no. 0019   no. 0019. Irregular.
1975-

A listing of physicists and students associated with the U.S. High Energy Physics Program, this volume is intended to indicate the situation as of January 1, 1978. The first part is an alphabetical listing by name and includes only the name, rank, and institution of high energy physicists and graduate students. The second part of the volume is arranged alphabetically by institution. Within each institution, the faculty (or permanent staff) and the graduate students are presented in separate alphabetical lists. For each person, the entry indicates birthdate, the year and institution of highest degree, rank and institutional affiliation with starting dates, up to three items selected from a list of research specialties, and sources of federal support. For graduate students, an estimated date for degree is indicated. Where appropriate, a person is listed at more than one institution.

375	E1.26 no. 0057	**National Solar Heating and Cooling Commercial Demonstration Program. Key Personnel Directory.** *See* entry 112.
376	E1.26 no. 0167	**State Energy Officials Directory.** *See* entry 306.
377	E1.28 DOE/TIC 11302	**Directory of Key Foreign Personnel-Solar Commercialization.** *See* entry 113.
378	E1.28 TID-4591-R9	**Directory of Librarians and Information Specialists in DOE and Its Contractor Organizations.** 9th rev. Compiled by Patsy Hendricks, et al. Energy Department. 1979. 103p. Contractor Research and Development report no. TID-4591-R9. Irregular.

Found in this directory are Department of Energy librarians and information specialists who are located at DOE regional offices, operations offices, and other laboratories and research centers. Also included is an alphabetical name arrangement of DOE contractor organizations and their librarians and/or information specialists. For the contractor organizations, each entry contains the following information: name, address, and telephone number(s); name of information specialist, title, telephone extension; and a historical statement and brief description of the library and its services. There is an alphabetical index of names, indicating pages where located.

379	E1.33-2 no. 10879-01	**Consumer Energy Atlas.** *See* entry 308.
380	E3.39	**Energy Data Contacts Finder.** *See* entry 166.
381	ED1.8 D63-3	**Educators with Disabilities: A Resource Guide.** Diane Merchant, Project Director. Education Department. 1981. 153p.

The objectives of this publication are (1) to provide a listing or directory of the more than nine hundred educators who contributed to the project—people who represent a vast pool of experience with disabilities and education, and who can be mutual resources to each other and to educational institutions; (2) to share cost-efficient and effective coping strategies used by educators with various handicapping conditions; (3) to show that despite progress since the passage of Section 504 of the Rehabilitation Act of 1973, barriers to training and employment continue to exist; and (4) to recommend strategies for change in the realm of professional teacher education, employment, and public awareness. The publication is organized chronologically according to typical stages of career preparation and employment in pursuing an education career, and is

114 / 8—Individuals

arranged in five parts. Part 1 is a discussion of the process of deciding on an education career, completing a teacher training program, and obtaining certification. It highlights specific barriers that disabled persons have faced in the process and suggests possible solutions. Part 2 takes us into the classroom itself and describes by category of disability the successful coping strategies used by disabled educators. Part 3 reports on a conference in which disabled and nondisabled educators defined barriers faced by disabled persons in education and suggested ways to eliminate or reduce those barriers. Of major interest in part 4 is a directory of the more than nine hundred educators with disabilities who participated in the project and agreed to be listed as resources. This part is arranged alphabetically by name and gives each educator's address, telephone number, degrees, most recent position, nature of disability and age when disabled, and consultant resource areas. Also included in this part are alphabetical name indexes by region, specialization, and disability. Part 5 includes other resources, both material and organizational, relating to handicapped persons in education.

382   ED1.111-3   **Education Directory. State Education Agency Officials.** By
       1965/66-   Joanell Porter. National Center for Education Statistics. 1981. 81p. Annual.

Provided in this directory is a listing of the principal officials, managers, and supervisors employed by each state department of education. Also included are the chief personnel of the seven vocational-technical education departments (Colorado, Hawaii, Indiana, North Dakota, Oklahoma, Washington, Wisconsin), a listing of the principal officials of the Council of Chief State School Officials, and an alphabetical name index with state and page number references. Each entry includes address, indicating time zone, telephone number, and the names of the chief officials indicating title and telephone number.

383   EP1.2   **Directory of State Agencies Engaged in Environmental Moni-**
       En8-8   **toring.** *See* entry 313.

384   EP1.2   **Water Quality Management Directory.** *See* entry 315.
       W29-35

385   EP1.2   **Who's Who in Federal Noise Programs. A Directory of**
       W62-2   **Federal Professionals Involved in Noise Abatement and Noise Research.** Environmental Protection Agency. 1977. v.p.

The purpose of this directory is to facilitate communications among members of the federal noise community. The document includes information on persons with disciplines in noise control engineering, health effects science, hearing conservation, law, land use planning, and noise abatement policymaking. The directory contains three indexes to aid in locating federal personnel and organizations with activity or expertise in noise-related fields. Section 1 contains the introduction and a glossary of federal agency acronyms. Section 2 is an alphabetical index of names and telephone numbers of federal noise personnel, indicating agency affiliation and page number for the organizational index. Section 3 is the organizational index, which lists the known federal organizations involved in noise, their noise-related activities and the names, telephone numbers, and job titles of their personnel. This section is arranged alphabetically by the name of the agency. Section 4 is the geographical index, which lists known federal noise people included within the geographical boundaries of the standard federal regions, indicating agency affiliation. (Washington, D.C., headquarters personnel are not included.)

386 EP1.74 **Who's Who IV in the Interagency Energy/Environment R&D**
W62 **Program.** Environmental Protection Agency. 1978. 32p.
4th ed. 1975- Irregular.

This directory provides a means of access to information on specific projects currently underway within the Interagency Program. It also provides a link between policymakers, research managers, and the interested public and the individuals and organizations, both inside and outside the Interagency Program, who are involved in related work. The directory is divided into four parts. Parts 1 and 2 provide a means of access to information on specific projects currently underway within the Interagency Program. The projects are divided into health and environment effects and environmental control technologies. Under each category, the project areas are listed by descriptive title, with characterization, measurement and monitoring. After each project title, the names of the project contact, the EPA coordinator, and the agency coordinator are given. Part 3 lists other sources of Energy/Environment R&D information. Those listed here are directly related to concerns addressed by the Interagency Program. Part 4 is the Interagency Program directory and index. This part is arranged alphabetically by name, and gives mailing address, telephone number, affiliation, and the page where the individual's project is described.

387 EP1.77 **Environmental Program Administrators.** *See* entry 316.

388 EP1.79-2 **Directory of Federal Coordinating Groups for Toxic Sub-**
no. 80-008 **stances.** *See* entry 317.

389 HE5.2 **A Directory of Graduate Deans at United States Universities,**
D34 **1872-1970.** Education Office. 1970. 47p.

The purpose of this directory is to provide certain historical and biographical information about the administration of graduate work at U.S. institutions of higher education that award the Ph.D. or similar degree, with the exception of those conferring only the Doctor of Theology degree. This edition includes 240 institutions and 1,125 individuals. Institutions are listed alphabetically by state. Each entry shows the name, place, zip code, the year the first earned doctorate was conferred, the year in which a separate unit for the administration of the graduate program was established, and, from the latter year, a chronological list of all individuals in charge, together with their academic fields and years of tenure. For the current deans, certain standard biographical data are included, such as academic field, birthdate, and date and place of degree.

390 HE20.2015-2 **Directory of State, Territorial, and Regional Health Authori-**
1971-72 **ties.** *See* entry 325.

391 HE20.3018 **NIH Public Advisory Groups. Authority, Structure, Func-**
1969- **tions, Members. January 1981.** National Institutes of Health.
1981. 365p. Occasionally on microfiche. Semiannual.

The National Institutes of Health (NIH) conducts and supports biomedical research to improve the health of the nation. In carrying out its mission, the NIH relies upon public

116 / 8—Individuals

advisory committees for counsel and critique with respect to both ongoing and proposed activities. These committees of consultants are divided into two broad categories: scientific review groups and program advisory groups. The scientific review groups are composed exclusively of experienced investigators with highly developed expertise in specific scientific disciplines or medical specialty areas. The primary function of these committees is to determine the scientific merit of research grant applications and contract proposals. The program advisory groups comprise not only biomedical scientists, but also leaders in such fields as education, law, social sciences, public health or public affairs. These committees provide the broad perspective on social needs that is essential to balanced and effective programs. The table of contents lists the committees by organizational structure. The two indexes at the end of the publication list the committees and members alphabetically. Each entry contains the authority, structure, functions, frequency of meetings, and membership of the committees. For each individual, the year term expires, title, affiliation, and address are given. The chief executive officer is indicated.

392   HE20.3152   **Membership Roster Cancer Clinical Trials Groups and Projects. September 1979.** National Cancer Institute. 1979. v.p. Annual.
         M51
         1977-

This publication is designed as an aid not only to those investigators participating in the groups and projects, but to those seeking advice about cancer treatment. The membership roster is organized into the six sections that follow. "Administrative Information" gives addresses and telephone numbers of the chairmen, project officers, or principal investigators of groups or projects, administrators of the operations offices, and statisticians for each group or project. "Groups and Projects" is arranged alphabetically by group or project, then alphabetically by member institutions, with satellite or affiliate institutions indented under the member. Included are investigators' names and specialties. "Names" is arranged alphabetically by last name of investigators. Included are institution, group and project membership, and addresses and telephone numbers. "Geographic" is a section arranged alphabetically by state, city, institutions, and investigators. "WHO Melanoma Study Group" includes the collaborating centers for evaluation and methods of diagnosis and treatment of melanoma. Addresses and principal investigators are provided. "EORTC" contains information about the European Organization for Research on Cancer Treatment. Included are names and addresses of the council members, chairmen and secretaries of the cooperative groups, project groups, clubs, working parties, and task forces.

393   HE20.4022   **Public Advisory Committees Authority, Structure, Functions, Members.** Food and Drug Administration. 1976. 151p. Irregular.
         1971-

The FDA's major task is to prevent adulteration or misbranding of foods, drugs, medical devices, and cosmetics. It is likewise concerned with the safety of a host of chemical products, biological products, and electronic equipment that emits radiation. In pursuing these activities, the Food and Drug Administration constantly seeks advice from sources outside the federal government; thus arose the public advisory committees that are composed of highly qualified individuals from specialized fields and with wide geographic distribution. The committees are arranged in this publication in six sections. These sections are the Office of the Commissioner, Bureau of Biologics, Bureau of Drugs, Bureau of Medical Devices and Diagnostic Products, Bureau of Radiological

Health, and National Center for Toxicological Research. Each entry includes authority, structure, function, and meetings, chief executive officer(s), and members, with degrees, titles, mailing addresses, and year of ending of term. Also included in this volume are two indexes listing committees alphabetically and members alphabetically.

394	HE20.4122 1970-	**Directory of Personnel Responsible for Radiological Health Programs. October 1981.** Radiological Health Bureau. 1981. 38p. Semiannual.

This is a directory of professional personnel who administer the radiological health program activities in state and local governmental agencies. Included in the directory is a listing of each state health officer or the head of the agency responsible for the radiological health program. The name, address, and telephone number of the radiological health program is listed, followed by the alternate contact, who, in many instances, may be chief of a larger administrative unit of which the radiological health program is a subunit. The address of the program is also included if it differs from the official health department or agency. Generally, the titles of the personnel listed will indicate the administrative status of the radiological health program. The directory also includes a list of the key names, addresses, and telephone numbers of selected key personnel in the federal agencies concerned (FDA, NRC, EPA, NBS, NIOSH, and DOE). An alphabetical roster of names is at the end of the volume.

395	HE20.5102 N21h-4	**NHSC Health Care Practitioners, Winter 1978-79.** Community Health Services Bureau. 1979. 26p.

The National Health Service Corps (NHSC) assures accessibility to health care in underserved areas of the United States by arranging for health professionals to provide direct health services in health manpower shortage areas. This list of health professionals includes those individuals who are part of NHSC. The list is arranged by the ten regions of the United States, and alphabetically by name within each region. Given for each individual is the practicing specialty and location. The practicing fields include the following: physician, nurse practitioner, medical technologist, nurse, pharmacist, health administrator, field coordinator, speech pathologist, sanitarian, health educator, dietician, audiologist, dental hygienist, podiatrist, ophthalmologist, psychologist, physical therapist, dentist, clinical coordinator, osteopath, physician assistant, nurse midwife, and social worker.

396	HE20.8215 Ser. 20 no. 2	**Directory of State Drug Abuse Prevention Officials.** Rev. ed., December 1972. National Clearinghouse for Drug Abuse Information. December 1972. 15p. Report series 20, no. 2. Irregular.

This directory is an alphabetical arrangement by state of those officials active in the drug abuse prevention field. Each entry contains the governor of the state and the state agencies with chief officers. The agencies are classified under such headings as drug education, law enforcement, and state drug program. Given for each entry is the individual's name, title, mailing address, and telephone number(s).

397	HE20.8302 Oc1-2	**Directory of Occupational Program Consultants.** National Institute on Alcohol Abuse and Alcoholism. 1975. 9p.

118 / 8—Individuals

Occupational program consultants (OPCs) are employed by the states they serve; however they work in close cooperation with NIAAA and other federal, state, local, and private agencies concerned with the prevention and treatment of alcoholism throughout the nation. This directory is an alphabetical arrangement by state of the OPCs. Each entry contains the individual's name, affiliation, mailing address, and telephone number.

398	HH1.2 M66-4	**Registry of Minority Contractors and Housing Professionals.** *See* entry 131.
399	I29.2 H62-9 v. 20	**The Presidents, from the Inauguration of George Washington to the Inauguration of Jimmy Carter.** *See* entry 014.
400	I49.2 En2-8	**Liaison Conservation Directory for Endangered and Threatened Species.** *See* entry 337.
401	J1.2 At8-6	**Attorneys General of the United States, 1789-1979.** Justice Department. 1980. 147p.

This directory contains the attorneys general of the United States from the inception of the office (in 1789) through 1979. It is a chronological arrangement along with a portrait, giving the ordinal number as attorney general (whether 1st, 2d, and so on), years served, and a brief biographical sketch, which includes birthdate and place, education, professional career, and the president who appointed him. Along with these sketches is the name and brief biographical sketch of the artist who did the portrait. Also included is an alphabetical index of names.

402	Ju10.2 J89-4	**Judges of the United States.** Judicial Conference of the United States. 1980. 550p.

In this biographical directory, we find information about every person who ever sat as a judge of the United States, from a time before our constitution was adopted until publication of this directory. The directory affords us insight into the wide variety of their regional, educational, and ethnic backgrounds. The directory will be revised periodically. The directory includes a table of abbreviations; an index by appointing president, chronologically; an index by year of appointment; an alphabetical name index; and the biographies. The biographies are arranged alphabetically by name, giving details of birth, death, school(s), nominations for appointment, employment, honors, publications, read law, year admitted to practice, memberships, and family.

403	Ju10.15 1977-	**Directory of United States Probation Officers. November 1981.** Administrative Office of the United States Courts. 1981. 146p. Semiannual.

Probation personnel in the United States are arranged alphabetically by state in this publication. It is organized into five sections. The first lists the personnel of the Division of Probation of the Administrative Office of the United States Courts, giving title, regional information and telephone numbers. The second section gives personnel of the Federal Bureau of Prisons, their addresses, regions, telephone numbers, and titles. The U.S. Parole Commission is identified in section 3, listing personnel and regional addresses and telephone numbers. The fourth section is the state listings, in which the states are subdivided into districts. Information given includes names, titles, addresses, telephone numbers, chief clerks, and counties served. Section 5 is a list of correctional facilities, giving zip codes and telephone numbers, and indicating whether male or female. These include United States Penitentiaries; federal correctional institutions; federal detention centers; metropolitan correctional centers, federal prison camps, medical centers for federal prisoners, and staff training centers.

404   Ju10.17   **United States Court Directory. September 1, 1981.** Administrative Office of the United States Courts. 1981. 336p. Semiannual.
            1978-

Provided in this directory is a list of names and addresses of all justices, judges, and clerks of the United States courts. The courts are arranged in this volume in the following manner: Supreme Court of the United States; U.S. Court of Appeals and other federal courts (U.S. Court of Claims, U.S. Court of Customs and Patent Appeals, and U.S. Court of International Trade); and the Judicial Panel on Multidistrict Litigations, U.S. Court of Military Appeals, U.S. Tax Court, U.S. District Courts, and Bankruptcy Courts. Personnel of the Administrative Office of U.S. Courts and the Federal Judicial Center are listed in the last two sections. The section on district and bankruptcy courts is arranged alphabetically by state and subdivided by districts. Also included in the entries are telephone numbers, librarians if appropriate, and magistrates.

405   L2.83   **Directory of the Business Research Advisory Council to the Bureau of Labor Statistics, Fiscal 1980.** Labor Statistics Bureau. 1979. 33p. Annual.
            1980-

Listed here are members of the Business Research Advisory Council, who are qualified technicians and practitioners in the area of research undertaken by the Bureau of Labor Statistics. Members are broad representatives of American business. Other qualified persons who are not members of the council serve on its various committees. The arrangement is an alphabetical list of names, giving union affiliation, address, telephone number, company, and assignment of council. The committee section lists members alphabetically with union affiliation.

406   L2.109   **Directory of the Labor Research Advisory Council to the Bureau of Labor Statistics. 1978-1980.** Labor Statistics Bureau. 1978. 42p. Biennial.
            1978-

Listed in this publication are the members of the council, who are union research directors and staff members. They serve in an advisory capacity with respect to technical problems arising out of the statistical work of the bureau, provide consultation concerning bureau programs, and offer their perspectives on bureau programs in relation to labor union needs. An alphabetical listing of names gives union affiliation, address, telephone number, company, and assignment of council. A committee section lists members alphabetically with union affiliation.

407   LC1.2   **Librarians of Congress, 1802-1974.** Library of Congress. 1977. 273p.
            L61-16

To mark the 175th anniversary of the Library of Congress, the *Quarterly Journal of the Library of Congress* in April 1975 inaugurated a series of biographical articles on the

120 / 8 — Individuals

eleven men who headed the institution from 1802 to 1974. The articles collected in this volume form part of the historical record of the nation's library. This volume is arranged in chronological order and presents a detailed biography of each librarian. Also included are references, illustrations, and portraits, where available. At the end of the volume is an index to the work.

408 LC24.7 **National Directory of Latin Americanists.** 2d ed., 1971.
no. 12   Library of Congress. 1972. 684p. Hispanic Foundation biblio-
1966-   graphical series, no. 12. Irregular.

The basic objective of this volume is to provide a variety of researchers with accurate and up-to-date information on specialists in various Latin American disciplines. This edition contains 2,675 biographies. U.S. citizens and noncitizens who are permanently residents in the United States are included. Foreign nationals, even temporary residents, were normally excluded. Entries are arranged alphabetically by name. The standard entry contains the following data, in this order: name; birthplace; birthdate; major discipline; degrees; professional career; fellowships and honors; membership in professional and honorary organizations; research specialties and interests; publications (limited to three); language knowledge; linguistic studies; and home and office addresses. The biographies are indexed by subject and area, arranged alphabetically by name.

409 PM1.2   **College Placement Directors and Major Federal Agencies in**
C67   **New England.** Personnel Management Office. 1981. 29p.

This directory provides a list of personnel involved in career counseling for the six New England states. It is divided into four sections, the first of which is an alphabetical arrangement by the states in New England, listing alphabetically by the name of the college the directors of placement and career counseling. The entries are separated by whether they are four-year colleges or junior and community colleges. Each entry contains the name of the college, address, name of the placement director with title, college newspaper and radio station(s), and the director's telephone number. The second section contains a list of major federal agencies in New England, arranged alphabetically by state and city. It contains only the larger government installations. The entries provide zip codes, name of agency and official to contact, telephone number(s), and number of employees. Section 3 provides a list of federal career advisors (FCAs) and their assigned schools and community action agencies. Federal career advisors are employees of federal agencies who, because of their interest in recruiting, have assumed the role of representing the federal government on college campuses and in community organizations. Arranged alphabetically by state, each entry contains the name, address, and telephone number of the FCA, and lists the schools and agencies to which assigned. The fourth section gives the office, address, area served, and telephone number of the federal Office of Personnel Management's Federal Job Information and Testing centers.

410 PrEx1.10 **Membership Directory.** President's Committee on Employ-
M51-2   ment of the Handicapped. 1979. 132p. Irregular.
1969-

As indicated by the table of contents to this volume, this directory provides the names and addresses of the President's Committee on Employment of the Handicapped. It is arranged into five sections preceded by a copy of the Member's Creed. Section 1 lists the executive committee members, with address and affiliation. Officers of the Executive Committee are indicated. Section 2 lists the names and addresses of the associate members (heads of federal executive agencies). Section 3 lists the officers and members of the Advisory Council, giving address and affiliation. Section 4 lists, first by organization and then by individuals, the members of the President's Committee. Organizations and individuals are arranged alphabetically by name, giving address, representative for the organization, and affiliation for individuals. Section 5 is arranged alphabetically by state, and lists the chairmen, vice-chairman, and secretaries of governors' committees on employment of the handicapped. Addresses and affiliations are given.

411   PrEx3.10-7   **National Foreign Assessment Center Publications.** Central
       Cr-numbers   Intelligence Agency. Revised periodically. Irregular.
       1977-

These publications list the officials and government structure of the Eastern bloc countries (Albania, Bulgaria, the People's Republic of China, Cuba, Czechoslovakia, the German Democratic Republic, the Hungarian People's Republic, the Democratic People's Republic of Korea, the Lao People's Republic, Poland, the Socialist Republic of Romania, the USSR, the Socialist Republic of Vietnam, and Yugoslavia). Also found in this series are the various Communist party structures and, in some instances, military organizations, and ministries of defense, foreign affairs, and foreign trade. These publications are folded posters that usually include pictures of the officials, their names, titles, dates of official designation, and sometimes include date of birth. Some of the issues are cumulative (i.e., *Soviet Leadership since Stalin: CPSU Politburo and Secretariat, 1952-1980*). These publications were prepared primarily for the use of U.S. government officials; they supersede the Reference Aids series, PrEx3.11.

412   S1.7   **Foreign Service List.** State Department. August 1975. 90p.
       1929-1975   3 per year.

The Foreign Service list, compiled primarily for the Department of State, the Foreign Service, and other United States government agencies, provides information on assignments of foreign service and other U.S. personnel in the field of foreign affairs. The list includes chiefs of mission; foreign service officers; foreign service reserve officers; foreign service staff personnel; and consular agents. It also includes officers of the Agency for International Development, the Peace Corps and international operations of ACTION, the United States Information Agency, the Foreign Agricultural Service of the United States Department of Agriculture, the departments of Army, Navy, and Air Force, and United States missions to international organizations. Information on the opening and closing of posts, posts changed in rank and status, and other pertinent data also appears in each issue. Divided into four main sections, the volume lists personnel assigned to foreign service posts, U.S. missions to international organizations, and contains an index of persons and a geographic index. The personnel section is arranged alphabetically by country and lists individuals alphabetically by section, giving position, rank, and service dates. The same information is given for section 2. The indexes are arranged alphabetically by name and by area.

413   S1.7-2   **Foreign Service Classification List. November 1977.** State
       1977-   Department. 1977. 93p. Irregular.

122 / 8 — Individuals

This publication includes all changes in rank effective through November 14, 1977, for foreign service personnel of the Department of State. Career ambassadors and career ministers are listed alphabetically by date of appointment to class. Chiefs of mission or executives not shown elsewhere are listed alphabetically. All other foreign service employees are listed by class, by salary step within class, and in alphabetical order within each salary step. One column shows the date of entry into the Department of State, without regard to the service entered. In cases involving a break in service, the most recent date of entry was used.

414   S1.8   **Diplomatic List.** State Department. November 1981. 78p.
         1893-   Quarterly.

This publication contains the names of members of the diplomatic staffs of all missions and their spouses. Members of the diplomatic staff are the members of the staff of the mission having diplomatic rank. These persons, with the exception of those identified by asterisks, enjoy full immunity under provisions of the Vienna Convention on Diplomatic Relations. This volume includes only those missions in Washington, D.C., and are arranged alphabetically by country. It includes addresses and telephone numbers. Also included is a list of the chiefs of missions in their order of precedence, a chronological list of national holidays, and the pertinent provisions of the Vienna Convention of Diplomatic Relations concerning immunity.

415   S1.8-2   **Employees of Diplomatic Missions.** State Department.
         1970-   November 1981. 84p. Quarterly.

Contained in this publication are the names of alien members of the administrative and technical staffs as well as service staffs of the diplomatic missions who are not permanent residents of the United States and who enjoy immunity under provisions of the Vienna Convention on Diplomatic Relations. These personnel are not printed in the diplomatic list. The list is arranged alphabetically by country and gives names, titles and addresses. Members of the service staff are identified by asterisks. Also included in the volume is a description of the immunity enjoyed by these employees.

416   S1.40-2   **Key Officers of Foreign Service Posts. Guide for Business**
         Of2   **Representatives.** State Department. September 1981. 78p.
         1964-   3 per year.

This pocket-sized directory lists key officers at foreign service posts with whom American business representatives would most likely have contact. All embassies, missions, consulates general, and consulates are listed. At the head of each U.S. diplomatic mission are the chief of mission (with the title of Ambassador, Minister, or Charge d'Affaires) and the deputy chief of mission. These officers are responsible for all components of the U.S. mission within a country, including consular posts. At larger posts, commercial officers represent U.S. commercial interests within their country of assignment. At smaller posts, U.S. commercial interests are represented by economic/commercial officers, who also have economic responsibilities. Other officers listed are financial attachés, political officers, labor officers, consular officers, administrative officers, regional security officers, scientific attachés, agricultural officers, AID mission directors, and public affairs officers. The directory is arranged alphabetically by country and gives addresses, telephone number(s), names, and titles. Also included is a geographical index (arranged by city) and an alphabetical index (arranged by state) of U.S. Department of Commerce district offices, with addresses and telephone numbers.

8—Individuals / 123

417 S1.69 **Foreign Consular Offices in the United States, 1981.** State
       no. 128 Department. 1981. 121p. Department and Foreign Service
       1966-   series, no. 128. Annual.

Contained in this publication is a complete and official listing of the foreign consular offices in the United States, together with their jurisdictions and recognized personnel. It is offered as a convenience to organizations and persons who must deal with consular representatives of foreign governments. The listing is arranged alphabetically by country, and by state and city within the United States. Each entry provides state, city, name, rank, jurisdiction, and date of recognition.

418 S1.69 **United States Chiefs of Missions, 1778-1973. (Complete to**
       no. 147 **March 31, 1973.)** By Richardson Dougall and Mary Patricia
       1973-   Chapman. State Department. 1973. 229p. Department and
                Foreign Service series, no. 147. Irregular.

This volume was issued as a supplement to the series Foreign Relations of the United States and as part of the contribution of the Department of State to the nation's bicentennial observances. The tables that make up the main body of the volume include all United States ambassadors, ministers (including those commissioned as sole ministers by the Continental Congress), ministers resident, charges d'affairs, charges d'affairs pro tempore, and diplomatic agents. They also include those commissioners who were accredited to foreign governments and served as heads of American legations. Finally, they include those individuals nominated for these positions who were not finally appointed to them and individuals appointed to such positions who did not actually serve in them. The basic arrangement of the volume is alphabetical by country of assignment. An alphabetical list of chiefs of mission is in appendix E. The entries for each chief are divided into seven columns, containing the following information: name, residence, career status, title, appointment, presentation of credentials, and termination of mission. Chiefs of mission to international organizations and ambassadors-at-large are listed in appendix A and appendix B, respectively. Appendix C lists the two secretaries of/for foreign affairs appointed by the Continental Congress, and appendix D lists the officers of the Department of State appointed by the president from 1789 to 1973. Appendix E is an alphabetical list of the chiefs, and a list of abbreviations used for diplomatic titles appears in appendix F. A 1974 supplement to this volume was issued in 1975, and an up-to-date issue was printed in 1982.

419 S1.69   **The Biographic Register, 1974.** State Department. 1974. 382p.
       no. 148   Department and Foreign Service series, no. 148. Annual.
       1860-1974

The Biographic Register provides concise biographic information on personnel of the Department of State and other federal agencies in the field of foreign affairs. Biographies are included for ambassadors, ministers, chiefs of missions, foreign service officers, foreign service information officers, foreign service reserve officers, foreign service staff officers of classes 1 through 4, and Civil Service employees of grade GS-12 and above. In addition to the Department of State, biographies are included for personnel of the United States Arms Control and Disarmament Agency, ACTION, the Agency for International Development, the United States Information Agency, the Foreign Agricultural Service of the Department of Agriculture, and the Overseas Private Investment Corporation. The register is arranged alphabetically by name.

124 / 8—Individuals

420   S1.69   **The Secretaries of State: Portraits and Biographical Sketches.**
       no. 162   2d ed., rev. State Department. 1978. 125p. Department and
       1956-   Foreign Service series, no. 162. Irregular.

Covered in this volume are the two secretaries for foreign affairs and all the secretaries of state. All except the last two secretaries (Henry Kissinger and Cyrus Vance) are depicted by photographic reproductions of the Department of State collection of oil portraits. The secretaries are arranged in the publication chronologically, with the biographical sketch and a brief statement regarding the artist and the portrait. Two appendixes contain secretaries of state ad interim and a chronological list of presidents of the United States, secretaries of state, and secretaries of state ad interim.

421   SE1.2   **Investment Adviser Directory.** *See* entry 141.
       In8-17

422   SI1.42   **In the Cause of Flight. Technologists of Aeronautics and**
       no. 4   **Astronautics.** By Howard S. Walko. Smithsonian Institution.
       1977-   1981. 121p. Smithsonian Studies in Air and Space, no. 4. Irregular.

Many of the individuals who made important contributions to the technology of flight have attracted little historical attention, although their accomplishments stimulated progress in aerospace development. This book is written to bring together as much biographical information as is likely to prove useful for those interested in this topic. It is neither an encyclopedic treatment of vital contributions to flight technology, nor a comprehensive source of those responsible for them. Instead, it represents a starting point to be expanded upon as time and resources permit. The 129 biographical sketches are arranged in a topical format. Each topic is introduced with an overview of events of technical interest. Biographies of principal contributors are arranged in the chronological order of their main contribution. The topics include buoyant flight; aerodynamics; air-breathing propulsion; materials, structure, and design; vertical flight; and rocketry and space flight.

423   TD4.8-5   **FAA Inspection Authorization Directory.** Federal Aviation
       no. 65-13   Administration. 1979. 134p. Advisory circular (AC) no. 65-13. Irregular.

This advisory circular provides a directory of all FAA-certificated mechanics who held an inspection authorization as of December 31, 1978. The directory is arranged alphabetically by state and by name within each state. Also included are listings for the District of Columbia, Guam, Puerto Rico, Virgin Islands, and foreign countries. Each entry includes name and mailing address.

424   TD4.8-5   **Designated Engineering Representatives.** Federal Aviation
       no. 183-29   Administration. 1981. 15p. Advisory circular (AC) no. 183-29. Annual.

Listed in this circular are the designated engineering representatives who are available for consulting work. Designated engineering representatives, as direct representatives of the Federal Aviation Administration, are authorized to approve engineering or flight test information as complying with the Federal Aviation regulations within particular categories and subject to prescribed limitations. The circular is arranged alphabetically by name within each category (structures; systems and equipment; radio; powerplant; engines; propellers; flight analysts; flight test pilots; and special-administrative). Each entry provides name, mailing address, region of country, and limitations.

| 425 | TD4.8-5 no. 183-30 | **FAA Designated Mechanic Examiners Directory.** Federal Aviation Administration. 1978. 14p. Advisory circular (AC) no. 183-30. Irregular. |

Provided in this circular is a directory of all FAA designated mechanic examiners as of March 31, 1978. Designated mechanic examiners (DMEs) may accept applications and conduct oral and practical tests necessary for issuing mechanic certificates. The directory is arranged alphabetically by state and includes Puerto Rico and foreign countries. Entries are arranged alphabetically by name within each state and contain addresses and rating legends (airframe or powerplant). See entry 426 for later editions.

| 426 | TD4.8-5 no. 183-32 | **Federal Aviation Administration Designated Maintenance Technician Examiners. Directory.** Federal Aviation Administration. 1981. v.p. Advisory circular (AC) no. 183-32. Annual. |

This advisory circular provides a consolidated directory of designated mechanic examiners (DMEs) and designated parachute rigger examiners (DPREs) as of April 21, 1981, under the authority of Federal Aviation Regulation, Part 183. DMEs may accept applications and conduct oral practical tests necessary for issuing mechanic certificates; their ratings are shown for airframe and powerplant. DPREs may accept applications and conduct oral and practical tests necessary for issuing parachute rigger examiner certificates. DPRE ratings include seat, back, chest, and lap. The directory is divided by DMEs and DPREs, and is arranged alphabetically by state and name within state. Each entry contains name, address, and rating legend. Also included is a list of repair stations.

| 427 | Y1.1-3 92-8 1964- | **Biographical Directory of the American Congress, 1774-1971. The Continental Congress September 5, 1774, to October 21, 1788 and the Congress of the United States from the First to the 91st Congress March 4, 1789, to January 3, 1971 Inclusive.** 11th ed. Senate, 92d Congress, 1st Session. 1971. 1972p. Senate document no. 92-8. Irregular. |

Designed to give up-to-date and authentic biographical data, this edition contains more than 10,800 individual biographies that have been carefully compiled from currently available biographical works, or revised in accordance with verified new information on earlier members, generally made available by historical associations and individuals interested in family genealogy. A new addition to this volume is the biographies of presidents of the United States who never served as members of Congress. The directory is divided into the following sections: (1) officers of the executive branch of the government, 1789-1971; (2) the Continental Congress—place and time of meeting, and officers of the congress and delegates, by states; (3) apportionment of representatives (constitutional, and from the first census [1790] through the nineteenth census [1970]; (4) the 1st through 91st congresses of the United States, listing officers, dates, and congress members by state; (5) members of the 92d Congress serving their first term; (6) the biographies (biographies of presidents who were not members of Congress, presented first). Each biographical sketch generally gives birth, death, education, and service-in-Congress dates, and where interred.

428 Y1.3   **A Necrology of United States Senators—Showing Those Who**
     N28   **Died during Their Terms of Office and All Who Have Died**
                 since 1789. Senate. 1975. 46p.

Divided into two sections, this volume provides, in the first section, a list of senators who died during their term of service, showing the dates of death in chronological order. The entries provide name, state, Congress number and session, and date of death, indicating whether the death followed the sine die adjournment of the Congress. The second section lists in alphabetical order those senators who have died since 1789. The entries include name, state, dates of service, and date of death. An asterisk (*) following the date of death indicates that the senator died in office.

429 Y3.H62-4:2   **The First Ladies.** By Margaret Brown Klapthor. White House
     F51   Historical Association. 1981. 89p. Irregular.
     1975

This book, first published in 1975 when President and Mrs. Ford occupied the mansion, offers lively one-page biographies and authentic likenesses of the women who presided here over family and social affairs. Not all are wives: daughters and daughters-in-law often took on the responsibilities to relieve ill mothers, or to assist fathers who were widowers. Arranged in chronological order with color photographs, the volume contains Martha Washington through Nancy Reagan.

430 Y3.M69-2:2   **Coordination Directory of State and Federal Agency Water**
     D62   **and Land Resources Officials.** Missouri River Basin Commission. 1979. 83p. Microfiche.

The Missouri River Basin Commission (MRBC) has prepared this coordination directory as an aid in carrying out its responsibilities in accordance with the Water Resources Planning Act of 1965, which provides that the commission "serve as the principal agency for the coordination of Federal, State, interstate, local, and nongovernmental plans for the development of water and related land resources ..." in the basin. The directory is designed to assist state and federal members represented on the Missouri River Basin Commission in interagency communication and for use by all federal, state, interstate, local, and nongovernmental interests concerned with the development, management, and conservation of basin water and related land resources. MRBC members are Colorado, Iowa, Kansas, Minnesota, Missouri, Montana, Nebraska, North Dakota, South Dakota, and Wyoming; the federal departments of Agriculture, Army, Commerce, Energy, Health, Education, and Welfare, Housing and Urban Development, Interior, and Transportation; the EPA, FEMA, Yellowstone River Compact Commission, Big Blue River Compact Administration; and Canada, as an observer. The directory contains names, titles, agencies, addresses, and telephone numbers of all concerned parties, including the chief executive of each state.

431 Y4.B47   **Women in Congress, 1917-1976.** Joint Committee on Arrangements for the Commemoration of the Bicentennial: Congress.
     W84   1976. 112p.

Discussed in this booklet are the careers of those women who have held national office: the ninety-five women who have served in the United States Congress. These are primarily legislative biographies devoted to the public careers of these unique political women. Of the ninety-five women who have served in Congress, eighty-five have served in the House of Representatives and eleven in the Senate (Margaret Chase Smith served in both houses of Congress). The volume is arranged into three sections. The first section lists, in alphabetical order, the former members of Congress; the second lists the current members in alphabetical order; and the third is a chronological list of the members arranged by Congress number, giving dates of service.

432   Y4.G74-9   **Federal Advisory Committees. Index to Membership of Federal Advisory Committees Listed in the Fifth Annual Report of the President to the Congress Covering the Calendar Year 1976.** Senate Committee on Governmental Affairs. 1977. 1340p. Annual.
      Ad9-2
      1972

The fifth annual report of Federal Advisory Committees showed 1,159 committees, commissions, boards, councils, and other panels in existence as of December 31, 1976, with a total reported membership of 23,375 persons. The fifth annual report is available to the public on microfilm at the Library of Congress. The public can also order the set from the National Archives and Records Service. The index provides three alphabetical listings of the membership information contained in the annual report, making it possible to look up the 23,375 individual members by name or by affiliation, or to determine at a glance the names and affiliations of all the members of any given advisory committee. The listings are as follows: (1) by affiliation, then by member name and by committee code; (2) by member name, then by affiliation and by the committee served; and (3) by committee code, then by member name and by affiliation. Pages on which the individual may be found in the annual report are indicated.

433   Y4.P93-1:1   **1981 Official Congressional Directory, 97th Congress.** Joint Committee on Printing, Congress. 1981. 1104p. Annual with supplements.
      1809-

Issued for each Congress, this volume gives brief biographies of each member of Congress, terms of service, committee assignments. It lists committees, their staffs, and other capitol officials. It also includes statistical tables on sessions of Congress and election results of recent congressional elections. Other material includes the officials of the executive, judicial, and legislative branches of the government, members of the press galleries, diplomatic representatives of foreign countries, and U.S. diplomatic representatives. Also included are maps for each state, showing the congressional districts. Supplements are issued occasionally.

434   Y4.P93-1:1p   **Congressional Pictorial Directory. January, 1981. 97th Congress.** Joint Committee on Printing, Congress. 1981. 198p. Biannual.
      1959-

This pictorial directory supplements the official *Congressional Directory* by listing photographs of the congressmen and the president and vice-president. Each photograph is accompanied by the name, place of residence, date elected to Congress, and political affiliation. The photographs are arranged by Senate and House leadership; officers of the Senate; officers of the House; chaplains and officials of the capitol; members, by states; and delegates. Other sections list state delegations (by districts) and senators and representatives (in alphabetical order).

128 / 8—Individuals

| 435 | Y4.Sci2
97L
1975- | **Astronauts and Cosmonauts: Biographical and Statistical Data.** 5th ed., rev. House Committee on Science and Technology. March 31, 1981. 311p. Committee Print. Irregular. |

Contained in this document are biographies and photographs of NASA astronauts, NASA astronaut candidates, X-15, X-20, and Manned Orbiting Laboratory (MOL) astronauts, and soviet-bloc cosmonauts. Other data included in the volume includes status of astronauts by group, education, experience, selection criteria, summary of astronauts, status of cosmonauts, and comparative data on American and Soviet space flights.

| 436 | Y4.V64-4
M46-2 | **Vietnam Era Medal of Honor Recipients, 1964-1972.** Senate Committee on Veterans' Affairs. 1973. 236p. Committee Print no. 8. |

Recorded in this publication are the names and deeds of those outstanding and brave individuals who have been recognized for their acts of heroism by our country's highest award: the Congressional Medal of Honor. More than one hundred servicemen of the Vietnam era and their acts of courage are chronicled in this volume. Part 1 gives a historical background of the Medal of Honor; part 2 lists the citations of awards of the Medal of Honor of the Vietnam War (1964-72); part 3 lists the Medal of Honor recipients by state; part 4 is an alphabetical index of Medal of Honor recipients; and part 5 gives a documentary background on the Medal of Honor.

| 437 | Y4.V64-4
M46-3 | **Medal of Honor Recipients, 1863-1978. "In the Name of the Congress of the United States."** Senate Committee on Veterans' Affairs. 1979. 1113p. Committee Print no. 3. |

This publication, prepared by the Senate Committee on Veterans' Affairs, records the names and deeds of the outstanding and brave individuals who have been recognized for their acts of heroism. This revision adds the names and other appropriate information concerning individuals who have received the medal since 1963 and is complete through 1976. This document includes all recipients in the five branches of the service: Army, Navy, Marine Corps, Air Force, and Coast Guard. The volume is divided into six parts. Part 1 gives a historical background on the Medal of Honor. Part 2 lists the citations of awards of the Medal of Honor by war, campaign, conflict, or era in chronological order, beginning with the Civil War and ending with the Vietnam era. Part 3 lists the Medal of Honor recipients by state, and part 4 lists foreign-born Medal of Honor recipients. Part 5 is an alphabetical index of Medal of Honor recipients, an alphabetical individual name index of persons mentioned in the volume other than Medal of Honor awardees; and an account of the number of Medals of Honor awarded by wars and campaigns. Part 6 is a documentary background on the Medal of Honor.

9
Information Sources and Systems

At first glance, this chapter may seem to be a duplication of chapter 4. Not so. There is a difference between data sources and information sources. Information sources and systems are usually the organizations, places, persons, and contacts where one might find information about travel, ongoing research, consumer tips, and so forth.

438 C47.12 **Consumer's Guide to Travel Information.** *See* entry 300.
       In3

439 C47.12 **Traveler's Guide to Information Sources.** Travel Service.
       T69   1976. 40p.

Names, addresses, and some telephone numbers are provided in this publication, which lists sources of travel information. A bibliography is also included. This guide is divided into four sections. The first section contains a list of sources of general tourist information, which includes state and city tourism offices, and some visitors' bureaus, convention centers, and chambers of commerce, arranged alphabetically by state and city within state; a list of highway welcome centers, arranged alphabetically by state and place (the name of the center usually indicates the nearest town unless otherwise indicated); and a select list of national parks, including a map of the United States showing these select national parks and a list of the National Park Service's regional offices. The second section lists the sources of language assistance for international visitors, including airports with multilingual gateway receptionists, hotels with language certifications, toll-free "Travel-Phone USA," language banks, and American Council for Nationalities Service offices. Section 3 lists the Deak-Perera Group and banks in various cities offering foreign currency exchange service. Section 4 lists under the heading of Emergency Assistance for International Visitors those agencies that are able to assist foreign visitors with their problems in traveling, including Travelers Aid International Social Service of America, Immigration and Naturalization Service regional and district offices, Federal Information Centers, and a partial listing of foreign embassies in the United States.

440 C51.2   **International Directory of Appropriate Technology**
       D63   **Resources.** *See* entry 041.

9—Information Sources and Systems

441 C51.11 **NTIS Sumstat Catalog.** *See* entry 156.
　　　Su6

442 C51.11-6 **JACS Directory. NTIS Journal Article Copy Service.** National
　　　1978-　　Technical Information Service. October 1978. 182p. Irregular.

This directory is intended for use with the National Technical Information Service's (NTIS) Journal Article Copy Service (JACS). JACS is a new NTIS service that provides NTIS deposit account customers with rapid delivery of journal article copies under copyright license from the journal publishers. NTIS serves as a broker, relaying orders for article copies from NTIS customers to fulfillment sources, such as libraries, information services, and publishers, who provide the article copies directly to the customer. The *JACS Directory* must be used to determine whether the desired article is available from JACS. Journal titles are listed in alphabetical order. Following each title listing is a journal identification number (normally the International Standard Serial Number [ISSN]), indication of the extent of coverage of the journal, and the article price. An article is available through JACS only if the journal appears in the *JACS Directory* and the article is in an issue included in the coverage period indicated.

443 C55.8 **Guide to Information on Research in Marine Science and**
　　　M33　　**Engineering.** National Oceanic and Atmospheric Administration. 1978. 55p.

This guide should improve user ability to obtain access to ongoing research information as well as a much greater range of federal and nonfederal data and information bases. This brochure also has descriptions of the ocean research and development responsibilities of several federal agencies, including source contacts for further assistance. The guide is divided into three sections. The first section lists the federal agency programs in marine science and engineering, describes the programs, and provides an address for further information. The second section contains a list of organizations/agencies that will provide access to marine scientific and technical data and information. Included in this section are names of current research information sources (for example, Smithsonian Science Information Exchange, Inc.), environmental data and information sources, and nongovernment sources of information. Each source provides an address for further information. The third section is an alphabetical list of subject terms for access to federal marine science and engineering project information, compiled by the Smithsonian Science Information Exchange.

444 D5.411 **Research Aids: Selected Sources of Information.** Compiled by
　　　R31　　Gregory Diercks, Publications Editor, and Evelyn Lakes, Research Assistant. National Defense University. 1978. 31p.

Research aids listed here are oriented toward researchers in the area of national security affairs who require a familiarity with a variety of basic reference sources. While this list is not exhaustive, it does present a wide range of resources that serve to indicate to the researcher the types of materials that are available. The publication is divided into three parts. Part 1, divided into four sections, lists general reference publications, such as bibliographies, book reviews, yearbooks, directories, indexes, and abstracts, and also publications in the areas of humanities and social sciences, science and technology, and other data sources of the U.S. government. Part 2 describes the Library of Congress Scorpio system (a computerized information retrieval system), and part 3 contains a list of Social Science Data Libraries (members of the Council of Social Science Data Archives), indicating name, address, type of data, and subject matter.

445   E1.28   **Wind Energy Information Directory.** Energy Department.
        SERI/SP 290   1979. 28p. Solar Energy Research Institute publication no. 290.

The *Wind Energy Information Directory* has been prepared to provide researchers, designers, manufacturers, distributors, dealers, and users of wind energy conversion systems with easy access to technical information. This directory lists organizations and publications (giving addresses and telephone numbers) that have the main objective of promoting the use of wind energy conversion systems, some organizations that can respond to requests for information on wind energy or make referrals to other sources of information, and some publications that occasionally include information on wind energy. The publication lists such organizations as manufacturers, dealers, and distributors; universities and colleges; computer programs; state energy offices; solar energy associations; and energy information databases.

446   E1.28   **Solar Energy Information Locator.** *See* entry 307.
        SERI/SP
        751-210

447   E1.33   **Conservation and Renewable Energy Resource Directory.**
        DOE/IR 0040   Energy Department. 1979. v.p. DOE/IR series, no. 0040. Irregular.

The purpose of this directory is to facilitate quick access to Department of Energy (DOE) offices responsible for conservation and renewable energy activities. Because several offices in DOE may have responsibility for various phases of a technology or service (i.e., research, development, demonstration, commercialization, information, and education), the directory lists the key contacts from the various phases by category. The directory is organized in five main categories plus an index and relevant appendixes. The categories are renewable energy technologies, complementary technologies, conservation technologies, environment, and support services. Each category is defined and the responsibilities for each subject area are given, along with the DOE offices responsible, contacts, addresses, and telephone numbers. Three appendixes contain (1) an alphabetical list of state energy offices, with chief executive officers, addresses, and telephone numbers; (2) an alphabetical contact listing; and (3) organizational charts for all DOE offices mentioned in the directory. Also included is an alphabetical subject index.

448   E1.46   **Energy Library—Guide to Services.** Rev. ed. Energy Depart-
        DOE/OAS   ment. June 1978. 12p. DOE/OAS series, no. 0010/1. Irregular.
        0010/1

The Energy Library is maintained to provide DOE headquarters staff with a wide variety of bibliographic and reference services and to function as a major repository of energy-related information. This booklet describes the services available from the three locations of the library. Those services include reference services, literature searches, selective dissemination of information (SDI), acquisitions, circulation/interlibrary loan, serials, classified documents control, translation service, public document room,

132 / 9—Information Sources and Systems

publications, and collection catalogs. An appendix provides a selected list of databases accessed by the Energy Library. Addresses are given for the three locations of the Energy Library, with hours.

| 449 | ED1.8 Ar2 1978- | **Resource Guide—Architectural Barriers Removal.** Handicapped Individuals Office. 1980. 34p. Annual. |

This guide was compiled to meet the information needs of persons working with architectural barriers. The publication lists available information resources, indicates where funding can be obtained, and describes existing publications available through federal agencies. Only national-level information sources are described, and funding sources concentrate on federal grants, loans, or tax credits. The publication is divided into three sections. The first lists, in alphabetical order by name, the organizations that provide information resources. Each entry contains name, address, telephone number, a brief description of the organization, information services, publications, and how to use the organization's services. Section 2 provides a list of current federal programs providing assistance for architectural barriers removal. The program descriptions were excerpted from the 1980 *Catalog of Federal Domestic Assistance.* Section 3 is an alphabetical list of publications available from federal sources, giving necessary information for ordering and an annotation.

| 450 | ED1.8 R26 1980- | **Resource Guide. Rehabilitation Engineering and Product Information.** Handicapped Individuals Office. 1980. 49p. Irregular. |

Rehabilitation engineering (the application of science and technology to improve the quality of life of persons with disabilities) is becoming an increasingly important field in an age in which education, transportation, and employment opportunities are expanding for the handicapped. Professionals in the fields of rehabilitation engineering, rehabilitation counseling, and others who provide information and direct services to handicapped persons are concerned about the dissemination of information about technological research and available products. It is for these professionals that this resource guide is intended, describing a wide array of national resources in this area. Resources included in this guide have information on sensory, mobility, and communication technology ("hard products," such as aids, devices, instruments, equipment, materials, appliances, tools, contrivances, and machinery) that assist handicapped individuals in daily living (educational, recreational, vocational, and transportation) activities. Divided into six sections, the guide provides addresses and telephone numbers of (1) major information sources—federal and private; (2) general information sources; (3) sources of financial assistance and loans for aids and equipment; (4) funding sources; (5) publications; and (6) future information sources on engineering products.

| 451 | ED1.8 R26-2 | **Resource Guide: Recreation and Leisure for Handicapped Individuals.** *See* entry 050. |

| 452 | EP1.2 Un3-10 1976- | **U.S. Directory of Environmental Sources.** 3d ed. Environmental Protection Agency. January 1979. v.p. Irregular. |

The United Nations Environment Program (UNEP) was created in 1972 as a direct result of the International Conference on Human Environment. In order to assist in

9—*Information Sources and Systems* / *133*

carrying out the goals of this organization, several programs were created within the UNEP structure, one of which was the International Referral System (UNEP/IRS). In January 1979, this referral system was renamed INFOTERRA. Composed of a network of more than eighty national and sectoral focal points, INFOTERRA is engaged in identifying and registering sources of environmental information, transmitting these sources in a unified format to the system's central data bank in Geneva, Switzerland, and serving as a point of contact for users who need referral services—national and international. INFOTERRA is a referral service designed to link those who need environmental information with those who have the desired information. This directory includes environmental information sources registered with the U.S. International Referral Center as of September 1, 1978. This edition includes 1,311 United States sources from among business and industry groups, consultants, engineering firms, federal agencies, information centers, laboratories, societies and associations, state and local governments, and universities. Section 1 is the subject attribute listing, which is arranged alphabetically according to the specific environmental subject terms (called attributes), which are included in INFOTERRA. The registered sources having information on these terms are listed alphabetically under each subject. Pertinent information about each source can be found in section 2, which is the directory of sources. This section is arranged numerically by assigned source numbers, which are obtained from sections 1, 3, and 4 of the directory. Each entry in this section contains name; assigned source number; address, telephone, telex, and cable of source; a brief explanation of the source's operation and information available; major sources of funding/control plus geographical area of sponsoring organization; main occupation of parent body; capacity in which source works; geographical limitation; language in which information is provided; conditions of available information; types of information available and format; and topics on which source has available information or expertise. Section 3 is an alphabetical listing of registered sources by organization name and assigned source identification number. Section 4 is a geographical listing of registered sources by state and city. It is arranged alphabetically by state and U.S. territory under the city in which the source is located. Information includes the name of the organization, the unit comprising the source, and the source identification number. The title of this publication in 1976 was *United States Directory of Sources: United States International Referral Center.*

453   EP1.17   **Resource Recovery Plant Implementation Guides for Munic-**
      no. SW157.8   **ipal Officials.** *See* entry 055.

454   EP1.95   **Environmental Hotline '81.** *See* entry 318.

455   GA1.22   **Federal Information Sources and Systems. A Directory Issued**
      In3   **by the Comptroller General.** General Accounting Office.
      1976-   1980. 1178p. Congressional Sourcebook series. Irregular.

The implementation of the inventory of information sources and systems and the publication of this sourcebook are part of the GAO's continuing responsibilities under Title II of the Legislative Reorganization Act of 1970, as amended by Title VIII of the Congressional Budget Act of 1974 (P.L. 93-344). Section 203(b) requires that "the Comptroller General, in cooperation with the Director of the Congressional Budget Office, the Secretary of the Treasury, and the Director of the Office of Management and Budget shall develop, establish, and maintain an up-to-date inventory and directory of sources and information systems containing fiscal, budgetary, and program-related data and information and a brief description of their content." Executive, independent, and legislative agencies are included in the inventory. The term *executive agency* is defined to include executive departments, government corporations, and independent establishments. Information was reported to the GAO on major federal programs and the supporting information sources and systems that are important in fulfilling the agencies' missions. The GAO does not stock copies of reports produced by the agencies' information sources and systems covered in this directory. Some information sources and systems contain data that are not publicly available for reasons of security, privacy, or proprietary interest. Where such restrictions were reported to GAO, the system was designated "internal use only." The publication contains a citation section and an index section. The citation section is divided into two files: the I-file information sources and the S-file information systems. Within each file, the entries are arranged by agencies/bureaus and give for each information source or system descriptive information and an abstract. The information elements include accession number, title/subtitle, date of publication or date when the facility was established, primary author, OMB funding title/code, program, *Catalog of Federal Domestic Assistance* number, congressional relevance, law authority, availability, geographic relevance, abstract, and agency contact. The index section provides the following seven indexes with references to both I and S files in one sequence: subject, title, agency, congressional, law, program, and budget function. Also included in the volume is a glossary of terms used.

456   GS4.107/a   **Privacy Act Issuances, 1980 Compilation.** 6 vols. Federal
       P939-2   Register Office. 1980. Annual.
       1976-

The Privacy Act was enacted in December 1974, to provide certain safeguards for individuals against invasion of privacy by federal agencies. The act, with a few exceptions, applies to all information maintained by the federal government that can be retrieved by reference to one's name or other identifier, such as social security number, fingerprints, and alien registration number. Under the act, you have the right to: (1) find out what, if any, information an agency has about you; (2) find out who has regular access to your records; (3) get a copy of your record from the agency; (4) have any errors in your record corrected; and (5) approve certain disclosures of your records to people who could not otherwise see them. This compilation contains descriptions of systems of records on individuals maintained by federal agencies, which were published in the *Federal Register* as required by the Privacy Act of 1974; rules of each agency that set out the procedures they will follow in helping individuals who request information about their records; and a volume of research aids (an expanded table of contents) containing the names of all the systems of records in the compilation, grouped by agency; a table showing the agencies included in volumes 1 through 5; a table of dates and pages, indexing all Privacy Act material published in the *Federal Register* from May 1975 through December 1980; and a table of Privacy Act regulations published by the agencies as they appear in the *Code of Federal Regulations.* Each system of records citation includes the following information: system's name; system's location; categories of individuals covered by the system; categories of records in the system; authority for maintenance of the system; routine uses of records maintained in the system, including categories of users and the purposes of such users; policies and practices for storing, retrieving, accessing, retaining, and disposing of records in the systems; storage; retrievability; safeguards; retention and disposal; system manager(s) and addresses;

notifications procedure; record access procedures; contesting record procedures; and record source categories. The 1976 edition was entitled *Protecting Your Right to Privacy* and was issued in one volume.

457   HE1.2   **A Training and Resource Directory for Teachers Serving**
       H19-5   **Handicapped Students, K-12.** Prepared by Peggy M. Kapisovsky et al., Technical Education Research Centers. Health, Education, and Welfare Department. 1979. 213p.

This directory has been compiled to alert elementary- and secondary-level regular class teachers to resources that will assist them in accommodating students with physical and mental handicaps. These resources include inservice training opportunities; the network of national, state, and local agencies and organizations that are sources of materials, services, and technical assistance; and literature and media on educational services for handicapped students. The directory is divided into three parts. The first part identifies national resources that provide information and literature on handicapping conditions, equipment, and/or inservice education. Addresses, telephone numbers, and other pertinent data are given. Part 2 is a state-by-state listing of inservice training programs for teachers, state agencies, service and consumer organizations, and directories of services. Names, addresses, and telephone numbers are given. An annotated bibliography of texts and of materials for inservice workshops is presented in part 3. Included are addresses and prices.

458   HE1.54   **Catalog of Human Services Information Resource Organiza-**
       no. 15   **tions.** *See* entry 057.

459   HE1.54   **Section 504 Resources Manual. A Guide for Small Institu-**
       no. 19   **tions to Useful Sources, Services, and Procedures for Locating and Applying for Funds to Meet Section 504 Mandates.** Lawrence W. Marrs, Project Share. Health and Human Services Department. 1981. 48p. Human Services Monograph series, no. 19.

The primary purpose of the *Section 504 Resources Manual* is to provide the grantseeker with information regarding commercially available materials that provide assistance in writing effective applications for funding. This publication is designed to guide the small institution—be it a special-purpose, nonprofit organization (such as a day care center), a hospital, a college, or a small municipality's government—to the most useful sources and services to aid in identifying, locating, and successfully applying for funds to support Section 504 implementation efforts. This volume is divided into four chapters and an appendix. Chapter 1 is the introduction. Chapter 2 contains brief statements on the content and applications of thirty-eight monographs, books, newsletters, and other sources and services containing information about where and how to obtain funding from foundations and state and federal agencies. Chapter 3 discusses a variety of compliance problems experienced by one or more of the fifty case studies investigated by Lawrence Johnson and Associates, Inc. (LJA), under contract to the DHHS. The chapter also discusses types of Section 504 compliance issues that have cost implications and types of recipients hit hardest by these costs. Chapter 4 provides directions for identifying and utilizing sources and services in creative ways. It includes a description of a process or tracking system that the user can follow in searching for funds. The appendix lists organizations utilized by the fifty case studies and the roles of local, state,

136 / 9—Information Sources and Systems

and federal agencies in helping users comply with Section 504. Addresses are given for the source/service items, and addresses and telephone numbers are given for the organizations in the appendix.

| 460 | HE19.202
D62
1978- | **Directory of ERIC Search Services. November 1978.** Prepared by Elizabeth Pugh, et al. National Institute of Education. 1979. 61p. Irregular. |

The *Directory of ERIC Search Services* lists and describes the organizations that are currently providing computerized searches of the ERIC database. The intent is to include all sites providing search services on a regular basis, irrespective of whether the service is available only to a circumscribed community (e.g., a state education department or a university campus) or to all users without restriction. The directory is organized geographically, with entries grouped by state, and, within state, by city. Foreign entries appear at the end. There are a total of 341 entries. The organizations are arranged in tables, and the information given includes the following: organization name with complete mailing address, telephone number(s), and person(s) to contact for further information; population served; files available; inquiry submission (how a request for a search should be submitted and the preferred format of such a request); search output (what the organization delivers back to the requesters); cost per search; turnaround time; search system used; notes (miscellaneous relevant information); and date entry prepared. Also included in the directory are: (1) vendors that provide online computer access to ERIC, with addresses, telephone numbers, and contacts; (2) a table of organization acronyms with city and state; (3) a table of databases, referenced with acronym and file name (source); and (4) a list of search systems providing the search system name, acronym, developer, and access mode.

| 461 | HE20.3170
D62
1977- | **Directory of Cancer Research Information Resources.** National Cancer Institute. 1981. 264p. Biennial. |

Found in this directory are sources of cancer information throughout the world, updated every two years by the ICRDB (International Cancer Research Data Bank) Program. The bibliography lists the publications used to identify the cancer research information resources included in this directory. The volume is organized into twelve sections covering the following: computer-based information systems and services; primary publications; secondary publications; research projects information sources; organizations (excluding U.S. government agencies); U.S. government agencies, products, and services; cancer registries; dial-access services; libraries; classification schemes; special collections; and audiovisual information sources. A separate introduction to each of these sections gives a detailed explanation of the scope of the listings within that section. Four indexes (title, CANCERLIT Citation Ranking [CCR], organizational, and geographic) provide easy access to each resource, listing sponsors, acronyms, and translations by which the service may be known. Cross-referencing is used, when appropriate, to refer the user from a primary source to other closely related entries. The entries provide name, address, scope, frequency, language, services, programs, meetings, publications, and other information, as applicable.

| 462 | HE23.2
H19-3 | **Directory of National Information Sources on Handicapping Conditions and Related Services.** *See* entry 064. |

463   I1.2   **Information Sources and Services Directory.** *See* entry 275.
      In3-2

464   I19.2   **Sources of Information, Products, and Services of the U.S.**
      In3-4   **Geological Survey.** Geological Survey. 1978. 23p. Irregular.
      1978-

This brochure describes and identifies the results, findings, and products of the scientific and technical work conducted by the U.S. Geological Survey (USGS), which are disseminated through a wide range of services and sources of information. Information is provided on the following items: maps and charts; book reports; cartographic data; water resources data; geologic inquiries; evaluation and classification; computer data; photographs and transparencies; motion picture films; technical exhibits; library services; and news media services. For each of these areas, a contact office and address are provided. Also included in the brochure are lists of USGS public inquiries offices with addresses, and principal addresses of the U.S. Geological Survey around the country.

465   I19.2   **The U.S. Geological Survey's Public Inquiries Offices: Focal**
      In7   **Points for Information.** By R. S. Ritchey and A. E. Jones.
      1975-   Geological Survey. 1980. 9p. Irregular.

The U.S. Geological Survey maintains ten public inquiries offices (PIOs), staffed by information specialists, to provide convenient public contact for obtaining information regarding the work of the USGS and its publications (book reports, maps, nontechnical publications, indexes, catalogs, and open-file reports). Inquiries may be made by letter, by telephone, or in person. This brochure provides an alphabetical state arrangement of PIOs, with addresses and telephone numbers, and indicates materials available from these offices.

466   I19.4-2   **A Guide to Obtaining Information from the USGS.** Rev. ed.
      no. 777   Compiled by Paul F. Clarke, Helen E. Hodgson, and Gary W.
      1978-   North. Geological Survey. 1981. 42p. Annual.

Since 1879, the USGS has served federal, state, and local governments and the public by collecting, analyzing, and publishing detailed information about the nation's mineral, land, and water resources. This guide has been prepared to assist in obtaining the information products released by the USGS and to aid in locating both general and specific information within the USGS. Besides the introduction and general instructions for ordering maps and books by mail, the guide consists of three parts. The first part gives a description of the offices from which information is available, information about publications, where publications can be obtained, and about specific or specialized subjects. Also included are USGS libraries and other libraries in which USGS publications can be consulted. Some of the offices in this section are sources for information only, and some are sources for both information and for maps, reports, and other information products. The second part of the guide is a list of the types of USGS maps, reports, and other information products, and the places where these products can be obtained. This list is in tabular form, and, for brevity, the sources are in a code that is keyed to the third list. The third list, which is in part 3 of the guide, contains the sources of USGS maps, reports, and other information products, arranged alphabetically by the codes used in the list of products. It provides their addresses and commercial and

138 / 9—Information Sources and Systems

government (FTS) telephone numbers. Addresses and telephone numbers are also listed in part 1.

467 I49.2 **Ecological Characterization of the Sea Island Coastal Region of South Carolina and Georgia. Directory of Information Sources. A Reference List of Data Sources Pertinent to the Natural Resources of Coastal South Carolina and Georgia.** Edited by John V. Miglarese, et al. Fish and Wildlife Service. 1979. 35p.
       Ec7-3

This directory provides easy access to 337 sources of information in South Carolina, Georgia, and elsewhere. It contains three sections: (1) a list of subject matter descriptors (e.g., "air quality") and page numbers; (2) a list and ranking of information sources by subject area; and (3) alphabetical lists of data sources under four headings (South Carolina, Georgia, federal, and other). The sources are numbered consecutively in alphabetical order, and the numbers serve to link the subject matter descriptors and the information sources. Also, to help the user avoid duplication of effort, the data sources listed for each subject matter area are ranked as primary or secondary sources. The information given includes names, addresses and telephone numbers.

468 J1.2 **Criminal Justice Audiovisual Materials Directory.** 3d ed. Law Enforcement Assistance Administration. January 1978. 150p. Irregular.
       Au2
       1974-

This directory is designed to serve as a resource guide for those in the criminal justice field seeking materials for education, training, and orientation. The directory, described in its foreword as a source directory, is divided into sections covering courts; police techniques and training; prevention; prisons and rehabilitation/corrections; and public education (miscellaneous, and production and distribution) sources. Each entry, arranged alphabetically by title within sections, includes the title; a brief description of the material; the type of material; rental fee or purchase price, if applicable; and the name of the distributor. The last section lists in alphabetical order, with addresses, the distributors or the sources of the materials listed.

469 J28.20 **Directory of Criminal Justice Information Sources.** 4th ed. Compiled by Christine Lundy, National Criminal Justice Reference Service. National Institute of Justice. 1981. 142p. Irregular.
       1977-

Issued by the National Criminal Justice Reference Service (NCJRS), this publication is part of the continuing effort by the National Institute of Justice to foster the exchange of information and to open channels of communication among those who have an interest in the field of criminal justice. By providing a reference tool such as this directory, NCJRS makes known to all who are concerned with law enforcement and the criminal justice system the available resources and services of many agencies. This fourth edition represents an attempt to update previous editions and is based on a 1981 survey of approximately 260 criminal justice agencies. This directory should not be considered an exhaustive compilation, although every effort was made to contact known criminal justice information sources. The agencies included here feature such information resources as computerized literature search services, interlibrary loan programs, reference services, and technical assistance to criminal justice professionals.

9—*Information Sources and Systems* / *139*

The organizations are listed in alphabetical order, and two indexes, organized by geographic location and criminal justice specialty, are provided to assist users. Also included is a list of the codes identifying areas of activity. Each entry gives the following data, if applicable: name of information center or library; parent organization or sponsoring agency; address(es) — both street and mailing, if different; telephone number(s); user restrictions; year established; head of center; number of staff (professional, support, volunteer); contact person and/or interlibrary loan officer; areas of activity; objectives; services offered; collection size and type; and publications.

470 J29.8 **1980 Directory of Criminal Justice Information Systems.**
        C86   Justice Statistics Bureau. 1980. v.p. Irregular.

Contained in this document are indexed listings of the automated criminal justice information systems used by police, courts, correctional institutions, and other justice agencies. Information was derived from the automated index of CJIS Systems, maintained by SEARCH Group, Inc. For each jurisdiction covered, the listing describes briefly the criminal justice information systems that are operational or being developed, who is doing the work, and the current status of the system. Approximately six hundred separately defined systems are listed. System overviews are presented in index 2, master listings of systems. The principal purpose of the directory is to serve as a new reference for criminal justice planners in developing new systems or in enhancing existing ones. It is intended to foster communications among developers and users of criminal justice information systems in order to facilitate the transfer or adaptation of exemplary systems, and to minimize duplication of effort. The volume is divided into five indexes and three appendixes. Also included are tables of data elements, abbreviations, and system functions. Index 1 deals with jurisdictions, organized alphabetically by state, with the county and local-level jurisdictions listed alphabetically beneath the state. Index 2 lists the system descriptions alphabetically by name under the state and city or county in which they are located. Data elements provided in index 2 include such items as population area served, contractors, microform, software, environment, interface, data processing contact, and narrative description. Index 3 is an alphabetical arrangement of systems described in the directory, indicating page number of the description. Index 4 lists the system functions alphabetically, then by state, jurisdiction, system name, and page. Index 5 covers systems by central processing unit (CPU); it is arranged alphabetically by name of hardware manufacturer, then by CPU model, system name, and page. Appendix A provides names and addresses of other organizations involved in the exchange of systems; and appendix B provides an alphabetical arrangement by state of state criminal justice planning agencies, with chief officer and address.

471 LC1.31 **A Directory of Information Resources in the United States.**
        D62-2   **Social Sciences.** Rev. ed. A National Referral Center publica-
        1965-   tion. Library of Congress. 1973. 700p. Irregular.

For the purposes of this directory, *social sciences* has been defined broadly to encompass even such activities as recreation, education, and business. Entries in the directory are based on a register of information resources that has been continuously expanded since the center was established in 1962. The entries are arranged alphabetically and numbered sequentially. The subject index is keyed to these numbers rather than to pages. Cross-references have been used liberally throughout the directory. Each entry contains the name of the organization and/or subdivision(s),

140 / 9—Information Sources and Systems

address(es), telephone numbers, brief statement of purpose, areas of interest, publications, and information services.

| 472 | LC1.31
D62-4
1967- | **A Directory of Information Resources in the United States. Federal Government. With a Supplement of Government-Sponsored Information Analysis Centers.** Rev. ed. A National Referral Center publication. Library of Congress. 1974. 416p. Irregular. |

This directory is the ninth in a series compiled by the National Referral Center under the general title *A Directory of Information Resources in the United States*. Unlike the other directories in the series, which are subject oriented, *Federal Government* covers all subjects. All federal organizations were eligible for inclusion, regardless of their areas of interest. Some organizations were omitted at their own request, however, and others were excluded because adequate information concerning them was not available. With some exceptions, entries in both the directory proper and the supplement are alphabetically arranged. In the directory the alphabetical arrangement is by federal agencies and then subagencies. Entries provide name, address, telephone number(s), statement of purpose, areas of interest, publications, and information services. The subject index refers to the entry numbers rather than the page numbers. Entries are numbered sequentially.

| 473 | LC1.31
D62-7
1965- | **A Directory of Information Resources in the United States. Biological Sciences.** A National Referral Center publication. Library of Congress. 1972. 577p. Irregular. |

This directory updates and extends the biological sciences coverage of *A Directory of Information Resources in the United States: Physical Sciences, Biological Sciences, Engineering*, issued in 1965 by the National Referral Center. An updated volume on the physical sciences and engineering alone was released in 1971. Entries in the directory are based on a register of information resources that has continuously expanded since the center was established in 1962. The entries are arranged alphabetically by name of the organization, and are numbered sequentially. The subject index is keyed to these numbers rather than to page numbers. Each entry provides the name of the organization, its address, telephone number, areas of interest, holdings, publications, and information services.

| 474 | LC1.31
D62-8
1970- | **Directory of Federally Supported Information Analysis Centers.** 4th ed., 1979. A National Referral Center publication. Library of Congress. 1980. 87p. Irregular. |

Given in this volume are descriptions of the mission, scope, document and data holdings, information services, and qualified users of 108 centers that share two common attributes: (1) they are part of, or sponsored by, the federal government, and (2) they produce new, evaluated information through the collection and analysis or synthesis of information by subject specialists. Also given, in addition to the name, address, and telephone number of each center, are the names of center directors or other persons to contact, the names of sponsors, the year started, the makeup of the staff, and a list of the center's principal publications. Four indexes are included: personal names, geographic, organizations, and subject. The centers are arranged in alphabetical order by name.

475 LC1.31   **A Directory of Information Resources in the United States.**
     Oc2   **Geosciences and Oceanography.** A National Referral Center publication. Library of Congress. 1981. 375p. Occasionally on microfiche.

For the purposes of this directory, *geosciences* and *oceanography* have been defined quite broadly, organizations' ranges of interest often being diffuse. The entries are arranged alphabetically by organization name and, to permit simultaneous computer preparation of the organization locator and the subject index, they are numbered sequentially. The organization locator and the subject index are both keyed to these numbers rather than to pages. A few cross-references have also been used in the directory proper. Each of the entries provides the following: name of organization, address, telephone number, areas of interest, holdings, publications, and information services.

476 LC19.2   **Library Resources for the Blind and Physically Handicapped.**
     L61-5   *See* entry 233.

477 NAS1.64 **Sources for Landsat Assistance and Services.** National Aeronautics and Space Administration. 1980. 39p. Earth Resources Satellite Data Applications series.
     L23

With the increasing interest in Landsat data by the private and public sectors, the availability of pertinent information for potential users is of vital concern. The introduction of the Earth Resources Satellite Data Applications series of publications is directed toward bridging the gap that often arises between fast-paced technology development and the availability of practical results to the user community. The intent of this publication is to provide directories of academic and commercial sources to assist the potential user of Landsat data and products. In addition, points of contact for federal and state agencies are provided. Divided into three sections (academic organizations, commercial organizations, and federal and state agencies), and arranged alphabetically by state, the entries provide the following: organization name, address, and contact person with telephone number; courses and/or hardware, remote-sensing and interpretation; research Landsat data processing; services Landsat data applications; application specialties; and comments.

478 NS1.2   **Information Services on Research in Progress. A Worldwide Inventory.** Edited by the Smithsonian Science Information Exchange. National Science Foundation. 1978. 432p.
     In2-7

The inventory was compiled as a follow-up to recommendations made at the first International Symposium on Information Systems and Services in Ongoing Research in Science, held in October 1975. It was there that the need for an international directory of existing information systems and services on ongoing research was fully realized. This directory is an aid to development of individual systems and as a significant step in international cooperation. The inventory contains three sections: the first is a state-of-the-art review of systems and services for information about scientific research in progress. It combines an examination of the contents of the inventory with a selective review of the available literature, and includes suggestions for future initiatives that might be taken to develop the field at international, regional, national, and subnational levels. An extensive bibliography completes this section. The second section consists of detailed profiles for 179 planned, pilot, and operational ongoing research information systems throughout the world: 43 international and regional systems, and 136 national and subnational systems. The profiles were obtained as the result of a data collection effort undertaken by the UNISIST program of UNESCO and SSIE. The third section contains indexes for organization and system names, organization and system acronyms, persons responsible, and subject coverage given in the inventory profiles. The profiles of nations are arranged alphabetically by country, and then by system name. Information given includes name, address, and telephone number(s); system status, person responsible, institutional affiliation; description of the system (scope, file description, subject indexing methods and techniques, and data processing methods and techniques); system services (information and availability); and additional comments.

479 Pr39.15   **Consumer's Resource Handbook.** *See* entry 343.
     C76

480 S1.2   **The Information Resources and Services of the United States.**
     R31-3   *See* entry 189.

10
Laws and Regulations

These are directories that are concerned with laws and regulations on particular subjects. They may be local, state, or federal.

481 A13.2 **Digest of State Forest Fire Laws.** Forest Service. 1979. 330p.
St29-3

The forest fire laws are organized by subject matter in an attempt to conform to the outline of suggested forest fire laws prepared by the Council of State Governments. The laws are arranged alphabetically by state within each subject area and refer to state statutes and regulations. The states included are Connecticut, Delaware, Illinois, Indiana, Iowa, Maine, Maryland, Massachusetts, Michigan, Minnesota, Missouri, New Hampshire, New Jersey, New York, Ohio, Pennsylvania, Rhode Island, Vermont, West Virginia, and Wisconsin. The subject areas include such items as fire codes, emergency restrictions, penalties and liabilities (for building improper fires, and so forth), and payments for fire fighting, as well as many others. Also included is a section on suggested state legislation approved by the Council of State Governments.

482 A101.10-2 **State-Federal Health Requirements and Regulations Governing the Interstate and International Movement of Livestock and Poultry.** Rev. ed. Animal and Plant Health Inspection Service. December 1979. v.p. Irregular.
91-17-7

This publication is issued for the convenience of livestock owners and shippers, transportation agents, truckers, and others concerned in the interstate and international movement of livestock and poultry, subject to state and federal regulations and laws pertaining to animal diseases. Divided into three sections, section 1 lists the rules and regulations that are the requirements of the respective states for the entry of livestock into each state. The states are arranged alphabetically, and at the end of the section is an alphabetical-by-state list of livestock health officials with addresses. Section 2 includes the federal regulations and laws administered by Veterinary Services of the Animal and Plant Health Inspection Service, and are reprints or portions of subchapters A, C, D, G, and I of Chapter 1, Title 9, Code of Federal Regulations. Section 3 lists the import regulations of Canada.

144 / 10—Laws and Regulations

483 C46.2   **Directory of Permits—State of Alaska. Including: Registra-**
        D62-2   **tions, Licenses, Certifications, Approvals, Plan Reviews,**
                 Inspections, etc. Economic Development Administration.
                 1979. v.p.

The ultimate purpose of this directory is to diminish unnecessary procedures and simplify the system of permitting in Alaska. It identifies the permits, describes them, and outlines the procedures for issuing them. The directory is divided into three parts: federal, state, and local permits. The permits are organized by department; however, within a department, the permits are grouped by divisions or agencies within that department and arranged in alphabetical order. The pages are "numbered" by abbreviations of department (i.e., "GOV" for Office of the Governor). Federal agency/department abbreviations are preceded by "US" to differentiate them from Alaska state departments. In addition to the table of contents and abbreviations explanation table, there is a subject index located in the back of the directory. This index cross-references, by subject, all the permits described in the directory. The abbreviations are used as part of the page numbers and in the subject index to assist the reader in locating each permit.

484 C57.2   **Foreign Regulations Affecting U.S. Textile/Apparel Exports,**
        T31-2   **1977.** Domestic and International Business Administration.
                 1978. 272p.

This study identifies the restrictions and requirements of 137 countries, which may affect U.S. textile and apparel export sales. Section 1 of this inventory includes regulations of foreign governments, such as embargoes, quotas, licensing requirements, prior authorization, and border taxes. Section 2 contains consumer-oriented requirements of major textile importing countries, including labeling requirements, flammability standards, and metrication. Reference is made to tariffs only when special tariffs are applied over and above the usual rates of duty. The dollar value of U.S. exports of textile and apparel products for 1974, 1975, and 1976 is included in column 3 of each country chart on a three-digit Standard International Trade Classification (SITC) basis. The countries are arranged alphabetically in each section.

485 HE19.102 **State and Federal Laws Relating to Nonpublic Schools.** Com-
        L44   piled and edited by Helen M. Jellison. Education Office. 1975.
                  391p.

The primary purpose of this study is to present a state-by-state compilation of constitutional and statutory provisions that affect nonpublic elementary and secondary schools and the children who attend these schools. In addition to the compilation of state provisions, this report contains five introductory chapters. The first three briefly describe the current status of nonpublic schools in this country, summarize the duties of the states in regulating nonpublic schools (using quotations from another publication), and describe the effects of federal laws on state responsibilities to nonpublic schools and school children, including a brief summary of relevant Supreme Court decisions. In the final two chapters, the constitutional and statutory provisions included in the state-by-state compilation are analyzed and discussed. The goal of this report is to provide a general reference for study and comparison of current state laws that affect nonpublic elementary and secondary schools and school children.

486 HE19.202 **State Legal Standards for the Provision of Public Education:**
        St2-3   **An Overview.** National Institute of Education. 1978. 153p.

This booklet represents the first part of the 7,400-page *Compendium of State Legal Standards for the Provision of Public Education*. The entire study is available through the Educational Resources Information Center (ERIC) microfiche collection. This volume includes the organizational outline and introduction to the entire compendium; it explains the components and uses of the compendium, providing a concise overview of the entire work. In addition, this volume contains twenty-three charts comparing important elements of various education laws and regulations. The final pages include bibliographic information and two multistate agreements dealing with educational standards and interstate cooperation. The charts citing regulations by state cover such areas as admission requirements, adult education, attendance enforcement agent, attendance requirements, curriculum, extracurricular activities, grade organization, guidance and counseling program, high school graduation requirements, individual pupil records, inservice training, libraries, promotion requirements, pupil load/class size, pupil-teacher ratio, pupil transportation, safety and health requirements, school calendar, teacher personnel policies, textbooks, general teacher certification, administrative officers' certification and existing certification requirements for job title.

487   HE20.5102   **Death Investigation: An Analysis of Laws and Policies of the United States, Each State and Jurisdiction as of January 31, 1977.** Community Health Services Bureau. 1978. 121p.
         D34

This study is designed to assemble and analyze existing state and territorial laws, policies, and regulations governing medicolegal death investigation. Its purpose is to assist the BCHS Office of Maternal and Child Health in developing a systematic surveillance of national medicolegal investigation of the sudden and unexplained deaths of infants. In addition to the fifty states, this study covers the District of Columbia, American Samoa, Guam, Puerto Rico, Panama Canal Zone, and the Virgin Islands. Local ordinances or regulations and policies adopted by governmental bodies below the state level are not included except in occasional instances where cited to clarify state law. The volume is divided into two sections plus an appendix of supplemental data with twelve tables. Section 1 is an alphabetical arrangement by state of the narrative description of operations of death investigation systems for each state and territory. Section 2 presents abstracts of statutory law for each state and territory in alphabetical order. The tables in the appendix include such data as a numerical summary of categories; jurisdictions presently maintaining statutory provisions referencing infant death, and those having received legislative bills, which did not become law, referencing infant death; state and territorial abbreviations; distribution by structure; qualifications; method of accession; authority to order; nature of structure per jurisdiction; and summary of categories.

488   HE20.5102   **Family Planning, Contraception, Voluntary Sterilization and Abortion: An Analysis of Laws and Policies in the United States, Each State and Jurisdiction as of October 1, 1976 with 1978 Addenda.** Community Health Services Bureau. 1979. 380p. Irregular.
         F21
         1971-

The study is designed to assemble and analyze existing federal, state, and territorial laws, policies, and regulations regarding contraception, voluntary sterilization, abortion, and the conditions under which minors may receive these services. In addition to the federal government and the fifty states, this study covers the District of Columbia, American Samoa, Guam, Puerto Rico, and the Virgin Islands. The volume is divided into two sections. Section 1 provides a summary, an analysis of federal laws relating to family planning, contraception, voluntary sterilization, and abortion, as well as profiles of federal laws and policies, and a summary and analysis of state laws relating to contraception, abortion, voluntary sterilization, sterilization of the mentally incompetent, contraceptive and abortion services to minors, and medicaid policies. Section 2 presents, in alphabetical order, profiles of laws and health, welfare and medicaid agency policies on family planning, contraception, voluntary sterilization, abortion, and services to minors.

489   HE20.5102   **State Laws and Regulations on Genetic Disorders, July 1980.**
      G28-4   Community Health Services Bureau. 1981. 80p.

Since the development in the early 1960s of the Guthrie test, which allowed for high-quality and inexpensive mass screening of newborns for the detection of phenylketonuria (PKU), and the enactment in 1963 by the state of Massachusetts of a law mandating the screening of all newborns for PKU, popular concern with legislation on genetic screening has continued. This publication is a compendium of statutes and regulations on genetic disorders promulgated by the individual states and the District of Columbia. At the present time neither the Commonwealth of Puerto Rico nor the U.S. territories of American Samoa, Guam, Mariana Islands, Trust Territory of the Pacific Islands, nor the Virgin Islands have enacted any laws or regulations on genetic disorders. This publication is divided into a section on laws and regulations and the appendixes. The laws and regulations are organized under the particular state or territory that has enacted them. The states are listed alphabetically, followed by the territories. For each, an introductory summary is given, followed by sections on newborn screening statutes, administrative regulations (i.e., newborn screening) and other relevant laws or regulations. The appendixes consist of a survey of newborn screening programs; maternal and child health and disabled children's service directors; and state legislative information offices. Addresses and telephone numbers are given for the directors and information officers.

490   HE20.7210   **State Legislation on Smoking and Health, 1979.** Centers for
      1975-   Disease Control. 1980. 89p. Occasionally on microfiche. Annual.

Widespread interest in smoking and health legislation on the part of both public and private agencies prompted the preparation of this report. Nationwide, reported legislation is categorized into seven topics: (1) limitations on smoking; (2) commerce; (3) smoking and schools; (4) advertising; (5) sales to or use by minors; (6) insurance; and (7) other legislation that cannot be included appropriately in the other categories. The 346 bills and 39 laws reported for 1979 are presented in the following four tables. Table 1 provides a summary of legislation introduced and passed in each category. Table 2 lists the laws passed in each category by state. Table 3 furnishes a state-by-state breakdown of bills introduced and passed and any resolutions introduced and adopted. Table 4 provides a capsule summary of laws passed pertaining to smoking and health that have been reported in the state legislation on smoking and health reports for 1975 through 1979.

491   HE20.7302   **Youth Camp. Compendium of State Laws and Regulations.**
      C73   Centers for Disease Control. 1979. 493p.

10—Laws and Regulations / 147

This compendium is based upon those laws and regulations applicable to youth camp operations provided by state agencies. All legislation specific to youth camp licensing and regulation is included. The definitions of camping identified by law or regulation may be found in the section concerning applicability. The compendium is organized into ten major categories and seventy operational areas or subcategories. Nine subcategories are further divided, including Personnel; Program Safety; Personal Health, First Aid, and Medical Services; Site and Facilities; Sanitation; Food Service; Transportation; Primitive Camping and Out-of-Camp Trips; and Day Camping and Travel Camps. Within each area the laws and regulations are presented by states alphabetically. Also included in the volume are a listing of present liaison officers by state, with addresses and telephone numbers; specific statutory and regulatory sources utilized for each state; and an index of states with page citations to laws or regulations for each state.

492   HH10.2   **Statutory Land Use Control Enabling Authority in the Fifty**
      St2   **States. Special Reference to Flood Hazard Regulatory Authority.** Federal Insurance Administration. 1976. 304p.

In this report are summaries and analyses of statutes authorizing local units of government and state agencies to adopt zoning regulations, subdivision controls, building codes, and special flood hazard regulations. Emphasis throughout is upon land-use control legislation authorizing regulation of flood-prone areas. The report also examines case law interpreting the general scope of enabling authority and lists and annotates flood plain regulation cases. The report begins in part 1 with a discussion of selected issues and conclusions pertaining to the scope of statutory enabling authority, including a summary of statutory approaches and case law interpretation from the fifty states. Part 2 contains summaries of enabling acts authorizing local units of government or state agencies to adopt flood plain regulations. Selected examples of enabling authority are also included. Part 3 includes an annotated, state-by-state list of flood-related land-use control cases and attorney general opinions. Part 4 summarizes principal land use control powers, state by state. Four pages are devoted to each state. A one-page narrative summary begins each state discussion, followed by individual charts for zoning, subdivision control, and building code enabling powers.

493   I49.2   **Selected List of Federal Laws and Treaties Relating to Sport**
      L44   **Fish and Wildlife.** Rev. ed., January 1979. Fish and Wildlife Service. 1980. 22p. Irregular.

The purpose of this leaflet is to provide a ready reference to the authorities most commonly associated with conservation of fish, wildlife, and plants, most of which provide direction for the work of the U.S. Fish and Wildlife Service. However, it is not a complete listing of all conservation-related acts or of all laws governing the work of the service. The laws and treaties with important amendments noted are arranged alphabetically by popular name, except that some statutes have been grouped together in the alphabetical listing under the following headings: Fish and Wildlife Conservation at Federal Reclamation Projects; Fish and Wildlife Conservation at Federal Water Resource Development Projects of the Corps of Engineers; National Fish Hatchery Acts; National Wildlife Refuge Acts; National Wild and Scenic Rivers System Acts; and National Wilderness Preservation System Acts. Cross-references are used.

494 J26.2   **Privacy and Security of Criminal History Information. Com-**
         P93   **pendium of State Legislation.** National Criminal Justice Information and Statistics Service. 1978. 858p. Occasionally on microfiche. Irregular with supplements.

In 1975, the Office of General Counsel of the Law Enforcement Assistance Administration (LEAA) published the initial collection of available state privacy legislation, entitled *Compendium of State Laws Governing the Privacy and Security of Criminal Justice Information.* Supplements for 1979 and 1981 update and refine the previous editions. The purpose of this document is to gather current state legislation dealing with the topic in the hope that it may be of use to those who are reviewing or developing a legislative program. This compendium is generally limited to state legislation, though occasionally state agency regulations or executive orders governing state agencies are included when they implement or are in lieu of legislation. The legislation has been organized by state alphabetically. Also included are two tables: a list of the categories utilized to classify the legislation and a description of definitions; and an analysis and discussion of the comparative results. Table 1 contains a detailed matrix summarizing the results of this survey, with references keyed to specific sections of state legislation. Table 2 is a matrix comparing results of the current survey with results of a similar survey conducted earlier.

495 L1.2   **Summary of Public Sector Labor Relations Policies—Statutes,**
         L11-33   **Attorney Generals' Opinions and Selected Court Decisions.**
         1971-   Labor-Management Services Administration. 1981. 69p. Irregular.

In response to the burgeoning organizing and collective bargaining activity at the state and local government levels, and in the absence of federal authority in this area, a large number of states have created a broad variety of public policies to deal with the relationship between labor and management. At the present time, thirty-nine states, the District of Columbia, and the Virgin Islands have statutes or executive orders that provide legal frameworks for collective bargaining covering some of their employees. Of these, twenty-four states, the District of Columbia, and the Virgin Islands have comprehensive statutes covering all public employees; eleven states have comprehensive legislation limited to specific groups of employees; and four states provide limited collective bargaining rights to some or all of their employees. This summary is a compilation of those existing statutes, executive orders, personnel policies, court decisions, and attorney general opinions. It is intended to provide a resource guide for researchers, practitioners, and others conducting more specific and detailed research. Arranged alphabetically by state, the summary is segmented into topical categories. A "selected" index deals with those subjects most frequently compared and relevant to the needs of labor relations practitioners and researchers. Before 1976 this publication was entitled *Summary of State Policy Regulations for Public Sector Labor Relations.*

496 L37.202   **Unemployment Insurance: State Laws and Experience.**
         St2   Employment and Training Administration. 1978. 50p.

This publication furnishes a graphic presentation of statutory provisions of state unemployment insurance laws and some of the pertinent experience under those provisions. It includes information on the major aspects of the unemployment insurance program, such as coverage, qualifying requirements, benefit amount, benefit

10—Laws and Regulations / 149

duration, disqualifications, and tax rates and reserves. The information is portrayed in the form of maps, presenting data for all fifty states, the District of Columbia, and Puerto Rico. A map gives the clearest and most direct representation of the type of data shown here, especially as an aid in making comparisons. In addition, some text has been included to help explain and clarify the general area of the program portrayed by each map, without attempting to interpret the data presented.

497 S1.2 **The Global Legal Framework for Narcotics and Prohibitive**
       N16-2 **Substances.** State Department. 1979. v.p.

In July of 1978, the Bureau of International Narcotics Matters (INM) in the Department of State solicited a broad range of information on narcotics and prohibitive substances from all American embassies. In 1979, after a follow-up request, a database was compiled of 153 countries, of which 80 countries (52.25 percent) have partially complete information and 29 countries (19 percent) have no information at all as of June 15, 1979. The laws are summarized in data display charts that are arranged alphabetically by country. The data display charts are in five sections covering cannabis and its derivatives, coca leaf and its derivatives, opium poppy and its derivatives, other prohibitive substances, and criminal procedures. For each of the four substance display charts per country, there is a detailed break-down of four categories of offenses and their punishments: possession, trafficking, cultivation and production, and financial. The criminal procedures display chart for each country relates general functionings of the arrest, trial, and detention processes currently operating in that country.

498 T70.5 **State Laws and Published Ordinances: Firearms.** Alcohol,
       F51-2   Tobacco, and Firearms Bureau. 1981. 207p. Occasionally on
       1980-   Microfiche. Annual.

Compiled in this volume are municipal ordinances as required by law to inform the consumers of local requirements that apply to firearms transactions at the place of sale, delivery, or other disposition. In most instances, this publication includes only those municipal provisions relevant to enforcement of the Gun Control Act of 1968. Also included are state firearms laws. The laws are arranged alphabetically by state, and by municipality within states. Municipal ordinances and state law provisions that share identical language have been cross-referenced.

499 TD8.2   **Traffic Laws Annotated, 1979.** Compiled by the National
       T67-11 Committee on Uniform Traffic Laws and Ordinances.
       1979-   National Highway Traffic Safety Administration. 1981. 374p.
               Occasionally on microfiche. Irregular with supplements.

Reviewed in this volume are state laws and regulations on rules of the road, scope of traffic ordinances, uniform traffic-control devices, accidents and accident reports, and certain definitions in the context of the *Uniform Vehicle Code* provisions covering those subjects. Its format is similar to that generally used in an annotated edition of a book of law: the text of each of the code's sections (or subsections) is reprinted in full and supplemented by historical note, a statutory annotation, and citations. Occasionally, a prefatory note has been added to present additional information or references to other materials. Included is a section in which words and phrases are defined, and the state laws are arranged by chapters as in the *Uniform Vehicle Code*. The publication is kept current by means of "pocket" supplements, published annually.

150 / 10—Laws and Regulations

500   TD8.5-3   **Driver Licensing Laws Annotated. 1980.** National Highway
         1978-   Traffic Safety Administration. July 1982. 245p. Basic volume
                          plus annual supplements.

In this volume we find reviews of state laws and regulations dealing with driver licensing, including relevant definitions, in the context of *Uniform Vehicle Code* provisions covering those subjects. It follows the organization and numbering system of the code. Its format is similar to that generally used in an annotated edition of a book of law, with the text of each code section (or subsection) reprinted in full and supplemented by historical note, a statutory annotation, and citations. Annotations have also been provided for some common state driver licensing provisions that are not found in the Uniform Vehicle Code. The sections pertain to definitions of words and phrases; issuance of licenses, expiration and renewal; cancellation, suspension, or revocation of licenses; violation of license provisions; and commercial driver training schools.

501   Y3.A11-2   **State Initiatives on Alcohol Fuels. A State-by-State Compen-**
         St2   **dium of Laws, Regulations, and Other Activities Involving**
                          Alcohol Fuels. National Alcohol Fuels Commission. 1980.
                          99p.

State governments have been very active in encouraging the development of an alcohol fuels industry, particularly evident in state tax incentives. By July 1980, twenty-five states had exempted alcohol fuels from all or part of their state excise taxes, compared to only eight states with such legislation in June 1979. In addition, ten states have exempted alcohol fuels from state sales, use, or gross receipts taxes. Seven states have exempted alcohol fuel production facilities from all or part of their state property taxes, and nine states have exempted alcohol fuel producers from all or part of their state income taxes. This publication describes, on a state-by-state basis, state alcohol fuels legislation (enacted and proposed) and regulations, as well as other significant state activity involving alcohol fuels. In all, forty-five states have enacted a total of 101 separate pieces of alcohol fuels legislation as of July 1980. State regulations affecting alcohol fuel include state permit requirements for gasoline and gasohol. The section for each state entitled "Other Important Alcohol Fuels Activity" includes major fleet tests; colleges and universities offering alcohol fuels workshops, seminars, and courses; and important research and development projects. Two maps show the states that have enacted alcohol fuels legislation and states that have enacted tax incentives. Five appendixes contain (1) a summary of state tax exemptions; (2) restrictions on state tax incentives; (3) a summary of state permit regulations; (4) state volatility specifications; and (5) a schedule of state legislative sessions.

502   Y4.V64-4   **State Veterans' Laws. Digests of State Laws Regarding Rights,**
         L44   **Benefits, and Privileges of Veterans and Their Dependents.**
         1975-   **Revised to December 31, 1978.** Senate Committee on Veterans
                          Affairs. 1979. 315p. Committee Print no. 2. Irregular.

This report is a compilation of information on the laws regarding veterans' benefits of the several states and the District of Columbia. This report contains, in section A, an analysis of existing state legislation affecting veterans benefits and includes enactments of the 1978 sessions of the state legislatures. Section B lists those states that have authorized the payment of a bonus to veterans of World War II, the Korean Conflict, or the Vietnam era. Section C indicates the amounts spent by various states for veterans' benefits in calendar years 1975 through 1977. The state laws are arranged alphabetically by state in a table format, providing the type of law, a resumé, and the statute or code citation.

11
Programs, Activities, Facilities, and Services

This chapter covers a wide area of concerns. It annotates directories offering information about programs, activities, facilities, and services of federal government departments and agencies, the exact nature of which is indicated by the titles (i.e., *Directory of Rural Health Care Programs*).

503	A1.2 D62 1980-	**Directory of Services.** Agriculture Department. 1980. 29p. Irregular.

A primary purpose of the Office of Operations and Finance is to provide management services for the Secretary of Agriculture, the general offices of the department, the offices and agencies reporting to the Office of the Assistant Secretary for Administration and, by agreement, other offices or agencies of the department. This directory of services provides the following: (1) an alphabetical grouping of services provided by the Office of Operations and Finance, indicating services, where to contact (branch, office, division, etc.), building, room number, and telephone number; (2) within the alphabetical grouping, a set of relevant services provided by entities other than Operations and Finance; and (3) a detailed alphabetical index.

504	A13.65-2 R31	**Research Program Directory.** Intermountain Forest and Range Experiment Station. Forest Service. 1981. 11p. Irregular.

As an aid to technology, this directory provides research users and others with information about current research programs at the Intermountain Station. The Intermountain Station's research program is coordinated with forestry and range organizations in western universities, state agricultural experiment stations, private companies, and other federal and state agencies. The directory contains the following: a map indicating the states and areas of the Intermountain Region (Idaho, Montana, Nevada, and Utah); addresses, personnel, and telephone numbers of the station headquarters; current investigations and scientific staff, by state, providing titles of studies, project leaders, area, telephone numbers, and purpose of the studies; an alphabetical name index of researchers; a list of research locations; and mailing addresses for each state.

11 – *Programs, Activities, Facilities, and Services* / 153

505   A107.2   **Services Available through the U.S. Department of Agriculture.** Rev. ed. Governmental and Public Affairs Office. 1980. 39p. Irregular.
        Se8

The U.S. Department of Agriculture (USDA) conducts the programs in this directory in cooperation with state and local governments to provide more efficient, direct, and appropriate service benefits to the public. Some cooperative programs involve grants. Others provide only an exchange of information. This directory lists services and programs of the USDA, explaining what these services and programs do and where and how to obain them. The directory is divided into seven areas of services: farms, forests, markets, communities, consumers, business and industry, and resources. The programs are named providing purpose, how the USDA can help, who may apply, and where to apply.

506   C1.8-3   **Guide to Federal Assistance Programs for Minority Business Development.** Minority Business Development Agency. 1980. 95p. Annual.
        M66-3
        1977-

This edition of the guide pulls together in one convenient reference book a list of federal programs that furnish capital, management assistance, and opportunities to minority business; and those general-purpose federal programs that may be of particular help to minority entrepreneurs. Any minority business or group can refer to this publication for information regarding the general terms of a program and whom to contact locally. This guide has six sections. The programs of the Minority Business Development Agency are listed first, followed by a section on programs offering business contract opportunities. The third section covers programs involving financial assistance. That section is followed by coverage of management assistance and information services programs. Specialized programs are described in section 5. Finally, an appendix lists addresses of the regional federal offices and various minority business offices. The individual programs in each section are listed in the table of contents. A program may cover more than one function, such as contract opportunities and management assistance. In that case, the program is placed in the guide to reflect its primary capability to assist minority business. Each listing provides name of program; agency; type of assistance; description; eligibility; how to apply; further information; and whom to contact.

507   C1.8-3   **A Small Business Guide. A Directory of Federal Government Business Assistance Programs for Women Business Owners.** Commerce Department. 1980. 71p.
        Sm1

This handbook is a joint publication of the Economic Development Administration (EDA), the U.S. Department of Commerce, and the Small Business Administration (SBA). It is designed to help small business owners, particularly women owners, have a better understanding of entrepreneurship and easier access to federal business assistance. While the majority of programs discussed are those of the SBA and the Department of Commerce, other member agencies of the Interagency Committee on Women's Business Enterprise (IACWBE) have also contributed material for this guide. The chapters of this directory are organized in terms of normal business problem areas. The focus of almost all of the chapters is the availability of government assistance directed toward overcoming these problems. While the assistance programs and services discussed are, in most cases, available to all small businesses, there are certain programs that are limited to disadvantaged firms or those located in economically depressed areas of the country. In those instances, the eligibility criteria are enumerated. Following certain chapters, a list of relevant publications is provided for those who want to acquire more specific information on the chapter topic. The five chapter topics are (1) organizing a business, (2) credit and capital formation, (3) management training and technical assistance, (4) federal loans and grant programs, and (5) the government market. The appendixes consist of listings of regional, district, and local field offices for many of the major departments and agencies. For easy reference, a table depicting the ten federal regions and the states that comprise them is provided at the beginning of this section. Finally, in addition to a general index, there is a separate program index, as well as an office/agency index provided in order to help the reader find information more quickly.

508   C1.8-3   **The Guide to the U.S. Department of Commerce for Women**
         W84-2   **Business Owners.** *See* entry 247.

509   C1.56   **Directory of Private Programs Assisting Minority Business.**
         1969   Minority Business Enterprise Office. 1970. 364p. Annual.

The Office of Minority Business Enterprise (OMBE) has published this title to help the various groups or individuals with whom it works to engage or participate in profitable business enterprises. It identifies the types of private assistance available for minority business enterprises and provides information concerning activities currently underway. The book also covers specialized federal government and existing municipally sponsored programs. The directory is divided into five sections. The first section lists, alphabetically by city, private minority business programs in fifty-nine cities. Each entry provides the program's name, address, telephone number, director, purpose, activities, and types of assistance to recipients. The second section lists, alphabetically by city, municipal programs in fifteen cities. Sections 3 and 4 list in alphabetical order national organizations and national technical and management assistance programs. The fifth section is an alphabetical arrangement of minority-owned financial institutions (savings and loan associations and banks) providing addresses, telephone numbers, and chief executive officer(s). Also included in the directory is an alphabetical index of organizations and an appendix listing minority business directories.

510   C46.2   **Directory of Economic Development Districts and Area**
         Ec7-4   **Grantees.** *See* entry 007.

511   CS1.2   **Directory of Federal Occupational Health Facilities.** Civil
         Oc1   Service Commission. 1977. v.p.

Occupational health programs are established by federal agencies to deal constructively with the physical and mental well-being of their employees. Public Law 79-658 (5 U.S.C. 7901) was enacted in 1946 to authorize heads of departments and agencies to provide occupational (or preventive) health services to federal employees. The most effective method for delivery of health services has proven to be an on-site health unit. The units are under the direction of licensed physicians with services provided by registered professional nurses. The directory is a compilation of 967 such health units in operation across the country as of January 1, 1977. The facilities are listed in zip code sequence. Data for each entry include the name, address, city, and state of the facility; the operator of the facility; the number of civilian employees served; the services available (therapeutic, screening examinations, advisory services, health guidance, and counseling); and the approximate annual per-employee cost of operation. Also included in the directory is a bibliography of publications that could prove useful to federal agency officials contemplating the establishment of occupational health facilities.

512 D301.35 no. 213-2 **Educational Opportunities on Air Force Bases.** Air Force Department. 1980. v.p. AF pamphlet no. 213-2. Irregular.

This publication provides information on the broad range of activities of the Educational Services Program of the United States Air Force. It is a directory of educational opportunities that are offered on or near Air Force installations and includes the institutions that offer them. Program opportunities contained in this publication will assist education service officers and staff members in advising Air Force personnel and their dependents. The programs are covered in ten chapters arranged in alphabetical order by bases within each Air Force unit (Air Force Logistics Command, Air Force Systems Command, and so forth). The name of the program, the institution where it is provided, accrediting agencies, credentials issued, and major areas offered are contained in each entry. Also included are the mailing addresses and education services officers of each installation. Two indexes list alphabetically by state the program areas in the continental United States and overseas.

513 E1.19 no. 0114 **Directory of Contractors Supported by Division of Nuclear Physics.** Energy Department. 1981. 133p. DOE/ER series, no. 0114. Irregular.

Presented in this publication is a list of the institutions (colleges and universities) and the Department of Energy (DOE) laboratories that have received grant monies from DOE and are providing programs of research. The institutions are arranged alphabetically by name. Each institution entry contains the name of the institution, principal investigator, contract number, title of the research project, address, telephone number, and personnel (faculty, postdoctorals, and graduate students). The laboratory entries contain the following: name, address, DOE division, telephone number(s), and personnel (permanent staff, postdoctorals and visitors, graduate students).

514 E1.26 no. 0206 **"Futures" for Energy Cooperatives.** Energy Department. 1981. 92p. DOE/CS series, no. 0206. Irregular.

The Office of Conservation and Solar Energy (CS) in the Department of Energy (DOE) is interested in energy cooperatives as part of its commercialization efforts. Co-ops, with community-scale application of conservation energy gains and solar technologies, will help achieve national renewable energy goals. This booklet has been produced as a result of a conference sponsored by CS with the National Consumer Cooperative Bank (NCCB), which focused on the need for technical assistance and funding. It contains four sections: a listing of federal agencies and programs with potential funding for community-scale cooperatives using conservation measures and solar technologies; profiles of existing community energy cooperatives describing their location, history, membership, services, sources of finance, and technical assistance; a condensed summary from the recent conference on energy cooperatives featuring notes on co-op members' experiences, problems, and opportunities; and a listing of contacts for additional information, including addresses and telephone numbers of U.S. Department of Energy regional offices, regional appropriate technology representatives, hot lines,

National Consumer Cooperative Bank regional offices, nonfederal sources of information, and state energy offices.

515 E1.28 **National Solar Energy Education Directory.** *See* entry 195.
SERI/SP
751-1049

516 E2.12 **Recreational Opportunities at Hydroelectric Projects Licensed by the Federal Energy Regulatory Commission, 1978.** Federal Energy Regulatory Commission. 1979. 70p. DOE/FERC series, no. 0025. Irregular.
no. 0025
1978-

Many of the hydroelectric projects licensed by the Federal Energy Regulatory Commission provide facilities for various recreational activities, such as swimming, fishing, and hunting. Along with the recreational activities such as those indicated above, several projects offer historical sites, natural history museums, guided tours of powerhouses, and other facilities for the enjoyment of the public. Many projects have visitor centers that offer educational facilities and information relating to the electric power industry as well as information describing specific recreational opportunities available at the project. In addition to the general information given about the recreational opportunities, each project is listed separately with a map of the area plus the following information: project name, location of the nearest town with a population of over twenty-five hundred, name of the company that licensed the project, and a listing of the project recreation facilities and activities. Also included is an alphabetical list of licensees of projects shown in this publication, giving their addresses. These licensees will supply additional information on individual projects. Further information, recreation maps, and other materials about recreational opportunities at or adjacent to FERC-licensed projects may also be obtained by contacting state and local government agencies.

517 ED1.2 **Educational Technology Programs.** Education Department. 1980. 9p.
Ed8-2

The educational technology programs of the Department of Education support television and radio programming, the use of technology in basic skills instruction, and demonstrations of telecommunications technology. These programs are administered by the Division of Educational Technology (DET) within the Office of Libraries and Learning Technologies of the Office of Educational Research and Improvement. Each entry in this booklet describes the program and its objectives, the name and brief descriptions of the funded projects, how to apply, and the address and telephone number of whom to contact for further information.

518 ED1.2 **International Education Programs of the U.S. Government. An Inventory.** Compiled by Helen R. Wiprud, Federal Interagency Committee on Education. Education Department. 1981. 401p.
Ed8-4

This publication makes available a comprehensive inventory of U.S. government programs concerned with improving international understanding and/or cooperation—or "international education," to use the inclusive term. It provides summary information on 181 programs in twenty-eight federal departments and agencies, essentially as of mid-1979. Included are a brief description of what occurs in each program and information concerning its basic characteristics, such as the agency or department administratively responsible, participants and beneficiaries, legislative authority, funding, countries involved, and how the program administrators may be contacted. Programs are listed by their administering agencies. An "agency page" sets the stage by giving the purpose and scope of the agency's activities in general, and then a summary of the agency's international education activities, covering both ad hoc activities and services and specific programs. The specific programs are listed by number. The overall pattern of federal involvement is best seen in the considerably expanded and improved appendixes, where the governmentwide data from the listed programs are summarized in a variety of ways. Appendix A shows the number of beneficiaries, direction of international travel, and program location of each program by agency. Appendix B shows which programs served which international education purposes or functions. Appendix C lists forty-five pieces of legislation authorizing the various programs, beginning with an act concerning the Library of Congress's law department in 1832 and extending to the recent Education Amendments of 1978. Appendix D indicates that 143 of the 181 programs, or 79 percent, were funded wholly or in part by the administering agencies themselves. Appendix E, which lists programs by country or region, shows the extent of world coverage that federal international education programs have achieved.

519 ED1.2   **Higher Education and the Handicapped. Resource Directory.**
H53   Education Department. 1981. 10p.

This resource directory has been designed to help colleges and universities develop campuswide programs that will encourage institutions to provide equal access to postsecondary education for all qualified students and employees, regardless of handicap. What is called for is the development of general plans and specific strategies for eliminating all types of discrimination that have previously occurred on the basis of handicap. In addition to removing physical barriers to program accessibility, colleges and universities now have a responsibility to eliminate attitudinal barriers similar to those historically confronted by women and minorities. Each of the resources mentioned provides brief descriptions and purposes, telephone numbers, addresses, and price of the publication mentioned.

520 ED1.2   **Library Programs.** Education Department. 1980. 16p.
L61

The Division of Library Programs manages programs designed to develop, improve, and support public library services, public library construction, interlibrary cooperative services, and state institutionalized services; to support the acquisition of elementary and secondary school library resources and instructional equipment; to assist in training persons for library careers; to support research and demonstration in library and information sciences; to assist institutions in higher education and other nonprofit agencies in the acquisition of library materials; and to assist major research libraries in maintaining and strengthening their collections and in making their holdings available to other libraries and users. Entries include the name of the program and its objectives, representative projects, application procedures, and addresses and telephone number for obtaining further information.

158 / 11—Programs, Activities, Facilities, and Services

521   ED1.2   **Selected List of Postsecondary Education Opportunities for Minorities and Women. 1981.** Compiled by Linda Byrd Johnson and Carol J. Smith. Education Department. 1981. 128p. Annual.
P84
1977-

The number of minorities and women entering institutions of higher education has increased significantly over the past decades. Despite the changes in student financial aid programs administered by the federal government and the rising costs of higher education, there are strong indications that the truly needy student will be able to obtain the financial aid needed to pursue a college degree or further career goals if he/she explores all available resources. One of the most important things to remember is that the federal government is only one of several sources that provides financial aid to students. Such opportunities are also provided by private and public organizations/associations as well as by state governments. Although this brochure is designed primarily for minorities and women, many of the listed opportunities are open to all students. Specific information is provided on loans, scholarships, and fellowship opportunities. Also provided is general information on how and where to seek out assistance to prepare oneself to pursue education and career goals. Addresses of the offices that administer the programs are provided to help readers obtain additional information. Selected opportunities in fields in which minorities and women are underrepresented (engineering, science, and international areas) are listed even though they are not expressly for these population groups. Detailed information on the different financial assistance programs administered by the U.S. Education Department is provided in a separate section at the end of the brochure. The opportunities are arranged by selected fields of study in alphabetical order.

522   ED1.8   **Resource Guide—Architectural Barriers Removal.** *See* entry 449.
Ar2

523   ED1.8   **Five Federal Financial Aid Programs, 1981-82. A Student Consumer's Guide.** Education Department. 1981. 16p.
F49

This booklet presents an up-to-date, detailed description of the five student financial aid programs offered by the U.S. Department of Education. These five programs are Basic Educational Opportunity Grants (BEOGs); Supplemental Educational Opportunity Grants (SEOGs); College Work-Study (CW-S); National Direct Student Loans (NDSLs); and Guaranteed Student Loans (GSLs). Each entry contains information on what the program is, how to apply, how much money can be obtained, where to apply, eligibility, deadlines, addresses, and so forth. In addition, general information is given on eligibility and need and student consumer rights and responsibilities. Also included in the booklet are other sources of information on the Guaranteed Student Loan Program, arranged alphabetically by state, and a glossary of important terms.

524   ED1.8   **Guide to Federal Funding in Career Education, Education and Work and Vocational Education.** By the Coordinating Committee on Research in Vocational Education. Education Department. 1980. 37p.
F96

The Coordinating Committee designed this brochure to inform prospective grantees and contractors of the various kinds of federal funding available to them for research, development, and demonstration projects in vocational education, career education,

11 – Programs, Activities, Facilities, and Services / 159

and education and work. Divided into several chapters, chapter 2 outlines the administrative echelons within the U.S. Department of Education. Succeeding chapters outline the work of those agencies within the U.S. Department of Education that are primarily concerned with funding programs and projects in vocational education, career education, and education and work. Addresses, telephone numbers, and contacts are provided. Also included is a list of the federal resources (publications) with addresses and costs.

525   ED1.8   **Resource Guide. Rehabilitation Engineering and Product Information.** *See* entry 450.
       R26

526   ED1.8   **Resource Guide: Recreation and Leisure for Handicapped Individuals.** *See* entry 050.
       R26-2

527   ED1.29   **Catalog of Federal Education Assistance Programs – 1980. An Indexed Guide to the Federal Government Programs Offering Educational Benefits to the American People.** By Renee B. Jasper. Education Department. 1980. 718p. Biennial.
       1976-

Presented in this catalog are brief descriptions of, and extensive indexes to, federal programs that provide educational benefits to the American public. It includes programs administered by the U.S. Department of Education as well as programs administered by other federal agencies in support of educational services, professional training, or library services available to the general public. The catalog includes various programs, activities, and services that can be requested or applied for by a state or states; territorial possession; country; city; other political subdivision, grouping, or instrumentality thereof; any domestic profit or nonprofit corporation; and institutions, or individuals, other than agencies of the federal government. The program descriptions portion of the catalog contains descriptions of the federal domestic assistance programs related to education. It is arranged in program number sequence, assigned in blocks by agency. Each program is described in terms of the specific type of assistance provided, the purpose for which it is available, who can apply for it, and where to apply. The federal offices to contact for additional information on each program are identified. The catalog provides six indexes to help users identify federal programs that provide the type of assistance they are seeking. Each program is given on a program description page and is identified by a unique number (e.g., 13.430). The indexes include (1) an authorization index, which cites assistance programs according to the name of the act that authorizes each program; (2) a public law index, listing assistance programs according to the public law that authorizes the program; (3) a U.S. Code index, which lists assistance programs according to the U.S. Code citation of the act that authorizes the program; (4) a general index of key words and phrases from selected portions of each assistance program description (key-word context), with the indexed words or phrases shown alphabetically; (5) a beneficiary index, which lists under special descriptions all those beneficiaries eligible for assistance programs; and (6) a program name index, arranged alphabetically by name (key-word out-of-context). Appendixes or programs referred to but not included in this catalog may be found in the *Catalog of Federal Domestic Assistance* (*CFDA*), from which the program information and numbers were drawn (see entry 601).

528   ED1.34   **Federal Assistance for Programs Serving the Handicapped, 1980.** Handicapped Individuals Office. 1981. 242p. Irregular.
       1979-

160 / 11 – Programs, Activities, Facilities, and Services

Information on the majority of programs listed in this directory was excerpted from the 1980 *Catalog of Federal Domestic Assistance (CFDA)* (see entry 601). Most of the listed programs provide assistance to handicapped persons or those who work with or for them. Some programs serve a more diverse segment of the population, but are mandated to spend a certain percentage of funds for serving the handicapped. Programs are not presented in agency order, but according to four categories: formula grants to states, project grants, direct payments, and nonfinancial assistance. An index of the federal departments and agencies represented in the directory, a subject index, and an index on applicant eligibility are provided. A selection of the most important state agencies serving the handicapped has been included, with addresses and telephone numbers. There is also a listing of resources for funding information and a small selection of bibliographic references to the numerous books in the funding field. Items indicated for each program are as follows: program description, uses and restrictions, types of assistance, formula and matching grants, application procedures, appropriations, applicant eligibility, beneficiary eligibility, program accomplishments, examples of funded projects, enabling legislation, and information contact(s).

529   EP1.23-5   **Directory of EPA, State and Local Environmental Quality Monitoring and Assessment Activities.** By John W. Scotton, et al. Environmental Protection Agency. 1974. 384p. Irregular.
          600/4-75-001

This directory presents descriptions of federal environmental quality monitoring or assessment programs within the EPA, juxtaposed with corresponding, though not necessarily administratively related, monitoring activities being undertaken at the national, state, and local levels. The directory may be used as a guide for contacting appropriate personnel at the federal, regional, state, or local levels who deal with monitoring the environment. In addition, it may be used as a reference source for statistics on, and descriptions of, monitoring efforts on a state-by-state basis. The directory is divided into seven sections covering air, water quality, interstate water carrier supplies, pesticides, radiation, noise, and solid waste. Each section begins with a description of the administration and the purpose of the office within the EPA charged with the responsibility of data collection or assessment in each of the seven areas. Each such description is followed by a statistical summary or profile of monitoring activities taking place at the national, state, and local levels.

530   HE1.2   **Federal Programs that Relate to Children.** Health, Education, and Welfare Department. 1979. 125p.
          C43-5

Identified with this report is the general nature and scope of ongoing U.S. federal government activities in 1979 that affect children. It does not intend to provide complete information on all government programs or projects, or on all government agencies whose programs affect children. Generally, from each agency you will find a brief description of its program; information on its authorizing legislation, its appropriations, and any recent program modifications; and names of any programs that have been authorized, but not funded. The agencies are arranged alphabetically from Agency on International Development to the Veterans Administration. Each entry provides the agency's address, telephone number, and agency representative, as well as names of the programs, with a brief summary and appropriations.

531   HE1.2   **A Training and Resource Directory for Teachers Serving Handicapped Students, K-12.** *See* entry 457.
          H19-5

11—Programs, Activities, Facilities, and Services / 161

532 HE1.2   **Directory of State and Local Resources for the Mentally**
     M52-16   **Retarded.** *See* entry 323.

533 HE1.2   **Directory of Rural Health Care Programs, 1979.** Health, Edu-
     R88-2   cation, and Welfare Department. 1980. 499p.

Identified and described in this directory are innovative organizations providing primary health care services in rural America. Organizations eligible for inclusion in the survey and directory were those located in rural areas or serving rural populations (for example, migrants) and offering some primary care services, such as internal medicine, family or general practice, pediatrics, or obstetrics/gynecology. Programs offering only mental health, dental, or other specialized medical services were not included. The survey was further limited to organizations: hospitals, clinics, corporations, projects, programs, centers, and the like. The directory is organized alphabetically by state and, within state, by city and place. The following information is included for each listing: program name, address, and telephone number; county in which the program is located; program contact person; year in which services were first offered by the program at any of its sites; type of program owner (private-for-profit, public, or private-nonprofit); presence or absence of a community board; total number of full-time-equivalent staff employed during the reporting year; total number of full-time physicians on staff during the reporting year; service area population; estimated unduplicated count of the number of persons using the program's services at least once during the reporting year; estimated number of encounters (face-to-face contacts between patients and health care providers) during the reporting year; type of fee structure; sources of current or past financial or personnel support; and total number of program delivery sites, with names, addresses, and telephone numbers of principal, and up to three additional, sites.

534 HE1.214   **National Directory of Educational Programs in Gerontology.**
                See entry 203.

535 HE1.508   **Guide to Federal Consumer Services.** Consumer Affairs
     C76-2   Office. 1976. 39p. Irregular.
     1979-

Found in this guide are answers to questions such as: What are the federal government's benefits and services for consumers? Which federal department or agency can help me? How do I obtain service? This publication reflects the federal government's response to consumers' right to know. The guide is arranged alphabetically by department/agency, and each entry provides a brief statement about the agency, lists its functions for consumers (with contact persons and telephone numbers), and gives names, addresses, and telephone numbers to contact for service. A table of contents by subject is included. Also included is a list of helpful federal government publications (resources) and an alphabetical arrangement by state of Federal Information Centers, with telephone numbers.

536 HE3.49   **Social Security Programs throughout the World, 1979.** Social
     no. 54   Security Administration. 1980. 269p. Social Security Admin-
     1937-   istration research report no. 54. Biennial.

Provided in this publication is a perspective on the methods used by different countries in designing and applying income-maintenance measures; it is used extensively as background in drafting social security legislation. The report serves as a reference in responding to inquiries from Congress, other agencies of government, business firms, labor unions, and others. It has also been useful in making decisions pertaining to the benefit rights of foreign nationals covered under the U.S. program, in providing technical assistance and services to countries, and in connection with the work of international and regional organizations dealing with social security matters. Arranged alphabetically by country, the information on the national social security system of each country is presented here in the form of a two-page chart. These charts are organized identically and are divided into eight vertical columns with the same headings for all countries: dates of basic laws and types of programs; coverage; source of funds; qualifying conditions; cash benefits for insured workers; permanent disability and medical benefits for insured workers; survivor benefits and medical benefits for dependents; and administrative organization. The five horizontal columns correspond to the major social security branches: old age, invalidity, death; sickness and maternity; work injury; unemployment; and family allowances.

537 HE5.2 **Directory of Representative Work Education Programs,**
W59-2 **1972-73.** Edited by Steven M. Frankel, et al. Education Office.
1973- 1973. 328p. Irregular.

This volume, when used in conjunction with its indexes and its table of contents, should prove a valuable resource in identifying work education programs with particular features and in developing a better understanding of the wide breadth of program configurations operating in the work education field. The programs included in this directory are listed by state. The states appear in alphabetical order as indicated by the table of contents. Within each state, the programs are grouped by educational level with all secondary level programs appearing first, postsecondary programs next, and programs operating at varied educational levels appearing last. For each program, a synopsis of its characteristics, as supplied by program personnel, is included. The specific items of information included are as follows: school(s) in which the program operates; educational level of the program; primary purpose of the program; inclusion of job-related instruction as a component of the program; industrial setting in which the program is located; presence of students who are under the age of sixteen and are working for pay; availability of academic credit for the time spent at the job site; percentage of students completing the program during the 1971-72 school year who were placed in jobs in the occupational field in which they worked while in the program; number of students enrolled in the program for the 1972-73 school year and the percentages who are female, physically handicapped, and members of minority groups; occupational areas in which the students are working; reimbursed expenses paid to employers participating in the program; and private support. The two indexes list programs by industrial setting, and programs by primary purpose.

538 HE19.102 **Directory of Services for the Handicapped in California.** 4th
H19-2 ed. 6 vols. Edited by Joan K. Honeycutt, Ed.D., and Gail
v. 1-6 Honeycutt, California Regional Resource Center, University of Southern California, Los Angeles. Education Office. 1979. Irregular.

11 – *Programs, Activities, Facilities, and Services* / 163

These volumes comprise the fourth edition of the title *Guide to Assessment, Prescriptive and Related Services for the Handicapped in California*, first published in December 1974. This edition reflects major revisions in scope, content, and format, as well as the new title. In addition to all agencies listed in the 1977 guide, the combined six volumes of the directory include 730 additional agency listings for a total of approximately forty-two hundred entries. The six volumes correspond to the California Office of Special Education service regions: volume 1 covers Region A; volume 2, Region B; volume 3, Region C; volume 4, Regions D and G; volume 5, Region E; and volume 6, Region F. They are organized alphabetically by county, and within each county, the agencies are arranged alphabetically in terms of the category of service provided. The service categories are further divided into subcategories, and each entry provides the following information as well: client types, eligibility requirements, and agency name and address, with zip code and telephone numbers. A map of California is included, indicating service regions. Also included is a very thorough introduction providing a history of the general organization of the directory and a good explanation of how to use the directory, as well as definitions and abbreviations of the categories and subcategories of services and client types.

539 HE19.102 **Federal Programs for Libraries: A Directory.** Compiled by
 L61-6 Lawrence E. Leonard and Ann M. Erteschik. Education Office. 1978. 64p.

This directory provides information regarding nine federal library programs and seventy-two federal library-related programs. Program summaries included in sections 2 and 4 contain information found in the 1978 edition of the *Catalog of Federal Domestic Assistance* (see entry 601), American Library Association's *Federal Grants: Where in the Bureaucracy to Find Them* and its *ALA Washington Newsletter*, the *Educational Media Yearbook*, program summaries prepared by staff members of the Division of Library Programs (U.S. Office of Education), and a number of other sources. The directory provides a guide to sources of funding, but only a guide. It is not meant to be a complete program information source; instead it is only intended to lead libraries to possible funding sources for projects that are proposed to meet their assessed needs. Section 1 is the introduction. Section 2 contains an annotated listing of twenty existing directories and other current or recent publications relevant to library-related funding sources. A number of section 2 publications also include funding sources sponsored by the private sector. Section 3 lists nine federal programs that provide direct support for library projects. Programs are arranged alphabetically by the name of the authorizing act. Program descriptions include the *CFDA* number, authorizing legislation, purpose of the program, uses to which funds may be applied, applicant eligibility requirements, the type of grant, level of funding, range of grants, average grant, application/program information source, and, when available, application closing date. Library-related federal programs are arranged alphabetically by program title, and descriptions follow the format of section 2 entries. Section 5 is a bibliography of publications on the grants application process. Section 6 is an index to the programs included in sections 3 and 4. The programs are indexed by federal agency responsible for the program; applicant eligibility; whether state or local government, an organization, individual, or a combination; authorization (an alphabetical listing of authorizing acts for the programs); *CFDA* number; and subject. State library agencies are the contact source for many of the included federal programs. Section 7 is a listing of all state/territorial library agencies arranged alphabetically by state, providing chief executive officer, address, and telephone number.

11 — Programs, Activities, Facilities, and Services

540 HE19.302 **Colleges and Universities Offering Accredited Programs by**
C68 **Accreditation Field.** *See* entry 207.

541 HE19.337 **Directory of Postsecondary Schools with Occupational Programs.** *See* entry 210.

542 HE20.2 **Public Health Service Profiles of Financial Assistance Programs.** Public Health Service. 1980. 105p. Biennial.
F49
1977-

Because the job of the Public Health Service is to protect and advance the nation's health, it is involved directly or indirectly in almost everything that happens in the two hundred billion dollar enterprise called the American Health Care System. Government traditionally, however, has looked to the health professionals who provide care from day to day, to the citizens who receive that care, and to the wide range of health-related agencies and institutions, both public and private, for help in developing and operating the kind of programs that the public wants and needs. This partnership of public and private initiative has been strengthened and its work immeasurably advanced by the many financial assistance programs administered by the Public Health Service and carried out by its recipient-partners. Annually these programs distribute more than six billion dollars to help finance thousands of projects in all parts of the country. This booklet describes these programs, agency by agency, in a uniform and detailed fashion: the Alcohol, Drug Abuse and Mental Health Administration, Centers for Disease Control, Food and Drug Administration, Health Resources Administration, Health Services Administration, National Institutes of Health, the Office of the Assistant Secretary for Health along with its sub-bureaus and institutions, and others. Each entry provides the program name and accompanying project grants with reference to the *CFDA*/program service entry number, purpose, legal basis, eligibility, basis for awarding funds, special requirements, applications, and address of the issuing agency. Also contained in the volume is a list of Public Health Service's programs subject to health systems agency, statewide health and coordinating council and A-95 review; and addresses and telephone numbers of U.S. Department of Health and Human Services regional offices and Indian Health Service area offices.

543 HE20.2402 **Directory of Halfway Houses for the Mentally Ill and Alcoholics, 1972.** National Institute of Mental Health. 1973. 133p.
H13

Information is provided here on the availability of halfway houses for the mentally ill and alcoholics throughout the United States. It is intended for use by referring professionals, families of potential residents, or the individuals for whom this type of facility would be appropriate. For the purposes of this directory, halfway houses are facilities that provide residential services primarily to the emotionally disturbed, alcoholics, or both. The directory is arranged in alphabetical order by state. Within each state the facilities are grouped by primary resident group served (mentally ill persons or alcoholics), and by Salvation Army residential facilities. The facilities within the broad categories are listed in city order. Items contained are name, address, telephone number, year established, geographic area served, auspices, capacity, ages served, sex(es) served, maximum stay permitted, number of re-admissions permitted, and admission requirements. For later information see entry 226.

544 HE20.3002 **Animal Resources. A Research Resources Directory.** National
     An5-3   Institutes of Health. 1980. 56p. Annual.
     1977-

The Animal Resources Program of the National Institute of Health's Division of Research Resources meets the need of biomedical researchers for well-nourished, disease-free animals, and specialized animal research facilities. The purpose of this directory is to inform researchers of the resources provided by the Animal Resources Program and where to access them. Examples of the services and facilities available at resource sites are modern analytical laboratory equipment; surgery, X-ray, and clinical pathology units; improved animal cages and holding facilities; materials and techniques for diagnosis of animal diseases; and so forth. The directory entries are organized by type of resource, and within each type, resources are arranged alphabetically by title. Each entry includes the name of the resource; name, address, and telephone number of the principal investigator or resource director; research emphasis of the resource; and the services provided. A geographical index to these animal resources is provided at the end of the directory. It lists the resources alphabetically by state and by title within each state, and includes the name of the cities in which they are located and the page on which each resource entry appears.

545 HE20.3002 **Biotechnology Resources. A Research Resources Directory.**
     B52-4   Rev. ed. National Institutes of Health. 1980. 64p. Annual.
     1977-

The facilities described in this directory provide the national biomedical community with new technologies and procedures for the conduct of biomedical investigations. To guide prospective users in identifying potential sources of research assistance, the directory details the instruments, services, and current research applications at the individual resources. Because of time and space limitations, most of the facilities have eligibility requirements for investigators and their proposed research. Operating policies also vary in other respects. For additional information, a user contact person is identified for each resource. The directory entries are organized by type of resource, and all available resources are listed alphabetically by state and by title within each state. The index provides the names of the cities in which the facilities are located and the page number on which each entry appears. Names, addresses, and telephone numbers are given for the principal investigator and a contact person.

546 HE20.3002 **General Clinical Research Centers. A Research Resources**
     C61-11   **Directory.** Rev. ed. National Institutes of Health. 1979. 86p.
     1978-   Annual.

This directory outlines facilities and investigations at all seventy-four DRR-supported General Clinical Research centers. As a guide for researchers interested in clinical studies of human disorders, it includes major topics of investigation, names of program directors, special assays and equipment, and names of instructional guides and booklets. The clinical research centers appear alphabetically by state and, within each state, alphabetically by host institution. A geographical index is similarly arranged and also identifies the names of the cities in which the centers are located. Page numbers are indexed by the name of the host institution. Names, addresses, and telephone numbers are provided for program directors, associate directors, principal investigators, and contact persons.

166 / 11 – Programs, Activities, Facilities, and Services

547 HE20.3002 **Minority Biomedical Support Program. A Research Resources**
M66 **Directory.** Rev. ed. National Institutes of Health. 1979. 67p.
1977- Irregular.

The major thrust of the Minority Biomedical Support (MBS) Program is to develop minority student, faculty, and institutional involvement in biomedical research. Through its grants, the Minority Biomedical Research Support (MBRS) Program supports its projects, which are designed to strengthen the biomedical capabilities of minority institutions and to expand the involvement of minority faculty and students in biomedical research. This directory is a guide to MBRS-supported research projects and facilities throughout the country. The directory entries are arranged alphabetically by state and, within each state, alphabetically by name of the grantee institution. The name of the program director appears with the address of the institution. Adjoining columns show the names of the individual project investigators, the title of each research project, and the number of participating students. Some of the programs provide a list of special laboratory instruments and facilities that may be available on a limited basis to other MBS programs in the area or region. A geographic index, arranged alphabetically by state and institution within the state, is provided.

548 HE20.3002 **Federal Programs for Minorities, Women, and the Handi-**
M66-3 **capped.** Excerpted from the *Catalog of Federal Domestic Assistance.* National Institutes of Health. 1980. 45p.

The information in this brochure was excerpted from the 1980 *Catalog of Federal Domestic Assistance* (see entry 601). The brochure incorporates programs administered by several different federal agencies. The programs are arranged under three subject headings (Minorities and Women, American Indian, and Civil Rights), and, within each subject area, by the *CFDA* number. Each entry provides the following information: name of the federal program; name of the federal agency offering the program; authorization; objectives; types of assistance; uses and use restrictions; eligibility requirements; application and award process; assistance considerations; post-assistance requirements; financial information; program accomplishments; regulations, guidelines, and literature; information contacts; related programs; examples of funded projects; and criteria for selecting proposals. An appendix lists by subject field additional federally supported health-related programs. It provides names of offices, addresses, and telephone numbers for information.

549 HE20.3174 **National Cancer Institute Fact Book.** *See* entry 270.

550 HE20.3202 **Directory of National, Federal and Local Sickle Cell Disease**
Si1-10 **Programs.** Rev. ed. National Heart, Lung, and Blood Insti-
1978- tute. 1981. 39p. Irregular.

This resource contains the names, addresses, and telephone numbers of those agencies and organizations in communities throughout the United States that are concerned in some capacity with sickle cell disease. It is divided into seven sections. Section 1 contains a list of comprehensive sickle cell screening centers. Section 2 is a list of sickle cell screening and education clinics. Section 3 presents, by the ten U.S. regions, the sickle cell programs in national centers for family planning services. A list of Veterans Administration hospitals that have sickle cell screening and education programs are provided in section 4, organized alphabetically by place. Sickle cell programs in Job

11 – *Programs, Activities, Facilities, and Services* / *167*

Corps regions are provided in section 5. An alphabetical arrangement of state health departments is provided in section 6; and section 7 contains an alphabetical listing of public and private organizations.

551 HE20.5102 **Clinical Programs for Mentally Retarded Children.** 10th ed.
C61 Community Health Service Bureau. 1978. 43p. Irregular.
1962/66-

In general, the clinics listed in this booklet can be defined as outpatient medical facilities providing comprehensive evaluation, treatment, or follow-up services primarily to children believed to be, or diagnosed as, mentally retarded. Initially developed to facilitate the exchange of new ideas, approaches, and techniques among these special programs, the list has also been used as a partial directory of specialized clinical services for mentally retarded children. Each clinic is staffed by an interdisciplinary team headed by a physician who takes medical responsibility for all patients seen and is in attendance at regularly scheduled hours. The entries are arranged alphabetically by state, and each contains the following: name, address, and telephone number of the facility; clinic director; area served; ages accepted; name of sponsor; clinic hours; and satellite offices, if any.

552 HE20.5102 **Directory of Community Health Centers.** Community Health
D62-2 Services Bureau. 1978. v.p.

This directory lists Community Health Centers by the ten standard federal regions of the United States. Within each region, the centers are arranged by program grant number. Each entry contains the grant number, grantee's name, and address; project title and center's address; and name of the project director.

553 HE20.5102 **Directory of Family Planning Grantees and Clinics.** *See*
D62-3 entry 059.

554 HE20.5302 **Foundations That Provide Support for Human Services. A**
F82 **Selected List.** Indian Health Service. 1978. 45p.

Presented in this document is a reference source of selected private foundations that provide support for human resources and is a revision of, and addition to, a previous publication prepared and distributed in 1973 by the Phoenix area office of the Indian Health Service. This new document is for people who work with native American groups and for communities that wish to apply for foundation grants for projects in the areas of health education, community development, and social services. The foundations listed are not exclusively for native Americans, however. The foundations are listed alphabetically by state and alphabetically by name within each state. Each entry contains the name, address, and a brief statement of purpose. Two appendixes list the addresses and telephone numbers of Indian Health Service area office contacts regarding resource development and Indian Health Service regional office contacts regarding resource development.

555 HE20.6102 **A Directory of Programs Training Physician Support Per-**
P56 **sonnel, 1974-75.** Health Resources Development Bureau. 1975. 29p.

168 / 11 — Programs, Activities, Facilities, and Services

The directory was prepared jointly by the Department of Health Manpower in the American Medical Association (AMA), and the Bureau of Health Resources Development in the Health Resources Administration (HRA). It provides a comprehensive list of programs training physician-support personnel and reflects increasing interest in efforts to train new types of physician support personnel to perform tasks that significantly extend the services of the physician. The programs in this directory are arranged alphabetically by state, title, and city within the following categories: (1) programs that train assistants to primary care physicians only; (2) programs that train assistants to physicians practicing a specialty; and (3) programs that train assistants for a primary care and/or specialty physician(s). Those programs approved by the AMA Council on Medical Education up to the present are identified. Excluded from this list are programs designed primarily to train nurses for an expanded role. The entries contain program title, director, and address; entrance requirements; length of program; when class begins; entering class capacity; credential awarded; and whether there is financial aid.

556	HE20.6202 F21	**Directory. Family Planning Service Sites — United States.** *See* entry 218.
557	HE20.6602 Ed8-3	**Area Health Education Centers. A Directory of Federal, State, Local and Private Decentralized Health Professional Education Programs.** Health Manpower Bureau. 1976. 22p.

The *AHEC* directory catalogs the federal, state, local, and private decentralized professional health education programs initiated in direct response to the recommendations of the 1970 report of the Carnegie Commission on Higher Education, *Higher Education and the Nation's Health: Policies for Medical and Dental Education.* This directory serves as a guide for government agencies and other interested groups concerned with the existing void of AHEC-type activities in both rural and urban areas. Tables, arranged alphabetically by state, present the number of AHEC-type programs listed in the directory by classification. Four maps of the United States pinpoint the nationwide Area Health Education Center (AHEC) systems' Carnegie sites; the HEW's Bureau of Health Manpower AHECs (Carnegie-type medical school-based); HEW regional medical program health services/education activities (non-Carnegie-type community-based); and Veterans Administration AHECs. The centers are arranged alphabetically by state, and by name within state. The entries provide information on classification, funding, and name of contact, with addresses and telephone number for obtaining more information.

558	HE20.6602 T68	**Health Occupations Training Programs Administered by Hospitals.** *See* entry 222.
559	HE20.6610 1974/75	**A Directory of Expanded Role Programs for Registered Nurses.** Health Manpower Bureau. 1979. 30p. Annual.

Provided in this directory is a list of educational programs designed to prepare registered nurses to work in an expanded role. The directory is divided into three sections: (1) programs awarding certificates; (2) programs awarding a master's degree; and (3) programs awarding a baccalaureate degree. An index of specialties precedes each section, and each section is arranged alphabetically by state. The programs are arranged alphabetically by the name of the institution, and the address, telephone number, and specialties are given for each. Inquiries regarding eligibility requirements,

11 — Programs, Activities, Facilities, and Services / 169

curriculum, application procedures, and financial assistance should be made directly to the institution offering the program.

560 HE20.7002 **Directory of STD [Sexually Transmitted Disease] Clinics.**
     Se9   *See* entry 223.

561 HE20.8102 **U.S. Facilities and Programs for Children with Severe Mental**
     C43   **Illnesses. A Directory.** 2d ed. National Institute of Mental
     1974-   Health. 1977. 504p. Irregular.

Programs and facilities listed in this directory include those that serve children diagnosed as autistic, schizophrenic, or as having any other childhood psychoses or severe mental disorders. The number of services for mentally ill children nationwide has continued to grow since the last directory was published, and the trends toward providing more day care facilities, more schools, and more treatment protocols involving parents have continued unabated. The facilities are listed alphabetically by state, and by city within state. Each entry contains the following: name of facility, address, and telephone number; residential and/or day; date established; capacity; admission criteria; staff; physical description; and parent participation. Also included is an alphabetical facility index indicating type of program; an appendix of other facilities that provide services to autistic children; lists with addresses of chapters of the National Society for Autistic Children and international societies, and representatives or contact persons for autistic children; other directories for further sources of information; a list of legal agencies; and a reading list.

562 HE20.8102 **Regional Directory: Rape Prevention and Treatment**
     R18-3   **Resources.** National Center for the Prevention and Control of
                Rape. 1979. 27p.

This directory, one of the ten regional directories compiled by the National Rape Information Clearing House, covers Region 4: Alabama, Florida, Georgia, Kentucky, Mississippi, North Carolina, South Carolina, and Tennessee. It will prove useful in indicating the various groups or individuals involved in providing rape prevention and treatment services, the types of services being provided, and, of course, the geographic locations of resources in this region. The directory is organized alphabetically by state or territory within the region, by city or county within each state or territory, and by program title within each city or county. Each entry contains the following: title of program or resource; mailing address; telephone number; hot line number, if different; hours of operation or hours of hot line; and services provided.

563 HE20.8102 **National Directory: Rape Prevention and Treatment**
     R18-4   **Resources.** National Center for the Prevention and Control of
                Rape. 1981. 150p.

The *National Directory* is a consolidation of the ten regional directories printed in 1979. The original listings have been updated and refined into the seven hundred included in this directory. The purpose of the publication is to provide a focal point for service delivery activities in the field of sexual assault; facilitate networks among concerned agencies and individuals; and serve as a central referral source that can be accessed by anyone in the country. The resources listed comprise a diverse array of groups and individuals. They include rape crisis centers, community mental health centers, medical

170 / 11—Programs, Activities, Facilities, and Services

facilities, women's centers and commissions, YWCAs, public departments, district attorneys' offices, state and local organizations and government agencies, university women's centers, medical and legal associations, and individuals who have expertise in problems resulting from sexual assault. The listings are arranged alphabetically by state and territory, and by city and county within each state. Canadian entries follow the state listings. Each entry contains the program title, address, telephone number, and, where available, hot line information. The services provided are also listed.

564   HE20.8108   **The Consumer's Guide to Mental Health and Related Federal**
      C76   **Programs.** Edited by John W. Cohrasen, et al. National Institute of Mental Health. 1979. 204p.

The federal government makes available to individual citizens a large number of programs and benefits. The National Institute of Mental Health offers this guide as a tool to assist consumers in understanding and applying for participation in federal programs. In addition to mental health services, it describes federal programs and benefits in the areas of social security, employment, housing, welfare, food, and transportation. The guide is divided into sections pertaining to health entitlements, education, employment, food, housing, transportation, the Veterans Administration, and rights, and includes appendixes. Each entry provides the name of the program, program description, who qualifies for benefits, and how to apply. The appendixes contain addresses and telephone numbers of federal agencies and departments that can supply further information (including Federal Information Centers, field agencies, and state employment security agencies).

565   HE20.8129   **Directory of Halfway Houses and Community Residences for the Mentally Ill.** *See* entry 226.

566   HE20.8202   **Alternatives for Young Americans: A Catalog of Drug Abuse**
      Al7-3   **Prevention Programs.** National Institute on Drug Abuse. 1979. 349p.

The major goal of this catalog is to facilitate communication among individuals involved in drug abuse prevention programs for our nation's youth. The information in this work is arranged under five major headings: National Models, State Selections, Honorable Mentions, List of Evaluated Programs, and Descriptions of Prevention Programs. All of the programs listed are viable means of helping youth to become healthy and productive citizens. In each section, entries are identified by state and listed alphabetically within each state according to program title. The descriptions of prevention programs also cross-references those programs found in the first four categories. Each entry has been designed to convey a maximum of information to the user: program name, address, contact person, telephone number, hours available (where applicable), and a general program description. Unique features and/or operational instruments are offered to define the successful ingredients of the programs.

567   HE20.8202   **National Directory of Drug Abuse Treatment Programs.**
      D84-19   National Institute on Drug Abuse. 1981. 157p. Microfiche and
      1972-   paper. Irregular.

A compilation of approximately thirty-five hundred federal, state, local, and privately funded agencies responsible for the provision of drug abuse treatment throughout the

11 — Programs, Activities, Facilities, and Services / 171

United States and its territories, the directory consists of three sections concerning (1) state agencies, (2) drug abuse treatment programs, and (3) VA medical centers' drug abuse programs. The directory is organized alphabetically by state, and, within each state, the entries are ordered alphabetically by city and then by program name within the city. Each entry consists of the unit's name, address, and telephone number.

568	HE20.8202 T71 1972-	**National Directory of Drug Abuse and Alcoholism Treatment Programs.** National Institute on Drug Abuse. 1979. 350p. Irregular.

The first joint effort by NIDA and NIAAA is this compilation of approximately ninety-one hundred federal, state, local, and privately funded agencies responsible for the administration or provision of alcoholism or drug abuse services throughout the United States and its territories. The directory has been prepared to serve as a resource tool for program managers, treatment personnel, and others interested in locating alcoholism and drug abuse units. Most of the units are treatment units. The publication consists of three sections on (1) state authorities, (2) drug abuse and alcoholism programs, and (3) VA medical centers. All sections are organized alphabetically. In states where there are separate alcoholism and drug abuse authorities, the alcoholism authority is listed first. Within each state, the entries are alphabetically by city, and then by program name within city. Each entry consists of the unit's name, address, telephone number, and focus. Later editions are divided into treatment programs (see entry 567).

569	HE20.8215 Ser. 5 no. 2	**Voluntary Action in Drug Abuse Prevention Programs. December 1973.** National Clearinghouse for Drug Abuse Information. December 1973. 15p. Report series 5, no. 2. Irregular.

This publication is intended as a general information source as well as a resource for individuals interested in establishing volunteer programs or in volunteering their time and talents. Although not exhaustive, this publication includes descriptions of representative types of volunteer activities on the national, state, and local levels, as well as organizations that sponsor such activities. Three sections identify the national, state, and local organizations in alphabetical order. Although addresses are not given, the place, purpose, services, and funding agencies are.

570	HE20.8215 Ser. 6 no. 2	**Religious Activities and Drug Abuse: Some Current Highlights. December 1973.** National Clearinghouse for Drug Abuse Information. 1975. 6p. Report series 6, no. 2. Irregular.

Designed for persons seeking information on drug abuse activities sponsored or supported by religious organizations, this report contains descriptions of drug abuse treatment, rehabilitation, information/education, and counseling programs. It is designed to provide the reader with examples of the types of activities that have been implemented. These religious organizations have been arranged alphabetically by name, with a brief statement of purpose and place of location.

571	HE20.8215 Ser. 10 no. 3	**Drug Abuse Programs: A Directory for Minority Groups. June 1978.** National Clearinghouse for Drug Abuse Information. 1973. 24p. Report series 10, no. 3. Irregular.

11—Programs, Activities, Facilities, and Services

Drug Abuse Programs is a resource for persons requiring information on drug abuse programs that serve communities populated predominantly by minority groups. Programs are selected for inclusion only if the minority group (American Indian, Asian-American, Puerto Rican, Mexican-American, and black) involvement equals at least 50 percent of the total client census. This directory lists 332 programs, the majority of which offer some type of treatment or rehabilitation services. Programs are arranged alphabetically by state and city within state. Contact persons, addresses, predominant minority, and type of program(s) are provided.

572   HE20.8215   **National Directory of Hotline Services. September 1972.**
      Ser. 23   National Clearinghouse for Drug Abuse Information. September 1972. 35p. Report series 23, no. 1. Irregular.
      no. 1

Calls received by hot line are concerned with drug abuse problems as well as a broad spectrum of other general and mental health problems. This directory is intended as a resource for persons desiring information on operating hot lines throughout the country. The directory reflects only those hot lines that have responded to the clearinghouse's requests for information and that have reported they are currently operational. Program name, address, telephone number, and hours of operation are provided in this directory, which is organized alphabetically by state and city. Programs within each city are listed alphabetically by street address.

573   HE20.8215   **Directory of Women's Drug Abuse Treatment Programs.**
      Ser. 44   *See* entry 331.
      no. 2

574   HE20.8302   **National Directory of Alcoholism Treatment Programs. 1980.**
      Al1-19   National Institute on Alcohol Abuse and Alcoholism. 1981.
      1972-   244p. Irregular.

Included in this publication are primarily those treatment programs intended to serve as a resource for those who seek treatment and referral information on alcoholism and alcohol-related problems. More than sixty-three hundred alcohol services facilities responded. The directory includes federal, state, local, and privately funded agencies and are basically treatment units. Each unit is identified according to its orientation as (1) alcoholism treatment, (2) alcoholism/drug treatment, (3) alcoholism services, or (4) alcoholism/drug services unit. The directory consists of three sections that deal with (1) state alcoholism authorities; (2) alcoholism programs for each state; (3) Veterans Administration medical centers. All sections are organized alphabetically by state. Within each state, the entries are alphabetical by city and by program name within city. Each entry consists of the unit name, address, telephone number, and orientation.

575   HE22.202   **Directory of Adult Day Care Centers.** *See* entry 227.
      Ad9

576   HE23.102   **International Directory of Mental Retardation Resources.**
      D62   *See* entry 332.

577   HE23.1002   **Promising Practices: Reaching out to Families.** Human Development Services Office. 1981. 61p.
      P94-2

11 – Programs, Activities, Facilities, and Services / 173

This publication is intended primarily for those interested in sharing creative ideas about services for families. *Promising Practices* pulls together selective efforts of various groups involved in identifying and dealing with concerns of families. Across the country, these groups are engaged in developing and delivering services and materials to help meet family needs. Educational, emotional, environmental, financial, physical, and social problems are dealt with from the perspective of family involvement. Chapters are organized according to broad themes that underlie their programs' designs. Chapter 1 examines programs that explore informal service approaches and the use of national support systems. Chapter 2 concerns programs that focus on particular groups' needs. Chapter 3 describes programs that address issues of the parent-child relationship, and chapter 4 explores the programs that seek to help the family develop as a strong, adaptable unit. Contact persons, addresses, and telephone numbers are provided, as well as a subject index.

578   HE23.1015   **Programs Providing Services to Battered Women.** 3d ed., 2d
            no. 1   rev. Compiled by Center for Women's Policy Studies. Administration for Children, Youth, and Families. 1980. 214p. National Clearinghouse on Domestic Violence Information series, no. 1. Irregular.

Contained in this directory are contact persons, services, and addresses for battered women. The programs are listed alphabetically by state, and then by city or town. Most entries contain name, address, contact person(s), services, telephone number(s), materials available, funding sources, and additional information, if applicable.

579   HE23.1102   **Directory: Full Year Head Start Programs, Summer Head**
            D62   **Start Programs, Head Start Parent and Child Centers.** Head
            1971-   Start Bureau. 1978. 145p. Irregular.

Grants are awarded by the HEW regional offices to local public and private nonprofit organizations and agencies for the purpose of operating Head Start programs at the community level. At the end of fiscal 1978, approximately thirteen hundred grants had been awarded to local groups, which provided for the enrollment of an estimated 400,000 three- to five-year-olds. The programs serve both rural and urban areas in all fifty states and in U.S. trust territories. There are also special programs for Indian and migrant children. The directory is divided into several sections listing the HEW regional offices, Indian Head Start programs, migrant Head Start programs, summer Head Start programs, Head Start parent and child centers, and the full year Head Start programs. The section on full-year programs is arranged alphabetically by state, and by city within state, then by grantee and delegate agencies and centers. Information given for each entry includes name, address, and zip code.

580   HE23.1202   **National Directory of Intercountry Adoption Service**
            Ad7   **Resources.** Prepared by the American Public Welfare Association. Children's Bureau. 1980. 212p.

This is the first directory that lists service resources in the United States for families seeking to adopt internationally. The directory is organized to provide families seeking to adopt internationally with basic information on United States agencies with foreign child-placement resource contacts, public and voluntary agencies providing adoption services, and adoptive parent support groups at the local, state, and national levels. It should serve as a useful referral and information source for local public and voluntary

174 / 11 – Programs, Activities, Facilities, and Services

agencies. It should provide federal authorities involved in processing international adoptions with a tool for contacting or referring others to adoption services and resources. The directory should serve as an important and useful source of information for all those who seek to identify service providers and to locate information on intercountry adoption. The directory is arranged alphabetically by state. Subdivisions within each state include the state public welfare agencies, domestic child-rearing agencies, United States-based international child-placing agencies, and adoptive parent groups involved with intercountry adoption. Entries other than state agencies provide address, agency director, agency contact person, telephone number, agency service requirements, restrictions, and so forth. State agency entries provide addresses, telephone numbers, and contact persons. Included in the directory is a list of specialized service resources, addresses of the offices of the Immigration and Naturalization Service, and an alphabetical index of agencies and parent groups.

581   HE23.1210   **Child Abuse and Neglect Helplines: A Special Report.**
       H36   National Center for Child Abuse and Neglect. 1978. n.p.

The helplines are to provide the parent or child caller with a sympathetic, nonjudgemental listener, and to offer information and referral services. The list of programs was compiled from information collected in semiannual national surveys of child abuse and neglect programs undertaken since 1975 (see entry 582). The programs are organized into regions 1 through 9, providing name of organization or agency, city, area code, telephone, and listing restrictions, if any. A short bibliography on child abuse telephone services is also provided.

582   HE23.1211   **Child Abuse and Neglect Programs.** National Center for Child
       1976-   Abuse and Neglect. 1978. v.p. Annual.

Contained in this directory are brief, up-to-date descriptions of more than twenty-two hundred service-oriented child abuse and neglect programs in the United States. Administered by private and public organizations and agencies, the programs were identified in national surveys conducted semiannually since 1975. The volume has two major sections. In the first section, descriptions of individual programs are presented by federal region and by state or territory within federal regions. Within states, the program descriptions are arranged alphabetically by organization name. Programs have also been arranged in sequence by their five-digit accession numbers. These accession numbers are displayed throughout indexes appearing in the second section of the volume. The programs are cross-referenced by a director index, administering organization index, and subject matter index. Each entry provides the following: program accession numbers, administering organization, organization address, program title, director, starting date, abstract, clientele, staffing, organization, coordination, and funding.

583   HH1.2   **Housing Management Training Programs.** *See* entry 229.
       M31-3

584   I19.2   **Sources of Information, Products, and Services of the U.S.**
       In3-4   **Geological Survey.** *See* entry 464.

585   I29.9-2   **Access National Parks: A Guide for Handicapped Visitors.**
       H19-2   *See* entry 018.

11 — Programs, Activities, Facilities, and Services / 175

586   I66.2   **Sources of Assistance for Developing Boating Facilities.** Out-
        B63   door Recreation Bureau. 1977. 14p.

Due to widespread interest in boating and the concomitant necessity now and in the future to provide boating facilities, this reference list is being published by the Bureau of Outdoor Recreation as an aid for private individuals and public officials who wish to provide facilities and services for the boater. While the list is designed as an "operations reference list," researchers and boat users may also find it useful. The listing provides the names and addresses of (1) federal agencies that can help, (2) focal points for state assistance, (3) private organizations for information and assistance; and (4) periodicals and miscellaneous literature.

587   I70.8   **Federal Assistance Guide for Park and Recreation Profes-**
        F31   **sionals.** Heritage Conservation and Recreation Service. 1981. 95p.

This guide has been prepared for use by professionals interested in ways of supplementing their current leisure service delivery programs through financial and other assistance provided by the federal government. The programs that have been included in this guide are those that appear to have the greatest applicability to local park and recreation agencies and related organizations. Parts 1 and 2 comprise an introduction, then the rest of the guide is made up of five more parts. Part 3 is keyed to help determine eligibility and type of assistance. It lists the programs in numerical order by the five-digit program identification number, and the program title in the guide for detailed information. Part 4 lists the programs in numerical order and categorizes them by six major subject areas of interest: recreation—land, construction, and facility; cultural affairs—education, arts, and humanities; population—elderly, disadvantaged, handicapped, and youth; community development; personnel resources and training; and conservation and resource management. Part 5 contains detailed descriptions of the federal assistance programs listed in parts 2 and 4. Among the information provided are program objectives, types of assistance, use and use restrictions, applicant eligibility, information contacts, and user tips. Part 6 lists additional sources of information. Part 7, the appendix, contains addresses and telephone numbers of the regional and local federal offices of many of the agencies described in the guide.

588   J1.2   **Resources for Corrections: Directory of Federal Programs.**
        D62   Robert C. Grieser, Project Director. National Institute of Corrections. 1981. v.p.

This directory has been developed to locate potential resources available from the federal government to correctional organizations staffs, and clients. Due to the curtailing of funds from the Law Enforcement Assistance Administration, alternative resources of criminal justice programs must be explored and identified. The directory contains four major components: part 1, the overview; part 2, the indexes; part 3, the correctional resource entries or agency program listings; and part 4, the appendixes. The indexes section includes the resource entries, which provide a complete listing of all programs in this directory by OMB catalog number (*Catalog of Federal Domestic Assistance*); a corrections functional index; and a beneficiary index, or "special groups" (groups eligible for assistance) index. Part 2 is the central component of the directory and contains listings of the resources and indicates authority, scope, eligibility requirements, resources, management, and information contacts. Part 4 is comprised of

176 / 11 – Programs, Activities, Facilities, and Services

the various appendixes containing addresses and telephone numbers of Federal Information Centers and regional councils, suggestions for proposal writing, and a glossary of terms.

589	J26.2 C73-5	**Directory of Community Crime Prevention Programs: National and State Levels.** *See* entry 071.

590	J26.2 C73-8/OH	**Local Community Crime Prevention Resources. Ohio.** National Criminal Justice Reference Service. n.d. n.p.

Compiled to provide information about community crime prevention programs and resources within the state of Ohio, this directory was based on a survey of known crime prevention programs conducted between January and May of 1979. The leaflet presents the programs alphabetically by locality (state items appear first). Each entry provides service area, name of program, sponsoring organization, address, telephone, and scope codes. The scope codes are identified in a separate listing.

591	J26.2 F31	**A Condensed List of the Catalog of Federal Domestic Assistance Programs. Compiled Especially for Use in Providing Technical Assistance to the Office of Community Anti-Crime Programs Grantees, 1978.** Law Enforcement Assistance Administration. 1979. 169p.

Listed here are specially selected domestic assistance programs compiled from the *Catalog of Federal Domestic Assistance* (see entry 601). These programs provide some form of support or service that is of particular interest to community organizations concerned with crime prevention. The programs are arranged in numerical order by the catalog identification number. Each entry contains the federal agency or department; catalog number; title of the program; objectives of the program; types of assistance; and addresses and telephone numbers of information contacts. A separate list provides the names, addresses, and telephone numbers of the fiscal year 1979 members of the National Association of Criminal Justice Planners.

592	J26.2 R87	**Runaway Youth Program Directory.** Juvenile Justice and Delinquency Prevention Office. 1979. 109p.

Runaway youth are the subject of considerable concern, controversy, and confusion among parents, juvenile justice practitioners, and social service agencies and schools. The 212 runaway programs in the directory exist for the most part outside the juvenile justice system and primarily serve the self-referred runaway and "throwaway" youth. Through this directory, every runaway youth program will have the capability to learn of the services and program innovations of other such programs. Along with the program descriptions, it provides a map of the United States pinpointing runaway programs and a list of selected resources such as hot lines, books, general information services, and relevant government agencies. The program descriptions are arranged alphabetically by state and then alphabetically by name. Each entry contains the address, contact person, telephone number, and a description with information about staff, residents, services, and the like.

593	M66	**Public Information Materials for Language Minorities.** National Institute of Justice. 1981. 23p.

11—Programs, Activities, Facilities, and Services / 177

Law enforcement agencies in communities with non-English-speaking minorities face special challenges. Public information programs conducted on an ongoing basis transmit information as to how law enforcement agencies serve the public and facilitate interaction between police and citizens when the need for service arises. Public information programs also contribute to community acceptance by answering frequently asked questions or by highlighting programs directed to a specific group within the community. This pamphlet describes the special information needs of an important segment of our population—those with limited knowledge of English—and illustrates how selected criminal justice agencies have responded to these needs. The public information programs are arranged alphabetically by city (place), and a description is provided in addition to an address and telephone number. Suggested readings and other programs funded by LEAA Discretionary Grant Program are also listed.

594 L37.2 T68 1977- **Training Opportunities in Job Corps.** Rev. ed. Employment and Training Administration. 1979. 48p. Annual.

This directory provides a list of vocational courses offered at 103 Job Corps centers located in forty-two states, the District of Columbia, and Puerto Rico. Authorized by Title IV of the Comprehensive Employment and Training Act (CETA), Job Corps provides intensive programs of education, vocational training, work experience, and counseling on a residential or nonresidential basis. These facilities and programs and the courses listed are available for training youth and adults who are out of work or not in school and who need additional skills to secure and hold meaningful employment. The centers are arranged alphabetically by the name of the city. Each entry provides the name of the center (type), address, telephone number, capacity, operator, courses, and, occasionally, travel directions. An address list of Job Corps regional offices is also provided.

595 LC19.4-2 no. 79-2 **Information for Handicapped Travelers. 1979.** National Library Service for the Blind and Physically Handicapped. 1981. 11p. Reference circular 79-2. Irregular.

Contained in this circular are a listing and some descriptions of services to assist handicapped persons when they decide to travel. It is divided into four sections, the first of which lists the travel information centers in the United States, giving addresses and services provided. Section 2 is an alphabetical arrangement by topic of transportation services in the United States. Section 3 lists addresses and services of organizations in foreign countries for disabled persons, and section 4 is a list of travel guides (name, description, and price).

596 NS1.2 T22-15 **Appropriate Technology: A Directory of Activities and Projects.** National Science Foundation/Research Applied to National Needs (RANN). 1977. 66p.

Innovators in the field have been developing technologies that incorporate a concern for maintenance of the ecological balance by increasing the use of renewable resources, extending recycling and diminishing waste, and fostering the resource independence of local areas. These technologies have begun to be called "appropriate" technologies. This directory is, in part, a compilation of the descriptions of activities of the survey individuals and groups about the scope of their activities, the legal and technological

178 / 11 – *Programs, Activities, Facilities, and Services*

problems they are facing in moving from idea to application, and recommendations for federal activities in support of appropriate technology. This information is reported in chapters 1 and 2. Chapter 3 gives a listing of certain sources of information, assistance, and federal activity in the Washington, D.C., area. Chapter 4 contains an annotated bibliography, including publications in which continuing updates of information and reportage activities will be available. Addresses and telephone numbers are provided.

597   PM1.8   **Hispanic Employment: A Recruitment Sources Booklet**
      H62   **Including Recruitment Sources in Puerto Rico.** *See* entry 082.

598   Pr38.8   **Finding Your Way: A Directory of Public Programs Available**
      R25/P96   **to Indochinese Refugees.** Interagency Taskforce for Indochina Refugees. 1975. 40p. Publication no. 12.

This directory contains a list of benefits available to Indochinese refugees (in English, Lao, and Vietnamese) on housing, employment, business opportunities, legal assistance, and medical aid. It gives information on the wide range of government services for which one may qualify, and the names, addresses, and telephone numbers of the agencies that provide the services. The directory section lists alphabetically by state the federal agencies and voluntary agencies, with addresses and telephone numbers, that will assist the Indochinese with their special problems.

599   Pr39.15   **Consumer's Resource Handbook.** *See* entry 343.
      C76

600   PrEx1.10-8   **Highway Rest Areas for Handicapped Travelers.** *See* entry
      H53   026.

601   PrEx2.20   **Catalog of Federal Domestic Assistance. 1981.** Management
      1965-   and Budget Office. 1981. v.p. Annual with 2 supplements.

The *Catalog of Federal Domestic Assistance* (*CFDA*) is a governmentwide compendium of federal programs, projects, services, and activities that provide assistance or benefits to the American public. It contains financial and nonfinancial assistance programs administered by departments and establishments of the federal government. As the basic reference source of federal programs, the primary purpose of the catalog is to assist users in identifying programs that meet specific objectives of the potential applicant and in obtaining general information on federal assistance programs. In addition, the intent of the catalog is to improve coordination and communication between the federal government and state and local governments. The catalog provides the user with access to programs administered by federal departments and agencies in a single publication. Program information is cross-referenced by functional classification, subject, applicants, deadlines for program application submission, popular name, authorizing legislation, and federal circular requirements. Programs in the catalog provide a wide range of benefits and services. They have been grouped into 20 basic functional categories and further into 176 subcategories that identify specific areas of interest. The catalog is divided into three basic sections: the indexes, the program descriptions, and the appendixes. Indexes include agency program, functional, popular name, subject, applicant, eligibility, and deadline. The program description sections includes program number, title, and popular name, federal agency; authorization; objectives; types of assistance; uses and use restrictions; eligibility requirements;

application and award process; assistance considerations; post-assistance requirements; financial information; program accomplishments; regulations, guidelines, and literature; information contacts; related programs; examples of funded projects; and criteria for selecting proposals. The appendixes list programs requiring circular coordination; authorization; commonly used abbreviations and acronyms; agencies' regional and local office addresses; and sources of additional information.

602 PrEx23.10 **Directory of Federal Technology Transfer.** 2d ed. Federal
         1975-   Coordinating Council for Science, Engineering, and Technology. 1977. 222p. Irregular.

The publication of this document represents a key step toward increasing utilization of science and technology in the public sector by bringing together in one place an indexed description of the program resources and contact points at the federal level that can be drawn upon by persons in industry, and particularly in state and local government. In its broadest sense, technology transfer encompasses the collection, documentation, and dissemination of scientific and technical information, including data on the performance and costs of using the technology; the transformation of research and technology into processes, products, and services that can be applied to public or private needs; and the secondary application of research or technology developed for a particular mission that fills a need in another environment. This directory is a guide to all these activities as carried out in departments and agencies of the federal government. Each section of the directory describes the agency's program, including the agency's research base, its technology transfer policy and objectives, areas of responsibility, methods of implementation, accomplishments and user organizations. Contact points through which one can find the most pertinent elements of the agency are provided. There is an index to help the reader locate activities or applications related to their areas of interest and also determine whether these areas are common to more than one federal agency.

603 S1.40-2   **Directory of Consular Services.** State Department. 1979. 12p.
         C76

This booklet is a reference guide to services provided by the State Department's Bureau of Consular Affairs. It lists the services provided and the telephone numbers for inquiries about those services. The Immigration and Naturalization Service (Justice Department) is included because it deals with the status of aliens in the United States. Services described are passport services, visa services, and overseas citizens' services. Addresses are also given for passport regional agencies.

604 S1.40-2   **A Guide to Visas, Passports, and Consular Services.** State
         V82   Department. 1978. 12p.

This two-part booklet, which is a reference guide to services provided by the State Department's Bureau of Consular Affairs, lists those services and telephone numbers for inquiries about them. The Immigration and Naturalization Service (Justice Department) has been included because it deals with the status of aliens who are presently in the United States. The first part describes the services of the Visa Office, the Passport Office, and the Office of Special Consular Services. The second part is a directory of the offices and agencies indicating addresses and telephone numbers.

605 SBA1.2 **Directory of State Small Business Programs.** 2d ed. Small
D62-3 Business Administration. 1980. v.p. Irregular.
1979

The major focus of this work is to build a framework of communication and cooperation in the government-small business relationship. As a source of information for the small business community, the directory tries to identify state officials and programs that demonstrate an understanding of small business, as well as individuals who can relate to the daily problems and operations of a small business. Another objective is to identify unique programs that stand above the crowd. Included are those programs that, in intent and purpose, are designed to reach out to small businesses. The directory is divided into three major parts. The first presents a survey chart of fifty states that indicates the types of services provided to small businesses. Part 2 is an alphabetical, state-by-state presentation of business programs and summaries. The state entries provide data as to small business assistance programs, loan programs, business development, Kentucky's Small Business Purchasing Act, Michigan Procurement Program, Illinois Procurement Program, Missouri Regulatory Analysis, and so forth. A section at the end of the volume describes the Office of Advocacy within the Small Business Administration, and lists the regional advocates, with addresses and telephone numbers.

606 SI1.2 **Museum Studies Programs in the United States and Abroad.**
M97-4 **April 1976. Addendum, October 1978.** Smithsonian Institution. 1979. v.p.

This directory was compiled in response to the multitude of requests for listings of museum training opportunities. The United States listings are followed by the foreign country listings, and a 1978 addendum is also included. The entries are organized by state, and by city within the state. The entries contain the name of the institution; affiliate museum or university (where applicable); type of program offered; department or official title by which the program can be identified; description of program and eligibility requirements; information concerning fees, salaries, or stipends, and dates; contact person (whenever possible) and the address; and, to the right of the name of the institution, a number by which the program is identified in the index (used instead of page numbers). Indexes by category (i.e., high school, graduate, fellowships) and by institution name are provided.

607 TD1.2 **Directory of Transportation Education.** *See* entry 235.
Ed8

608 TD1.20-8 **State Technical Assistance Programs and Manuals on Rural**
81-6 **Public Transportation.** 2d ed., 1980. Transportation Department. 1981. 22p. Information report 81-6. Irregular.

Described in this document are the technical assistance activities of some forty states and Puerto Rico dealing with rural public transportation. It is not intended as a detailed review of the specific elements of each program, but more as an indication of the wide variety of state initiatives that have occurred in this area. The directory is arranged alphabetically by state. Each entry contains the following: contact name, address, telephone number, management programs; studies; manuals (whether completed or still in developing stage, if copies are available, and person to contact for information if different from other contact); and legislation/executive orders; and Section 18 management plan information.

609   Y3.Ad6:2   **Directory of Administrative Hearing Facilities.** Administrative
         1981-   Conference of the United States. 1981. 210p. Irregular.

This directory is designed to help persons who are scheduling administrative hearings and conferences to locate appropriate sites. It lists and describes courtrooms, conference rooms, hearing rooms, and other locations across the United States in which these proceedings may be held. The site listings were submitted in response to questionnaires by agencies that use administrative law judges or have contract or grant appeals boards. The directory is only a compilation of information forwarded. It is arranged alphabetically by state, and then by city within each state. The maps therein show the geographical locations within state by those cities where there are hearing sites. Each entry provides city, facility (name, and, if provided, street address); contact (name, if possible, or title, and telephone number); size (physical dimensions and/or seating capacity); remarks (helpful general information about facility); and source (abbreviations of source agency). Four appendixes present (1) a list of agencies contributing to the directory, with initials or abbreviations; (2) an update form; (3) a list of state court administrations arranged alphabetically by state, with addresses and telephone numbers; and (4) a copy of the Administrative Conference of the United States's Recommendation 68-1, concerning adequate hearing facilities.

610   Y3.H62:2   **Federal Programs for Neighborhood Conservation.** Advisory
         N31   Council on Historic Preservation. 1975. v.p.

Described in this publication are federal agency programs that have been devised to assist in conserving older neighborhoods. It should be of significant interest to leaders in government, business, program planning/design, and social action, as well as individuals who wish to explore pragmatic methods for conserving older neighborhoods of special urban character. The pamphlet is divided into three sections. Section 1 describes the departmental programs; section 2 lists the independent agency programs; and section 3, the appendix, provides a list of agency contacts (names and titles). The sections are arranged alphabetically by agency name. Each entry in sections 1 and 2 contains the following: program or activity name; type of assistance; objectives; eligibility; authorization; comments; and contact (office, address, and telephone number).

611   Y4.Ag4-2   **Innovative Developments in Aging: Area Agencies on Aging.**
         Ag4-6   **A Directory Compiled by the University of California.** House Select Committee on Aging, 96th Congress, 1st Session. December 1979. 571p. Committee publication no. 98-197.

This report, a 1979 update of the area agencies section of the *Project IDEA Directory* (originated at the University of California, San Francisco, in 1976), contains profiles of local-level activities reported by Area Agencies on Aging (AAAs) and their associates across the country. These profiles give an overview of national trends in aging services and policies, and provide an important central and broad reference source for state and local innovations in aging. The detailed index will assist persons with interest in specific types of programs, funding sources, or geographic areas to locate needed information. The directory is divided into the following sections: introductory materials, profiles organized within thirteen subject topics, index, and appendixes. The profiles of topics contain summaries of programs, policies, and legislation and provide follow-up contact sources. The thirteen categories are: Administration/Planning; Advocacy/Ombudsperson; Day Care/Home Care; Economic Resources; Education/Training; Employment; Health/Mental Health; Housing/Living Arrangements; Information and Referral/Outreach; Legal Issues and Services; Nutrition; Transportation/Escort Services; and Additional Programs/Services. The alphabetical subject index includes keywords and states. The appendixes (three in all), list the contact persons alphabetically by state and city under the headings of Resource Lists, Area Agencies on Aging, and Additional Contacts.

612 Y4.In 2-11 As7 1978- **Federal Programs of Assistance to American Indians.** Prepared by Richard S. Jones. Senate Select Committee on Indian Affairs, 97th Congress, 1st Session. 1981. 345p. Committee Print. Irregular.

Information contained in this report concerns (1) programs specifically designed to benefit Indian tribes and individuals; (2) programs that specifically include Indians or Indian tribes as eligible beneficiaries; and (3) programs that may not specifically denominate Indians or Indian tribes as eligible beneficiaries, but are deemed to be of special interest to Indians. Numbers, where used in related program entries, refer to numbers in the *Catalog of Federal Domestic Assistance* (see entry 601). The format of the entries is as follows: name of program; its nature or purpose; eligibility requirements (assistance prerequisites); how to apply (application deadlines and approval deadlines); who to contact for information regarding program; printed information available concerning the program; authorizing legislation; administering agency; available assistance; use restrictions; appropriations for the last four years; obligations incurred; Washington contacts and local contacts throughout the country; and related programs.

12
Miscellaneous Subjects

This is a catch-all chapter that includes those items that did not seem to fit into the other ten categories, and yet were too important to be left out.

613   A13.2   **Fishing Directory. Okanogan National Forest.** Forest Service,
         F53-3/Ok   Pacific Northwest Region. n.d. n.p.

Management of fishing and fish habitats in the Okanogan National Forest is a cooperative effort of the Washington State Department of Game and the U.S. Forest Service. This directory contains information to help people locate fishing spots in the forest. It is designed to use with the forest's recreation map, which can be purchased from the forest supervisor's office. Fishing waters are divided into three categories: (1) rivers and streams, (2) lakes and reservoirs accessible by road, and (3) back country lakes. Each entry in the directory is accompanied by a description of the location, size, fish species, access, and recreation facilities (if present). The forest supervisor's address is provided.

614   A13.2   **Fishing Directory. Deschutes National Forest.** Forest Service,
         F53-3/Des   Pacific Northwest Region. n.d. n.p.

The Deschutes National Forest (Oregon) contains cold water fishing opportunities for all classes of anglers. Only bodies of water actually containing fish are reported in this directory, which contains information about where to find the fishing spots. The directory is designed for use with the Forest Recreation Map, which can be purchased from the forest supervisor's office. Fishing waters are subdivided into three categories: (1) rivers and streams, (2) lakes and reservoirs accessible by road, and (3) backcountry lakes. Each entry is accompanied by a description of the location, size, depth, fish species, access, and recreation facilities (if present). For further information, the forest supervisor and the Oregon Department of Fish and Wildlife should be contacted. Addresses are provided.

615   A88.56   **Warehouses Licensed under U.S. Warehouse Act, as of**
         1980-   **December 31, 1980.** Agricultural Marketing Service. 1981. 64p. Annual.

The U.S. Warehouse Act was passed by Congress in 1916 to improve this country's agricultural warehousing industry. Currently licensed under the act are 228 cotton warehouses, 1,834 grain elevators, and 69 warehouses storing other agricultural commodities. These represent about 60 percent of the commercial cotton storage capacity and about 40 percent of the commercial grain elevator space in this country. At any given time, the aggregate value of warehouse receipts, which represent the actual stored products in federally licensed warehouses, may be $7 billion or more. This directory is arranged alphabetically by the type of warehouse (cotton, grain, dry bean, cottonseed, nut, syrup, wool), and then alphabetically by state and city within state. Only names of the warehouses are provided. A list of area offices of the Warehouse Service Branch, Agricultural Marketing Service, USDA, is provided, giving addresses and telephone numbers for those who want further information.

616 C13.46 **Software Exchange Directory for University Research Administration.** By Zella G. Ruthberg and Gloria R. Bolotsky. National Bureau of Standards. 1976. 215p. Technical note no. 916. Irregular.

The Institute for Computer Sciences and Technology (ICST) at the National Bureau of Standards (NBS) developed this directory with the idea that this type of exchange of information could prove very useful to the University research community by saving many man-hours of work that would otherwise be used in developing the same programs at different institutions and by yielding a state-of-the-art overview in this area. It was decided that information to be included in the directory would consist of descriptions of the administrative environment in which automated research administration programs were being used, along with the summaries of the software packages themselves. Seventy-five institutions sent responses suitable for eighty-three directory entries under Administrative Information and 315 directory entries under Software Package Summaries. An administrative entry contains information on the reporting unit, the basic administrative structure and parameters, computer usage, automated functional areas, and comments. A package entry contains a functional description, software and hardware characteristics, history, availability, and comments. The administrative entries have been indexed by funding size, size of research staff, number of federal granting agencies, and number of contracts and grants awarded in fiscal year 1974. The software packages have been indexed by function, computer used, and language used. The detailed entries and indexes should help open communication channels for this community of computer users and thus maximize transferability of these programs between institutions. The universities are arranged alphabetically by name.

617 C39.202 **Bulk Carriers in the World Fleet. Oceangoing Merchant Type**
B87 **Ships of 1,000 Gross Tons and Over (Excludes Vessels on the**
1966- **Great Lakes) as of December 31, 1978.** Maritime Administration. 1980. 139p. Occasionally on microfiche. Annual.

This publication presents a list and statistical data on the world's bulk carrier fleet. The United States is listed first and other countries follow in alphabetical order. The ships included have been placed in various categories (general bulk, Colliers, ore carriers, and ore/bulk/oil), and within each category, they are listed alphabetically by name. Five basic ship characteristics are displayed for each vessel: the year built, gross tonnage, deadweight tonnage, speed in knots, and draft in feet. Class totals are presented at the end of each category of ship, with a total for all classes of ships appearing as the last entry for each respective nation. Country totals have been added to provide a grand total for the world bulk carrier fleet in a summary table.

618 C39.217 **Vessel Inventory Report as of June 30, 1980.** Maritime Admin-
    1975- istration. 1980. 61p. Semiannual.

Contained in this report is information on all United States registered merchant ships of 1,000 gross tons and over. This inventory of vessels, which amounted to 23.6 million deadweight tons, includes all merchant vessels in the United States flag fleet, whether privately or government-owned. The report is in five parts. Part 1 contains an alphabetical listing by vessel name of all merchant ships in the United States merchant fleet, whether privately owned or Maritime Administration-owned, showing each vessel's type, owner or operator, design type, and deadweight tonnage. Part 2 presents the same information as part 1, arranged as an alphabetical listing by owner or operator together with their respective vessels, whether privately or Maritime-Administration-owned. Part 3 lists Reserve Fleet sites maintained by the Maritime Administration and merchant and military vessels in lay-up at each site, with the design type summaries for individual sites and for the Reserve Fleet as a whole. Part 4 lists military vessels currently in the National Defense Reserve Fleet by name, type, Reserve Fleet site, and design type. Part 5 lists military and privately owned vessels currently in custody of the National Defense Reserve Fleet by name, type of Reserve Fleet site, and design type.

619 C47.17 **Festivals USA, 1973.** Travel Service. 1972. 66p. Irregular.
    1971-

This publication was prepared for the use of travel agents and tour operators abroad. Because of the interest of the U.S. public in these events, however, it is also distributed within the United States. The 1973 listing includes more than seven hundred events occurring in the United States in 1973. In addition to listing major festivals, it also includes those "fun" festivals that are peculiar to the United States, such as the National Egg Striking Contest, the Jumping Frog Rodeo, the Brick and Rolling Pin Throwing Contest, and a host of others. This edition includes a section listing major sporting events in the fields of horseracing, auto racing, tennis, golf, boating, surfing, and skiing. The first section lists the events chronologically by month and date (January-December). Each event is named, and date(s) and place of occurrence are given. A brief statement of description may be provided. Long-run events are listed in the second section by month and date (if appropriate), providing the same information as section 1; and the third section contains the major U.S. sporting events in the areas already mentioned.

620 C60.12 **1980 World's Submarine Telephone Cable Systems.** 2d ed.
    80-6 Prepared by H. H. Schenck. National Telecommunications Information Administration. 1980. 353p. NTIA Contractor report 80-6. Irregular.

Provided here is detailed technical, cost, and ownership information on all of the commercial underseas telephone cable systems in the world that contain at least one submerged electronic amplifier (repeater) and were in operation as of the end of 1979. The volume is divided into nine sections. Section 1 gives a general summary of the submarine telephone cable systems. Section 2 contains a list of the systems arranged in approximate chronological order and by the system's reference number. Provided are

186 / 12—Miscellaneous Subjects

nationality(ies), identification, and date in service or (retired). Immediately following the list is an alphabetical index of the systems grouped by countries, terminal sites, and landing points, as well as acronyms and system names. Section 3 lists the future undersea telephone cable systems and includes an alphabetical index. The Seacable System data profiles are presented in section 4. They are arranged by the system reference number. Section 5 provides an alphabetical arrangement by country of cable-owning and -operating agencies with addresses. Maps of submarine telephone cable systems are depicted in section 6, while sections 7, 8, and 9 contain abbreviations and short names, a glossary, and a bibliography, respectively.

621　C61.10-2　**Commercial News USA. New Products Annual Directory.** *See* entry 105.

622　D101.22　**Credit Unions Serving Army Personnel.** Army Department.
　　　210-5　1979. 18p. Pamphlet no. 210-5. Irregular.
　　　1979-

Credit unions serving Army personnel are dedicated to providing financial services to Department of Army military and civilian personnel and their families. This directory, with some exceptions, lists those credit unions chartered to serve specific groups of Army personnel (for example, active duty personnel assigned to a particular installation/activity, retired personnel authorized to use installation facilities, and Reserve and National Guard personnel in the immediate vicinity of the installation). The credit unions are arranged alphabetically by state and place within the state. Each entry includes the name, address, and zip code. Also included are overseas credit union services arranged alphabetically by country.

623　E1.28　**Solar Events Calendar and Call for Papers as of August 1980.**
　　　SERI/SP　Energy Department. 1981. 58p. Solar Energy Research Insti-
　　　751-811　tute publication 751-811. Irregular.

Listed in this publication are conferences, symposiums, workshops, and other formal meetings pertaining to the solar technologies. It has been compiled by the staff of the Solar Energy Information Data Bank to provide a wide variety of information on developing solar technologies to government, the scientific and university communities, and the public. The calendar is organized into four main sections. These sections include an alphabetical subject index and a location index containing name and date, an international call for papers section, and the body of the publication, which is a chronological listing of each event, its locations, sponsor, and the name of an individual or organization to contact for additional information.

624　ED1.111-2　**Education Directory: Local Education Agencies. Fall 1980.**
　　　1965/66-　By Jeffrey W. Williams and Warren A. Hughes. National Center for Education Statistics. 1980. 175p. Annual.

This directory continues a series of directories begun by the Office of Education, formerly entitled *Education Directory: Public School Systems*. It provides a current listing of operating and nonoperating local public school systems in the United States. The purpose of this annual is to list all local agencies providing free public elementary and secondary education in the United States and its outlying areas. "Local" denotes those agencies closest to the actual operation of the educational programs. This may include town, district, county, or even state agencies (as in Hawaii). The systems are arranged alphabetically by state and by name within state. The regular operating school systems are presented first and are followed by the nonoperating districts. Where supervisory unions or county-administered systems are included, they and their component districts are listed last. Information for the outlying areas of the United States is given following the alphabetical listing of states and the District of Columbia. Unless otherwise noted in the introduction, the following information is given for each system listed: name, address, county, grade span, number of pupils, and number of schools.

625   EP1.84   **Women/Consumer Calendar of Events, 1979-80.** Environ-
      1979-   mental Protection Agency. 1979. 4p. Irregular.

The first issue of this calendar contains the location, date, and theme of conferences and meetings to be held by women/consumer associations and organizations. The calendar was developed by the Constituent Development Unit of the Office of Public Awareness of EPA in response to a request for help in reaching members of the women/consumer constituency. Arranged by month and date (April-December), the organizations are listed with themes for the conferences, locations, and telephone numbers. An address list of EPA regional public information offices is provided as well as a name list of other women's consumer organizations.

626   FEM1.102   **Detector Directory.** Prepared by K. R. Mniszewski and T. E.
      D48   Waterman of IIT Research Institute and S. W. Harpe of
                    Underwriters Laboratories, Inc. Fire Administration. 1978.
                    173p.

Provided in this directory is a large collection of information on fire detectors, technical reports, and manufacturer's catalogs and brochures. The state of the art of fire detection technology is presented here in a summary table of fire detector devices, a listing of manufacturers and suppliers of nontemperature-sensing fire detectors, and a bibliography of papers and reports related to fire detection. Appendix A (table 1), provides a list of fire detection devices organized primarily by the fire characteristic being detected. It is further subdivided by detection technique. A description of the mode of operation of each device is summarized, known or expected applications of each device are listed, and unique characteristics or other remarks on each device are given. References cited in table 1 are listed at the end of the table and identify sources of further information on each device. Table 2, presented as appendix B, lists all known fire detectors of the nontemperature-sensing types that are presently on the market. They are listed in alphabetical order by the name of the manufacturer or supplier. Each manufacturer's model names or numbers also are given. Presented in table 2 are power source requirements of each detector. Appendix C contains a computer printout of all literature holdings arranged in alphabetical order by author. Information is provided on author, title, reporting institution, publication source, and date. The KWIC (key word in context) index, which is actually a subject (key word) index, is found in appendix D. The index is generated by alphabetizing all nouns, pronouns, verbs, adjectives, and adverbs in every document title in the file. Appendix E is a document number index of fire detection literature.

627   GS8.10   **Federal Travel Directory. December 1981.** General Services
      1981-   Administration. 1981. 49p. Monthly.

188 / 12—Miscellaneous Subjects

This directory, published monthly by the General Services Administration (GSA), contains schedules and fares for the federal contract airlines and information on certain other transportation discounts offered to federal travelers. Listed also are contract airline telephone reservation numbers, contract air service use guidelines, and ground transportation information, including all the GSA contract car rental companies' locations and telephone numbers. This directory may include additional connecting flights not shown in the *Official Airline Guide* (*OAG*). The directory is organized into sections containing transportation guidelines; information on how to use airline schedules; a list of city-pairs-contract airlines/AMTRAK; airline abbreviations and reference marks; contract airline schedules; helicopter schedules; AMTRAK schedules and information; ground transportation information (guidelines for GSA car rental use); contract airline codes, names, reservations, telephone numbers, and fare basis; and a list of federal travel management centers.

628 HE20.4012 **National Drug Code Directory.** 6th ed., 1980. 2 vols. Drugs
1969- Bureau. 1981. Irregular with quarterly supplements.

The 1980 edition of this directory is again limited to prescription drugs and selected over-the-counter (OTC) products. The directory is composed of four sections: an alphabetical index by product trade name, a numerical index of products by National Drug Code (NDC), a numerical index of products by drug class, and an alphabetical index by short name of the labeler/vendor. The first three sections contain drug product information and the last section contains drug establishment information. The data elements included in the first section are product trade name or catalog name, labeler's/vendor's short name, drug class, OTC designation (if applicable), active ingredient(s), labeler code, product code, dosage form and routes of administration, strength, unit, and trade package size and type for product. Section 2, the drug classes, are arranged in alphabetical order by major drug class, and subordinate, minor drug classes are in numerical order. The data contain the NDC labeler and product codes, the product trade name or catalog name, the dosage form, the strength, and unit. The numerical index of products by NDC section is arranged numerically by labeler code and then by product code. The first line contains the labeler code and the short name of the labeler. Subsequent lines list each product for that labeler. Each of these lines contains the NDC labeler and product code, the trade name or catalog name, and the dosage form. The strength and unit may also be present. Section 4 contains the names and addresses of establishments whose products appear in the directory. It is arranged alphabetically by labeler short name. Four tables explain the dosage forms, routes of administration, and unit codes, and identify drug classes.

629 HE20.4030 **National Health Related Items Code Directory.** 2d ed. Medical
1974- Devices and Diagnostic Products Bureau. 1975. v.p. Irregular.

This directory is the product of a cooperative effort to establish a uniform identification system for computer processing of health-related items information. Included in the National Health Related Items Code (NHRIC) system are medical and surgical treatment products (including medical devices and in vitro diagnostics) and other health-related items generally used in the diagnosis, care, and treatment of patients. The listing of a health-related item in the directory is not intended to imply that the product has been approved by the FDA. The NHRIC system is designed to list trade packages only, and for the purposes of this system a trade package is defined as the smallest individual unit of sale that moves intact from the manufacturer through the distributor to the purchasing entity (e.g., surgical supply outlet, pharmacy, or hospital), complete with identification of labeler and contents, and with any necessary overwrap. Divided into three sections, section A contains an index of class terms arranged alphabetically. All like products of the different labelers are grouped together and listed alphabetically by labeler within a category. Section B presents the NHRIC code index/company listing in ascending sequence. Section C is a listing that correlates the abbreviated labeler short names to the labeler codes and the labelers' full names and addresses. Each product description includes the catalog name, item size or description (optional), package size, and package type.

630   HE20.4202   **Common Poisonous and Injurious Plants.** Drugs Bureau.
       P69   1981. 29p.

Provided in this illustrated booklet is a description of some house and garden plants and a few wild-growing species that are poisonous. The plants are presented in full color and arranged alphabetically by popular name. Each entry provides the generic name, history of the species, description of the plant, symptoms if eaten, antidote, and some procedures to follow for recovery.

631   HH1.2   **U.S. Housing Developments for the Elderly or Handicapped.**
       El2-10   Housing and Urban Development Department. 1979. 119p.

In this directory is a listing of all elderly housing developments funded under sections 202, 231, and 236 of the Housing Act of 1937, as amended, prior to the enactment of the Housing and Community Development Act of 1974. New construction under Section 236 and the Section 221(d)(3) Market Rate Rent Supplement Program has been terminated since the adoption of the 1974 Act. Additional projects may be built under public housing and sections 202 or 231, with rental asistance under Section 8 of the U.S. Housing Act of 1937, as amended. The housing developments are arranged alphabetically by state and then by city. Each entry provides the name of the unit and address, the number of units, and type of project (Section 202, 236, etc.).

632   I19.16   **Historical Survey of U.S. Seismograph Stations.** By Barbara
       no. 1096   B. Poppe. Geological Survey. 1979. 389p. Professional paper
                      1096. Irregular.

Found in this publication is a compilation of detailed information about seismograph stations in the United States, the trust territories, Panama, and the Commonwealth of Puerto Rico current to June 1977. Its principal purpose is to provide information on availability of records. The data are presented alphabetically by state and then by the operating institution. In the upper right-hand corner of each page is the state name and the city in which the operating organization is located. Pages are arranged alphabetically, first by in-state addresses and then by out-of-state addresses. Although most networks are confined to one state, those networks that overlap more than one have been split so that the address of the network operator is listed in each state with those stations of the network that are in it. The station listings include the following: general information—operator, address, telephone number, and address to obtain records; site information—code, station name, latitude, longitude, elevation, date opened, date closed, foundation, and geologic age; instrumentation; and a short history (information on origin, development, or role in particular research). The appendixes contain (1) a listing of the states in which each organization operates stations; (2)

190 / 12 — Miscellaneous Subjects

response curves for eleven instrument systems that are broadly used; (3) a cross-reference of stations in alphabetical order, including station name, state, operating organization, and page reference; and (4) the stations coded by National Earthquake Information Service (NEIS) plotted on region maps.

633	I20.2 C12-2 1970-	**American Indian Calendar, 1979.** Indian Affairs Bureau. 1979. 96p. Annual.

Ceremonials, dances, feasts, and celebrations of many kinds are held throughout the year on or near American Indian reservations. Most of these occasions occur in the summer, but colorful events take place year-round. Non-Indians and Indians from other tribes become aware of the traditions and ancient heritage of their hosts at these gatherings. This calendar is a guide to the most well known events. The events are arranged alphabetically by state, then chronologically by date. The entries provide time of year, the celebration or event name (occasionally including activities), and location (city). A list of Bureau of Indian Affairs area offices with addresses and telephone numbers is provided.

634	J26.2 C12 1978-	**Criminal Justice Calendar of Events, February-May 1979.** National Criminal Justice Reference Service. 1978. n.p. Irregular.

In this calendar of events is a selected list of meetings and workshops of interest to the criminal justice professional. Each event is arranged chronologically by date and provides the following: date and place, title, description of event, and address of contact person or organization. The telephone number is also provided.

635	J29.8 Sy8-2	**A National Directory of 911 Systems. Final Report, September 1980.** By B. K. Yamaoka and T. J. Yung. Justice Statistics Bureau. 1980. 626p.

In 1968, the telephone industry reserved the digits 9-1-1 as the universal emergency telephone number. Since then, the Law Enforcement Assistance Administration (LEAA) has helped a large number of state and local agencies to implement emergency 911 services. This directory provides a compilation of information on operating 911 systems for ready use by community planners who are contemplating the implementation of a 911 system. A key objective of this document is to facilitate the nationwide exchange of 911 information available from the 911 systems that presently serve approximately 26 percent of the nation's estimated 218 million people. Information on the 911 systems is organized alphabetically by state. Each state section may comprise as many as three parts: (1) 911 systems descriptions, (2) survey non-respondents, and (3) 911 systems not contacted. The descriptions within each state are presented in alphabetical order by Public Safety Answering Point (PSAP) name, which is generally the city or county in which the PSAP is located. The PSAP name appears in the upper right-hand corner of the page. Each 911 system is described according to the following categories: community, historical background, telephone system, PSAP administration and operations, legal, fiscal, problem areas, and PSAP director, with address and telephone number. A comprehensive chapter on how to use the directory is provided. As a reference tool, a cross-index to the 911 system descriptions is provided at the back of the directory. A glossary of terms is also provided.

12—Miscellaneous Subjects / 191

636   P1.2   **Express Mail, Los Angeles Next Day Service City Directory.**
        Ex7-4   Postal Service. 1980. 59p.

This directory was developed primarily for out-next-day express mail customers. In it are those cities and countries to which one can mail on a nonscheduled basis. This directory is divided into several sections. General sections include items on insurance, acceptance post office locations, express mail collection boxes, preparation instructions, and late charts (both post office to addressee and post office to post office). An alphabetical listing of express mail cities identifies the cities throughout the United States where express mail next-day delivery can be made from Los Angeles. Addresses, stations, and zip codes are provided. The next section, "International Express Mail Service," identifies the foreign countries in alphabetical order where express mail service is available. These entries contain areas served, what can be sent, customs declaration form required, weight limit, delivery time, rates per pound, and so forth. Also included is a list of express mail cities ordered alphabetically by state and a list of cities to which express mail same-day airport service is available.

637   PM1.10   **Federal Job Information Centers Directory.** Personnel Man-
        BRE-9   agement Office. November 1981. n.p. Pamphlet BRE-9.
        1974-   Irregular.

The Office of Personnel Management operates Federal Job Information Centers (FJICs). FJICs can provide general information on federal employment, explain how to apply for specific jobs, and supply application materials. You can get information by mail, by telephone, or by visiting an FJIC. The centers are arranged alphabetically by state and by city within state, if there is more than one center. Addresses and telephone numbers are provided.

638   SBA1.3   **National Directories for Use in Marketing.** Small Business
        no. 13   Administration. 1981. 9p. Small Business bibliography no. 13.
        1958-   Irregular.

The selected titles in this directory are of primary interest to those seeking lists of business firms that buy goods for resale. However, the selected references of information are also helpful to those who purchase or sell specific types of merchandise and services. Only national directories are listed. The directories are listed under categories of specific business or general marketing areas in an alphabetical subject index. Information given for each directory includes name, frequency of publication and latest edition available, price, a brief description, and address.

639   TD2.2   **License Plates, 1981.** Federal Highway Administration. 1981.
        L61   n.p. Annual.
        1980-

Presented in this brochure are color illustrations of vehicle license plates of the fifty states, territories of the United States, U.S. inaugural license plates, and plates of Canada and Mexico. They are arranged alphabetically by state (or jurisdiction) name. A table gives a brief narrative description of the plates identifying such items as colors and reflectorization, type of plate, validation, number of plates used, disposition on sale of car, slogan and other items on plate, personalized (vanity) plate, expiration date, enforcement date, date plates go on sale, and earliest display date. A brief history of the inaugural license plates is also given.

192 / 12 — Miscellaneous Subjects

640   TD4.12   **Airport Directory, Spring-Summer 1978.** Federal Aviation
        pt. 2   Administration. 1978. 403p. Airman's Information Manual,
        1966-1978   part 2. Semiannual.

This airport directory has been issued semiannually (March and September) for almost fourteen years. With this issue it was terminated by the FAA. Part 2 and part 3 of the *Airman's Information Manual* will be combined in a new seven-volume issuance entitled *Airport Facility Directory*, and will be produced and sold by the National Ocean Survey. This directory covers the conterminous United States, Puerto Rico, and the Virgin Islands. It contains a directory of all airports, seaplane bases, and heliports available for civil use. It includes all their services, except communications, in codified form. Also included are U.S. entry and departure procedures, including airports of entry and landing rights airports, as well as a listing of flight service station and National Weather Service telephone numbers. Arranged alphabetically by state and by city within state, each entry provides the following: location identification (name, place, telephone number, nautical miles and direction from center of referenced city, and geographical coordinates); elevation; runway's length, weight-bearing capacity, and end data; runway lighting; airport rotating beacon; repairs data; fuel data; UNICOM; oxygen; airport remarks; indication of certification; and other information.

641   TD5.12-2   **Merchant Vessels of the United States, 1979. (Including**
        1976-   **Yachts).** 2 vols. Coast Guard. 1980. Annual.

Contained in this publication are names of American merchant vessels and yachts having uncanceled marine documents (registers, enrollments and licenses, or licenses) on January 1, 1979. The vessels are listed in alphabetical order by name, except for those vessels that only have digits as names, which are listed first. Volume 1 lists the vessels, with a section explaining terms and abbreviations. Volume 2 presents special sections on the following: signal letters, present names of merchant vessels showing former names, former names showing present names, vessels lost, vessels sold or transferred to aliens, vessels abandoned or removed for other causes, and an index of managing owners. Information on the vessels listed in volume 1 includes official number, signal and radio call letters, rig, name, tonnage (gross, net), dimension in feet (length, breadth, depth), hull, when built, where built, service, horsepower, name of owner, and home port.

642   TD7.2   **A Directory of Regularly Scheduled, Fixed Route, Local Pub-**
        D62   **lic Transportation Service.** Urban Mass Transportation
        1978   Administration. July 1979. 17p. Occasionally on microfiche.
                          Irregular.

Contained in this directory is information on 647 local transit operations in 279 urbanized areas (UZAs) with populations of over 50,000. For the purposes of this compilation, a transit operation is a fixed route, regularly scheduled service available to the general public, offering rides wholly within, or commuter rides from outside, a particular UZA. The publication is in two parts. Part 1 presents the 106 urbanized areas with populations of over 200,000, and part 2 presents the 173 urbanized areas with populations of 50,000 to 200,000. UZA listings are in the order of population rank. Two indexes identify the UZAs alphabetically by state and place, and provide population rank and page reference. The listings provide name of the urbanized area, population, and a listing of transit services with the following data: whether member of American Public Transit Association (APTA), peak requirement of vehicles, whether privately owned, contact person, mailing address, city, zip code, telephone number, and management firm. Also included is an alphabetical state arrangement of American Association of State Highway and Transportation officials with their names and titles, departments, street addresses, (including city and zip), and telephone numbers.

643   TD7.2   **A Directory of Regularly Scheduled, Fixed Route, Local Rural**
       D62-2   **Public Transportation Service.** Urban Mass Transportation
       1980-   Administration. February 1981. 17p. Occasionally on microfiche. Irregular.

Contained in this directory is data on 339 regularly scheduled, fixed route local transit operations serving rural areas. These are nonurbanized areas with populations of less than 50,000 that have services available to the general public scheduled every weekday. Arranged alphabetically by state, the transit operations are listed, with population served, number of buses required for peak service, contact person, mailing address, post office, zip code, telephone number, whether private, and if member of American Public Transit Association. Addresses and telephone numbers of the Standing Committee on Public Transportation of the American Association of State Highway and Transportation officials and state representatives responsible for the administration of Section 18 Formula Grant programs are provided as well as an alphabetical listing of state and regional public transportation associations, with chief officer, address, and telephone number.

644   TD7.11   **Roster of North American Rapid Transit Cars, 1945-1976.**
       DC-06-0121-   Urban Mass Transportation Administration. 1977. 239p.
       -77-1   Technical report no. UMTA-DC-06-0121-77-1. Irregular.

Compiled in this document is data on rapid transit cars ordered or built in the United States, Canada, and Mexico between 1945 and 1976. The book is arranged alphabetically by transit authority, and under each authority, the car data is presented in chronological order. The authorities included are BART (San Francisco Bay Area Rapid Transit District), CTA (Chicago Transit Authority), GCRTA (Greater Cleveland Regional Transit Authority), MBTA (Massachusetts Bay Transportation Authority), MUCTC (Montreal Urban Community Transit Commission), NYCTA (New York City Transit Authority), PATCD (Port Authority Transit Corporation), PATH (Port Authority Trans-Hudson Corporation), SEPTA (Southeastern Pennsylvania Transportation Authority), STC (Sistema de Transporte Colectivo Organismo Publico Descentralizado, Mexico City), TTC (Toronto Transit Commission), and WMATA (Washington Metropolitan Area Transit Authority). General data for each authority is given (number of cars, year purchased, when placed in service, car builder, type of car, and bid price per car), followed by such technical data as performance, dimensions, weights, electrical equipment, heating and ventilation systems, traction motors, propulsion equipment, lighting systems, trucks and suspensions, and so forth. Also included is an appendix of photographs of the exterior of each transit car series.

645   Y3.El2-3:2   **Votingsystems Users 81. A Directory of Local Jurisdictions.**
       V94-3   National Clearinghouse on Election Administration. 1981. v.p.

There are more than thirteen thousand election jurisdictions that are responsible for administering federal elections. This volume is an attempt to provide information on the variety of voting systems available. It lists the jurisdictions and what equipment they now use. Arranged alphabetically by state, and by county within state, each entry provides county seat and telephone number, 1980 population, 1980 general election registration, total precincts, and abbreviation of the manufacturer of the equipment used. A companion volume, *Voting Systems Vendors 81*, SuDocs class no. Y3.El2-3:2:V94-4, will provide one with more information on the systems and addresses of manufacturers.

Appendix 1
Regional Federal Depository Libraries

FEDERAL DEPOSITORY LIBRARY PROGRAM*

AUBURN UNIV. AT MONTGOMERY LIBRARY
Documents Department
Montgomery, AL 36193
(205) 279-9110

UNIVERSITY OF ALABAMA LIBRARY
Documents Dept., Box S
University, AL 35486
(205) 348-6046

DEPT. OF LIBRARY, ARCHIVES AND PUBLIC RECORDS
Third Floor, State Cap.
Phoenix, AZ 85007
(602) 255-4035

UNIVERSITY OF ARIZONA LIB.
Government Documents Dept.
Tucson, AZ 85721
(602) 626-4871

CALIFORNIA STATE LIBRARY
Govt. Publications Section
P. O. Box 2037
Sacramento, CA 95809
(916) 322-4572

UNIV. OF COLORADO LIB.
Government Pub. Division
Boulder, CO 80309
(303) 492-8834

DENVER PUBLIC LIBRARY
Govt. Pub. Department
1357 Broadway
Denver, CO 80203
(303) 573-5152

CONNECTICUT STATE LIBRARY
Government Documents Unit
231 Capitol Avenue
Hartford, CT 06115
(203) 566-4971

UNIV. OF FLORIDA LIBRARIES
Library West
Documents Department
Gainesville, FL 32601
(904) 392-0367

UNIV. OF GEORGIA LIBRARIES
Government Reference Dept.
Athens, GA 30602
(404) 542-8949

UNIV. OF HAWAII LIBRARY
Govt. Documents Collection
2550 The Mall
Honolulu, HI 96822
(808) 948-8230

UNIV. OF IDAHO LIBRARY
Documents Section
Moscow, ID 83843
(208) 885-6344

*SEND NO CHECKS OR ORDERS TO THESE LIBRARIES.

ILLINOIS STATE LIBRARY
Information Services Branch
Centennial Building
Springfield, IL 62756
(217) 782-7597

INDIANA STATE LIBRARY
Serials and Documents Section
140 North Senate Avenue
Indianapolis, IN 46204
(317) 232-3678

UNIV. OF IOWA LIBRARIES
Govt. Publication Department
Iowa City, IA 52242
(319) 353-3318

UNIVERSITY OF KANSAS
Doc. Collect, Spencer Lib.
Lawrence, KS 66045
(913) 864-4662

**UNIV. OF KENTUCKY
 LIBRARIES**
Govt. Pub. Department
Lexington, KY 40506
(606) 257-2639

LOUISIANA STATE UNIV. LIB.
BA/Docs. Dept.
Middleton Library
Baton Rouge, LA 70803
(504) 388-2570

**LOUISIANA TECHNICAL UNIV.
 LIBRARY**
Documents Department
Ruston, LA 71272
(318) 257-4962

UNIVERSITY OF MAINE
Raymond H. Fogler Library
Documents Depository
Orono, ME 04469
(207) 581-7178

UNIVERSITY OF MARYLAND
McKeldin Lib., Doc. Div.
College Park, MD 20742
(301) 454-3034

BOSTON PUBLIC LIBRARY
Government Docs. Dept.
Boston, MA 02117
(617) 536-5400, ext. 295

DETROIT PUBLIC LIBRARY
Sociology Department
5201 Woodward Avenue
Detroit, MI 48202
(313) 833-1000

MICHIGAN STATE LIBRARY
P. O. Box 30007
735 E. Michigan Avenue
Lansing, MI 48909
(517) 373-0640

UNIVERSITY OF MINNESOTA
Govt. Pub. Division
409 Wilson Library
Minneapolis, MN 55455
(612) 373-7813

UNIV. OF MISSISSIPPI LIB.
Documents Department
University, MS 38677
(601) 232-7091, ext. 7

UNIV. OF MONTANA
Mansfield Library
Documents Division
Missoula, MT 59812
(406) 243-6700

NEBRASKA LIBRARY COMM.
Federal Documents
1420 P Street
Lincoln, NB 68508
(402) 471-2045

**UNIVERSITY OF NEBRASKA-
 LINCOLN**
D. L. Love Memorial Library
Documents Division LL201N
Lincoln, NB 68508
(402) 472-2562

UNIVERSITY OF NEVADA LIB.
Govt. Pub. Department
Reno, NV 89557
(702) 784-6579

NEWARK PUBLIC LIBRARY
Social Services Division
5 Washington Street
Newark, NJ 07102
(201) 733-7812

UNIVERSITY OF NEW MEXICO
Zimmerman Library
Government Pub. Dept.
Albuquerque, NM 87131
(505) 277-5441

NEW MEXICO STATE LIBRARY
Reference Department
P. O. Box 1629
Santa Fe, NM 87503
(505) 827-2033

NEW YORK STATE LIBRARY
Empire State Plaza
Albany, NY 12230
(518) 474-5563

UNIV. OF NORTH CAROLINA AT CHAPEL HILL LIBRARY
BA/SS Div. Documents
Chapel Hill, NC 27514
(919) 933-1151

NORTH DAKOTA STATE UNIV. LIBRARY
Govt. Documents Department
Fargo, ND 58105
(701) 237-8886
(in cooperation with)

UNIV. OF NORTH DAKOTA
Chester Fritz Library
Documents Department
Grand Forks, ND 58202
(701) 777-4646

STATE LIBRARY OF OHIO
Documents Department
65 South Front Street
Columbus, OH 43215
(614) 466-9511

OKLAHOMA DEPT. OF LIBRARIES
Government Documents
200 NE 18th Street
Oklahoma City, OK 73105
(405) 521-2502

OKLAHOMA STATE UNIV. LIB.
Documents Department
Stillwater, OK 74078
(405) 624-6546

PORTLAND STATE UNIV. LIB.
Documents Department
P. O. Box 1151
Portland, OR 97207
(503) 229-3673

STATE LIBRARY OF PENN.
Government Pub. Section
P. O. Box 1601
Harrisburg, PA 17105
(717) 787-3752

TEXAS STATE LIBRARY
Public Service Department
P. O. Box 12927
Austin, TX 78711
(512) 475-6725

TEXAS TECH UNIV. LIBRARY
Govt. Documents Department
Lubbock, TX 79409
(806) 742-2268

UTAH STATE UNIVERSITY
Merril Library, U.M.C. 30
Logan, UT 84321
(801) 750-2682

UNIVERSITY OF VIRGINIA
Alderman Lib., Public Doc.
Charlottesville, VA 22901
(804) 924-3133

WASHINGTON STATE LIBRARY
Documents Section
Olympia, WA 98504
(206) 753-4027

WEST VIRGINIA UNIV. LIB.
Documents Department
Morgantown, WV 26506
(304) 293-3640

MILWAUKEE PUBLIC LIBRARY
814 West Wisconsin Avenue
Milwaukee, WI 53233
(414) 278-3000

STATE HIST. LIB. OF WISCONSIN
Government Pub. Section
816 State Street
Madison, WI 53706
(608) 262-4347

WYOMING STATE LIBRARY
Supreme Ct. & Lib. Building
Cheyenne, WY 82002
(307) 777-7281

Appendix 2
GPO Sales Publications Reference File (PRF)

Introduction

The "GPO Sales Publications Reference File" or PRF is a 48X microfiche catalog of publications sold by the Superintendent of Documents, Government Printing Office. The PRF lists all publications currently for sale by the Superintendent of Documents as well as forthcoming and recently out-of-stock items.

Frequency of Issue

There are two parts to the PRF: the cumulative file of approximately 300 microfiche and a supplement, called "GPO New Sales Publications," that is usually 1 or 2 microfiche. The cumulative file is issued to subscribers and Depository Libraries every two months—in January, March, May, July, September, and November. The supplement, issued monthly, lists new and reprinted publications added to the active sales inventory in the past month.

A weekly edition of the cumulative PRF is issued to GPO personnel and is available to subscribers for a special higher rate.

Who Can Use the PRF?

PRF can be used by anyone interested in Federal Government documents—bookstore staff, librarians, students, teachers, business people, researchers, and others. PRF can be used:

To identify specific publications sold by the Superintendent of Documents; to determine their availability, prices, and stock numbers.

To find out what the Government is publishing on a particular subject; to supplement other information sources on Federal Government publications.

To identify Government publications which may be used in GPO Depository Libraries. Over 1300 libraries in the United States have GPO depository collections open to the public. About 1150 of these libraries receive the PRF.

Scope

Almost any subject can be discussed in a Government document: solar energy, gardening, home building, geology, space exploration, occupations, military history, public transportation—as well as Government reports, laws, and regulations.

Publications include books, pamphlets, periodicals, maps, posters, microfiche and other materials supported and published by the United States Government and sold by GPO.

About 25,000 titles are in stock at any one time. PRF includes bibliographic citations to documents from over 60 major Federal departments and agencies, as well as from smaller Federal bureaus.

Most of the publications on PRF were issued in the last five years. However, PRF does cite many earlier publications still available from GPO.

Arrangement

The microfiche has three sequences:

(1) The "stock number sequence" starts with microfiche #1. The stock numbers are arranged in numerical sequence, from 001−000−00006−3 to 099−000−03865-9 as of this writing.

(2) The "catalog number sequence" begins with A 1. and continues through Y 10. Catalog numbers for "Forms" follow in a separate sequence. The catalog number is the "Superintendent of Documents classification number" or "SuDoc class number." In this manual, it is called simply the catalog number.

(3) The "alphabetical sequence" is a dictionary arrangement, in alphabetical order, of all titles, series, key words, key phrases, subjects, and personal authors.

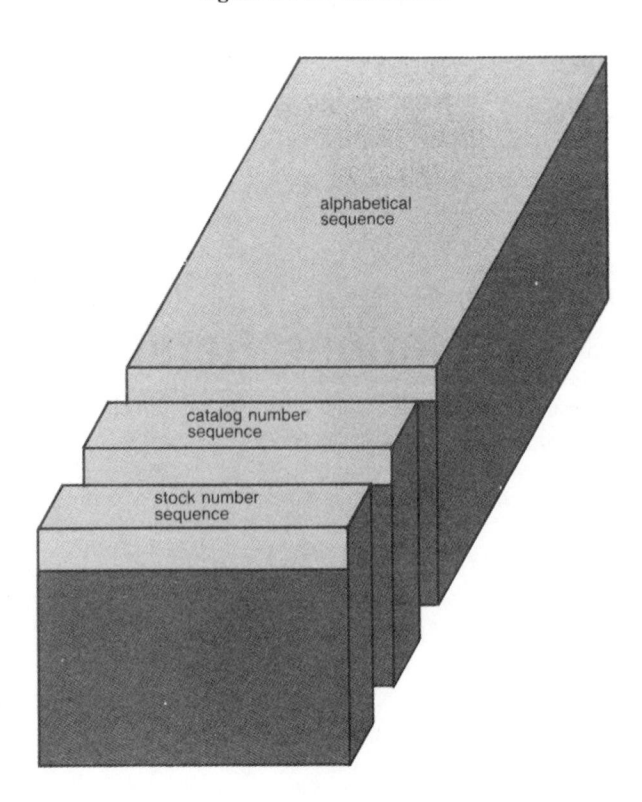

Figure 1 PRF Microfiche

Finding the Right Microfiche

The color stripe at the top of each microfiche is the header. The header works like a telephone directory page guide: it gives the first and last entries on each microfiche. In the example shown in Figure 2, the first entry is for "Minnesota Dulut" and the last entry is for "Money Income An." The words are cut short on the header because of space limitations. The "203 of 290" in the upper right corner indicates this is number 203 in the set of 290 microfiche. These numbers simplify refiling microfiche after use. The microfiche in this example was produced on January 22, 1981.

Microfiche Grids

A grid system is used to locate information on the microfiche. Each microfiche is divided into rows and columns: rows are lettered A to O; columns are numbered 1 to 18. Each frame is designated by a letter and a number: A1, B6, J12, etc.

There are 270 frames on a microfiche and an average of 2 or 3 records to a frame. The last frame (O18) is the index frame.

Using the Index Frame

Once you find the microfiche you need, refer to the index frame in the bottom right corner (frame O18). The index lists the first heading on each frame and gives the frame number.

Part of an index frame is shown in Figure 3. If you were looking for publications about the Mississippi River, you would look on frames 08 through F9.

Figures 2 and 3 are shown on page 202.

Figure 2 Sample Microfiche

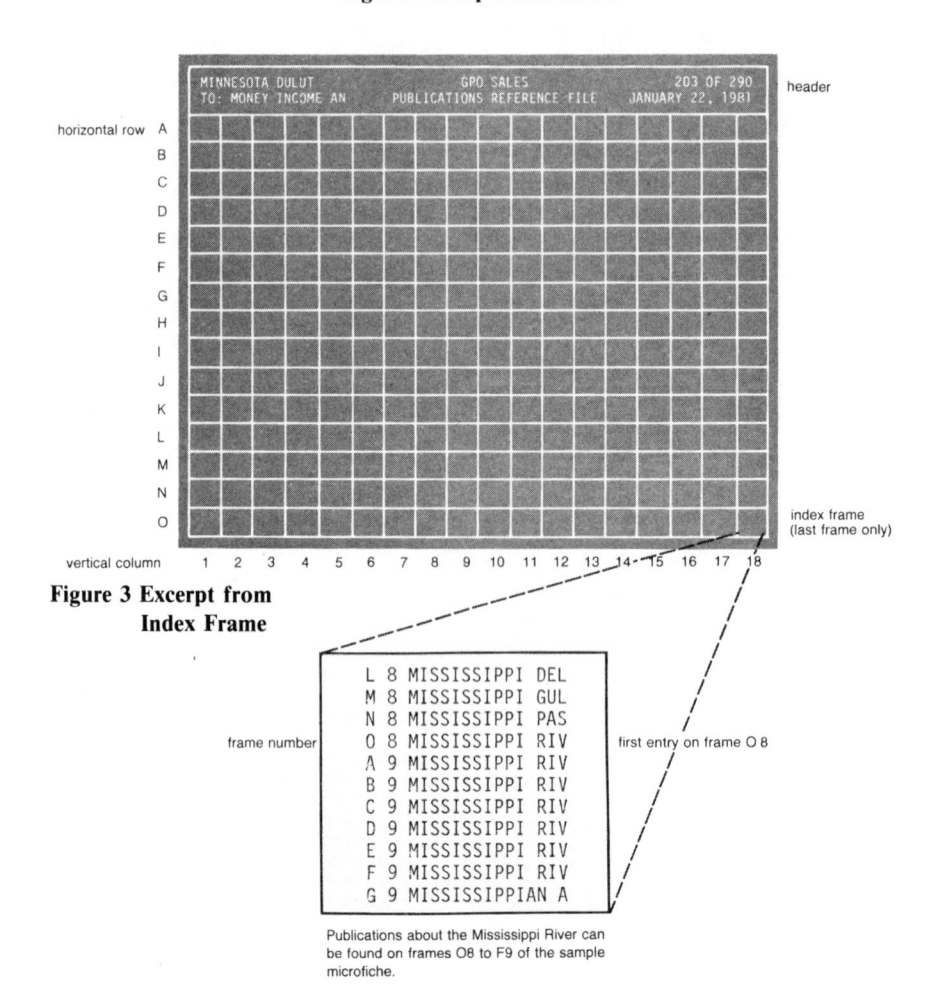

header: MINNESOTA DULUT TO: MONEY INCOME AN / GPO SALES PUBLICATIONS REFERENCE FILE / 203 OF 290 JANUARY 22, 1981

horizontal row A–O

vertical column 1–18

index frame (last frame only)

Figure 3 Excerpt from Index Frame

frame number

```
L 8 MISSISSIPPI DEL
M 8 MISSISSIPPI GUL
N 8 MISSISSIPPI PAS
O 8 MISSISSIPPI RIV
A 9 MISSISSIPPI RIV
B 9 MISSISSIPPI RIV
C 9 MISSISSIPPI RIV
D 9 MISSISSIPPI RIV
E 9 MISSISSIPPI RIV
F 9 MISSISSIPPI RIV
G 9 MISSISSIPPIAN A
```

first entry on frame O 8

Publications about the Mississippi River can be found on frames O8 to F9 of the sample microfiche.

Appendix 2—GPO Sales Publications Reference File / 203

Figure 4 Sample Record (showing a typical entry on the PRF)

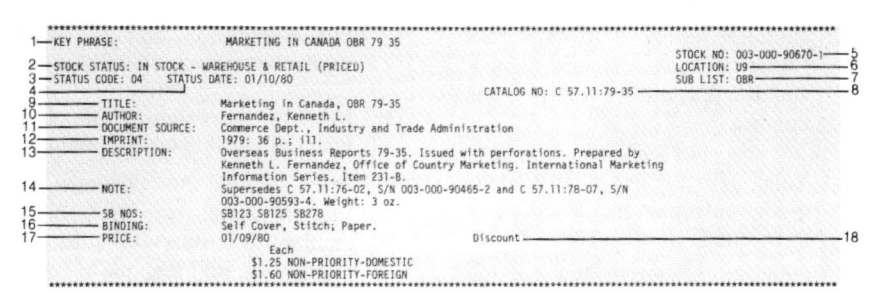

```
1—KEY PHRASE:            MARKETING IN CANADA OBR 79 35
                                                                        STOCK NO: 003-000-90670-1——5
2—STOCK STATUS: IN STOCK - WAREHOUSE & RETAIL (PRICED)                  LOCATION: U9——————————————6
3—STATUS CODE: 04    STATUS DATE: 01/10/80                              SUB LIST: OBR————————————7
4—                                              CATALOG NO: C 57.11:79-35—————————————————————————8
9———————TITLE:           Marketing in Canada, OBR 79-35
10——————AUTHOR:          Fernandez, Kenneth L.
11——————DOCUMENT SOURCE: Commerce Dept., Industry and Trade Administration
12——————IMPRINT:         1979: 36 p.; ill.
13——————DESCRIPTION:     Overseas Business Reports 79-35. Issued with perforations. Prepared by
                         Kenneth L. Fernandez, Office of Country Marketing. International Marketing
                         Information Series. Item 231-B.
14——————NOTE:            Supersedes C 57.11:76-02, S/N 003-000-90465-2 and C 57.11:78-07, S/N
                         003-000-90593-4. Weight: 3 oz.
15——————SB NOS:          SB123 SB125 SB278
16——————BINDING:         Self Cover, Stitch; Paper.
17——————PRICE:           01/09/80                        Discount ————————————————————————————————18
                         Each
                         $1.25 NON-PRIORITY-DOMESTIC
                         $1.60 NON-PRIORITY-FOREIGN
```

Parts of the Record

(1) **Key Phrase** Any heading that indexes the publication and sorts on the microfiche. The term "key phrase" refers to any access point: stock number, catalog number, title, author, series, subject heading, as well as key words from the title.

(2) **Stock Status** Tells whether or not an item is available for sale from GPO. Most publications listed are available, but some are forthcoming or out-of-stock.

(3) **Status-Code** Numerical symbol for the stock status.

(4) **Status-Date** Date the status of the publication was changed.

(5) **Stock Number** The unique 12-digit hyphenated number (000–000–00000–0) that GPO Sales uses to identify a publication or subscription. This number should be used when ordering a publication.

(6) **Location** Symbol for the unit in the GPO retail warehouse where copies of the item are stored.

(7) **Sub List** Symbol used by GPO Sales to identify a subscription, or a publication available on standing order service.

(8) **Catalog Number** Superintendent of Documents classification number. Many Depository Libraries use catalog numbers to arrange documents on shelves in their collections.

(9) **Title** Name of document. Usually taken from the title page. May be taken from the cover, envelope, or mailing carton of items without a title page.

(10) **Author** Person(s) who wrote the document. May also refer to editors, illustrators, compilers, or task force leaders named prominently in the publication.

(11) **Document Source** Name of the Federal agency that issued or released the document. Often it is what librarians refer to as the "corporate author."

(12) **Imprint** Gives the year the publication was printed, the number of pages, and related information.

(13) **Description** Provides other information about the publication. Includes, as applicable: departmental series, report number, complete title, alternate titles, additional information about

personal/corporate authors, scope note or brief abstract, department contract number, ISBN, ISSN, Library of Congress card number, and the Depository Library item number.

(14) **Note** This paragraph is used for special information. Includes, as applicable: weight of the publication, supersession information, SL number (number assigned to the publication when listed in GPO's *Selected U.S. Government Publications*), CIC number (number assigned the publication when listed in the *Consumer Information Catalog*), reprint information, and other sales information.

(15) **SB Nos** Numbers of the GPO Subject Bibliographies in which this publication and others on similar subjects are to be listed.

(16) **Binding** Gives binding, cover material, and related information.

(17) **Price** Gives the domestic and foreign prices for non-priority mailing, the date the price was established, and the unit of issue.

(18) **Discount** "Discount" means the price will be discounted for customers ordering certain bulk quantities and for bookdealers. "No Discount" means bookdealers and bulk orders will not receive discounts.

Appendix 2 – GPO Sales Publications Reference File / 205

Figure 5 How a Typical Publication Is Indexed

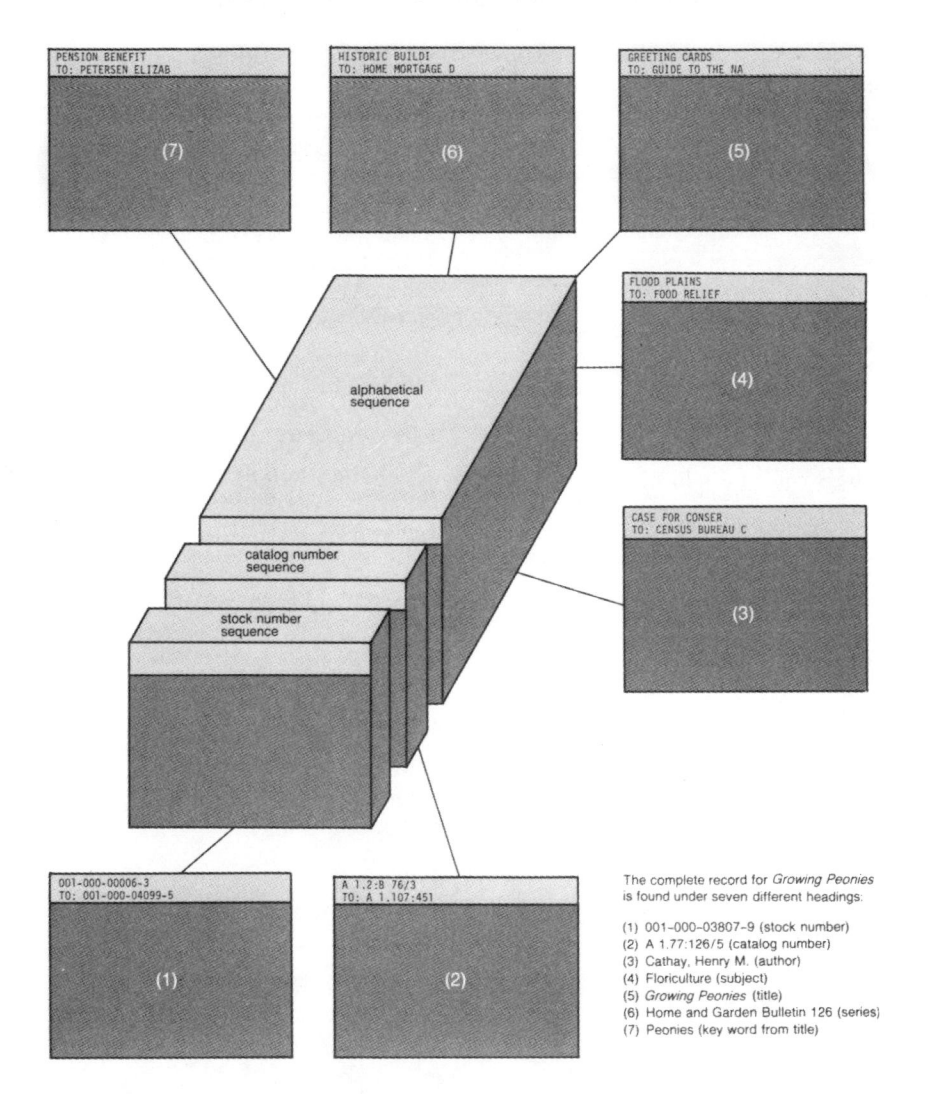

PENSION BENEFIT
TO: PETERSEN ELIZAB
(7)

HISTORIC BUILDI
TO: HOME MORTGAGE D
(6)

GREETING CARDS
TO: GUIDE TO THE NA
(5)

FLOOD PLAINS
TO: FOOD RELIEF
(4)

CASE FOR CONSER
TO: CENSUS BUREAU C
(3)

alphabetical sequence

catalog number sequence

stock number sequence

001-000-00006-3
TO: 001-000-04099-5
(1)

A 1.2:B 76/3
TO: A 1.107:451
(2)

The complete record for *Growing Peonies* is found under seven different headings:

(1) 001-000-03807-9 (stock number)
(2) A 1.77:126/5 (catalog number)
(3) Cathay, Henry M. (author)
(4) Floriculture (subject)
(5) *Growing Peonies* (title)
(6) Home and Garden Bulletin 126 (series)
(7) Peonies (key word from title)

GPO New Sales Publications Microfiche

GPO New Sales Publications, a monthly supplement to the PRF, is included as part of the PRF subscription. Consisting of one or two microfiche, it lists "new" publications offered for sale during the past month. The publications are listed in only one sequence, alphabetically by title.

"New" publications include:

(1) forthcoming publications with prices;
(2) new publications in stock for the first time;
(3) reprints of older publications that have come back in stock.

On reprinted publications, the capitalized word REPRINT appears in the Note field. This can alert you to the fact that the publication has been in existence for some time. If you are using the file for acquisitions, a reprinted publication may already be in your collection.

All publications on the GPO New Sales Publications microfiche are also indexed on the PRF.

The latest issue of the GPO New Sales Publications microfiche can be used for ordering publications. When you order, always use the latest issue of either the cumulative PRF or the GPO New Sales Publications microfiche. Prices and statuses are constantly changing and information on older microfiche may be outdated and inaccurate.

Figure 7 GPO New Sales Publications Microfiche

Issued as a monthly supplement to the PRF, this single microfiche lists new and reprinted publications in alphabetical order by title.

```
ADMINISTRATIVE        GPO NEW SALES PUBLICATIONS            1 OF   1
TO: YOUR ENERGY WOR                                  JANUARY 22, 1981
```

Exhausted GPO Sales Publications Reference File (EPRF)

What Is It?

Each January, a number of out-of-stock publications are removed from the PRF. These out-of-stock publications are transferred to the Exhausted GPO Sales Publications Reference File (EPRF).

EPRF is a 48X microfiche index of out-of-stock publications. It is not included as part of the PRF subscription, but is sold separately as a companion file.

As of 1981, there are two editions of the EPRF: 1980 and 1981.

The EPRF published in 1980 covers documents that went out-of-stock over a six year period—from 1972 to December 1978. The file cites over 25,000 documents; it is composed of 136 microfiche.

The EPRF published in 1981 is a supplement to the 1980 EPRF. It covers documents that went out-of-stock over an eighteen month period—from January 1979 to June 1980. The file cites about 9000 documents; it is composed of 76 microfiche.

In the future, GPO plans to update the EPRF by issuing supplementary cumulations once a year.

EPRF is identical to the PRF in its indexing and microfiche format. It can be searched in the same way as the PRF.

How Can EPRF Be Used?

The EPRF provides a ready reference file of historical bibliographic information that can be helpful in identifying older publications. While the EPRF does not claim to be the final authoritative source for identifying all Government documents, it does serve as a useful companion volume to the PRF.

If you do not find a publication listed on PRF, you can search the EPRF to determine if the publication was sold by GPO in the past. Bibliographic information on the EPRF may aid in locating a copy of the publication in a Depository Library or from the issuing agency. If a publication cannot be found on either PRF or EPRF, it can be searched in the *Monthly Catalog* and/or other indexes.

PRF Searching Aid for Depository Library Users

The GPO Sales Publications Reference File (PRF) is a microfiche catalog of all publications for sale by the United States Government Printing Office. It is arranged in three sequences:

(1) GPO stock numbers
(2) catalog numbers (Superintendent of Documents classification numbers)
(3) alphabetical arrangement of titles, key words, subject headings, personal authors, agency series, subtitles, alternate titles, and other headings.

The most useful sequence for library users is the alphabetical section. If you search under a good title, key word, or subject heading, you will probably find what you are looking for easily.

Each microfiche has a header which works like a telephone directory page guide by indicating the first and last entries on that microfiche. On the microfiche, entries are arranged in columns, from top to bottom, and then from left to right.

Many Government documents collections use the catalog number (found near the upper right corner of most records) to arrange documents on their shelves. Documents in these collections can be requested by catalog numbers. Publications that are not yet in stock may not yet have catalog numbers, and may not be in a collection.

Most publications can be found under at least 7 different headings. The record shown below is indexed under:

(1) stock number 001–000–03807–9
(2) catalog number A 1.77:126/5

AND in the alphabetical sequence under:

(3) *Growing Peonies* (title)
(4) Cathey, Henry M. (author)
(5) Home and Garden Bulletin 126 (series)
(6) Peonies (key word)
(7) Floriculture (subject heading)

Figure 12

```
*KEY PHRASE:            GROWING PEONIES                                                    STOCK NO: 001-000-03807-9
                                                                                           LOCATION: U1
*STOCK STATUS: IN STOCK - WAREHOUSE & RETAIL (PRICED)
*STATUS CODE: 04    STATUS DATE: 09/08/78
                                                                 CATALOG NO: A 1.77:126/5
         TITLE:         Growing Peonies
         AUTHOR:        Cathey, Henry M.
         DOCUMENT SOURCE: Agriculture Dept., Science and Education Administration
         IMPRINT:       1978: 11 p.; ill. revised ed.
         DESCRIPTION:   Home and Garden Bulletin 126. Item 11.
         NOTE:          Supersedes A 1.77:126/4, S/N 001-000-01283-5. Weight: 1 oz. 1980 SL 2400
         SB NOS:        SB301
         BINDING:       Paper Cover, Stitch; Paper.
         PRICE:         07/19/78                     Discount
                        Each
                        $.80 NON-PRIORITY-DOMESTIC
                        $1.00 NON-PRIORITY-FOREIGN
```

Appendix 3
U.S. Government Bookstores

In addition to the mail-order service provided by the Office of the Superintendent of Documents, U.S. Government Printing Office, there are retail bookstores in Washington, D.C., and several cities throughout the United States, each of which has in stock approximately 1,500 of our most popular titles. You are invited to stop in any time. The locations of these stores are shown below:

Atlanta Bookstore
Room 100, Federal Building
275 Peachtree Street NE.
Atlanta, Georgia 30303
Telephone: (404) 221-6947

Birmingham Bookstore
9220 Parkway East-B
Roebuck Shopping City
Birmingham, Alabama 35206
Telephone: (205) 254-1056

Boston Bookstore
Room G25, John F. Kennedy
  Federal Building
Sudbury Street
Boston, Massachusetts 02203
Telephone: (617) 223-6071

Chicago Bookstore
Room 1463—14th Floor
Everett McKinley Dirksen Building
219 South Dearborn Street
Chicago, Illinois 60604
Telephone: (312) 353-5133

Cleveland Bookstore
First Floor
Federal Building
1240 East 9th Street
Cleveland, Ohio 44199
Telephone: (216) 522-4922

Columbus Bookstore
Federal Office Building, Room 207
200 North High Street
Columbus, Ohio 43215
Telephone: (614) 469-6956

Dallas Bookstore
Room 1C50
Federal Building—U.S. Courthouse
1100 Commerce Street
Dallas, Texas 75242
Telephone: (214) 767-0076

Denver Bookstore
Room 117
Federal Building—U.S. Courthouse
1961 Stout Street
Denver, Colorado 80294
Telephone: (303) 837-3964

210 / Appendix 3 – U.S. Government Bookstores

Detroit Bookstore
Patrick V. McNamara Federal Building
477 Michigan Avenue, Suite 160
Detroit, Michigan 48226
Telephone: (313) 226-7816

Houston Bookstore
45 College Center
9319 Gulf Freeway
Houston, Texas 77017
Telephone: (713) 226-5453

Jacksonville Bookstore
Room 158
Federal Building
400 West Bay Street
Jacksonville, Florida 32202
Telephone: (904) 791-3801

Kansas City Bookstore
Room 144, Federal Office Building
601 East 12th Street
Kansas City, Missouri 64106
Telephone: (816) 374-2160

U.S. Government Bookstore
ARCO Plaza, C Level
505 South Flower Street
Los Angeles, California 90071
Telephone: (213) 688-5841

Milwaukee Bookstore
Room 190
Federal Building
519 East Wisconsin Avenue
Milwaukee, Wisconsin 53202
Telephone: (414) 291-1304

New York Bookstore
Room 110
26 Federal Plaza
New York, New York 10007
Telephone: (212) 264-3825

Philadelphia Bookstore
Federal Office Building
Room 1214
600 Arch Street
Philadelphia, Pennsylvania 19106
Telephone: (215) 597-0677

Pittsburgh Bookstore
Room 118, Federal Building
1000 Liberty Avenue
Pittsburgh, Pennsylvania 15222
Telephone: (412) 261-7165

Pueblo Bookstore
Majestic Building
720 North Main Street
Pueblo, Colorado 81003
Telephone: (303) 544-3142

Pueblo Distribution Center
Public Docs. Distribution Center
P. O. Box 4007
Pueblo, Colorado 81003
Telephone: (303) 544-5277

San Francisco Bookstore
Room 1023, Federal Office Building
450 Golden Gate Avenue
San Francisco, California 94102
Telephone: (415) 556-0643

Seattle Bookstore
Room 194
Federal Building
915 Second Avenue
Seattle, Washington 98174
Telephone: (206) 442-4270

Washington, D.C., Area Bookstores

U.S. Government Printing Office
710 North Capitol Street
Washington, D.C. 20402
Telephone: (202) 275-2091

Department of Commerce
Room 1604, First Floor
14th & E Streets NW.
Washington, D.C. 20230
Telephone: (202) 377-3527

Washington, D.C., Area Bookstores (cont'd)

Department of State
Room 2817, North Lobby
21st and C Streets NW.
Washington, D.C. 20520
Telephone: (202) 632-1437

Health and Human Services Bookstore
Room 1528
330 Independence Ave., SW.
Washington, D.C. 20201
Telephone: (202) 472-7478

Int'l Communication Agency
1776 Pennsylvania Avenue NW.
Washington, D.C. 20547
Telephone: (202) 724-9928

Laurel Bookstore
8660 Cherry Lane
Laurel, Maryland 20810
Telephone: (301) 953-7974

Pentagon Bookstore
Main Concourse, South End
Washington, D.C. 20301
Telephone: (202) 557-1821

Appendix 4
U.S. Government Departments and Agencies

Provided here is an alphabetical list of agencies that appear as issuers, or publishers, in this directory. Prefixes of Superintendent of Documents (SuDocs) classification numbers and historical data have been provided, where available. A list of abbreviations and/or acronyms for parent bodies and other agencies used in this appendix precede the alphabetical list of agencies. An asterisk (*) in the abbreviations list indicates a parent body. In the list of full names, abbreviations appearing in parentheses after an agency indicate parent body or bodies; further, "(HEW, HHS)" signifies a change in parent body from HEW to HHS. Occasionally, abbreviations other than the parent body will be cited, e.g., "(PHS, HEW, HHS)" and "(NOAA, CD)." This indicates, first, a well-known agency under which a title may be sought, although that agency is not the parent body, followed by the abbreviation for the parent body or bodies. See the abbreviations list to find the names of these agencies. Parent bodies in the full names list do not have abbreviations or acronyms following their names. Those agencies in the full names list that are no longer in existence are preceded by a dagger (†).

Abbreviations

AA	Aging Administration
*AD	Agriculture Department
ADAMHA	Alcohol, Drug Abuse, and Mental Health Administration
*CAB	Civil Aeronautics Board
*CD	Commerce Department
CDC	Centers for Disease Control
*CRC	Civil Rights Commission
*CSA	Community Services Administration
*CSC	Civil Service Commission
CYFA	Children, Youth and Families Administration
*DoD	Department of Defense
*DOE	Department of Energy
*DOT	Department of Transportation
*ED	Department of Education
*EEOC	Equal Employment Opportunity Commission
*EOP	Executive Office of the President

213

214 / Appendix 4—U.S. Government Departments and Agencies

*EPA	Environmental Protection Agency
*ERDA	Energy Research and Development Administration
*FCC	Federal Communications Commission
*FDA	Food and Drug Administration
*FDIC	Federal Deposit Insurance Corporation
*FEA	Federal Energy Administration
*FEC	Federal Election Commission
*FEMA	Federal Emergency Management Agency
*FHLBB	Federal Home Loan Bank Board
*FPC	Federal Power Commission
*GAO	General Accounting Office
*GSA	General Services Administration
HDSO	Human Development Services Office
*HEW	Health, Education, and Welfare Department
*HHS	Health and Human Services Department
HRA	Health Resources Administration
*HUD	Housing and Urban Development Department
*ID	Interior Department
JCS	Joint Chiefs of Staff
*JD	Justice Department
*LC	Library of Congress
*LD	Labor Department
LEAA	Law Enforcement Assistance Administration
*NASA	National Aeronautics and Space Administration
*NCUA	National Credit Union Administration
NIDA	National Institute on Drug Abuse
NIH	National Institutes of Health
NIMH	National Institute of Mental Health
NOAA	National Oceanic and Atmospheric Administration
*NRC	Nuclear Regulatory Commission
*NSF	National Science Foundation
OE	Office of Education
*OPM	Office of Personnel Management
PHS	Public Health Service
*SBA	Small Business Administration
*SD	State Department
*SEC	Securities and Exchange Commission
*SI	Smithsonian Institution
*TD	Treasury Department
*USPS	United States Postal Service
*VA	Veterans Administration

Full Names, Publications Information, and Parent Bodies

Administrative Conference of the United States
   Y3.Ad6, 1964- .

Administrative Office of the United States Courts
   Ju10, 1939- .

Advisory Council on Historic Preservation
   Y3.H62, 1966- .

Aging Administration
   HE1.200, 1973-1977; HE23.3000, 1977- . (HEW, HHS)

Agricultural Marketing Service
   A88, 1972- . (AD)

Agriculture Department
   A1. 1861- .

Air Force Department
   D301, 1949- . (DoD)

Alcohol, Drug Abuse, and Mental Health Administration
   HE20.8000, 1973- . (PHS, HEW, HHS)

Alcohol, Tobacco, and Firearms Bureau
   T70, 1972- . (TD)

American Folklife Center
   LC39, 1976- . (LC)

Animal and Plant Health Inspection Service
   A101, 1972- . (AD)

Army Corps of Engineers
   D103, 1949- . (DoD)

Army Department
   D101, 1949- . (DoD)

Automated Data and Telecommunications Service
   GS12, 1972- . (GSA)

†Cabinet Committee on Opportunity for Spanish Speaking Peoples
   Y3.Sp2-7:2, 1969-1974.

Census Bureau
C3, 1903-1972, 1975- ; C56.200, 1972-1975. (CD)

Center for Military History
D114, 1974- . (DoD)

Centers for Disease Control
HE20.7000, 1973- . (PHS, HEW, HHS)

Central Intelligence Agency
PrEx3.10, 1961- . (EOP)

Children, Youth and Families Administration
HE23.1000, 1977- . (HEW, HHS)

Children's Bureau
HE23.1200, 1977- ; HE1.450, 1975-1977; HE21.100, 1970-1975.
(HEW, HHS)

Civil Aeronautics Board
C31.200, 1940-1978. (CD)
CAB1, 1978- .

Civil Rights Commission
CR1, 1957- .

†Civil Service Commission
CS1, 1883-1978.
Later, Personnel Management Office.

Coast Guard
TD5, 1966- . (DOT)

Commerce Department
C1, 1913- .

Community Health Services Bureau
HE20.5100, 1973- . (PHS, HEW, HHS)

Community Services Administration
CSA1, 1975- .

Congressional Publications. *See also names of specific committees under* U.S.
Congress
Y, 1789- .
Y1.2, House of Representatives.
Y1.3, Senate.
Y4, Committee publications (Hearings, Prints).

Consumer Affairs Office
    HE1.500, 1973- . (HEW, HHS)

Customs Service
    T17, 1973- . (TD)

Defense Civil Preparedness Agency
    D14, 1972- . (DoD)

Defense Contract Audit Agency
    D1.46, 1965- . (DoD)

Defense Department
    D1, 1949- .

†Domestic and International Business Administration
    C57, 1972-1977. (CD)
    Later, Industry and Trade Administration, 1977-1980, and International Trade Administration, C61, 1980- .

†Domestic Commerce Bureau
    C57.500, 1974-1980. (CD)
    Later, Industrial Economics Bureau.

Drugs Bureau
    HE20.4200, 1971- . (FDA, HEW, HHS)

Economic Development Administration
    C46, 1965- . (CD)

Economic Regulatory Administration
    E4, 1977- . (DOE)

Education Department
    ED1, 1979- .

†Education Office
    HE5, 1970-1972; HE19.100, 1972-1979. (HEW)
    Later, Education Department.

Employment and Training Administration
    L37, 1975- . (LD)

Employment Standards Administration
    L36, 1971- . (LD)

Energy Department
    E1, 1977- .

Energy Information Administration
E3, 1977- . (DOE)

†Energy Research and Development Administration
ER1, 1975-1977.
Later, Energy Department.

Environmental Data and Information Service
C55.200, 1970- . (NOAA, CD)

Environmental Protection Agency
EP1, 1970- .

Equal Employment Opportunity Commission
Y3.Eq2, 1965- .

Executive Office of the President
PrEx1, 1961- .

Extension Service
A43, 1970-1978; A106, 1978-1981; A43, 1981- . (AD)

Federal Aviation Administration
TD4, 1967- . (DOT)

Federal Committee on Ecological Reserves
Y3.F31-22.

Federal Communications Commission
CC1, 1934- .

Federal Coordinating Council for Science, Engineering, and Technology
PrEx23, 1976- .

Federal Deposit Insurance Corporation
Y3.F31-8, 1933- .

Federal Election Commission
Y3.El2-3, 1974- .

Federal Emergency Management Agency
FEM1, 1979- .

†Federal Energy Administration
FE1, 1974-1977.
Later, Energy Information Administration.

Federal Energy Regulatory Commission
E2, 1977- . (DOE)

Federal Executive Board
Y3.F31-20, 1962- .

Federal Highway Administration
TD2, 1966- . (DOT)

Federal Home Loan Bank Board
FHL1, 1955- .

Federal Insurance Administration
HH10, 1868-1979; FEM1.200, 1979- . (HUD, FEMA)

†Federal Power Commission
FP1, 1930-1977.
Later, Federal Energy Regulatory Commission.

Federal Register Office
GS4.100, 1949- . (GSA)

Fish and Wildlife Service
I49, 1940- . (ID)

Food and Drug Administration
HE20.4000, 1970- . (PHS, HEW, HHS)

Food and Nutrition Service
A98, 1969- . (AD)

Food Safety and Inspection Service
A110, 1981- . (AD)

†Food Safety and Quality Service
A103, 1977-1981.
Later, Food Safety and Inspection Service.

Foreign Agricultural Service
A67, 1953- . (AD)

Forest Service
A13, 1905- . (AD)

General Accounting Office
GA1, 1921- .

General Services Administration
GS1, 1949- .

Geological Survey
I19, 1879- . (ID)

Government Financial Operations Bureau
T63.100, 1974- . (TD)

Governmental and Public Affairs Office
A107, 1978- . (AD)

Handicapped Individuals Office
HE23.4000, 1977-1979. (HEW, HHS)
ED1, 1979- . (ED)

Head Start Bureau
HE21.200, 1970-1977. (HEW)
HE1.800, 1977. (HEW)
HE23.1100, 1977- . (CYFA, HHS)

Health and Human Services Department
HE1, 1979- .

Health Care Financing Administration
HE22, 1977- . (HEW, HHS)

†Health, Education, and Welfare Department
HE1, 1970-1979.
Later, Health and Human Services Department and Education Department.

Health Manpower Bureau
HE20.6600, 1975- . (PHS, HEW, HHS)

†Health Planning and Resources Development Bureau
HE20.6100, 1976-1978. (PHS, HEW)

Health Planning Bureau
HE20.6100, 1978- . (PHS, HEW, HHS)

†Health Resources Development Bureau
HE20.6100, 1973-1976. (PHS, HEW)

†Health Services and Mental Health Administration
HE20.2000, 1970-1973.
Later, Health Services Administration and Health Resources Administration.

Heritage Conservation and Recreation Service
I70, 1978-1981. (ID)
Later, National Park Service, I29.

Housing and Urban Development Department
HH1, 1965- .

Human Development Services Office
HE23, 1977- . (HEW, HHS)

Appendix 4 – U.S. Government Departments and Agencies / 221

Immigration and Naturalization Service
J21, 1940- . (JD)

Indian Affairs Bureau
I20, 1947- . (ID)

Indian Arts and Crafts Board
I1.84. (ID)

Industrial Economics Bureau
C62, 1980- . (CD)

†Industry and Trade Administration
C57, 1977-1980. (CD)
Later, International Trade Administration, C61, 1980- .

†Interagency Task Force for IndoChina Refugees
Pr38, 1975.

Interior Department
I1, 1849- .

Internal Revenue Service
T22, 1953- . (TD)

†International Commerce Bureau
C57.100, 1972-1977. (CD)

International Trade Administration
C61, 1980- . (CD)

John E. Fogarty International Center for Advanced Study in the Health Sciences
HE20,3700, 1970- . (PHS, HEW, HHS)

Judicial Conference of the United States
Ju10.

Justice Department
J1, 1870- .

Justice Statistics Bureau
J29, 1979- . (JD)

Juvenile Justice and Delinquency Prevention Office
J26. (LEAA, JD)

Labor Department
L1, 1913- .

Labor-Management Services Administration
L1. 1974-19? (LD)

Labor Statistics Bureau
L2, 1913- . (LD)

Land Management Bureau
I53, 1946- . (ID)

Law Enforcement Assistance Administration
J26, 1978- . (JD)

Library of Congress
LC1, 1800- .

Management and Budget Office
PrEx2, 1970- . (EOP)

†Manpower Administration
L1.39, 1953-1975. (LD)
Later, Employment and Training Administration, L37, 1975- .

Maritime Administration
C39.200, 1950- . (CD)

†Medical Devices and Diagnostic Products Bureau
HE20.4300, 1971-1977. (FDA)
Later, Medical Devices Bureau.

Medical Devices Bureau
HE20.4300, 1977- . (FDA, PHS, HEW, HHS)

Minority Business Development Agency. *See* Commerce Department

Minority Business Enterprise Office
C1.56. (CD)

Missouri River Basin Commission
Y3.M69-2, 1972- .

National Aeronautics and Space Administration
NAS1, 1958- .

National Alcohol Fuels Commission
Y3.Al1-2, 1978- .

National Bureau of Standards
C13, 1934- . (CD)

National Cancer Institute
HE20.3150, 1970- . (NIH, PHS, HEW, HHS)

National Center for Child Abuse and Neglect. *See* Children's Bureau

National Center for Education Statistics
ED1.100, 1979- . (ED)

†National Center for Educational Statistics
HE19.300, 1972-1979. (OE, HEW)
Later, National Center for Education Statistics, ED1.100.

National Center for Health Services Research and Development
HE20.6500, 1973- . (HRA, PHS, HEW, HHS)

National Center for Health Statistics
HE20.6200, 1973- . (PHS, HEW, HHS)

†National Center for Productivity and Quality of Working Life
Y3.P94, 1976-1978.

National Center for the Prevention and Control of Rape. *See* National Institute of Mental Health

National Clearinghouse for Drug Abuse Information
PrEx13, 1970-1973. (EOP)
HE20.8200, 1973- . (NIDA, HEW, HHS)

National Clearinghouse on Aging
HE23.3100, 1977- . (AA, HEW, HHS)

National Clearinghouse for Poison Control Centers. *See* Food and Drug Administration

National Clearinghouse on Domestic Violence. *See* Children, Youth and Families Administration

National Credit Union Administration
NCU 1, 1970- .

National Criminal Justice Information and Statistics Service
J1, 1968-1978; J26, 1978- . (LEAA, JD)

National Criminal Justice Reference Service. *See* Law Enforcement Assistance Administration

National Defense University
D5.400, 1977- . (JCS, DoD)

National Heart, Lung, and Blood Institute
    HE20.3200, 1975- . (NIH, PHS, HEW, HHS)

National Highway Traffic Safety Administration
    TD8, 1970- . (DOT)

National Institute for Occupational Safety and Health
    HE20.2800, 1971-1974; HE20.7100, 1974- . (CDC, PHS, HEW, HHS)

National Institute of Corrections. *See* Justice Department

National Institute of Education
    HE19.202, 1975-1979; ED1.300, 1979- . (OE, HEW, ED)

National Institute of Justice
    J28, 1979- . (JD)

National Institute of Law Enforcement and Criminal Justice
    J26, 1978- . (LEAA, JD)

National Institute of Mental Health
    HE20.2400, 1970-1973; HE20.8100, 1973- . (ADAMHA, PHS, HEW, HHS)

National Institute on Alcohol Abuse and Alcoholism
    HE20.8300, 1973- . (ADAMHA, PHS, HEW, HHS)

National Institute on Drug Abuse
    HE20.8200, 1973- . (ADAMHA, PHS, HEW, HHS)

National Institutes of Health
    HE20.3000, 1970- . (PHS, HEW, HHS)

National Library Service for the Blind and Physically Handicapped
    LC19, 1978- . (LC)

National Oceanic and Atmospheric Administration
    C55, 1970- . (CD)

National Park Service
    I29, 1916- . (ID)

National Science Foundation
    NS1, 1950- .

National Security Council
    PrEx3, 1961- . (EOP)

National Technical Information Service
    C51, 1970- . (CD)

National Telecommunications and Information Administration
C60, 1978. (CD)

National Weather Service
C55.100, 1970- . (NOAA, CD)

Nuclear Regulatory Commission
Y3.N88, 1975- .

†Office of Education
HE5, 1970-1972; HE19.100, 1972-1979. (HEW)

Office of Libraries and Learning Technologies. *See* Education Department

†Outdoor Recreation Bureau
I66, 1962-1977. (ID)

Patent and Trademark Office
C21, 1975- . (CD)

Pension Benefit Guaranty Corporation
Y3.P38-2, 1974- .

Personnel Management Office
PM1, 1978- .

Postal Service
P1, 1970- .

†Presidential Commission on Hunger
Pr39.8: W89/H89, 1977-1980.

President's Committee on Employment of the Handicapped
PrEx1.10, 1961- . (EOP)

President's Committee on Mental Retardation
Pr36.8:M52, 1971-1977; HE23.100, 1978- . (HDSO, HEW, HHS)

Public Health Service
HE20, 1970- . (HEW, HHS)

†Science and Education Administration
A106, 1978-1981. (AD)

Securities and Exchange Commission
SE1, 1934- .

Selective Service System
Y3.Se4, 1948- .

Small Business Administration
SBA1, 1953- .

Smithsonian Institution
SI1, 1846- .

Social Security Administration
HE3, 1970- . (HEW, HHS)

Solar Energy Research Institute
E1.28: SERI, 1977- . (DOE)

State Department
S1, 1789- .

†Telecommunications Office
C1.60, 1970-1978. (CD)

Transportation Department
TD1, 1966- .

Treasury Department
T1, 1789- .

U.S. Congress

House Committee on Science and Technology
Y4.Sci2, 1958- .

House Select Committee on Aging
Y4.Ag4-2, 1961- .

† Joint Committee on Arrangements for the Commemoration of the Bicentennial
Y4.B47, 1976.

Joint Committee on Printing
Y4.P93-1, 1809- .

Senate Committee on Governmental Affairs
Y4.G74-9, 1977- .

Senate Committee on Veterans' Affairs
Y4.V64-4.

Senate Select Committee on Indian Affairs
Y4.In2-11.

United States Fire Administration
C58, 1978-1979. (CD)
FEM1.100, 1979- . (FEMA)

United States Travel Service
C47, 1961- . (CD)

Urban Mass Transportation Administration
   TD7, 1968- . (DOT)

Veterans Administration
   VA1, 1930- .

Water Resources Council
   Y3.W29, 1965- .

White House Conferences
   Y3.W58, 1930- .

White House Historical Association. *See* Advisory Council on Historic
   Preservation

Women's Bureau
   L36.101, 1971- . (LD)

Title Index

All numbers are entry numbers rather than page numbers.

Access National Parks: A Guide for Handicapped Visitors, 018

Accessibility Assistance. A Directory of Consultants on Environments for Handicapped People, 108

Accredited Postsecondary Institutions and Programs—Including Institutions Holding Preaccredited Status, 199

Address List: Regional and Subregional Libraries for the Blind and Physically Handicapped, 232

Address List for Regional Airports Divisions and Airports Districts/Field Offices, 348

Address List of State Offices of Emergency Medical Services, 349

Airport Directory, 640

Allied Health Education Programs in Junior and Senior Colleges, 219, 220

Alphabetic List of Lenders, 129

Alternatives for Young Americans: A Catalog of Drug Abuse Prevention Programs, 566

American Association of Spanish-speaking and National Association of Minority Certified Public Accounting Firms, 097

American Indian Calendar, 633

Animal Resources. A Research Resources Directory, 544

Annotated Acronyms and Abbreviations of Marine Science Related International Organizations, 042

Appropriate Technology: A Directory of Activities and Projects, 596

Area Health Education Centers. A Directory of Federal, State, Local and Private Decentralized Health Professional Education Programs, 557

Arson Resource Directory, 056

Asian American Reference Data Directory, 170

Astronauts and Cosmonauts: Biographical and Statistical Data, 435

Attorneys and Agents Registered to Practice before the U.S. Patent and Trademark Office, 367

Attorneys General of the United States, 1789-1979, 401

Beef Cattle Publications and Visual Materials, 033

Biographic Register, The, 419

Biographical Directory of the American Congress, 1774-1971, 427

Biotechnology Resources. A Research Resources Directory, 545

Bulk Carriers in the World Fleet. Ocean-going Merchant Type Ships of 1,000 Gross Tons and Over, 617

Bureau of Land Management Office Directory, 277

Buyers Guide to Products Manufactured on American Indian Reservations, 103

Buyer/Seller Codes Authorized for Reporting to the Federal Energy Regulatory Commission, 123

Camp and Picnic in the National Forests of the Intermountain Region, 001

Campground Directory. Idaho Panhandle National Forests, 004

Camping in the National Park System, 019

Camping on the Public Lands, 022

Catalog of Federal Domestic Assistance, 601

Catalog of Federal Education Assistance Programs, 527

Catalog of Human Services Information Resource Organizations. An Exploratory Study of Human Services Information Clearinghouses, 057

Catalog of Security Equipment, 101

230 / Title Index

Catalog of Selected Offices of the Office of Surface Mining, Bureau of Land Management, and Geological Survey Relating to Coal, 336
Centers of Population for States and Counties, 1950, 1960, and 1970, 009
Child Abuse and Neglect Helplines: A Special Report, 581
Child Abuse and Neglect Programs, 582
Civil Rights Directory, 044
Classification, Assets and Location of Registered Investment Companies under the Investment Company Act of 1940, 139
Classified Information Directory for the Central Office, 285
Clinical Genetic Service Centers. A National Listing, 217
Clinical Programs for Mentally Retarded Children, 551
Coal Distribution Companies in the United States, 119
College Placement Directors and Major Federal Agencies in New England, 409
Colleges and Universities Offering Accredited Programs by Accreditation Field, Including Selected Characteristics, 207
Commercial News USA. New Products Annual Directory, 105
Commercially Available Small Wind Systems and Equipment, 111
Commissions, Committees, and Councils on the Status of Women, 078
Common Poisonous and Injurious Plants, 630
Computer Science and Technology: Guide to Computer Program Directories, 155
Condensed List of the Catalog of Federal Domestic Assistance Programs, A, 591
Congressional Pictorial Directory, 434
Conservation and Renewable Energy Resource Directory, 447
Consumer Energy Atlas, 308
Consumer Health Education. A Directory, 061
Consumer's Guide to Mental Health and Related Federal Programs, 564
Consumer's Guide to Travel Information. Helpful Information Sources, 300
Consumer's Guide to Travel Information. State and Territorial Tourism Offices, 301
Consumer's Resource Handbook, 343
Contractors Listing. Volume II of Directory of Federal Contract Audit Offices, 109

Coordination Directory of State and Federal Agency Water and Land Resources Officials, 430
Counselor's Guide to Occupational Information, A, 179
Credit Unions Serving Army Personnel, 622
Criminal Justice Agencies: In Regions 1-10, 338
Criminal Justice Audiovisual Materials Directory, 468
Criminal Justice Calendar of Events, 634
Critical Surveys of Data Sources, 154
Cumulative List of Organizations Described in Section 170(c) of the Internal Revenue Code of 1954, 088
Current Listing and Topical Index to the Vital and Health Statistics Series, 1962-1977, 173

DCPA National Directory of Fallout Shelter Analysts and Their Associated Architectural and Engineering Firms, 110
Death Investigation: An Analysis of Laws and Policies of the United States, Each State and Jurisdiction, 487
Designated Engineering Representatives, 424
Detector Directory, 626
Digest of State Forest Fire Laws, 481
Diplomatic List, 414
Directory (Transportation Department), 289
Directory. Family Planning Service Sites—United States, 218
Directory: Federal, State and Local Government Consumer Offices, 324
Directory. Federally Funded Community Mental Health Centers, 224
Directory: Full Year Head Start Programs, Summer Head Start Programs, Head Start Parent and Child Centers, 579
Directory. Pacific States Region—National Wildlife Refuges and Fish Hatcheries, 020
Directory. Region 6, 276
Directory. State Agencies on Aging and Regional Offices, 333
Directory and Field Office Listing, 245
Directory for Reaching Minority and Women's Groups, 079
Directory of Administrative Hearing Facilities, 609
Directory of Adult Day Care Centers, 227
Directory of Air Quality Monitoring Sites, 311

Title Index / 231

Directory of Animal Disease Diagnostic Laboratories, 191
Directory of Area Wage Surveys, 183
Directory of Aviation Majors and Curricula Offered by Colleges and Universities, 239
Directory of Blood Establishments Registered under Section 510 of the Food, Drug, and Cosmetic Act, 214
Directory of BLS Studies in Employee Compensation, 1947-1971, A, 180
Directory of BLS Studies in Industrial Relations, 1960-74, 181
Directory of Business Education Programs and Courses of Academic and Commercial Interest for Small and/or Minority Entrepreneurs in the State of Maryland, A, 236
Directory of Cancer Research Information Resources, 461
Directory of Coal Production Ownership, 120
Directory of Community Crime Prevention Programs: National and State Levels, 071
Directory of Community Health Centers, 552
Directory of Community High Blood Pressure Control Activities, 058
Directory of Companies Required to File Annual Reports with the Securities and Exchange Commission under the Securities Exchange Act of 1934, 142
Directory of Computer Software and Related Technical Reports, A, 157
Directory of Computerized Data Files, Software and Related Technical Reports, A, 157
Directory of Consular Services, 603
Directory of Contacts for International Educational, Cultural and Scientific Exchange Programs, 086
Directory of Contractors Supported by Division of Nuclear Physics, 513
Directory of Cooperating Agencies, 298
Directory of Criminal Justice Degree Programs Offered by Institutions of Post-Secondary Education Participating in the Law Enforcement Education Program (LEEP), 230
Directory of Criminal Justice Information Sources, 469
Directory of Criminal Justice Information Systems, 470
Directory of Data Files, 153
Directory of Data Sources on Racial and Ethnic Minorities, 178
Directory of DCAA Offices, 253

Directory of Economic Development Districts and Area Grantees, 007
Directory of EDA Qualified Areas under the Public Works and Economic Development Act of 1965, as Amended May 1978, 008
Directory of Education Associations, 051
Directory of Elementary and Secondary School Districts and Schools in Selected School Districts, 197
Directory of Energy Data Collection Forms, 309
Directory of Environmental Groups. Region 7, 312
Directory of Environmental Life Scientists, 372
Directory of EPA, State and Local Environmental Quality Monitoring and Assessment Activities, 529
Directory of ERIC Search Services, 460
Directory of Expanded Role Programs for Registered Nurses, A, 559
Directory of FAA Certificated Aviation Maintenance Technician Schools, 238
Directory of Family Planning Grantees and Clinics, 059
Directory of Federal Agencies Engaged in Energy Related Activities, 319
Directory of Federal Agency Education Data Tapes, 171
Directory of Federal Coordinating Groups for Toxic Substances, 317
Directory of Federal Energy Data Sources. Computer Products and Recurring Publications, 169
Directory of Federal Occupational Health Facilities, 511
Directory of Federal Regional Structure, 263
Directory of Federal Statistical Data Files, 158
Directory of Federal Technology Transfer, 602
Directory of Federally Supported Information Analysis Centers, 474
Directory of Field Contacts for the Coordination of the Use of Radio Frequencies, 303
Directory of General Hospitals Providing Walk-in Emergency Mental Health Services, 211
Directory of Governors and State Officials Responsible for Disaster Operations and Emergency Planning, 321
Directory of Graduate Deans at United States Universities, A, 389

232 / Title Index

Directory of Halfway Houses and Community Residences for the Mentally Ill, 226
Directory of Halfway Houses for the Mentally Ill and Alcoholics, 543
Directory of Important Labor Areas, 024
Directory of Industry and Municipal Government Wage Surveys and Union Wages and Hour Studies, 1960-75, 182
Directory of Information Resources in the United States, A. Biological Sciences, 473
Directory of Information Resources in the United States, A. Federal Government, 472
Directory of Information Resources in the United States, A. Geosciences and Oceanography, 475
Directory of Information Resources in the United States, A. Social Sciences, 471
Directory of Institutions for Mentally Disordered Offenders, 212
Directory of International Organizations Concerned with Metric Building, 066
Directory of Job Corps Centers, 231
Directory of Key Contacts and Services. Who's Where in Commerce, 246
Directory of Key Foreign Personnel—Solar Commercialization, 113
Directory of Labor-Management Committees, 091
Directory of Law Enforcement and Criminal Justice Associations and Research Centers, 040
Directory of Librarians and Information Specialists in DOE and Its Contractor Organizations, 378
Directory of Library Networks and Cooperative Library Organizations, 052
Directory of Local Employment Security Offices, 341
Directory of Medicare/Medicaid Providers and Suppliers of Services, 204
Directory of Minority Contractors with a Maritime Capability, 102
Directory of Minority Media, 098
Directory of Minority Vendors. State of Oregon, 146
Directory of National, Federal and Local Sickle Cell Disease Programs, 550
Directory of National Health, Education, and Social Service Organizations Concerned with Youth, A, 060
Directory of National Information Sources on Handicapping Conditions and Related Services, 064

Directory of National Unions and Employee Associations, 076
Directory of Nonprofit Immigration Counseling Agencies, 070
Directory of Occupational Program Consultants, 397
Directory of Occupational Wage Surveys, 185
Directory of Operating Small Business Investment Companies, 135
Directory of Organizations Serving Minority Communities, 069
Directory of Permits—State of Alaska, 483
Directory of Personnel Offices. Regional and Headquarters, 274
Directory of Personnel Responsible for Radiological Health Programs, 394
Directory of Postsecondary Schools with Occupational Programs, 210
Directory of Preceptorship Programs in the Health Professions, A, 221
Directory of Private Programs Assisting Minority Business, 509
Directory of Productivity and Quality of Working Life Centers, 092
Directory of Professional Workers in State Agricultural Experiment Stations and Other Cooperating State Institutions, 357
Directory of Programs Training Physician Support Personnel, A, 555
Directory of Public Employee Organizations, A. A Guide to the Major Organizations Representing State and Local Public Employees, 074
Directory of Public Employment Relations Boards and Agencies, A. A Guide to the Administrative Machinery for the Conduct of Public Employee-Management Relations within the States, 339
Directory of Public Housing Agencies, 334
Directory of Public Management Organizations, A, 075
Directory of Regularly Scheduled, Fixed Route, Local Public Transportation Service, A, 642
Directory of Regularly Scheduled, Fixed Route, Local Rural Public Transportation Service, A, 643
Directory of Representative Work Education Programs, 537
Directory of Research Natural Areas on Federal Lands of the United States of America, A, 030
Directory of Resources for Affirmative Recruitment, A, 090

Directory of Rural Health Care Programs, 533
Directory of Security Consultants, 133
Directory of Selected Private Civic-Service Organizations for Cooperative 4-H Programing, 035
Directory of Services (Agriculture Department), 503
Directory of Services for the Handicapped in California, 538
Directory of Spanish Speaking Organizations in the United States, 093
Directory of Special Purpose Facilities for the Education of the Handicapped, 198
Directory of Standards Laboratories, A, 193
Directory of State Agencies Engaged in Environmental Monitoring, 313
Directory of State and Area Agencies on Aging, A, 356
Directory of State and Local Resources for the Mentally Retarded, 323
Directory of State, County, and City Government Offices, 324
Directory of State Drug Abuse Prevention Officials, 396
Directory of State Extension Horticultural Specialists, 361
Directory of State Government Energy-related Agencies, 320
Directory of State Merit Systems, 304
Directory of State Small Business Programs, 605
Directory of State, Territorial, and Regional Health Authorities, 325
Directory of STD [Sexually Transmitted Disease] Clinics, 223
Directory of the Agricultural Research Service, 241
Directory of the Business Research Advisory Council to the Bureau of Labor Statistics, 405
Directory of the Labor Research Advisory Council to the Bureau of Labor Statistics, 406
Directory of Transportation Education, Institutions Offering Programs at Degree and Non-Degree Levels, Including Seminars, Institutes and Workshops, 235
Directory of Unions and Associations with Exclusive Recognition in the Federal Service, 045
Directory of U.S. Export Management Companies, A, 104

Directory of United States Probation Officers, 403
Directory of United States Standardization Activities, 039
Directory of Wage Chronologies, 1948 to June 1975, 184
Directory of Women Business Owners, 128
Directory of Women's Drug Abuse Treatment Programs, 331
Directory/Poison Control Centers—United States and Territories, 216
District Export Councils Membership Directory, 369
DoD Activity Address Directory, 254
Doing Business with the Department of Energy Directory, 257
Driver Licensing Laws Annotated, 500
Drug Abuse Prevention: A Guide to Speakers, 063
Drug Abuse Programs: A Directory for Minority Groups, 571

Ecological Characterization of the Sea Island Coastal Region of South Carolina and Georgia. Directory of Information Sources, 467
Education Directory, Colleges and Universities, 200
Education Directory: Local Education Agencies, 624
Education Directory. State Education Agency Officials, 382
Educational Institution Numeric List, 205
Educational Opportunities on Air Force Bases, 512
Educational Technology Programs, 517
Educators with Disabilities: A Resource Guide, 381
Election Directory, 353
Employees of Diplomatic Missions, 415
Energy Data Contacts Finder, 166
Energy Information Directory, 310
Energy Library—Guide to Services, 448
Environmental Hotline, 318
Environmental Organizations Directory. A Directory of Environmental Organizations for Alaska, Idaho, Oregon, and Washington, 053
Environmental Program Administrators, 316
Environmental/Socioeconomic Data Sources, 165

234 / Title Index

ESA Directory of Offices, 280
Establishments and Products Licensed under Section 351 of the Public Health Service Act, 215
Express Mail, Los Angeles Next Day Service City Directory, 636

FAA Designated Mechanic Examiners Directory, 425
FAA Directory, 290
FAA Inspection Authorization Directory, 423
Facts at Your Fingertips. A Guide to Sources of Statistical Information on Major Health Topics, 172
Family Planning, Contraception, Voluntary Sterilization and Abortion: An Analysis of Laws and Policies in the United States, Each State and Jurisdiction, 488
FDA Location Directory, 271
Federal Advisory Committees. Index to Membership of Federal Advisory Committees Listed in the Fifth Annual Report of the President to the Congress, 432
Federal and State Indian Reservations and Indian Trust Areas, 005
Federal Assistance for Programs Serving the Handicapped, 528
Federal Assistance Guide for Park and Recreation Professionals, 587
Federal Aviation Administration Certificated Maintenance Agencies Directory, 144
Federal Aviation Administration Designated Maintenance Technician Examiners. Directory, 426
Federal Environmental Data: A Directory of Selected Sources, 188
Federal Information Centers, 322
Federal Information Sources and Systems. A Directory Issued by the Comptroller General, 455
Federal Job Information Centers Directory, 637
Federal Laboratories and Research Facilities with Noise Capabilities. A Directory, 314
Federal Programs for Libraries: A Directory, 539
Federal Programs for Minorities, Women, and the Handicapped, 548
Federal Programs for Neighborhood Conservation, 610
Federal Programs of Assistance to American Indians, 612

Federal Programs That Relate to Children, 530
Federal Statistical Directory, 345
Federal Travel Directory, 627
Festivals USA, 619
Financial Organization Directory, 143
Finding Your Way: A Directory of Public Programs Available to Indochinese Refugees, 598
Fire Research Specialists: A Directory, 366
Firms in the 8(a) Business Development Program, 136
First Ladies, The, 429
Fishing Directory. Deschutes National Forest, 614
Fishing Directory. Okanogan National Forest, 613
Five Federal Financial Aid Programs. A Student Consumer's Guide, 523
Food and Agricultural Export Directory, 036
Foreign Consular Offices in the United States, 417
Foreign Regulations Affecting U.S. Textile/Apparel Exports, 484
Foreign Service Classification List, 413
Foreign Service List, 412
Forest Service Organizational Directory, 243
Forestry Schools in the United States, 190
Foundations That Provide Support for Human Services. A Selected List, 554
Franchise Opportunities Handbook, 106
Free Universities and Learning Referral Centers, 208
"Futures" for Energy Cooperatives, 514

General Clinical Research Centers. A Research Resources Directory, 546
Geographical Areas Serviced by Bell and Independent Telephone Companies in the United States, 100
Global Legal Framework for Narcotics and Prohibitive Substances, The, 497
Government Depository Libraries. The Present Law Governing Designated Depository Libraries, 240
Guide and Map: National Parks of the United States, 017
Guide for Business, A. U.S. Commercial Offices and the Foreign Commercial Service Posts, 302
Guide to Characteristics of Civil Service Regions. Statistical Data, 251
Guide to EPA Libraries, 202

Guide to Federal Assistance Programs for Minority Business Development, 506
Guide to Federal Consumer Services, 535
Guide to Federal Data Sources on Manufacturing, A, 162
Guide to Federal Funding in Career Education, Education and Work and Vocational Education, 524
Guide to Foreign Trade Statistics, 161
Guide to High School Recruitment: School Districts with Significant Hispanic Student Enrollment, A, 194
Guide to Information on Research in Marine Science and Engineering, 443
Guide to Local Occupational Information, 187
Guide to Obtaining Information from the USGS, A, 466
Guide to Recurrent and Special Governmental Statistics, 150
Guide to the U.S. Department of Commerce for Women Business Owners, The, 247
Guide to U.S. Army Museums and Historic Sites, 011
Guide to USDA Statistics, 148
Guide to Visas, Passports, and Consular Services, A, 604
Guideline Codes for Named Populated Places and Related Entities of the States of the United States, 006

Health Occupations Training Programs Administered by Hospitals, 222
Health Systems Agencies, State Health Planning and Development Agencies, and Statewide Coordinating Councils, 326
High Energy Physicists and Graduate Students, 374
Higher Education and the Handicapped. Resource Directory, 519
Highway Rest Areas for Handicapped Travelers, 026
Hispanic Employment: A Recruitment Sources Booklet Including Recruitment Sources in Puerto Rico, 082
Historical Survey of U.S. Seismograph Stations, 632
Home Economics Communicators, 360
Horse Publications and Visual Materials, 031
Housing Data Resources. Indicators and Sources of Data for Analyzing Housing and Neighborhood Conditions, 149
Housing Management Training Programs. A Directory, 229
How to Get It: A Guide to Defense Related Documents, 164

Idaho Recreation Guide, 021
In the Cause of Flight. Technologists of Aeronautics and Astronautics, 422
Index: National Park System and Related Areas, 016
Index of Active Registered Investment Companies under the Investment Company Act of 1940 and Related Investment Advisers, Principal Underwriters, Sponsors (i.e., Depositors) and Underlying Companies, 140
Indian Land Areas, General: Indian Lands and Related Facilities, 012
Information for Handicapped Travelers, 595
Information Resources and Services of the United States: An Introduction for Developing Countries, The, 189
Information Services on Research in Progress. A Worldwide Inventory, 478
Information Sources and Services Directory, 275
Innovative Developments in Aging: Area Agencies on Aging. A Directory Compiled by the University of California, 611
Institutions of Higher Education Index by State and Congressional District, 209
Interim Climate Data Inventory: A Quick Reference to Selected Climate Data, The, 159
Intermountain Region Offices, 244
International Directory of Appropriate Technology Resources, 041
International Directory of Mental Retardation Resources, 332
International Education Programs of the U.S. Government. An Inventory, 518
Inventory of Federal Statistical Programs Relating to Older Persons, 176
Inventory of Power Plants in the United States, 122
Investment Adviser Directory, 141

JACS Directory. NTIS Journal Article Copy Service, 442
Judges of the United States, 402

Key Officers of Foreign Service Posts, 416

236 / Title Index

Labor Offices in the United States and Canada, 340
Large-Scale Alcohol Fuels Plants Directory, 114
Liaison Conservation Directory for Endangered and Threatened Species, 337
Librarians of Congress, 1802-1974, 407
Library of Congress Directory, 281
Library Programs, 520
Library Resources for the Blind and Physically Handicapped. A Directory of NLS Network Libraries and Machine-Lending Agencies, 233
License Plates, 639
List of Certificated Pilot Schools, 237
List of Certified U.S. Air Carriers, 107
List of Companies Registered under the Investment Company Act of 1940, 138
List of Local Boards of the Selective Service System, 354
List of Speakers on Issues Concerning Hispanic Women, A, 370
Local Community Crime Prevention Resources, 590
Location of New Federal Offices and Other Facilities, The, 242

Marine Advisory Service Directory, 368
Marine Geology and Geophysics Data Services and Publications, 160
Maritime Folklife Resources. A Directory and Index, 234
Market Development Directory for Solar Industrial Process Heat Systems, 115
Measuring Markets: A Guide to the Use of Federal and State Statistical Data, 163
Meat and Poultry Inspection Directory, 096
Medal of Honor Recipients, 1863-1978, 437
Medical Staff Directory: The Clinical Center, 266
Medicare/Medicaid Directory of Medical Facilities, 228
Members of the Federal Home Loan Bank Board System, 126
Membership Directory (President's Committee on Employment of the Handicapped), 410
Membership Directory. President's Export Council, Regional Export Councils, District Export Councils, 364
Membership Roster Cancer Clinical Trials Groups and Projects, 392
Mental Health Directory, 225
Merchant Vessels of the United States, 641

Metropolitan Planning Organizations and State Transportation Agencies— Directory, 347
Minority Biomedical Support Program. A Research Resources Directory, 547
Museum Studies Programs in the United States and Abroad, 606

National Basic Intelligence Factbook, 028
National Cancer Institute Fact Book, 270
National Clearinghouse for Census Data Services. Address List, 151
National Contingency Plan (National Oil and Hazardous Substances Pollution Contingency Plan) Emergency Response Contacts Listing Directory, 350
National Contingency Plan (National Oil and Hazardous Substances Pollution Contingency Plan) Emergency Response Contacts, Federal Region IV, 351
National Directories for Use in Marketing, 638
National Directory: Rape Prevention and Treatment Resources, 563
National Directory of Alcoholism Treatment Programs, 574
National Directory of Clearinghouses, 344
National Directory of Drug Abuse and Alcoholism Treatment Programs, 568
National Directory of Drug Abuse Treatment Programs, 567
National Directory of Educational Programs in Gerontology, 203
National Directory of Hotline Services, 572
National Directory of Intercountry Adoption Service Resources, 580
National Directory of Latin Americanists, 408
National Directory of Minority Manufacturers, 099
National Directory of 911 Systems, A, 635
National Drug Code Directory, 628
National Five Digit ZIP Code and Post Office Directory, 025
National Foreign Assessment Center Publications, 411
National Health Related Items Code Directory, 629
National Historic Landmarks. A Preservation Program of the National Park Service, 015
National Organizations Concerned with Visually and Physically Handicapped Persons, 080

National Organizations Issues Resource Book, 094
National Register of Historic Places, The, 023
National Solar Energy Education Directory, 195
National Solar Heating and Cooling Commercial Demonstration Program. Key Personnel Directory, 112
National Weather Service Offices and Stations, 248
NCI Fact Book, 270
Necrology of United States Senators—Showing Those Who Died During Their Terms of Office and All Who Have Died since 1789, A, 428
NHSC Health Care Practitioners, 395
NIH Almanac, 267
NIH Public Advisory Groups. Authority, Structure, Functions, Members, 391
1980 World's Submarine Telephone Cable Systems, 620
NTIS Sumstat Catalog. Federal Summary Statistical Data Project, 156
Numeric List of Lenders, 130
Nursing-related Data Sources, 175

Occupational Safety and Health Directory, 330
Official Congressional Directory, 433
Official U.S. and International Financing Institutions. A Guide for Exporters and Investors, 043
OMBE Funded Organizations Directory, 037
Online Literature Searching and Databases at the U.S. Environmental Protection Agency Environmental Research Center Library, 168
Operating Banking Offices, 145
Organization of Federal Executive Departments and Agencies, 296
Owners of Nuclear Power Plants, 147

Plant and Ownership List Supplementary to the Maps #1-11, Entitled Principal Electric Facilities, 121
Presidents, from the Inauguration of George Washington to the Inauguration of Jimmy Carter, The. Historic Places Commemorating the Chief Executives of the United States, 014
Privacy Act Issuances, 456

Privacy and Security of Criminal History Information. Compendium of State Legislation, 494
Private Assistance in Outdoor Recreation. A Directory of Organizations Providing Aid to Individuals and Public Groups, 068
Professional Minority Consulting Firms, 124
Programs Providing Services to Battered Women, 578
Promising Practices: Reaching Out to Families, 577
Public Advisory Committees Authority, Structure, Functions, Members, 393
Public and Private Sources of Funding for Sexual Assault Treatment Programs, 062
Public Health Service Profiles of Financial Assistance Programs, 542
Public Information Materials for Language Minorities, 593
Public Records Directory, 352

Recreation Sites in Southwestern National Forests, 002
Recreational Opportunities at Hydroelectric Projects Licensed by the Federal Energy Regulatory Commission, 516
Recruitment Sources for Women, 077
References and Data Sources for Implementing an Affirmative Action Program, 186
Regional Directory—Leafy Spurge Control . . . Rocky Mountain Forest and Range Experiment Station, 359
Regional Directory: Rape Prevention and Treatment Resources, 562
Register of Federal Employee Unions, 073
Register of Reporting Labor Organizations, 072
Registry of Minority Contractors and Housing Professionals, 131
Registry of Private Fair Housing Organizations/Groups, 065
Religious Activities and Drug Abuse: Some Current Highlights, 570
Research Aids: Selected Sources of Information, 444
Research Program Directory, 504
Resource Guide—Architectural Barriers Removal, 449
Resource Guide: Recreation and Leisure for Handicapped Individuals, 050
Resource Guide. Rehabilitation Engineering and Product Information, 450

238 / Title Index

Resource Recovery Plant Implementation Guides for Municipal Officials: Further Assistance, 055
Resources for Corrections: Directory of Federal Programs, 588
Roster. Emergency Electric Power Administration, 258
Roster of North American Rapid Transit Cars, 1945-1976, 644
Runaway Youth Program Directory, 592

Scientific Directory; Annual Bibliography, 268
SEC Corporation Index. Active Companies and Companies That Have Become Inactive, 137
Secretaries of State: Portraits and Biographical Sketches, The, 420
Secretaries of War and Secretaries of the Army. Portraits and Biographical Sketches, 373
Section 504 Resources Manual. A Guide for Small Institutions to Useful Sources, Services, and Procedures for Locating and Applying for Funds to Meet Section 504 Mandates, 459
Seed and Planting Stock Dealers: A Directory of Dealers That Sell the More Common Forest and Shelterbelt Seeds and Plants, 095
Selected List of Federal Laws and Treaties Relating to Sport Fish and Wildlife, 493
Selected List of Postsecondary Education Opportunities for Minorities and Women, 521
Service Organizations' Representatives Currently Recognized in the Presentation of Claims before the VA, 089
Services Available through the U.S. Department of Agriculture, 505
Sheep Publications and Visual Materials, 034
Small and Disadvantaged Business Utilization Specialists: Designated to Assist Small, Minority, and Labor Surplus Area Businessmen, 305
Small Business Guide, A. A Directory of Federal Government Business Assistance Programs for Women Business Owners, 507
Small Producer Certificate Dockets Sequenced by Docket Number Authorized for Use in Reporting to the Federal Energy Regulatory Commission, 117

Small Producer Certificate Holders and Co-owners, Listed Alphabetically, 118
Social Security Programs throughout the World, 536
Software Exchange Directory for University Research Administration, 616
Soil, Water, Air Sciences Directory, 362
Solar Energy Information Locator, 307
Solar Energy Technical Training Directory, 196
Solar Events Calendar and Call for Papers, 623
Source Directory. Native American Owned and Operated Arts and Crafts Businesses, 132
Sources for Landsat Assistance and Services, 477
Sources of Assistance for Developing Boating Facilities, 586
Sources of Data Related to Dentistry: A Catalog, 174
Sources of Information, Products, and Services of the U.S. Geological Survey, 464
Sources of U.S. Geological Survey Publications, 177
Soviet Biomedical Institutions: A Directory, 213
Sports and Games for Handicapped Persons, 081
Staff Report on Retired Hydropower Plants in the United States, 116
Standard Metropolitan Statistical Areas, 027
State and Federal Laws Relating to Nonpublic Schools, 485
State and Local Agencies Preparing Population Estimates and Projections: Survey, 299
State and Local Environmental Libraries. A Directory, 201
State Energy Officials Directory, 306
State Initiatives on Alcohol Fuels. A State-by-State Compendium of Laws, Regulations, and Other Activities Involving Alcohol Fuels, 501
State Laws and Published Ordinances: Firearms, 498
State Laws and Regulations on Genetic Disorders, 489
State Legal Standards for the Provision of Public Education: An Overview, 486
State Legislation on Smoking and Health, 490

Title Index / 239

State Technical Assistance Programs and Manuals on Rural Public Transportation, 608
State Veterans' Laws. Digests of State Laws Regarding Rights, Benefits, and Privileges of Veterans and Their Dependents, 502
State/City List of Lenders, 130
State-Federal Health Requirements and Regulations Governing the Interstate and International Movement of Livestock and Poultry, 482
Status of the World's Nations, 029
Statutory Land Use Control Enabling Authority in the Fifty States, 492
Summary of Public Sector Labor Relations Policies—Statutes, Attorney Generals' Opinions and Selected Court Decisions, 495
Summary Tape Processing Centers and State Data Centers. Address List, 152
Survey of International Intergovernmental Organizations: The Strategies That They Use to Abate Pollution, A, 054
Survey of the National Metric Speakers Bureau, A, 365
Swine Publications and Visual Materials, 032

Tahoe National Forest Camping and Picnicking, 003
Telephone Directory.
   Administrative Office of the United States Courts, 278
   Brookhaven National Laboratory, Energy Department, 256
   Civil Aeronautics Board, 249
   Customs Service, 288
   Defense Department, 252
   Education Department, 259
   Environmental Protection Agency, 260
   Federal Communications Commission, 250
   Federal Emergency Management Agency, 261
   General Services Administration, 264
   Health and Human Services Department, 265
   House of Representatives, 291
   Housing and Urban Development Department, 273
   Human Development Services Office, 273
   Labor Department, 279
   National Aeronautics and Space Administration, 283
   National Credit Union Administration, 284
   National Institutes of Health, 269
   Nuclear Regulatory Commission, 294
   Pension Benefit Guaranty Corporation, 295
   Senate, 292
   State Department, 286
   Transportation Department, 289
   Treasury Department, 287
Traditionally Black Institutions of Higher Education: Their Identification and Selected Characteristics, 206
Traffic Laws Annotated, 499
Training and Resource Directory for Teachers Serving Handicapped Students, K-12, A, 457
Training Opportunities in Job Corps, 594
Transportation Energy Activities of the United States Department of Transportation. A Technical Assistance Directory of Programs, Projects and Contacts, 346
Traveler's Guide to Information Sources, 439
Try Us. National Minority Business Directory, 134

Unemployment Insurance: State Laws and Experience, 496
United States Army Installations and Major Activities, 010
United States Chiefs of Missions, 1778-1973, 418
United States Contributions to International Organizations, 087
United States Court Directory, 404
U.S. Directory of Environmental Sources, 452
U.S. Facilities and Programs for Children with Severe Mental Illnesses. A Directory, 561
U.S. Geological Survey's Public Inquiries Offices: Focal Points for Information, The, 465
United States Government Manual, 262
U.S. Housing Developments for the Elderly or Handicapped, 631
U.S. Nuclear Regulatory Commission Functional Organization Charts, 293
USAF Installation Directory, 255

Vessel Inventory Report, 618
Vietnam Era Medal of Honor Recipients, 1964-1972, 436

Visitor Accommodations, Facilities, and Services, 013
Voluntary Action in Drug Abuse Prevention Programs, 569
Votingsystems Users. A Directory of Local Jurisdictions, 645

Warehouses Licensed under U.S. Warehouse Act, 615
Water Quality Management Directory, 315
Water Resources Coordination Directory, 355
Where to Write for Birth and Death Records: United States and Outlying Areas, 327
Where to Write for Divorce Records: United States and Outlying Areas, 328
Where to Write for Marriage Records: United States and Outlying Areas, 329
Who's Involved with Hunger: An Organization Guide, 084
Who's Who IV in the Interagency Energy/Environment R&D Program, 386
Who's Who in Federal Noise Programs. A Directory of Federal Professionals Involved in Noise Abatement and Noise Research, 385
WIC Program Directory of Local Agencies, 297
Wind Energy Information Directory, 445
Women. A Documentary of Progress during the Administration of Jimmy Carter, 1977-1981, 083
Women and Business. A Directory of Women-owned Businesses in Washington, Oregon, Idaho, and Alaska, 127
Women in Congress, 1917-1976, 431
Women/Consumer Calendar of Events, 625
World's Submarine Telephone Cable Systems, 620
Worldwide Directory of National Earth-Science Agencies, 335
Writers Guide to NASA, The, 282

Youth Camp. Compendium of State Laws and Regulations, 491

Subject Index

All numbers are entry numbers rather than page numbers.

Abbreviations, oceanographic, 042
Abortion, laws and policies in the United States, 488
Access control. *See* Security
Accounting firms
  minority, 097, 131
  Spanish-speaking, 097
Acronyms, oceanographic, 042
Administration on Aging, regional offices, 333
Administrative Office of the United States Courts
  probation division, 403
  telephone directory, 278
Adolescence. *See* Youth
Adoption, intercountry services, 580
Adult day care centers, 227
Advisory committees
  business research, 405
  Federal, 432
  Food and Drug Administration, 393
  labor research, 406
  National Institutes of Health, 391
  President's Committee on Employment of the Handicapped, 410
Aeronautics
  astronauts and cosmonauts, 435
  aviation curricula of colleges and universities, 239
  aviation maintenance technician schools, 238
  flight technologists, 422
  history of, 422
  pilot schools, certificated, 237
Affirmative action. *See* Discrimination in employment
Aged
  associations and organizations, 227
  data sources on, 176
  day care centers for, 227
  gerontology educational programs, 203

  housing for, 631
  medical assistance programs for, 204
  programs and services for, 611
  state agencies on, 333, 356, 611
  statistics on, 176
Aging. *See* Aged
Agricultural experiment stations, professional workers, 357
Agricultural products
  exporting, 036
  warehouses, 615
Agriculture. *See also* Agricultural products
  federal services, 503, 505
  statistics, 148
  USDA services, 505
Agriculture Department
  Agricultural Research Service directory, 241
  services, 503, 505
  statistics, 148
Air
  pollution associations and organizations, 053, 054
  quality, monitoring of, 311, 313, 529
  sciences, research personnel in, 362
Air carriers, certificated U.S., 107
Air Force
  educational opportunities on bases, 512
  installations, 255
Air pollution, associations and organizations, 053, 054
Aircraft
  aviation maintenance technician schools, FAA-certificated, 238
  engineering representatives, 424
  maintenance agencies, FAA-certificated, 144
  mechanics, FAA-certificated, 423
Airlines, certificated U.S., 107
Airplanes. *See* Aircraft

241

242 / Subject Index

Airports
  directory of, 640
  district/field offices, 348
  regional divisions, 348
Alarm systems, 101
Alaska
  campgrounds, 022
  environmental organizations, 053
  native villages, 005
  permits, listing of, 483
  women-owned businesses, 127
Albania, chiefs of state and cabinet members, 411
Alcohol fuels
  large-scale plants, 114
  state laws and regulations, 501
Alcoholics. *See* Alcoholism
Alcoholism
  halfway houses, 543
  occupational program consultants, 397
  treatment programs, 568, 574
Ambassadors
  biographies of, 419
  chiefs of missions, U.S., 418
  foreign, in United States, 417
  foreign service post officers, 416
  lists of, 412, 414, 417, 418, 419
American Indians. *See* Indians of North America; Minorities
Animals. *See also* Cattle; Horses; Sheep; Swine
  disease diagnostic laboratories, 191
  endangered species conservation, 337
  meat and poultry inspection, 096
  resources programs of National Institutes of Health, 544
Appropriate technology. *See* Science and Technology
Architects
  accessibility assistance, 108
  fallout shelter analysts, 110
  minority, 131
  solar heating and cooling, 112
Architectural barriers. *See* Handicapped
Arizona
  campgrounds, 002, 022
  national forests, 002
Armed forces. *See also* Air Force; Army; Installations (military)
  Medal of Honor recipients, 436, 437
Army
  credit unions serving personnel of, 622
  installations, 010, 011, 622
  museums, 011

  secretaries of the Army, 373
  secretaries of war, 373
Arson. *See* Fire(s)
Arts and crafts, native American, 103, 132
Asian Americans. *See also* Minorities
  data sources on, 170, 178
  health, education, and social welfare data sources, 170
Associations. *See subjects of associations (air pollution; civic; etc.)*
Astronautics. *See also* Aeronautics
  astronauts, 435
  cosmonauts, 435
  flight technologists, 422
Astronauts, 435
Attorneys
  attorneys general, 401
  Patent and Trademark Office, registered to practice before, 367
Automobile drivers, licensing laws, 500
Aviation. *See* Aeronautics

Banks and banking, 143, 145
  American Savings and Loan League members, 102
  Federal Home Loan Bank system members, 126
  international, 043
  minority, 102, 131
  and student loans, 129, 130
Battered women, 578
Biological products, 215
Biological sciences. *See* Biology
Biology
  biological products, 215
  information resources, 473
  Soviet research, 213
Biomass energy. *See also* Solar energy
  key foreign personnel, 113
Biomedicine
  animal resources, 544
  biotechnology resources, 545
  minorities, biomedical support program for, 547
  Soviet biomedical institutions, 213
Biotechnology. *See* Biomedicine
Birth control
  associations and organizations, 059
  laws and policies, 488
  service sites for family planning, 218
Birth records, 327, 352
Blacks. *See also* Minorities
  colleges and universities, 206
  media, 098

newspapers, 098
radio and television stations, 098
Blind. *See* Handicapped
Blood banks, 214
Blood pressure, associations and organizations, 058
Boats and boating, sources of assistance, 586
Builders. *See* Contractors; Shipbuilders
Bulgaria, chiefs of state and cabinet members, 411
Bureau of Indian Affairs. *See* Indian Affairs Bureau
Bureau of Labor Statistics. *See* Labor Statistics Bureau
Business. *See also* Small business; *specific types of businesses*
  arts and crafts, 132
  Business Research Advisory Council to Bureau of Labor Statistics, 405
  commercial news, 105
  courses and education programs, Maryland, 236
  franchising, 106
  marketing, 638
  minority, 134, 146
  women-owned businesses, 127, 128
Business education. *See also* Vocational education
  programs in Maryland, 236

Calibration services, 193
California
  campgrounds, 003, 022
  services for handicapped, 538
  Tahoe National Forest, 003
Camping. *See also* Recreation
  Alaska, 022
  Arizona, 002, 022
  California, 022
  Colorado, 022
  Idaho, 001, 004, 021, 022
  Montana, 022
  National Park System, 019
  Nevada, 001, 022
  New Mexico, 002, 022
  Oregon, 022
  on public lands, 022
  Tahoe National Forest, 003
  Utah, 001, 022
  Washington, 022
  Wyoming, 001, 022
Camps, youth, 491

Cancer. *See also* National Cancer Institute
  information resources, 461
  research, 392, 461
  treatment, 392
Career counseling, New England, 409
Career education. *See* Vocational education
Cartography. *See* Maps and charts
Cattle
  associations and organizations, 033
  publications and visual materials, 033
Census
  data files, 153
  data services, 151, 152, 165
  governmental statistics, 150
Charts. *See* Maps and charts
Child abuse and neglect. *See* Children; Families
Children. *See also* Families
  abuse and neglect of, 581, 582
  federal programs, 530
  food and nutrition programs, 297, 298
  Head Start programs, 579
  intercountry adoption services, 580
  mentally retarded children, programs for, 551
  with severe mental illnesses, facilities and programs for, 561
China, chiefs of state and cabinet members, 411
Cities and towns
  geographic codes, 006
  population, 027
  zip codes, 025
City planning
  contractors and housing professionals, minority, 131
  housing data resources, 149
Civic organizations, 044
Civil defense, fallout shelter analysts, 110
Civil rights. *See also* Discrimination in employment
  associations and organizations, 044, 079
Civil service
  affirmative recruitment, 077, 082, 090
  classified information, 285
  Hispanic recruitment, 082
  regions, characteristics of, 251
  women, recruitment sources for, 077
Civilian Conservation Corps Centers, 231
Climate
  data sources, 159
  offices and stations of National Weather Service, 248

244 / Subject Index

Clinics
  General Clinical Research centers, 546
  genetic service centers, 217
  programs for mentally retarded children, 551
  sexually transmitted disease clinics, 223
Coal
  distribution companies, 119
  production ownership, 120
  surface mining offices, 336
Coastal ecology, Sea Island region, 467
Collective bargaining. *See also* Labor unions
  public sector labor relations policies, 495
Colleges and universities, 199, 200
  accreditation, 199, 200, 207
  agricultural experiment stations at, 031, 032, 033, 034, 357
  aviation education, 239
  black institutions, 206
  business education, 236
  criminal justice degree programs, 230
  educational opportunities for minorities and women, 521
  energy research programs, 513
  forestry programs, 190
  free, 208
  gerontology programs, 203
  graduate deans, 389
  handicapped and higher education, 519
  housing management training, 229
  land-grant, 031, 032, 033, 034, 357
  learning referral centers, 208
  museum studies, 606
  New England college placement directors, 409
  occupational programs, 210
  placement directors, New England, 409
  software exchange, university research administration, 616
  solar energy education, 195, 196
  Soviet biomedical institutions, 213
  by state and congressional district, 209
  student loans, 129, 130
  transportation education, 235
Colorado, campgrounds, 022
Commerce
  statistics, 161
  trade associations, 037, 039, 115
Commercial education. *See* Vocational education
Commercial products, 105. *See also* names of products
Communist countries, chiefs of state and cabinet members, 411
Community health services, 552

Community mental health services, 225. *See also* Mental health services
  federally funded centers, 224
  halfway houses and residences, 226
Computer files. *See* Computer programs
Computer programs, 155, 156, 157, 158, 168
  federal energy, 169
  university research, 616
Computers. *See* Computer programs
Congress of the United States, 262, 427, 433, 434
  House telephone directory, 291
  Senate necrology, 428
  Senate telephone directory, 292
  women in, 431
Congressional districts, 433
  higher education institutions by, 209
Congressional Medal of Honor, recipients of, 436, 437
Consuls
  consular services, 603, 604
  diplomatic mission employees, 415
  diplomats, 414, 415
  foreign, in United States, 417, 433
Consultants
  accessibility assistance, 108
  minority firms, 124
  security, 133
Consulting services. *See* Consultants
Consumer protection
  federal consumer services, 324, 535
  offices, 324
  resource handbook, 343
Contraception. *See* Birth control
Contractors
  Defense Contract Audit Agency listing of, 109
  maritime, 102
  minority, 102, 131
Corporations, SEC index of, 137
Correctional institutions. *See* Corrections
Corrections. *See also* Criminal justice; Parole
  federal programs, 588
  institutions and facilities, 212, 338, 403
  local jails, 338
  police departments, 338
  prisons, 338
  public defenders, 338
Cotton, warehouses, 615
Counties
  population, 027
  unemployment, 024

Courts
  Administrative Office of U.S. Courts, telephone directory, 278
  criminal justice agencies, 338
  hearing facilities, administrative, 609
  judges, U.S., 402
  U.S., directory of, 404
Credit unions
  for Army personnel, 622
  National Credit Union Administration directory, 284
  and student loans, 129, 130
Crime and criminals. *See also* Criminal justice
  associations and organizations on, 040, 071
  correctional institutions and facilities, 212, 338, 403
  correctional resources, 588
  federal programs on, 588, 591
  prevention, 071, 590, 591
  mentally disordered offenders, 212
  911 systems, 635
  Ohio crime prevention resources, 590
Crime prevention. *See* Crime and criminals
Criminal justice. *See also* Crime and criminals
  administrative hearing facilities, 609
  agencies, 338
  associations and organizations, 040
  audiovisual materials, 468
  calendar of events, 634
  criminal history information, privacy and security of, 494
  degree programs in, 230
  education, training, and orientation materials, 468
  federal programs, 588, 591
  information sources, 469
  information systems, 470
  language minorities, public information programs for, 593
  legal service agencies, 044, 338
Criminal offenders. *See* Crime and criminals
Cuba, chiefs of state and cabinet members, 411
Cultural exchanges. *See* International exchanges
Cytogenetics, clinics, 217
Czechoslovakia, chiefs of state and cabinet members, 411

Data sources. *See subjects*
Databases. *See subjects (education, libraries, etc.)*

Day care centers for aged, 227
Death
  investigation of, laws and policies, 487
  records, 327, 352
Death records, 327, 352
Defense, national, 164
Defense Civil Preparedness Agency, fallout shelter analysts, 110
Defense contractors, 109
Defense contracts
  contractors listing, 109
  Defense Contract Audit Agency offices, 253
  small and disadvantaged business utilization specialists, 305
Dentistry, data sources, 174
Department of Energy
  contractors, Division of Nuclear Physics, 513
  data collection forms, 309
  energy cooperatives, 514
  librarians and information specialists, 378
  libraries, 448
  organization of, 257, 310
  personnel, 257, 310
Department of Transportation
  energy activities, 346
  telephone directory, 289
Depository libraries, 240
Diplomatic and consular service, 603, 604
  diplomatic mission employees, 415
  diplomats, 414
  foreign consuls in United States, 417, 433
Disabled. *See* Handicapped
Disaster relief
  Federal Emergency Management Agency directory, 261
  state officials, 321
Discrimination. *See also* Discrimination in employment
  associations and organizations, 044, 079
Discrimination in employment
  affirmative action data sources, 079, 090, 186
  equal employment opportunity data sources, 186
  of Hispanics, 082
  minority recruitment sources, 070, 082
  women recruitment sources, 070, 077
Diseases
  animal, 191
  sexually transmitted, 223
Divorce records, 328, 352
Domestic violence. *See* Families
Drivers. *See* Automobile drivers

Drug abuse
  hot line services, 572
  minority groups, programs for, 571
  prevention, 369, 566, 569
  religious activities, 570
  speakers' bureau, 063
  state prevention officials, 396
  treatment programs, 567, 568
  volunteers in prevention, 569
  women's programs, 331
Drugs. *See also* Drug abuse
  manufacturers, 215
  product code directory, 628
  products, licensed, 215

Earth Resources Observation Systems, data center, 177
Earth resources technology satellites, information sources, 477
Earth sciences, worldwide agencies, 335
East Germany, chiefs of state and cabinet members, 411
Economic conditions, 008
Economic development, 008
  districts, 007
  federal assistance, 246, 601
Economic Development Administration, 246
  regional offices, 007
Education. *See also* Colleges and universities; Educators; Health education; Schools; Students; Vocational education
  accrediting agencies, 199, 200, 207
  associations and organizations, 051
  educational technology programs, 517
  ERIC search services, 460
  federal assistance programs, 527, 601
  federal data sources, 171
  and handicapped, 198, 519
  international programs, 518
  local agencies, 624
  opportunities for, on Air Force bases, 512
  state legal standards, for public, 486
Education Department
  education assistance programs, 527, 601
  educational technology programs, 517
  library programs, 520
  student financial aid programs, 523
  telephone directory, 259
Educational associations and organizations, 051
Educational exchanges, 518
Educational Resources Information Center, search services, 460

Educators
  chief state school officials, council of, 382
  college placement directors, New England, 409
  at colleges and universities, 200
  with disabilities, 381
  education agency officials, state, 382
  graduate deans at U.S. colleges and universities, 389
  of handicapped, 457
Elderly. *See* Aged
Election(s)
  jurisdictions, 645
  state agencies, 353
Electric power plants, 121, 122
  Emergency Electric Power Administration roster, 258
  inventory, 122
  ownership list, 121
Elementary schools, districts, 197
Emergency medical services
  mental health, 211
  state offices, 349
Emergency telephone numbers, 635
Employee associations. *See* Labor unions
Employee-management relations. *See* Employees
Employees. *See also* Government officials and employees; Labor unions
  compensation, 180
  data sources, 180
  labor offices, United States and Canada, 340
  labor relations agencies, 339
  local employment security offices, 341
  national unions and associations, 076
  public, organizations of, 074
  public, and relations with management, 075
Employment. *See also* Discrimination in employment; Employees
  federal job information centers, 637
  handicapped, 410
  Hispanics, 082, 194
Employment security. *See* Unemployment insurance
Endangered species
  conservation organizations, 337
  laws and treaties, 493
Energy. *See also* Physics; Solar energy; Wind power
  conservation, 447
  cooperatives, 514
  data sources, 166, 169, 309, 448
  Department of Energy libraries, 448
  and environment, R & D program, 386

federal agencies, 308, 310, 319
organizations, 308, 310
programs, 346
renewable resources, 447, 596
research, 346, 386
state officials, 306, 308, 310, 320
statistics, 169
and transportation, 346
Energy conservation, 447
Energy research, 346, 386
Engineers
accessibility assistance, 108
engineering firms and fallout shelter analysts, 110
solar heating and cooling, 112
Environment. *See also* Air; Water
associations and organizations, 053, 054, 312
data sources, 165, 168, 188
environmental groups, 312, 318
environmental libraries, state and local, 201
environmental quality monitoring and assessment, 529
environmental sources, 452
EPA libraries, 202
hazardous substances, 350, 351
oil spills, 350, 351
research, 362, 386
state agencies, 313, 316, 318
Environmental life scientists, 372
Environmental Protection Agency
environmental quality monitoring and assessment, 529
libraries, 202
noise laboratories, 314
regional offices, 053, 312, 316, 318
telephone directory, 260
Equal employment opportunity. *See* Discrimination in employment
Equal rights, associations and organizations, 044, 079
ERIC search services, 460
EROS data center, 177
Exporting. *See* Exports
Exports
agricultural products, 036
associations and organizations, 036, 043
commercial service offices, 302
export councils, 364, 369
export management companies, 104
new products, 105
statistics, 161
textile/apparel exports, foreign regulations affecting, 484

Fair housing. *See* Housing
Fallout shelters, 110
Families
battered women, services to, 578
child abuse and neglect, 581, 582
food and nutrition programs, 297, 298
organizations concerned with, 094
services to, 094, 577
Family planning. *See* Birth control
Farms, services available from USDA, 505
Federal agencies. *See* Government agencies
Federal aid. *See subjects (education; students; etc.)*
Federal Aviation Administration, 290
engineering representatives, 424
mechanic examiners, 425, 426
mechanics, certificated, 423
maintenance agencies, 144
maintenance technician schools, 238
regional divisions, 290, 348
Federal employees. *See* Government officials and employees
Federal Energy Regulatory Commission, hydroelectric projects, recreational opportunities at, 516
Federal government. *See also* Government agencies
information analysis centers, 474
information resources, 472
information services, 322
information sources, 455, 456
manual, 262
regional structure, 263
Federal lands. *See* Public lands
Festivals. *See* Special days, weeks, and events
Financial instructions. *See* Banks and banking; Savings and loan associations
Firearms, state laws and published ordinances, 498
Fire(s)
associations and organizations, 056
control, 056
detectors, 626
forest, laws concerning, 481
prevention, 056
research specialists, 366
Fish and fishing
in Deschutes National Forest, 614
hatcheries, Pacific states region, 020
in Okanogan National Forest, 613
and wildlife conservation, 493
Fisheries. *See* Fish and fishing
Fishing. *See* Fish and fishing
Folklife, maritime, 234

248 / Subject Index

Folklore, maritime, 234
Food
  associations and organizations, 084
  exporting, 036
  meat and poultry inspection, 096
  and nutrition programs, 297, 298
  safety, 096, 245
  supplemental food program, 297
Food and Drug Administration
  blood establishments, 214
  drug codes, 628
  health-related item codes, 629
  location directory, 271
  public advisory committees, 393
  regional and field offices, 096
Foreign countries. *See also names of individual countries*
  capitals, 028, 029
  consular offices, 417, 433
  criminal justice organizations, 040
  diplomatic mission employees, 415
  diplomats, 414
  economy, 028
  export regulations of, affecting U.S. textile/apparel exports, 484
  government, 028
  intercountry adoption service resources, 580
  land area, 028, 029
  law enforcement organizations, 040
  maps, 028
  population, 028, 029
  social security programs, 536
  solar energy industries, 113
  and U.S. textile/apparel exports, 484
Foreign service
  chiefs of missions, U.S., 418
  classification list, 413
  list, 412
  officers, 416, 418, 419
  personnel, 419
  secretaries of state, 420
Foreign trade, statistics, 161
Foreign trade promotion
  new products, 105
  commercial service offices, 302
Forest fires, laws concerning, 481
Forest Service. *See also* National forests
  agencies and offices, 001, 002, 004, 243, 244
  Intermountain Forest Range Experiment Station, 504
  Intermountain Region, 244
  organizational directory, 243
Forestry. *See* Forests and forestry

Forests and forestry. *See also* Forest Service; National forests
  fire, laws concerning, 481
  research in Intermountain Region, 504
  schools, 190
  seed and planting stock dealers, 095
  USDA services, 505
4-H clubs, associations and organizations involved with, 035
Franchising opportunities, 106
Free universities, 208

Genetic(s)
  clinics, 217
  disorders, state laws and regulations, 489
Geographic codes, 006
Geological Survey. *See also* Interior Department
  information, sources of, 464, 465, 466
  offices relating to coal, 336
  public inquiries offices, 465
  publications, sources of, 177
Geology
  geosciences information resources, 475
  sources, 177, 464, 466
Georgia, ecological characteristics of Sea Island coastal region, 467
Geosciences, information resources, 475
Germany, East, chiefs of state and cabinet members, 411
Gerontology. *See also* Aged
  educational programs, 203
Government agencies
  aging, 333, 356, 611
  air quality, 311, 313, 316
  birth control, 059
  children, 530, 551, 561, 581, 582
  civil rights, 044
  coal mines and mining, 336
  consumer protection, 324, 343
  criminal justice, 338
  disaster relief, 321
  drug abuse programs, 063, 333
  earth sciences, 335
  education assistance, 527
  election, 353
  emergency medical services, 349
  employee-management relations, 339
  employment security, 341
  employment standards, 280
  endangered species, 337
  energy, 306, 308, 310, 319, 320, 346
  environmental, 053, 312, 313, 316, 318, 529
  federal domestic assistance, 601

federal executive, 296
Federal Information Centers, 322
federal job information centers, 637
federal regional structure, 263
fire prevention and control, 056
food and nutrition, 084, 297, 298
handicapping conditions, 050, 528
health, 325, 326
human services, 057, 060
information sources of, 455
intergovernmental cooperation, 344
international education, 086, 518
labor, 340
libraries, 201, 202, 232, 233, 240, 281, 378, 520
mental health, 564
mentally handicapped, 323, 332
merit systems, 304
minority communities, 069
national parks, 300
New England, major federal agencies in, 409
new federal offices and facilities, 242
noise pollution and control, 314, 316, 385
occupational safety and health, 330
oil pollution, 350, 351
population forecasting, 299
public housing, 334
radiation control, 316
radio frequency allocation, 303
sexual assault treatment, 062
solar energy, 307
tourism, 300, 301
toxicology, 317
transportation, 347
U.S. federal, 262
vital statistics, 327, 328, 329, 352
youth, 060
Government offices. *See* Government agencies
Government officials and employees
associations and organizations, 045, 073
attorneys general, 401
federal, 262, 433
labor offices, United States and Canada, 340
local employment security offices, 341
major federal employee population centers, 251
management relations, 339
occupational health facilities, 511
secretaries of the Army, 373
secretaries of state, 420
secretaries of war, 373
travel directory, 627

Grain, warehouses, 615
Grants-in-aid. *See also specific subjects*
education assistance, 527
federal domestic assistance, 601
Section 504 resources, 459
student financial aid programs, 523

Halfway houses
for alcoholics, 543
for mentally ill, 225, 226, 543
Handicapped
accessibility assistance, 108
architectural barriers removal, 449
associations and organizations, 050, 064, 080, 081, 085
education, 198, 519
educators with disabilities, 381
federal assistance programs, 528, 548, 601
higher education, 519
highway rest areas, 026
housing developments, 631
libraries, regional and subregional, 232
national parks, accessibility of, 018
President's Committee on Employment of the Handicapped, 410
recreation and leisure resources, 050
rehabilitation engineering and product information, 450
and Section 504, 459
services for the handicapped, California, 538
sports and games, 081
training for teachers of, 457
travel, 595
Hazardous substances. *See also* Waste products
contingency plan emergency response contacts, 350, 351
Hazardous waste. *See* Hazardous substances; Waste products
Head Start programs, 579
Health. *See also* Community health services; Indian Health Service; Mental health facilities; Mental health services; Occupational safety and health
agencies, regional, state, and territorial, 325
data sources, 172, 173
financial assistance programs of Public Health Service, 542
government agencies, 325, 326
handicapped, federal programs for, 548
minorities, federal programs for, 548
planning and development agencies, 326

Health (cont'd)
  rural health care, 533
  smoking and health, state legislation on, 490
  statistics, 172, 173
  systems, agencies on, 326
  women, federal programs for, 548
Health agencies. *See* Government agencies; Health
Health care practitioners, 395. *See also* Dentistry; Health education; Nurses; Physicians
Health education, 061
  allied programs in, 219
  area centers of, 557
  consumer, 061
  expanded role programs for registered nurses, 559
  nurses training programs, 222
  physician support personnel training programs, 555
  training programs administered by hospitals, 222
Health occupations. *See* Dentistry; Health education; Nurses; Physicians
High blood pressure, associations and organizations, 058
High energy physicists, 374
High schools
  districts, 197
  enrollment, 194, 197
  with Hispanic student enrollment, 194
  local systems, 624
  nonpublic, state and federal laws, 485
Higher education. *See* Colleges and universities
Highways. *See* Roads and highways
Hispanic(s). *See also* Minorities
  accounting firms, Spanish-speaking, 097
  associations and organizations, 044, 082, 093
  criminal justice, 593
  employment, 370
  recruiting, 082, 194
  women, speakers on issues concerning, 370
Historic sites, 011, 014, 023
  commemorating chief executives of United States, 014
  national historic landmarks, 015
Holidays. *See* Special days, weeks, and events
Home economics, communicators, 360
Horses
  associations and organizations, 031
  publications and visual materials, 031

Horticulture, state extension specialists in, 361
Hospitals. *See also* Mental health facilities
  health occupations training programs, 222
  Medicare/Medicaid providers and suppliers, 204, 228
  walk-in emergency mental health services, 211
Housing. *See also* Contractors
  associations and organizations, 229
  data resources, 149
  for elderly, 631
  fair, organizations and groups, 065
  for handicapped, 631
  minority housing professionals, 131
  public, agencies, 334
Housing management. *See* Housing
Human services
  associations and organizations, 057, 060
  federal domestic assistance for, 601
  foundations providing support for, 554
  information resources, 057
  youth, 060
Hungary, chiefs of state and cabinet members, 411
Hunger. *See also* Food
  associations and organizations, 084
Hydroelectric generators
  projects licensed by FERC, 516
  retired plants, 116
Hydroelectric power. *See* Hydroelectric generators
Hypertension, associations and organizations, 058

Idaho
  campgrounds, 021, 022
  environmental associations and organizations, 053
  national forests, 001, 004, 021
  recreation, 021
  women-owned businesses, 127
Illinois, environmental groups and agencies, 318
Immigrants, counseling agencies for, 070
Immigration and emigration, counseling agencies, 070
Imports, statistics, 161
Indian Affairs Bureau, 275
  area offices, 633
  field offices, 012
Indian Health Service, area and regional offices, 554
Indian lands, 012

Indian reservations, 005, 006
  arts and crafts businesses on, 132
  products manufactured on, 103
Indiana, environmental groups and agencies, 318
Indians of North America. *See also* Minorities
  Alaskan native villages, 005
  arts and crafts businesses, 132
  calendar, 633
  human service foundations for, 554
  programs assisting, 612
  native villages, 005
  population, 005
  reservations, 005
  tribes, 005
Indochina, programs for refugees of, 598
Industrial relations. *See also* Labor unions
  associations and organizations, 075, 091
  boards and agencies, 339
  data sources, 181
  public management organizations, 075
  public sector labor relations policies, 495
Installations (military)
  Air Force, 255
  Air Force bases, educational opportunities on, 512
  Army, 010, 011, 622
  Army museums, 011
Insurance companies
  life, 126
  minority, 102, 131
  and student loans, 129, 130
Intergovernmental cooperation, clearinghouses for, 344
Interior Department
  information sources and services, 275
  personnel offices, 274
Interior designers, as accessibility assistance consultants, 108
International education programs, 518
International exchanges
  associations and organizations, 086
  contacts for, 086
  education programs, 518
International organizations, 087
  exporting, 043
  law enforcement and criminal justice, 040
  metric building, 066
  oceanography, 042
  pollution, 054
Investment advisers, 140, 141

Investment companies
  active registered, 140
  advisers, 140, 141
  registered under Investment Company Act, 139, 140
Iowa, environmental groups and agencies, 312

Jails. *See* Corrections
Job Corps
  centers, 231
  training opportunities in, 594
Judges
  court directory, U.S., 404
  of United States, 402

Kansas, environmental groups and agencies, 312
Korea (Democratic People's Republic), chiefs of state and cabinet members, 411

Labor. *See also* Employees; Industrial relations; Labor unions; Migrant agricultural laborers
  areas, 024
  offices and agencies, 340
Labor organizations. *See* Labor unions
Labor relations agencies, 339
Labor Statistics Bureau
  Business Research Advisory Council to, 405
  Labor Research Advisory Council to, 406
  offices, 262, 279
  personnel, 279
  regional offices, 279
Labor unions, 072, 076, 091
  government officials and employees, 045, 073
  Labor Research Advisory Council to Labor Statistics Bureau, 406
  register of reporting, 072
Laboratories
  animal disease diagnostic, 191
  animal research, 544
  biotechnology, 545
  clinical genetic, 217
  noise capability, 314
  standardization activities, U.S., 039
  standards, 193
Labor-management relations. *See* Industrial relations

252 / Subject Index

Land
   resources information, 464, 465, 466
   resources officials, 430
   -use control, 492
Land use, 492
Landmarks. *See* Historic sites
Landsat satellites, information sources, 477
Landscape architects, as consultants on environments for handicapped, 108
Laos, chiefs of state and cabinet members, 411
Latin Americanists, 408
Law enforcement. *See also* Criminal justice
   agencies, 338
   associations and organizations, 040
   audiovisual materials, 468
   information sources, 469
Leafy spurge control, 359
Legal service agencies, 044, 338
Librarians
   of Congress, 407
   of DOE, 378
   ERIC search services, 460
Libraries
   associations and organizations, 052, 054
   for blind and physically handicapped, 232, 233
   Department of Education programs, 520
   depository, 240
   of DOE, 378
   environmental, 201, 202
   federal programs for, 539
   librarians of Congress, 407
   Library of Congress directory, 281
   networks, 052
Life insurance companies, 126
Life sciences, environmental, 372
Livestock
   animal disease diagnostic laboratories, 191
   cattle associations and organizations, 033
   horse associations and organizations, 031
   meat and poultry inspection, 096
   movement of, interstate and international, 482
   sheep associations and organizations, 034
   swine associations and organizations, 032
Los Angeles, express mail, 636
Low-income housing. *See* Public housing

Mail. *See* Postal Service
Manufactures and manufacturers. *See also* names of products
   of American Indian reservations, 103
   federal data sources, 162
   new products, 105

Manufacturing. *See* Manufactures and manufacturers
Maps and charts, sources of, 177, 464, 465, 466
Marine geology and geophysics. *See* Oceanography
Marine sciences. *See* Oceanography
Maritime
   folklife resources, 234
   minority contractors, 102
Market surveys, 163
Marketing
   measuring markets, 163
   national directories for use in, 638
Marriage records, 329, 352
Maryland, business education programs, 236
Meat, inspection of, 096
Medals. *See* Congressional Medal of Honor
Medicaid. *See* Medical care
Medical care. *See also* Health; Hospitals
   Medicare/Medicaid facilities, 228
   providers and suppliers of services, 204
Medical devices, codes, 629
Medical facilities. *See* Hospitals; Mental health facilities
Medical research
   National Cancer Institute, 270
   National Institutes of Health, 267, 268
   Soviet, 213
Medical schools. *See also* Colleges and universities
   expanded role programs for registered nurses, 559
   physician support personnel training programs, 555
   preceptorship programs, 221
Medicare. *See* Medical care
Mental health facilities, 225. *See also* Mental health services
   children with severe mental illnesses, facilities for, 561
   halfway houses and community residences, 226, 543
   mentally disordered offenders, institutions for, 212
   mentally retarded children, clinical programs for, 551
Mental health services. *See also* Community mental health services
   associations and organizations, 225
   for children, 561
   emergency, 211
   facilities and programs, 225, 561
   federal programs, 564
   halfway houses, 543

hot lines, 572
  for mentally disordered offenders, 212
Mental retardation services
  for children, 551
  international, 332
  state and local, 323
Mentally handicapped. *See* Mental retardation services
Mentally ill. *See* Mental health services
Merit systems, state, 304
Metallurgy, data sources, 154
Metals, data sources, 154
Methanol, large-scale alcohol fuel plants, 114
Metric system
  metric building organizations, 066
  speakers bureau, 365
Metropolitan areas, 027
  planning, 347
Michigan, environmental groups and agencies, 318
Migrant agricultural laborers, supplemental food program for, 297
Minerals, resources information, 464, 465, 466
Minnesota, environmental groups and agencies, 318
Minorities. *See also names of specific minority groups*
  accounting firms, 097, 131
  affirmative recruitment organizations, 077, 079, 082, 090
  American Indian reservations, products manufactured on, 103
  American Indians, arts and crafts businesses of, 132
  architects, 131
  arts and crafts businesses, 132
  associations and organizations, 044, 079
  banks and banking, 102, 131, 509
  biomedical support programs, 547
  business assistance programs and organizations, 037, 102, 106, 135, 136, 506, 509
  businesses, 132, 134
  city planners, 131
  consulting firms, 124
  contractors, maritime, 102
  contractors and housing professionals, 131
  data sources, 178
  drug abuse programs, 571
  federal domestic assistance, 601
  federal programs, 548
  franchise opportunities, 106
  insurance companies, 102, 131
  language, criminal justice information for, 593
  manufactures and manufacturers, 099, 103, 132, 134
  maritime contractors, 102
  media, 098
  native Americans, arts and crafts businesses of, 132
  organizations serving, 069
  postsecondary education opportunities, 521
  real estate appraisers and brokers, 131
  savings and loan associations, 102, 131, 509
  vendors, in Oregon, 146
Minority Business Development Agency, 506
Minority Business Enterprise Office (OMBE), 246, 247
  -funded organizations, 037, 102
  private programs assisting minority business, 509
Missouri, environmental groups and agencies, 312
Missouri River Basin Commission, water and land resources officials, 430
Montana, campgrounds, 022
Motor vehicle operators. *See* Motor vehicles
Motor vehicles
  driver licensing laws, 500
  license plates, 639
  traffic laws, 499
Museums
  Army, 011
  maritime folklife resources, 234
  museum studies programs, 606

Narcotics. *See also* Drug abuse
  laws, worldwide, 497
National Cancer Institute, 266, 267, 268, 269. *See also* Cancer
  clinical trial groups and projects, 392
  fact book, 270
National defense, information resources, 164
National forests
  Arizona, 002
  Deschutes, 614
  Idaho, 001, 004
  Indian lands, 012
  Intermountain Region, 001
  Nevada, 001
  New Mexico, 002
  Okanogan, 613
  Oregon, 614
  Southwestern Region, 002
  Tahoe, 003

National forests (cont'd)
  Utah, 001
  Washington, 613
  Wyoming, 001
National Health Service Corps, health care practitioners of, 395
National historic landmarks. See Historic sites
National Institutes of Health, 266, 267, 268, 269
  almanac, 267
  animal resources program, 544
  annual bibliography, 268
  biomedical support program for minorities, 547
  biotechnology program, 545
  clinical research centers, 546
  public advisory groups, 391
  scientific directory, 268
  telephone and service directory, 269
National monuments
  commemorating chief executives of United States, 014
  on Indian lands, 012
National Oceanic and Atmospheric Administration, sea grant program, 368
National Park System. See National parks
National parks, 016, 017
  accommodations, facilities, and services, 013
  camping, 019
  and handicapped, 018
  on Indian lands, 012
  map, 017
  and related areas, 016
National recreation areas
  Idaho, 001
  Utah, 001
  Wyoming, 001
National security, research aids, 444
National Technical Information Service
  computer software and related technical reports, 157
  journal article copy service, 442
  Sumstat catalog, 156
National Wildlife refuges, 012
Native Americans. See Indians of North America
Natural gas
  buyer/seller codes, 123
  data sources, 166
  small producer certificate dockets, 117
  small producer certificate holders, 118
Natural resources, on public lands, 030

Nebraska, environmental groups and agencies, 312
Neighborhoods, federal programs for conservation of, 610
Nevada
  campgrounds, 001, 022
  national forests, 001
New England
  college placement directors, 409
  federal agencies, 409
New Jersey, women business owners in, 128
New Mexico
  campgrounds, 002, 022
  national forests, 002
New York, women business owners, 128
Newspapers, minority-oriented, 098
Noise pollution and control
  environmental quality monitoring and assessment, 314
  federal laboratories and research facilities, 314
  federal professionals involved in, 385
  government agencies, 385
  research, 385
Nonprofit organizations, 088. See also subject areas
Nuclear physics, 513
Nuclear power plants, 122, 147
Nurse practitioners. See also Nurses
  National Health Service Corps, 395
Nurses
  data sources, 175
  registered, expanded role programs for, 559
Nursing
  data sources, 175
  statistics, 175
Nutrition
  agencies, government, 297, 298
  agencies, local, 297
  associations and organizations, 084
  programs, 297, 298

Occupational education. See Health education; Vocational education
Occupational information. See Occupations
Occupational safety and health
  agencies, federal, state, and local, 330
  federal facilities, 511
  program consultants, 397
Occupational training. See Health education; Vocational education

Subject Index / 255

Occupations. *See also* Vocational education
  information sources, 179, 187
  occupational program consultants, 397
  park and recreation professionals, federal assistance guide, 587
Oceanography
  acronyms, 042
  associations and organizations, 042, 475
  data services, 160
  information resources, 475
  marine science specialists, 368
  research in marine science and engineering, 443
Offenders. *See* Crime and criminals
Office of Minority Business Enterprise. *See* Minority Business Enterprise Office
Ohio
  community crime prevention resources, 590
  environmental groups and agencies, 318
Oil spills, emergency response contacts, 350, 351
Older persons. *See* Aged
Oregon
  campgrounds, 022
  environmental associations and organizations, 053
  minority vendors, 146
  women-owned businesses, 127
Organizations. *See subjects (air pollution; civic; etc.)*
Outdoor recreation. *See* Recreation

Parks. *See also* National parks
  federal assistance for, 587
Parole. *See also* Criminal justice
  agencies, 338
  probation officers, U.S., 403
Passports and visas, 604
  consular services, 603, 604
Patents, attorneys dealing with, 367
Pest control
  environmental quality monitoring and assessment, 529
  leafy spurge, 359
Pesticides. *See* Pest control
Petroleum
  data sources, 166
  refineries, 117, 118
  small producer certificate dockets, 117
  small producer certificate holders, 118
Phenylketonuria, state laws and regulations, 489
Photovoltaic power commercialization, key foreign personnel, 113

Physical security. *See* Security
Physically handicapped. *See* Handicapped
Physicians
  National Health Service Corps practitioners, 395
  preceptorship programs, 221
  support personnel, training programs for, 555
Physicists. *See* Physics
Physics
  contractors supported by DOE's Nuclear Physics Division, 513
  high energy physicists, 374
  nuclear, research projects, 513
Picnicking, 001, 002, 003, 004
PKU, state laws and regulations, 489
Plants, poisonous and injurious, 630
Poison(s)
  control centers, 216
  poisonous and injurious plants, 630
Poland, chiefs of state and cabinet members, 411
Police departments. *See* Corrections
Pollution. *See* Air; Environment; Water
Population
  centers, 009
  forecasting, 299
  Indian reservations and trust areas, 005
  Standard Metropolitan Statistical Areas, 027
Post offices, 025
Postal Service
  express mail, Los Angeles, 636
  post offices, 025
  zip codes, 025
Postsecondary education. *See* Colleges and universities
Poultry
  inspection, 096
  movement of, interstate and international, 482
Poverty, associations and organizations, 084
Preceptorship programs, 221
Prenatal diagnosis, clinics, 217
President's Committee on Employment of the Handicapped, 410
Presidents of the United States, 262, 433
  first ladies, 429
  from George Washington to Jimmy Carter, 014
  historic places commemorating, 014
Prisons. *See* Corrections
Privacy, right of
  criminal history information, 494
  federal government records, 456

256 / Subject Index

Probation
    agencies, 338
    officers, U.S., 403
Productivity, centers for, 092
Products, commercial, 105. *See also names of products*
Prohibitive substances, 497. *See also* Drug abuse
Psychiatric care. *See* Mental health services
Public defenders, 338
Public employees. *See* Government officials and employees
Public Health Service, 262, 265
    financial assistance programs, 542
Public housing
    agencies, 334
    for elderly, 631
    for handicapped, 631
Public lands
    camping, 022
    natural resources, 030
Public records, 352. *See also* Vital statistics

Radiation. *See* Radioactivity
Radiation control
    environmental quality monitoring and assessment, 529
    state program administrators, 316
Radio frequency allocation, field contacts, 303
Radio stations, minority-oriented, 098
Radioactivity
    environmental quality monitoring and assessment, 529
    fallout shelter analysts, 110
    fallout shelter architectural and engineering firms, 120
Radiology, medical, 394
Rape. *See* Sexual assault
Real estate
    minority contractors and housing professionals, 131
    minority real estate professionals, 131
Recreation. *See also* Camping; National forests; National parks
    Arizona, 002
    California, 003
    federal assistance for, 587
    handicapped, 050, 081
    at hydroelectric projects, 516
    Idaho, 001, 004, 021
    Nevada, 001
    New Mexico, 002
    outdoor, organizations, 068
    picnicking, 001, 002, 003, 004
    Utah, 001
    Wyoming, 001
Recruiting. *See* Civil service; Minorities
Recycled materials
    appropriate technology activities and projects, 596
    associations and organizations, 055
    resource recovery, 125
Recycling. *See* Recycled materials
Regional planning, 007
Rehabilitation
    engineering, 450
    and Section 504, 459
Renewable energy resources, 447, 596
Representatives, congressional. *See* Congress of the United States
Research
    aids, 444
    air sciences, 362
    biomedical, 213, 268, 544, 545, 547
    cancer, 266, 267, 268, 270, 461
    energy, 448
    ERIC search services, 460
    health, 266, 267, 268, 270
    in progress, information services on, 478
    soil sciences, 362
    Soviet biomedical, 213
    university, 616
    water sciences, 362
Research centers
    civil rights, 044
    criminal justice, 040
    general clinical, 547
    information analysis, government sponsored, 472
    law enforcement, 040
Resource recovery. *See* Recycled materials
River Basin commissions, 355
    Missouri, 430
Roads and highways
    rest areas, 026
    traffic laws annotated, 499
Romania, chiefs of state and cabinet members, 411
Rural communities. *See also* Cities and towns
    health care programs, 533
    public transportation service, 608, 643
Russia. *See* Union of Soviet Socialist Republics

Savings and loan associations, 143
  American Savings and Loan League
    members, 102
  Federal Home Loan Bank Board system
    members, 126
  minority-owned, 102, 131, 509
  and student loans, 129, 130
Schools. *See also* High schools
  elementary, 197
  enrollment, 194, 197
  for handicapped, 198
  nonpublic, state and federal laws, 485
Science and technology
  associations and organizations, 041
  data sources, 189
  federal technology transfer, 602
  research in progress, information services
    on, 478
  publications, 041
  thermal technology companies, 113
  United States, 189
Scientific exchanges. *See* International
  exchanges
Scientists
  annual bibliography of, 268
  cancer clinical trials groups and projects,
    392
  environmental life, 372
  public advisory committees, FDA, 393
  public advisory groups, NIH, 391
  scientific directory, 268
  state agricultural experiment stations,
    professional workers at, 357
Secondary schools. *See* High schools
Securities and Exchange Commission
  companies required to file annual reports
    with, 142
  corporation index of, 137
  investment companies registered with, 138,
    139, 140
Security
  consultants, 133
  equipment, 101
Seed crops, 095
Seeds, 095
Seismograph stations, historical survey of,
  632
Seismology, stations, 632
Selective Service System, local boards, 354
Senators. *See* Congress of the United States
Sexual assault
  associations and organizations, 062
  prevention resources, 562, 563
  crisis centers, sources of funding, 062
  treatment programs, sources of funding,
    062
  treatment resources, 562, 563
Sexually transmitted diseases, clinics, 223
Sheep
  associations and organizations, 034
  publications and visual materials, 034
Shipbuilders, minority contractors, 102
Ships
  bulk carriers, 617
  U.S. merchant vessels, 618, 641
Sickle cell anemia, disease programs, 550
Small business
  business education programs, Maryland,
    236
  DOE, doing business with, 257
  8(a) business development program firms,
    136
  federal government assistance, 507
  investment companies, 135
  programs for, state, 605
  utilization specialists, 305
Smoking and health, state legislation on, 490
Social sciences
  information resources, 471
  socioeconomic data sources, 165
Social security programs, worldwide, 536
Soil, research personnel, 362
Solar cooling. *See* Solar energy
Solar energy
  associations and organizations, 115, 307
  commercialization of, key foreign
    personnel, 113
  cooling, commercial demonstration program, 112
  cooperatives, 514
  education, 195
  events calendar, 623
  foreign personnel in commercialization
    of, 113
  heating, commercial demonstration program, 112
  industrial process heat systems, 115
  industries, 112, 113, 115
  information locator, 307
  manufactures and manufacturers, 113, 115
  technical training, 196
Solar heating. *See* Solar energy
Solid wastes. *See* Waste products
South Carolina, ecological characterization
  of Sea Island coastal region, 467
Soviet Union. *See* Union of Soviet Socialist
  Republics

258 / Subject Index

Spanish-speaking people. *See also* Hispanics; Minorities
  accounting firms for, 097
  associations and organizations, 093
Special days, weeks, and events
  American Indian calendar, 633
  festivals, 619
  solar events calendar, 623
Spouse abuse. *See* Families
Standard Metropolitan Statistical Areas (SMSAs), 024, 027
  population (1970), 027
  unemployment, 024
Standards and standardization
  associations and organizations, 039
  laboratories, 193
State Department, 262, 433
  foreign service personnel, 412, 413, 416, 418, 419
  secretaries of state, 420
  telephone directory, 286
State departments of education, officials of, 382
Statistics
  federal data files, 156, 158, 345
  foreign trade, 161
  government, 150
  manufacturing, 162
  market surveys, 163
Sterilization. *See* Birth control
Student aid. *See* Students
Student loan program. *See* Students
Students
  colleges and universities eligible for student loans, 205
  federal education assistance programs, 527, 601
  financial assistance, 129, 130, 523, 601
  minorities and women, postsecondary education opportunities for, 521
Swine
  associations and organizations, 032
  publications and visual materials, 032

Teachers. *See* Educators
Technological innovations. *See also* Science and technology
  associations and organizations, 041
  data sources, 189
  publications, 041
Technology. *See* Science and technology
Teenagers. *See* Youth

Telephone
  companies, 100
  911 systems, 635
  undersea telephone cable systems, 620
Textile industry, foreign regulations affecting exports, 484
Thermal technology, 113
Tourist trade. *See* Travel
Toxic substances. *See* Toxicology
Toxicology. *See also* Cancer; National Cancer Institute
  toxic substances federal coordinating groups, 317
Trade associations, 037, 039, 115
Traffic laws, 499
Transit systems. *See* Transportation
Transportation
  education programs, 235
  intermodal planning process, 347
  North American rapid transit cars, 644
  public, 642
  public, rural, 608, 643
  state agencies, 347
Travel
  federal agencies, 300
  for federal employees, 627
  handicapped, information for, 595
  information sources, 300, 301, 439, 595
  state agencies, 300
  tourism offices, 300, 301, 439
  visitors' bureaus, 439

Unemployment, hard-hit areas of, 024
Unemployment insurance
  local employment security offices, 341
  state laws and experience, 496
Union of Soviet Socialist Republics
  biomedical institutions and research, 213
  chiefs of state and cabinet members, 411
  Communist party structure, 411
Unions. *See* Labor unions
United States Congress. *See* Congress of the United States
Universities. *See* Colleges and universities
Urban planning. *See* City planning
USDA. *See* Agriculture Department
USSR. *See* Union of Soviet Socialist Republics
Utah
  campgrounds, 001, 022
  national forests, 001

Subject Index / 259

Veterans
  rights, benefits, and dependents, state laws regarding, 502
  service organizations representatives, 089
Veterinarians, 096, 191, 357
Vietnam
  chiefs of state and cabinet members, 411
  era, Medal of Honor recipients of, 436
Visas. *See* Passports and visas
Visually handicapped. *See* Handicapped
Vital statistics
  birth records, 327, 352
  death records, 327, 352
  divorce records, 328, 352
  marriage records, 329, 352
  public records, 352
Vocational education. *See also* Colleges and universities
  federal funding, 524
  Job Corps training opportunities, 594
  occupational programs, 210
  state education agency officials, 382
  work education programs, 537
Voter registration, state agencies, 353
Voting systems, 645

Wages, data sources, 180, 182, 183, 184, 185
Warehouses
  cotton, 615
  grain, 615
  licensed under U.S. Warehouse Act, 615
Washington (state)
  campgrounds, 022
  environmental associations and organizations, 053
  national forests, 613
  women-owned businesses, 127
Waste disposal. *See* Waste products
Waste management
  resource recovery, 125
  state agencies, 313
Waste products
  appropriate technology, 596
  environmental quality monitoring and assessment, 529
  recycling associations and organizations, 055
  resource recovery, 125

Water
  data sources, 177
  pollution associations and organizations, 054
  professional research personnel, 362
  quality, management agencies for, 315
  quality, monitoring and assessment of, 313, 529
  resources agencies, 355, 430
  resources information, 464, 465, 466
  resources officials, 430
Weather, offices and stations of National Weather Service, 248
Wildlife
  conservation, 337, 493
  refuges, 012
  and sport fish, federal laws and treaties, 493
Wind energy. *See* Wind power
Wind power
  information resources, 445
  key foreign personnel, 113
  small wind systems and equipment, 111
Wisconsin, environmental groups and agencies, 318
Women
  associations and organizations, 044, 078, 079, 083
  business owners, 127, 128
  business owners, federal government business assistance programs for, 507
  business owners, guide to U.S. Department of Commerce for, 247
  calendar of events, 625
  civil rights, 044
  commissions, committees, and councils on status of women, 078
  congresswomen, 431
  drug abuse treatment programs, 331
  federal programs for, 548
  Hispanic, speakers on issues concerning, 370
  postsecondary education opportunities, 521
  recruitment sources for, 077, 370
  resources, 083
Work, productivity and quality of working life centers, 092
Wyoming
  campgrounds, 001, 022
  national forests, 001

Young people. *See* Youth
Youth. *See also* Children
   camps, laws and regulations, 491
   drug abuse prevention programs, 566
   health, education, and social service
     organizations, 060
   runaway youth programs, 592

Yugoslavia, chiefs of state and cabinet members, 411

Zip codes, five-digit, 025